The Ethics of Bioethics

The Ethics of Bioethics

Mapping the Moral Landscape

Edited by

LISA A. ECKENWILER
Associate Professor and Co-director
Institute for Ethics and Public Affairs
Department of Philosophy and Religious Studies
Old Dominion University
Norfolk, Virginia

and

FELICIA G. COHN
Associate Professor and Director of Medical Ethics
School of Medicine
University of California, Irvine
Irvine, California

The Johns Hopkins University Press
Baltimore

For Thom and John

© 2007 The Johns Hopkins University Press
All rights reserved. Published 2007
Printed in the United States of America on acid-free paper
2 4 6 8 9 7 5 3 1

The Johns Hopkins University Press
2715 North Charles Street
Baltimore, Maryland 21218-4363
www.press.jhu.edu

Library of Congress Cataloging-in-Publication Data
The ethics of bioethics : mapping the moral landscape /
edited by Lisa A. Eckenwiler and Felicia G. Cohn.
p. ; cm.
Includes bibliographical references and index.
ISBN-13: 978-0-8018-8609-6 (hardcover : alk. paper)
ISBN-10: 0-8018-8609-0 (hardcover : alk. paper)
ISBN-13: 978-0-8018-8612-6 (pbk. : alk. paper)
ISBN-10: 0-8018-8612-0 (pbk. : alk. paper)
1. Medical ethics. 2. Bioethics. 3. Professional ethics.
I. Eckenwiler, Lisa A., 1967– . II. Cohn, Felicia.
[DNLM: 1. Bioethics. 2. Ethics, Professional.
3. Politics. WB 60 E8463 2007]
R724.E8242 2007
174'.957—dc22   2006033237

A catalog record for this book is available from the British Library.

Contents

Contributors

Felicia G. Cohn, Ph.D., Associate Professor and Director of Medical Ethics, School of Medicine, University of California, Irvine

Lisa A. Eckenwiler, Ph.D., Associate Professor and Co-director, Institute for Ethics and Public Affairs, Department of Philosophy and Religious Studies, Old Dominion University, Norfolk, Virginia

Judith Andre, Ph.D., Professor, Center for Ethics and Humanities in the Life Sciences and Department of Philosophy, Michigan State University, East Lansing, Michigan

Robert Baker, Ph.D., Chair, Alden March Bioethics Institute, Professor of Bioethics, Graduate College of Union University, and Professor of Philosophy, Union College, Schenectady, New York

Françoise Baylis, Ph.D., Canada Research Chair in Bioethics and Philosophy, Dalhousie University, Halifax, Nova Scotia, Canada

Allen Buchanan, Ph.D., James B. Duke Professor of Philosophy and Public Policy, Duke University, Durham, North Carolina

Tod Chambers, Ph.D., Associate Professor of Medical Humanities and Bioethics and of Medicine, Feinberg School of Medicine, Northwestern University, Chicago, Illinois

R. Alta Charo, J.D., Warren P. Knowles Professor of Law and Bioethics, University of Wisconsin Law and Medical Schools, and Associate Dean for Research and Faculty Development, University of Wisconsin Law School, Madison, Wisconsin

James F. Childress, Ph.D., Hollingsworth Professor of Ethics and Professor of Medical Education, and Director, Institute for Practical Ethics, University of Virginia, Charlottesville, Virginia

Debra A. DeBruin, Ph.D., Assistant Professor and Director of Graduate Studies, Center for Bioethics, University of Minnesota, Minneapolis, Minnesota

Carl Elliott, M.D., Ph.D., Professor, Center for Bioethics, University of Minnesota, Minneapolis, Minnesota

H. Tristram Engelhardt Jr., M.D., Ph.D., Professor, Rice University, and Professor Emeritus, Baylor College of Medicine, Houston, Texas

Nancy M. P. King, J.D., Professor of Social Medicine, Department of Social Medicine, School of Medicine, University of North Carolina, Chapel Hill, North Carolina

Mark G. Kuczewski, Ph.D., the Fr. Michael I. English, SJ, Professor of Medical Ethics and Director, Neiswanger Institute for Bioethics and Health Policy, Stritch School of Medicine, Loyola University Chicago, Maywood, Illinois

Carol Levine, M.A., Director, Families and Health Care Project, United Hospital Fund, New York, New York

Hilde Lindemann, Ph.D., Associate Professor, Department of Philosophy, Michigan State University, East Lansing, Michigan

Mary Faith Marshall, Ph.D., Associate Dean for Social Medicine and Medical Humanities, College of Medicine, and Professor of Bioethics, Center for Bioethics, University of Minnesota, Minneapolis, Minnesota

Jonathan D. Moreno, Ph.D., University Professor of Medical Ethics and the History and Sociology of Science, University of Pennsylvania, Philadelphia, Pennsylvania

E. Haavi Morreim, Ph.D., Professor, College of Medicine, University of Tennessee Health Science Center, Memphis, Tennessee

Catherine Myser, Ph.D., Founder, Partnerships for Public, Cross-Cultural and International Bioethics, Oakland, California

James Lindemann Nelson, Ph.D., Professor and Acting Chair, Department of Philosophy, Michigan State University, East Lansing, Michigan

David Orentlicher, M.D., J.D., Samuel R. Rosen Professor of Law, Co-director, Center for Law and Health, Indiana University School of Law–Indianapolis, Core Faculty, Indiana University Center for Bioethics, Adjunct Professor of Medicine, Indiana University School of Medicine, and State Representative, House District 86, Indianapolis, Indiana

Lisa S. Parker, Ph.D., Associate Professor and Director of Graduate Education, Center for Bioethics and Health Law, University of Pittsburgh, Pittsburgh, Pennsylvania

Virginia A. Sharpe, Ph.D., Medical Ethicist, National Center for Ethics, Veterans Health Administration, Washington, D.C.

M. L. Tina Stevens, Ph.D., Lecturer, Department of History, San Francisco State University, San Francisco, California

Griffin Trotter, M.D., Ph.D., Associate Professor, St. Louis University Center for Health Care Ethics, St. Louis University, St. Louis, Missouri

Leigh Turner, Ph.D., Associate Professor, Biomedical Ethics Unit and Department of Social Studies of Medicine, Faculty of Medicine, McGill University, Montreal, Québec, Canada

Laurie Zoloth, Ph.D., Professor of Medical Humanities and Bioethics and of Religion, Director, Center for Bioethics, Science, and Society, Feinberg School of Medicine, Northwestern University, Chicago, Illinois

Foreword

JONATHAN D. MORENO, PH.D.

This collection of essays marks an important milestone in the maturation of bioethics. In 1995 I published a book on the nature of moral consensus called *Deciding Together*. As should happen when an author is truly grappling with the material, I was surprised by the direction I felt impelled to pursue in the last chapter. Having explored bioethical consensus from various disciplinary perspectives, including a theory of morally justifiable consensus processes, I found myself wondering what hazards a field that engaged in moral consensus building would face if the coherence and legitimacy of its intellectual mission were called into question, a development I guessed was inevitable. At that more innocent time in bioethics I did not fully perceive how this might happen, but it was clear that any group of self-appointed professionals who presented themselves as (in some sense or other) experts on ethics was setting itself up for one hell of a lot of scrutiny.

As events have unfolded over the ensuing decade the sheer volume of that scrutiny and the raw feelings it has often engendered exceeded anything I then imagined. There were two sources and types of controversy that in retrospect should not have been surprising. One source that was latent in the field from the very beginning was a deep disagreement about the acceptability in principle of technologies that manipulated the products of human reproduction processes, especially when the research or the technologies themselves involved creating, altering, or destroying human embryos. The morality of abortion itself was such an incendiary topic within bioethics circles that, with few exceptions, it seems to have been studiously avoided as a matter of professional discourse. Many concluded that the subject was so hopelessly politicized that no progress could be made in thinking in new ways about the issue, much less constructively influencing public policy.

The de facto agreement not to join this issue, which I have elsewhere called the Great Bioethics Compromise, fell apart in the late 1990s (Moreno 2005). The cloning of Dolly the sheep in 1996 and the isolation of human embryonic stem cells in 1998 created public confusion about the related but distinct issues raised by each breakthrough. When President George W. Bush announced his policy of extremely limited funding of embryonic stem cell research and appointed a bioethics advisory council chaired by a bioethicist who has long been perhaps the leading skeptic of artificial reproductive technologies, both professional and popular media carried the voices of an unprecedented, politically supercharged bioethics debate. Academic bioethicists found that someone had crashed the party: A neoconservative Washington policy institute with staff connections to the President's Council on Bioethics began a journal of commentary on biotechnology, theologically conservative think tanks declared bioethics programs, and journalists began referring with far greater frequency to "liberal" and "conservative" bioethicists. Many of the newcomers declined to pursue traditional means of entry to the field through several prestigious university centers believed to typify the left-leaning academy. It became clear that the genteel compromise among those who called themselves bioethicists was at an end.

It is true that before the end of the compromise there was one sustained "immanent critique" (to borrow the language of critical theory) of the institution of bioethics. Feminist bioethicists raised questions about the selection of issues and the sorts of theoretical strategies dominant in the field (Sherwin 1992; Warren 1992; Wolf 1996). But this discussion nonetheless took place in the polite language and conditions of the academy. However challenging feminist bioethics has been and continues to be of bioethics orthodoxy, it has never abandoned the assumption that mainstream bioethics could and should be saved from itself.

The operative question now is, can a scholarly field retain its intellectual legitimacy, both internally and in the eyes of the public, when some of its core topics seem matters of ideology rather than, or at least as much as, expertise? It might be argued that other fields, like economics and sociology, have long been characterized by similar ideological colorings and disputes yet they have retained at least a measure of credibility and cohesion. A critical difference, however, is that bioethicists believe themselves to be engaged in a normative as well as descriptive enterprise, a self-understanding that has given rise to a small but important literature. Through the eighties and nineties there was a low-intensity but continuing debate about how bioethicists could avoid being co-opted, and their credibility undermined, by powerful forces like the medical profession and medical schools. Worries about doing ethics in the midst of institutional politics now seem nearly quaint as the stakes associated with the moral expertise notion have been transformed into such questions as: Can such a field sustain its mission while navigating the treacherous currents of culture wars? Can an avowedly political bioethics be ethical?

A second source of the reexamination of bioethics is still more painful, as it has both been stimulated by bioethicists themselves—or at least their fellow travelers who may decline to call themselves bioethicists but participate in its institutions—and calls into question the professional practices, and perhaps even the moral character, of some of the field's practitioners. These critics within the family circle have questioned the association of high-visibility colleagues or their centers with private industry, urging that only a wholly disinterested bioethics can function as a trustworthy critic of the medical-industrial complex. Setting aside the issue of how widespread the activities in question really are, these associations can range from sitting on corporate ethics advisory boards to accepting grants to engage in bioethics projects. In response, it is argued that certain conditions on these relationships, such as full disclosure, editorial control, and carefully modulated compensation, can prevent abuses that may be associated with financial conflicts of interest (Brody et al. 2002). It is also observed that in order for bioethics to be effective in a market economy it must be "at the table" where important decisions about the development of new ideas and the investment of capital are made.

In one sense the issues raised by this debate are routine in the history of a profession that at a certain point goes self-conscious about its substantive responsibilities and its public image. The institution of bioethics is now sufficiently independent of medicine, philosophy, law, and its other originating professions that a strong case can be made for a distinct role-based morality for its practitioners. Ethics codes and other modes of professional self-regulation are one plausible response, as are external watchdogs. The fact that these ethical conundrums arise in the context of a profession devoted to ethics may stimulate a momentary intellectual vertigo but doesn't necessarily distinguish the underlying problem from that facing other fields whose members may be said to be operating as fiduciaries for the larger public.

My sense is that the sudden emergence of bioethics at ground zero of the culture wars, and the debate about its relation to the corporate world, have somehow combined to foster a certain unease about the intellectual soundness of the field. Yet interestingly, there is little overlap between these two sources of criticism of the bioethics establishment. Those who charge that the field is in thrall to liberal academics do not, for the most part, take it to task for association with private industry. Cultural conservatives and critics of capitalist values do not often appear in the same body. Nonetheless, the more or less simultaneous appearance of these controversies has to some degree rattled the profession's self-confidence. When controversies like these first emerge in a profession they are bound to generate more heat than light. This landmark collection will do much to illuminate the terrain and, I feel sure, help move bioethics into a sadder but wiser future.

NOTE

Disclosures: I am a senior fellow of a nonpartisan Washington policy institute often described as liberal, the Center for American Progress. I also was a member of a bioethics advisory board for a small genomics company; that association lasted less than two years and ended when all board members resigned following the company's acquisition by new owners.

REFERENCES

Brody, B., Dubler, N., Blustein, J., Caplan, A., Kahn, J. P., Kass, N., Lo, B., Moreno, J. D., Sugarman, J., and Zoloth, L. 2002. Bioethics consultation in the private sector. *Hastings Center Report* 32(3): 14–20.

Moreno, J. D. 1995. *Deciding Together: Bioethics and Moral Consensus.* New York: Oxford University Press.

———. 2005. The end of the Great Bioethics Compromise. *Hastings Center Report* 35(1): 14–15.

Sherwin, S. 1992. *No Longer Patient: Feminist Ethics and Health Care.* Philadelphia: Temple University Press.

Warren, V. L. 1992. Feminist directions in medical ethics. *HEC Forum* 4(1): 19–35.

Wolf, S. M., ed. 1996. *Feminism and Bioethics: Beyond Reproduction.* New York: Oxford University Press.

Acknowledgments

This book was inspired by our experiences as two professionals now in the early middle of our careers working in bioethics. One of us is a philosopher by training, working in an academic philosophy department, while the other is grounded in religious studies and based in a university medical center. One participates in ethics consultation and the other in policy settings. Both of us teach, conduct research, and write in bioethics. We came to this project from our passion for the field and its potential—passion that began when we were undergraduate students exposed to bioethics by extraordinary teachers at the University of Wisconsin–Madison and the University of Virginia—and our frustration, indeed, awe, over what we were witnessing as maturing professionals: the influence of money, a certain myopia when it came to the concerns that gained our colleagues' attention, a tendency to see "the usual suspects" wherever we turned—in meetings, in the media, in speaking and consulting engagements, and people treating each other callously.

This book is a constructive tribute to our optimism. Our wish is to contribute to the conversation, or rather, the many conversations, about the future of the field and above all, its moral compass.

A few people deserve special mention: our partners, Thom and John, for their unwavering devotion; our parents, for, well, everything; Amanda, for whom we hope to help make the world a better place; and our mentors, some of whom appear here, who helped to pave the way, offered us opportunities and encouragement, and inspired us to be our best. Thanks are also owed to our editors and reviewers who significantly improved this book, to Sam Berger, and to Ashley Gonzalez for her invaluable assistance at every stage of the project. It is also worth expressing our appreciation to those who have helped to show us what we do not want to become, as individuals or as a field. Without these people, this book would not have been possible.

Introduction

Over the course of four decades, bioethics has come to be recognized as an authoritative field. Indeed, many would argue that the field has come of age. Increasingly, bioethicists are sought after for their expertise—in clinical research and in government, legal, corporate, and community contexts—by universities, hospitals, businesses, policy makers, and the media. The rising demand for the contributions of these professionals has spurred the growth of graduate programs and centers—both free standing and university based—devoted to the study and practice of bioethics.

Bioethicists have long been called on to comment on a wide variety of topics, but bioethics is increasingly becoming a topic for comment itself. As the field has matured, there has been considerable controversy and critique concerning its work and the behaviors of those doing the work. This is to be expected in a profession that focuses on deeply contentious issues. More disturbing is the wide array of allegations that, all told, call into question the ethics of bioethics.

Some argue, for example, that the field tends to focus on isolated issues and "hot topics" that gain easy notoriety, and so functions in a way that ultimately diverts attention from other problems—perhaps more important and complex ones—like violence, health disparities, the relationship between health and the environment, and global inequalities. Critics wonder whether, whatever their intentions, the field and its practitioners engage in narrow and distorted analyses and serve ultimately to perpetuate existing relations of power. They claim that bioethicists, as they participate in a growing number of settings and find themselves in new kinds of relationships, and even careers, may be enhancing the power of certain individuals and institutions rather than serving the citizenry as "watchdogs" or social critics, challenging injustice and strengthening the ethical capacities integral to a pluralistic democracy.

Some allege that, as a field, bioethics has identifiable biases and, as a result, cannot be trusted to assess issues from all relevant perspectives. Others object to its neutrality as a collective, that is, its unwillingness to "take stands" on specific ethical, political, and policy issues. By failing to take substantive public positions, these critics claim, bioethics abandons its responsibility and undermines its effectiveness. Further, many wonder whether bioethicists act unethically by not explicitly and systematically attending to questions about the "public face" of bioethics. For instance, who in the field's fold gains access to the venues—such as advisory panels, government commissions, and the media—where analyses and recommendations are formed? To what extent do the faces and voices that emerge in the public sphere represent the field? Are opportunities to serve fairly distributed?

Still another line of criticism comes from those whose experience and observations lead them to conclude, ironically, that bioethicists do not always behave ethically toward their colleagues and their students when they work together in bioethics centers, programs of study, funded projects, or task forces. In recent years this concern has taken on a new urgency, with increased polarization and mounting acrimony between so-called liberal and conservative bioethicists. Many worry that the field is becoming less collegial and more politicized, and that this will serve to undermine fair-minded, thoughtful inquiry and the credibility of bioethics and bioethicists. These critiques, which come from external observers of the field as well as its own practitioners, concern the direction and indeed the ethics of bioethics. At stake are the integrity and credibility of the field and its members, and above all, the trust and welfare of the public they purport to serve.

While international organizations have crafted codes and declarations (Partners in the BIOMED II Project 2000; Scientific Committee of the International Society of Bioethics 2000; UNESCO 2005) and scholars in Canada have developed a model code of ethics for the field (Canadian Bioethics Society 2003), divergent understandings of the field's origins and its proper scope, methods, and objectives contribute to the absence of any authoritative consensus on defining values and principles, or even a shared understanding of what bioethics is. With varied interpretations of its history—we can trace its roots to different thinkers with distinct agendas in Washington, D.C., Madison, Wisconsin, and more broadly, to the responsible science movement of the 1960s and 1970s—it is not so surprising that some see the principal domains of bioethics as clinical research and practice, while others argue that the field also should encompass global public health and environmental policy. Moreover, with its multidisciplinary membership, we might expect to find at work the methods of moral philosophy, history, and literary criticism, the teachings of particular religious traditions, and the techniques of social science, and to see practitioners aim variously at facilitating sound moral reasoning and judgment, building moral community, or nurturing moral development. Combined, these factors make it challenging, to say the very least, to develop shared understandings of what bioethics is, descriptively and normatively, to determine what its problems are, and to reach consensus about our moral grounding and core values. However bioethicists come to understand themselves and their work, they now must confront the fact that they are subject to criticism similar to that which once faced medicine—and ironically, that compelled the creation of bioethics.

This collection begins a critical and, we hope, constructive discussion about the "moral landscape" of North American bioethics, primarily (though not exclusively) as it exists in the United States. We bring together a collection of engaging and provocative original essays that situate the field and its members at this historical juncture, explore the nature and scope of the distinctive terrains they traverse in their work as educators, scholars, consultants, and activists, and most critically, that reflect upon the moral grounding and future direction of the field. Most authors here are recognized figures within the field; we sought out external critics but found few ready or willing to join the conversation.

We asked the contributors to think about some of the key questions at the root of the critiques of bioethics and bioethicists: How should we understand and use our expertise—which is, at once, increasingly courted and subject to scrutiny? How should we understand our role in society? In an international context? What, ethically speaking, are the contributions that bioethics and bioethicists make and what kinds should we make? How can bioethics and bioethicists cause harm? What are our creation myths and what of ethical importance can be found therein? In a liberal, pluralistic, capitalistic society what is the proper relationship between bioethics and the public? Between the field and the private sector? In what ways are we myopic, and how can we resist or correct this? How might we maintain our integrity, and that of the profession, under ethically compromised conditions? What responsibilities do we have to our colleagues, students, and future members of the profession? Are there any defining values or principles we can identify for bioethics and bioethicists? How might we evaluate ourselves as individuals and our work as a field? What will be the legacy of bioethics? What should it be? Not only did the contributors address these questions with clarity and grace, but they raised many others that will need to be addressed if we are to reach any authoritative consensus on the ethics of bioethics.

SITUATING BIOETHICS: WHERE HAVE WE BEEN? WHERE SHOULD WE BE GOING?

We begin by examining the identity of bioethics: what it is, how it emerged, and how it has evolved, ethically speaking. Charting a path through bioethics' beginnings is the challenge taken up by Carol Levine in the opening chapter, "Analyzing Pandora's Box: The History of Bioethics." Levine astutely distinguishes between the origins of the term *bioethics* and the origins of the field, describing how it broke out of the confines of the academy and entered the public consciousness by means of dramatic events. From arguably radical origins—indeed, in its early days it might have been called a "social movement"—she charts how the field rapidly became institutionalized. In tracing this history Levine highlights fundamental tensions that persist and complicate efforts to identify fundamental values for the field, which she describes, notably, as a healing profession.

Robert Baker continues from a historical perspective, raising the question of whether, given the field's evolution and the experiences of its members, the time has come to formulate a binding code of ethics for bioethics in the United States. Applauding earlier efforts to articulate ethical ideals and professional standards, Baker, in "A History of Codes of Ethics for Bioethicists," argues for advancing beyond what he regards as reactive, piecemeal, and merely advisory instruments. He takes into account the arguments of "anti-code skeptics" yet concludes that a code is necessary to provide authoritative guidance and protection for the field and its members, to prevent abuses of power, and to assert integrity to employers, the media, and the public at large.

BIOETHICS AND THE PROBLEMS OF EXPERTISE

In the second section we address concerns regarding "expertise" as it relates to bioethics. Perceptions of and claims to expertise raise moral quandaries about how we represent ourselves, use our knowledge and skills, and embed ourselves within institutions.

In "The Tyranny of Expertise," Carl Elliott ruminates on whether bioethicists have become self-important and are rightly invested with moral authority. Especially troublesome, according to Elliott, is the authority given to bioethicists not merely because of their knowledge and abilities but because of the social and institutional positions some have come to occupy and, in particular, their links to larger, bureaucratic power structures. He calls for bioethicists to take considerably more care in how we wield our expertise lest we tarnish our own moral character, threaten the public good, and undermine the moral agency of others. While his analysis suggests a need for social, institutional, and organizational reforms, it might also be seen as entreating us to consider Socratic humility and Aristotelian proper pride as defining values for the field.

Like Elliott, James Lindemann Nelson wonders whether bioethicists should be trusted. Nelson examines the ethical implications of exerting influence on the formation of people's moral beliefs, given the potential for "corrupting" them, leading them astray, and promoting "servility." His focus, then, is not on the corrosive effects of institutional power but, instead, on our well-meaning efforts to use our expertise in the service of helping people navigate their moral lives. Calling for an invigorated discussion of "expertise," Nelson concludes that there are good reasons for trusting bioethicists, and that it is possible for us to avoid harming others by diminishing their moral capacities. He cautions, however, that the concerns here—which lie at the very heart of the professional endeavors of many in the field—are not amenable to codes of ethics or attempts at standardization.

CONTRIBUTIONS AND CONFLICTS: POLICY AND POLITICS

In the third section we move to questions about the varied contributions of bioethics and bioethicists. How do we contribute to society and to institutions? What are our roles and responsibilities, and how do we ethically discharge them? What ethical concerns arise from those contributions, or our failures to contribute?

M. L. Tina Stevens opens the third section by arguing for a fundamental obligation of the field to educate the public and to serve as a resource for strengthening the moral agency of the citizenry and, ultimately, public policy. Stevens, a historian, is among those external critics of bioethics. She has censured the field for working to maintain the status quo and supporting the interests of the powerful rather than serving the public as social critic. In "Intellectual Capital and Voting Booth Bioethics: A Contemporary Historical Critique," she expands her analysis of what she sees as a long-standing tendency for the field to "foster quiescence" and issues it a specific challenge: to take on the role of public educator so that citizens can more effectively participate in science and technology policy. She uses the passage of California's Proposition 71—which allows for human embryonic stem cell research—as a cautionary tale demonstrating what can happen when powerful financial incentives obscure important information and the expertise bioethicists might offer in the public arena seems elusive if not altogether absent.

Also convinced that bioethicists have an obligation to participate in the formation of legislation and public policy is David Orentlicher, a bioethicist who won a seat in his state's house of representatives. In "Bioethics and Society: From the Ivory Tower to the State House," Orentlicher discusses how precisely bioethicists—whether they have the privilege of serving as elected officials or not—can contribute to the democratic process, elevate the level of ethical discourse, and help to ensure that public policy rests on sound ethical analysis. With its portrayal of a bioethicist-legislator, his essay also contributes to the field's collective wisdom on how to maintain integrity under political and other pressures in different professional roles and environs.

Throughout their history, bioethicists have served the public as members of government bioethics commissions. In "Democratic Ideals and Bioethics Commissions: The Problem of Expertise in an Egalitarian Society," Mark Kuczewski recognizes the tensions surrounding claims of expertise in the field and considers what makes for ethical (and effective) government bioethics commissions in pluralistic, liberal democracies. Bioethics commissions offer one way to help us, as members of a moral community, engage in public discussions of how science, medicine, and technology can and should shape our pursuit of a good life. These bodies can be seen as ethically ideal mechanisms in that they allow for deliberation guided by expertise and organized around the democratic ideals of accountability and transparency. They can help us to avoid the ethical perils associated with self-interested politics and tyrannical rule, and they have the potential to enhance citizens' moral agency. Kuczewski calls for caution, however. Bioethics commissions can also fall short of democratic ideals and can—depending upon how they operate—"fail the public."

It is precisely this concern that motivates the essay by R. Alta Charo. With a critical eye aimed at President George W. Bush's Council on Bioethics, her essay "The Endarkenment," describes the interlocking relationships between the President's Council on Bioethics and the neoconservative movement and questions whether such connections are ethically appropriate for a public body in a pluralistic democracy. Intent on highlighting how ethical analysis should operate in the context of public bioethics bodies, Charo is sharply critical of cloistered commissions used for the purposes of organizing political coalitions and advancing predetermined policy agendas.

If there are identifiable biases in bioethics, it is the left-leaning tendencies of the field that should most concern us, according to Griffin Trotter. In "Left Bias in Academic Bioethics: Three Dogmas," he acknowledges the neoconservative influences that distress Charo but claims that liberal propensities are the greater problem. Trotter distinguishes between two kinds of conservatism and argues that one variety in particular, "stasis conservatism," pervades bioethics, rendering left-liberalism an unscrutinized habit, while the other, "partisan conservatism," is absent from usual bioethics dialogue. He then identifies three "dogmas" to illustrate the liberal tendencies of the field. Such leanings are ethically suspect, according to Trotter, for they threaten legitimate inquiry and hold troubling implications for public policy. Given what he sees as bleak prospects for moral consensus, bioethicists should refrain from making substantive recommendations and instead confine themselves to helping clarify the meaning and implications of different moral arguments and perspectives.

H. Tristram Engelhardt Jr., like Trotter, contends, in "Bioethics as Politics: A Critical Reassessment," that the reality of moral pluralism is an insurmountable hurdle to true ethical consensus. After offering a historical account of the social authority of bioethics, he argues that the field cannot fulfill the promise of providing a common, secularly accessible morality to society. The ordering of basic human needs will remain controversial; thus negotiated policies cannot offer definitive moral conclusions. In the end, he concludes, the pursuit of consensus is better sacrificed to a search for appropriate political structures.

Unlike Engelhardt, Mary Faith Marshall argues that consensus on ethical standards is attainable, and sometimes essential. She draws on her experience speaking out against her institution's policy of facilitating the incarceration of pregnant, drug-abusing women (described earlier in this volume by Baker). As a result of her experience, the American Society for Bioethics and Humanities (ASBH) revised its bylaws to allow the organization to take positions on professional matters. In "ASBH and Moral Tolerance," Marshall challenges ASBH and the field as a whole to go further, exhorting bioethicists to publicly decry unethical policies and practices. Citing the example of physicians' involvement in prisoner abuse at Abu Ghraib, she questions the ethics of the field's refusal to take stands against injustice. Like Stevens, she wonders where the voices of bioethicists are on ethical issues of public importance.

Lisa S. Parker brings needed clarity to conversations about the relationship between bioethics, deliberative democracy, and activism. Parker considers the meaning, methods, and goals of each and argues that bioethics reflects elements of both deliberative democracy and activism. Her work "Bioethics as Activism" offers an intriguing response to allegations that the field fails to challenge structures of power and address inequalities and has come up short on serving the public good.

CONTRIBUTIONS AND CONFLICTS: CONSULTATION
IN THE CLINIC AND THE CORPORATE WORLD

Earlier generations of bioethicists faced criticism for aligning themselves with hospitals, physicians, and other sources of institutional power. While concern over this persists, it is work in business and corporate settings that has received more recent scrutiny. The institutional landscape(s) in which bioethicists now find themselves present new perils. We must navigate within and around new kinds of economic structures and relationships, new models of health care delivery, a rapidly changing, increasingly complex clinical research enterprise, and arguably, a more polarized and confused polity; at the same time, we are working to shape the future of bioethics by educating students and seeking out new opportunities to broaden and deepen the field's contributions. When the topics bioethicists work on and the methods we use are shaped, even distorted, by our institutional contexts, how do we uphold the dignity of the profession? How do we maintain its moral legitimacy? When we find ourselves in the employ of institutions, or individuals, with tarnished ethical ideals, how do we keep from becoming a field full of Mr. Stevenses—the ever-faithful butler in Kazuo Ishiguro's *The Remains of the Day?* The authors in the fourth section consider how work in ethically challenged contexts might be carried out in ethically acceptable ways.

In "Ethics on the Inside?" Debra A. DeBruin examines the perception that bioethicists have "sold out." DeBruin offers a nuanced analysis of the meaning of "insider," exploring alternative ways of conceptualizing the role of the bioethicist-in-institution and enriching our understanding of how we can be morally compromised and how we might avoid it. She argues that ultimately individuals and institutions share responsibility for protecting and promoting the field's dignity, that is, its moral legitimacy. DeBruin concludes with concrete ideas on how institutions and professional organizations might do their part, emphasizing the importance of cultivating conditions of authentic academic inquiry and freedom.

Virginia A. Sharpe's essay, "Strategic Disclosure Requirements and the Ethics of Bioethics," highlights the role of market forces in science, academia, and increasingly, bioethics. Sharpe takes for granted that the field and its professionals in this contemporary context are vulnerable to organizing research agendas around money (and power) and to being used in the service of shielding corporate (and other) entities from scrutiny. In the absence of collective refusal to accept corporate dollars, she argues that we must reckon with the ways economic structures and relationships can seep in to twist the inquiries, analyses, and judgments of bioethicists. She examines the potential for disclosure—a minimal condition—to uphold the integrity of bioethics and stay true to its moral grounding, namely public service, or "enabling people to make informed decisions." Along with Elliott, Nelson, and Stevens, Sharpe is particularly concerned about the field's potential to lead people astray and to disempower them as moral agents, a matter made more urgent by the growing influence of industry. She sets the stage for her argument by offering an inventory of the factors that obscure our ability to see our efforts as part of larger social, political, and economic structures and relationships.

In "Ties without Tethers: Bioethics Corporate Relations in the AbioCor Artificial Heart Trial," E. Haavi Morreim argues by example that corporate involvement without conflict of interest is possible and even desirable. She describes her experience with ABIOMED, the small corporation that designed the AbioCor artificial heart and, notably for bioethics, the Independent Patient Advocacy Council (IPAC), an advisory group charged with giving ethical guidance for the company's clinical trial of the device. She highlights features of the IPAC's structure that, she maintains, enabled her and other members to support ABIOMED in its commitment to promoting ethical ideals without feeling constrained or otherwise ethically compromised by the corporate tie. She ends with insights on what makes for effective and ethical consulting relationships for others who actively seek or will otherwise find themselves at an industry conference table in the future.

DEFINING VALUES AND OBLIGATIONS

In exploring the ethical challenges facing the field, the authors herein speak of humility, honesty, and transparency and the need to promote—even restore—dignity and trust. This section offers a more explicit discussion of defining values and obligations for bioethics and bioethicists. Which ones should govern the field and guide those working within it? How might they inform research agendas, educational programs, methods of inquiry, and collegial relations?

Building upon her work on the importance of character, and in particular, moral courage, Françoise Baylis considers the role of integrity in the life of the ethics consultant. In "Of Courage, Honor, and Integrity," she identifies ways in which the exercise of moral courage can be thwarted for ethics consultants working to make "health care institutions, practices, and policies more just in their impact on individuals and groups." Yet Baylis's principal aim in this essay is to cast light on the perils of misperception and misinterpretation for ethics consultants, or more specifically, the potential for moral achievement, courage, and integrity to be mistaken for arrogance. In a rich and inspiring analysis, Baylis clearly distinguishes arrogance from integrity and describes how integrity can serve as a cardinal virtue for bioethics.

Laurie Zoloth calls for shifting to an ethic of hospitality. In "I Want You: Notes toward a Theory of Hospitality," she asks how we are to treat our "neighbors." She contends that accounts of moral agency that arise from Kantian notions of autonomy and dignity neglect the complexity of human relationships and concerns of justice. "Hospitality" refers to an opening away from the self and toward the other, and so serves as a better guide for the praxis of bioethics. In prose drawing on Levinas and both religious and secular thinkers, she lays out a compelling conception of hospitality that can inform work in bioethics.

Judith Andre considers the role of what she calls "second-order moral perception" in bioethics. Second-order moral perception refers to appreciation not merely of the moral worth of others and the ethical dimensions of issues or circumstances but also of the fact that people are moral perceivers who see the moral landscape in a particular way. In "Learning to Listen: Second-Order Moral Perception and the Work of Bioethics," Andre takes three examples—the burden of disease in the developing world, the lack of universal health coverage in the United States, and the suffering of animals in intensive agriculture—to illustrate why second-order moral perception should be a defining ethical capacity for the field, enabling bioethicists to greatly enhance the breadth and depth of their contributions.

For the sake of social justice, Leigh Turner challenges bioethicists to expand their research agendas. In "Global Health Inequalities and Bioethics"—which continues the thread of discussion on how and for whom we should use our intellectual and other resources—Turner analyzes why certain topics tend to be neglected by bioethicists and why this can represent moral failure. In the end he offers recommendations for how bioethicists might refocus their moral attention to help remedy this form of myopia and thereby redress global injustices, an obligation for the field.

Concern about our methods is what motivates Catherine Myser's essay "White Normativity in U.S. Bioethics: A Call and Method for More Pluralist and Democratic Standards and Policies." Taking aim at the "dominance and normativity of whiteness in the cultural construction of [U.S.] bioethics," Myser argues that the field and its members risk perpetuating inequalities and undermining social justice by failing to scrutinize the theories and methods used for "managing" ethical issues. She recommends community-based participatory research as a remedy that can support egalitarian, democratic decision making and generate policy that promotes social justice.

In thinking about the ethics of bioethics, we would be remiss if we neglected to consider obligations to colleagues—present and future. James F. Childress writes about our obligations to future generations and explores the importance of mentoring in "Mentoring in Bioethics: Possibilities and Problems." After analyzing of the role of the mentor in general, he considers the implications for bioethics in particular and elaborates on how experienced bioethicists can uphold obligations to future generations, namely their students and junior colleagues.

As a final contribution for this section, Hilde Lindemann outlines the shared moral obligations involved in the processes of publication: writing, editing, publishing, reviewing, and for many, mentoring graduate students. In "Obligations to Fellow and Future Bioethicists: Publication," she details the responsibilities and pitfalls of each activity. For what and how bioethicists publish reflect the field's values and commitments, shape the values of others, and, in part, determine our own and future professionals' opportunities.

ASSESSING BIOETHICS AND BIOETHICISTS

As bioethics evolves and continues to face criticism, questions of assessment and professional reflection naturally arise. To date, discussions concerning the evaluation or assessment of bioethics and bioethicists have centered on strategies such as certification or credentialing (Aulisio, Arnold, and Youngner 1999, 2000). The authors included here propose less conventional and more broadly inclusive methods.

Tod Chambers, in "The Virtue of Attacking the Bioethicist," considers the value of ad hominem critiques and argues that the field should embrace them. Highlighting three varieties—motivation, bias, and what we might call "moral identity" ad hominem arguments—Chambers shows how such critiques can promote self-reflexivity in moral reasoning, expand and strengthen the analysis of ethical issues, and more radically, facilitate a kind of moral identity therapy for individual bioethicists.

Allen Buchanan, concerned about the field's epistemic reliability, and in turn, ethical performance, takes aim at the standard methodologies of bioethics. In "Social Moral Epistemology and the Role of Bioethicists" he describes the nature and utility of social moral epistemology, which scrutinizes the relationship between social practices and institutions, true beliefs, and right actions. Using the examples of medical paternalism and eugenics, Buchanan shows how this variety of moral epistemology can remedy serious deficiencies in the analyses generated by the field and also serve as a method for individual bioethicists to embrace in assessing themselves.

Nancy M. P. King's essay, "The Glass House: Assessing Bioethics," problematizes the matter of what it means to assess bioethics. Highlighting the works of the contributors in this collection, King considers what exactly should be assessed: who we are? what we do? the focus of our work? What might be the objective of assessment? How should it be accomplished? After considering these questions, she asks whether bioethics would benefit from the usual methods proposed, or if a strategy of cultivating a certain kind of "disposition"—toward high standards for scholarship, openness, and humility—might better serve us, and those who look to us for help.

We are honored to present this volume, a collection of voices and ideas brought together in what will be an ongoing and we hope respectful and constructive conversation about the future of the field. Developing an authoritative consensus on the issues discussed in these essays is a vital next step for bioethics. It is vital for the purpose of satisfactorily addressing the full range of ethical questions confronted by a wide array of professionals working in diverse contexts. And it is vital for us to be able to promote appreciation for the functions and contributions of bioethics and bioethicists, to defend our integrity, and to justify the resources and trust others—patients, families, scientists, health professionals, policy makers, and others—invest in us.

REFERENCES

Canadian Bioethics Society. 2003. Model Code of Ethics for Bioethics. Available at www .bioethics.ca/draftcode.pdf

Partners in the BIOMED II Project. 2000. Barcelona Declaration. Final Project Report: Basic Ethical Principles in European Bioethics and Biolaw, Institut Borja de Bioètica, Barcelona, and Centre for Ethics and Law, Copenhagen.

Scientific Committee of the International Society of Bioethics. 2000. Bioethics Declaration of Gijón. Available at www.sibi.org/ingles/ddc/bio.htm

UNESCO. 2005. Draft Declaration on Universal Norms in Bioethics. Available at www .unesco.org

PART I

Situating Bioethics

Where Have We Been? Where Should We Be Going?

CHAPTER ONE

Analyzing Pandora's Box

The History of Bioethics

CAROL LEVINE, M.A.

The definitive history of bioethics has yet to be written. That is not surprising since bioethics in its modern American incarnation is only about fifty years old. But the future historian will have a mountain of source material, for nearly everyone involved in the field has written about some clinical dilemma, legal ruling, policy option, philosophical analysis, or personal experience. All the many public commissions and advisory boards that have examined specific issues have produced a flood of documents.

The future historian will also have the benefit of several publications by some of the major participants themselves—notably books by David Rothman (1992), Al Jonsen (1998), H. Tristram Engelhardt Jr. (1996), and members of the Kennedy Institute of Ethics (Walter and Klein, 2003) and articles by Stephen Toulmin (1988), Daniel Callahan (1999, 2005), Renée C. Fox and Judith P. Swazey (2005), David Thomasma (2002), and Daniel Kevles (2000), among others. The various editions of the *Encyclopedia of Bioethics* (1978, 1995, 2003) are a rich resource. Some accounts criticize bioethics in terms of its founding principles and current practice (Stevens 2000; Evans 2002; Short 2003; and Smith 2002), seeing capitulation to the demands of transplantation or other technology (Stevens), hubris (Evans and Smith), or plain misreading of the basic philosophical texts (Short).

There are also a few attempts to revise the conventional wisdom about some of the early debates. For example, it is often stated that the Report of the Harvard Ad Hoc Committee to Examine the Definition of Brain Death developed the concept of "brain death" in 1968 to facilitate procuring organs for transplantation. In reviewing the original documents, especially the papers of Henry Beecher, one of the most prominent committee members, and interviews with surviving members, Gary Belkin concluded that "a more careful history of the Report pushes interest in transplantation to the side, and sees it as a subset of the primary problem of coma and hopelessness" (Belkin 2003, 357). It is likely that future historians may also revise other articles of faith within bioethics about early decisions and reports.

Increasingly, writing about bioethics analyzes not just the issues that concern the field, but the field itself. What started as a largely academic, fairly modest endeavor has moved rapidly onto the center stage of media, political, and public attention. While some of the ideas were radical for their time, and bioethics at its beginnings had many elements of a social movement, institutionalization set in rather quickly.

As a participant over the past thirty years in some of the major ethical debates, I do not claim to be totally objective. Nevertheless, I hope to provide in this chapter as unbiased a view as possible, relying on my own experience and those elements of the historical record that are easily available. The founding fathers (and they were indeed mostly fathers or Fathers) would undoubtedly be amazed that their efforts had created so much controversy. The widespread interest in matters bioethical today confirms the premise that bioethics addresses critical issues affecting the way we live and die; however, some of the internal focus also threatens to distract attention from the issues themselves. Will this revolution, like so many others, end by eating its own children?

WHERE DID BIOETHICS COME FROM?

This question can be answered in two ways: the origin of the term and the origin of the field. The term *bioethics* itself was born twice—in Wisconsin and in Washington, D.C. Influenced by the work of land ethicist and conservationist Aldo Leopold (1949), Van Rensselaer Potter, a cancer specialist at the University of Wisconsin, published an article in 1970 called "Bioethics, the Science of Survival." In it he proposed "bioethics" as a global movement integrating concern for the environment and ethics (Potter 1970). He extended these views in his book *Bioethics: A Bridge to the Future* (1971), which proposed bioethics as a link between science and humanities. Later, as Potter saw mainstream bioethics focusing more on technology and genetics, he modified his original term and called his position "global bioethics" (Potter 1998). Without using the term, Hans Jonas, a German philosopher-in-exile who taught at the New School for Social Research for many years, focused on many of the same issues in his philosophical writing, especially the "imperative of responsibility" to sustain the planet for future generations (Jonas 1984).

As Peter Whitehouse, Potter's student and disciple, put it, "The original formulation of bioethics by Van Rensselaer Potter included a profound commitment to the future that the world desperately needs bioethicists to rediscover" (Whitehouse 2003, W26). Potter's concerns were relatively dormant within bioethics for many years but have surfaced recently in the controversy over genetic manipulation of food and other environmental issues and a more global focus in the field.

Also in 1970 Sargent Shriver, husband of Eunice Kennedy Shriver, came up with the term *bioethics* in discussions with André Hellegers, a Dutch physician and Jesuit priest, and others about the creation of an institute at Georgetown University that would apply moral philosophy to medical dilemmas (Reich 1994, 1995). These discussions resulted in the creation in 1971 of the Joseph and Rose Kennedy Center for the Study of Human Reproduction and Bioethics, now known as the Kennedy Institute of Ethics. While Potter's use of *bioethics* was the first to be published, it was the Kennedy Institute's use of the term, focusing on medicine and an institutional base for scholarly discussion, which came to dominate the field.

What were the origins of bioethics as a field of inquiry? An anthropologist might observe that its followers tell different creation stories. In one version, bioethics in Western thought starts with the Hippocratic corpus. Another goes back to the British physician Thomas Percival's 1803 book *Medical Ethics*, which argued for professional codes of ethics and which influenced the first American codes of medical ethics a half century later. Early codes of ethics were largely but not exclusively focused on the guild aspects of medicine and mutual obligations among practitioners.

When it comes to America in the mid-twentieth century, the creation stories are often summarized in a word—"Nuremberg," "Tuskegee," "Willowbrook," and more. All of these stand for part of but not the whole story. In its foundational beliefs in individual autonomy, bioethics had a distinctly American cast. In warning against American "bioethics imperialism," however, Moreno (2004) cites the experience of Weimar Germany in the early 1930s when a few physicians created a journal called *Ethics* to discuss various theories of eugenics, then the dominant social philosophy of medicine. Moreno calls the devolution of this journal into a Nazi tract for racial purification a warning that an intellectual movement can slide into disaster.

Hanauske-Abel (1996) interprets the situation differently. Rather than the German medical community being a "victim of circumstances," he contends that it set its own course. Medical organizations voluntarily placed the resources and loyalties of their profession at the service of the state. Within a short period in 1933 doctors in some respects even outpaced the Nazi regime in enthusiastically carrying out eugenic sterilizations. (Several other countries, including the United States, permitted forced sterilization, with the imprimatur of the U.S. Supreme Court's 1927 decision in *Buck v. Bell,* into the 1960s [Kevles 2000].)

Moreover, in 1931 a federal law in Germany was passed that clearly specified the obligations of physicians and the rights of patients in medical research (Sass 1983). Even stricter in some ways than the Nuremberg Code that followed the trial of German doctors in 1947, these rules were not repealed under the Nazis. Nevertheless, in the Nazi period German physicians carried out some of the most heinous and cruel abuses ever conducted under medical aegis. If their digression illustrates one overriding theme, it is that medical ethics is inextricably entwined with the social and political forces of its time and place.

In our time and our place, bioethics emerged in the late 1950s and 1960s, a turbulent era in which authorities of all kinds—parental, academic, political, medical, military—were challenged. In this version of the creation story, one need name only the key events of the period to realize the impact on all sectors of society: Vatican II, with its appeal to modernize the Catholic Church; the Vietnam War and its dissenters; college campuses turned into battlefields; the birth control pill that revolutionized women's control over reproduction; various rights movements, starting with civil rights for black Americans, then women's rights, gay and lesbian rights, abortion rights, disability rights, animal rights, and more. Some of these social movements directly affected the emergence of bioethics; others contributed to the general tenor of the times.

This was also a period in which scientific advances were creating startling and often unsettling new possibilities in controlling and facilitating reproduction, modifying behavior, and understanding genetics. People who would have died in earlier eras could be sustained on life-prolonging machinery, not just feeding tubes but also dialysis machines and ventilators. Extremely premature infants could be kept alive, albeit with significant health problems. Decisions had to be made about allocating kidney dialysis machines, then a scarce resource. Organ transplantation became feasible, if there were enough organs to transplant. So many of these inventions have become so commonplace and so accepted, and in some cases inappropriately used, that it is worth remembering that they did not always exist. The agonizing decisions that make up so much of modern bioethics discussion are the outcomes of modern technology introduced with great hopes but little forethought. In this brave new world most physicians assumed, as they had for centuries, that they were the only appropriate decision makers. Against this background it seemed inevitable that patients would begin to challenge physicians' authority.

Partnership in decision making is now often presented as the ideal, especially given the often overwhelming amount and easy access to medical information of variable quality. But when bioethics emerged, physicians had almost total control of information and decision-making power. The women's movement of the 1960s and 1970s was a front-line attack on this patriarchal and authoritarian model. In the "good old days" of the 1950s doctors frequently performed "one-step" mastectomies—breast biopsies followed immediately by radical surgery—without the patient's knowledge or consent (Lerner 2001). Why trouble the little woman, they said, when I can just tell her husband what I am going to do? In the early 1980s women's groups succeeded in getting state legislation requiring informed consent and disclosure of alternatives for breast cancer treatments. The right to be heard and to be treated as full moral and political agents was not just a rallying cry; it was at the core of the women's movement.

In recalling his early days in promoting a patient-centered ethic as opposed to a physician-dominated ethic, Veatch says: "The arrogance of the medical professional claiming that he or she (mostly 'he') had the authority to decide, even against a patient's wishes, what was best for the patient was morally indefensible. Physicians were deciding not only that continued tortuous life support was in a dying person's best interest but that the physician's 'order' justified continued infliction of that torture. That ethic seemed so wrong, so contrary to any moral decency, that it was only natural to challenge it in the name of patients' rights" (Veatch 2002, 345).

Those who determined to provide some reflection on all these issues—the founders of bioethics—came largely from a religious or philosophical background or were philosophically inclined physicians or scientists. Among the physicians were Eric Cassell, Fritz Redlich, Robert Morison, and Robert F. Murray Jr. Scientists included Theodosius Dobzhansky, Rene Dubos, and Ernst Mayr. Among the most prominent nonscientists were Richard McCormick, a Jesuit priest; Warren Reich, a Catholic philosopher; K. Danner Clouser, the first philosopher to teach ethics in a medical school (Pennsylvania State University); and Sam Gorovitz, a philosopher at Case Western Reserve University. Prominent Protestant theologians involved in bioethics included William F. May of Southern Methodist University, James Gustafson of the University of Chicago, Ralph Potter of the Harvard Divinity School, Stanley Hauerwas, now at Duke University Divinity School, and Paul Ramsey of Princeton University, whose book *The Patient as Person* (1970) was a major statement of the primary goal of medicine. Joseph Fletcher, an Episcopalian priest turned atheist, taught at Harvard Divinity School and then at the University Virginia; his 1954 book *Morals and Medicine,* and his 1966 work *Situation Ethics,* offered an approach in which rules were meant to be reviewed, not necessarily followed and in which decisions should be made on the basis of a Christian love.

In 1969 in Hastings-on-Hudson, New York, Daniel Callahan, a philosopher and former editor of the liberal Catholic journal *Commonweal,* and Willard Gaylin, a psychiatrist, formed the Institute of Society, Ethics, and the Life Sciences, later changed to the Hastings Center. Institutes, centers, and departments of medical ethics and medical humanities sprang up around the country soon after. The Kennedy Institute was a collection of scholars working and teaching more or less independently. The Hastings Center had a different model: it convened research groups from among its fellows (elected from scholars and others around the country) and led by a staff member. The Hastings Center chose the independent "think tank" model but only after considering and rejecting university affiliation (Callahan 1999). As a staff member and participant in Hastings Center meetings from 1975 to 1987, I can attest to their abstract nature and rarefied tenor during the early years, the absence of media interest, and the limited dissemination of the results, either through publication in the *Hastings Center Report* or another scholarly journal or book. The meetings were often stimulating and spirited but in the way that seminars can be stimulating and academic debates can be spirited. There wasn't a twenty-second sound bite to be heard. Nor can I recall more than a handful of conversations that escaped the bounds of civility.

The university-based model had certain advantages for the early bioethics ventures. Affiliation brought credibility, an administrative and financial home (although supporting funds had to be raised), academic appointments for scholars, and often access to medical schools and clinical services. On the other hand, university affiliations placed bioethics squarely in the academic world with all its "ivory tower" connotations, and subjected bioethics to the vagaries of university politics and policies. Medical centers connected with universities usually have their own administrations and priorities; integrating bioethics into a world controlled by physicians required the ability to get along in this environment, not always a comfortable position for a nonmedical outsider. Universities welcomed bioethics because they saw an opportunity to be in the forefront of a new wave of public interest and government funding.

Scholars had varying reasons to take this new career path but were influenced by a combination of the compelling and stimulating nature of the questions being discussed and dissatisfaction with the prevailing currents in disciplines such as philosophy. As Thomasma recalled, "ethics was not where the action was in philosophy . . . and applied philosophy was the lowest possible kind of philosophy in the hierarchy of the department" (Thomasma 2002, 339). In the title of a classic article, Stephen Toulmin, a British philosopher of science, put it bluntly: medicine saved ethics (1982).

Once scholars began to find new homes in universities, they began to do what scholars in any field do: they banded together, sought funding, found new outlets for their writing, convened conferences, and promoted their interests among students and administrators. New journals appeared linking medicine and ethics, such as the *Journal of Medicine and Philosophy, Theoretical Medicine and Bioethics,* and *Perspectives in Biology and Medicine.*

The Society for Health and Human Values (SHHV) was established by a collaboration of the Protestant and Methodist United Ministries in Education in 1970. The Society was funded by the National Endowment for the Humanities and the Russell Sage Foundation. Edmund Pellegrino, a physician, became the chairman of the Institute on Human Values in Medicine, which was focused on education in medical schools. After much deliberation about the advantages and disadvantages of having separate societies with similar missions, in January 1998 the SHHV merged with the American Society for Bioethics and the Society for Bioethics Consultation (SBC) to form the American Society for Bioethics and Humanities (ASBH). The ASBH now has over fifteen hundred individual and institutional members. Future historians of bioethics organizations will find eleven linear feet of shelf space devoted to the archives of the SHHV at the University of Texas Medical Branch in Galveston.

If one were to list all the names of all the people who were involved in bioethics in these early years, the list would include at most seventy-five to one hundred people, nearly all with academic appointments in philosophy, theology, or medicine. When Al Jonsen convened a conference on "The Birth of Bioethics" in 1992, he limited the invitations to "pioneers"—those who had been named in the first edition of the *Bibliography of Bioethics* (1975) and continued to work in the field— a total of sixty people (Jonsen 1993). Only a few women (Karen Lebacqz of the Pacific Institute of Religion, Patricia King of Georgetown Law Center, Sissela Bok of Harvard, Ruth Macklin of Case Western Reserve University and then the Hastings Center, and Loretta Kopelman of East Carolina University) and a few lawyers (King, Harold Edgar of Columbia University, and Alexander Morgan Capron) were involved. Renée Fox of the University of Pennsylvania and Judith Swazey of Boston University represented the social sciences. Robert Murray, a medical geneticist at Howard University, and King were the only prominent African Americans, and other minority groups were not represented at all.

In their early years bioethics programs depended on the generosity of individuals (the Kennedys) or foundations (Rockefeller Foundation, Russell Sage Foundation, Ford Foundation, and others). Government support came from the National Library of Medicine and the National Endowment for the Humanities. There was little or no corporate support.

Several events brought bioethics out of the seminar room into the glare of politicians, the public, and the media. The first was a series of congressional hearings convened by Senator Walter Mondale, a fellow of the Hastings Center, in 1975 around issues of experimentation that resulted in the establishment of the National Commission for the Protection of Human Subjects of Biomedical and Behavioral Research and ultimately the system of institutional review boards (IRBs) that has oversight over federally funded research. Research scandals were the impetus for the National Commission—Beecher's 1966 article on unethical experimentation in the United States, the 1972 revelations about the forty-year history of the Tuskegee syphilis study, and concerns about fetal experimentation and prisoners as research subjects. The National Commission was the first of six (so far) national commissions under different names and sponsorships; it proved, according to Albert Dzur and Daniel Levin, that "bioethics and advisory commissions were made for each other" (2004, 334).

The second event to bring attention to bioethics was the case of Karen Ann Quinlan, a young New Jersey woman who in 1975 suffered irreversible brain damage and whose parents sought to have her ventilator removed. The 1976 decision in the legal case led to the creation of ethics committees in hospitals around the country to advise on end-of-life dilemmas and other controversies. Along with bioethics representation on IRBs to review research protocols, bioethicists were enlisted as members of these hospital or institutional ethics committees. Bioethics began to look less and less like the solitary pursuit of truth and justice and more like employment as the designated ethics hitter on a variety of clinical and policy teams.

Other events also played a role. As early as 1962 the public became aware of resource allocation issues when Shana Alexander, a journalist, published an article in *Life* magazine, then a leading source of America's news and public opinion, called "They Decide Who Lives, Who Dies." (The thirtieth anniversary of this publication was the occasion for Jonsen's "Birth of Bioethics" conference.) The subject was the deliberations of a Seattle hospital committee, which included nonphysicians, charged with deciding which of the several candidates for the new and scarce kidney dialysis machines would get them. The use of "social worth" criteria by the "God Committee" became a flashpoint for controversy. When a person with end-stage kidney disease was dialyzed in the halls of Congress, legislators bowed to public opinion and created the federal End-Stage Renal Disease (ESRD) program under Medicare. They justified this exception for a single disease as an interim step before national health insurance was passed. When the ESRD program was begun in 1973, it served 10,000 people on dialysis; there are now more than 320,000 patients, and the number and the cost keep growing.

In 1984 the "Baby Doe" rules were promulgated to address the care and treatment of infants born with birth defects. This issue, raised by the specific case of an Indiana baby whose parents opted against surgery, on the advice of physicians, brought to the fore questions of parental rights, decision making on behalf of an incompetent person, and the role of concepts such as "best interests of the child." The first rules, based on section 504 of the Rehabilitation Act of 1973, were replaced in 1985 by rules based on amendments to the Child Abuse and Protection and Treatment Act. In order to receive federal funding, states must have in place procedures for reporting and addressing cases of withholding "medically indicated" treatment. Even now, these rules are controversial (Kopelman 2005).

The National Commission for the Protection of Human Subjects of Biomedical and Behavioral Research and the various commissions that followed brought what had been an academic or a clinically focused enterprise squarely into the public policy arena. The Quinlan case brought the kind of agonizing decision that had been largely unexamined and private into the open and into the media. The Seattle dialysis committee raised awareness of allocation issues. And the Baby Doe rules started a public discussion of the appropriate care of infants born with serious birth defects who would have died in earlier periods.

These shifts created the at times uneasy and ill-defined role of bioethics in public policy and clinical decision making. For all that bioethicists proclaim that they do not "make decisions" but only "lay out the options and the moral reasoning behind them," and only "advise" on public policy, there continue to be critics who assign ulterior motives or believe that bioethicists have no special expertise in determining what is ethical and what is not.

THE EARLIEST BIOETHICS ISSUES

In the early years, as bioethics was defining itself, it also got to choose its agenda, in contrast to the situation today, when to a large degree the bioethics agenda follows the news or policy makers' or corporate interests. Although some individuals have written extensively on important social and political questions in medicine, such as health care for the uninsured or disparities in health care based on race or ethnicity or the inadequacy of the acute care model of health care for an aging population, or firearm-related violence (Turner 2005), these problems have not been at the core of bioethics. On the other hand, other topics—stem cell research comes to mind—are almost obsessively pursued.

As already noted, one of the first issues to be raised on the new bioethics agenda was research ethics. This came about less as an echo of Nuremberg than as publicity about domestic scandals. Nevertheless, the Nazi experience was clearly a stimulus for Jay Katz, a psychiatrist who had lost family members in the Holocaust. In an apt description of the path of many at the time and even later, Katz says that he "wandered into bioethics" in the 1960s at Yale University's Law School. Recalling his first public lecture on human experimentation in 1965, he says that the senior physicians—his colleagues—in the audience were not pleased: "[They] told me afterwards, in polite but no uncertain terms, that the subject of human experimentation was not something to talk about and surely not in the way I had done it" (Katz 1994, 89). The cardinal sin that Katz had committed—less than two decades after the Nuremberg trials of Nazi doctors—was to suggest that there were complexities in the relationships between physician-investigators and patient-subjects and that disclosure of risks and obtaining of consent ought to be part of the research process.

The areas chosen by the Hastings Center as its focus were death and dying, genetics, reproductive biology and population issues, and behavior control (Callahan 1999, 60). All these issues (with the possible exception of population control) are still with us, albeit in different forms. Research on fetuses—one of the original stimuli for the creation of the National Commission—is governed by federal regulations; stem cell research has taken its place as one of the most divisive issues. In vitro fertilization, still thought of as science fiction in the 1960s, is now so commonplace that a whole industry has built up around strollers and other supplies for twin and triplet babies. Yet in 1978 the birth of Louise Brown, the first IVF baby, was a media sensation. Despite the U.S. Supreme Court decision in *Roe v. Wade* in 1973, legal abortion remains bitterly debated. Other permutations of reproductive technology—multiple births and births to older women, for example—are newer examples of the older debates about what is "natural" and to what extent medicine can or should control human reproduction.

When Willard Gaylin, co-founder of the Hastings Center, published a serious article with the tabloid title of "The Frankenstein Myth Becomes a Reality: We Have the Awful Knowledge to Make Exact Copies of Human Beings," cloning was still another science fiction theme (Gaylin 1972). While no one has yet cloned a human being, success in cloning animals (real, not fraudulent) has brought the possibility to the bioethics agenda, this time for real.

Some of the early debates on behavior control—psychosurgery, for example—have been resolved and that infamous procedure ceased to be performed. But others continue. The use of drugs to make children less hyperactive or to enhance athletic or academic performance are current issues with historical resonance. Of all the scientific advances, genetics is undoubtedly the one with the most dramatic implications. Early debates around genetics focused on screening—the possibility of stigmatizing or misleading populations such as African Americans by encouraging sickle cell screening, for example—employed techniques that, compared with knowledge about the human genome, seem primitive. Yet the basic question remains: What are the appropriate uses of genetic knowledge, especially given its uncertainties and implications for other aspects of a person's life? While early debates focused on detecting genes that cause disease, today's debates focus more on genetics to enhance human possibilities.

One of the Hastings Center's earliest research groups was devoted to "Death and Dying." That phrase, along with "terminal" illness, is now outmoded and bioethicists and others talk about end-of-life care. One of the earliest essays published in the *Hastings Center Report* (June 1971) was William F. May's "On Not Facing Death Alone: The Trauma of Dying Need Not Mean the Eclipse of the Human." Decades later, we are still trying to put that ideal into practice. Undoubtedly hospice and now palliative care have made a difference for some people, yet for many others death is still accompanied by unwanted and ineffective interventions, unrelieved pain and suffering, and a loss of personal dignity and autonomy. Advocates have moved from urging people to sign living wills to recommending advance directives and especially health care proxies, but no one has figured out a way to make people who do not want to think about death take that step and to ensure that those wishes are followed or, as the President's Council on Bioethics argues (2005), set aside on the grounds of the "authenticity of the person that is, not the person that was" (122). These legal documents are probably neither as flawed as critics would have it nor as fail-safe as proponents would like to believe.

International population control was on the agenda of the early bioethics movement, at least at the Hastings Center. Undoubtedly some of that interest came from the Rockefeller Foundation's own efforts to introduce family planning in developing countries, but the fear of explosive population growth was high all around, fueled in part by Paul Ehrlich's influential 1968 book *The Population Bomb*. The Hastings research group focused on ethical issues in governmental programs that encouraged sterilization in countries like India.

Apart from this issue, international dilemmas and public health concerns generally were not high on the early U.S. bioethics agenda. Today there is a much less parochial vision (Keenan 2005) and many contacts with colleagues in other countries. Some issues resonate more deeply with European colleagues, such as broad philosophical concepts such as the goals of medicine (Callahan 1999) or the ethics of genetically enhanced food. Asian and African societies still, for the most part, have desperate gaps in resources and coexisting Western and traditional medical systems. Many American bioethicists today urge the field to turn its attention to issues of fairness—what the rich and developed countries owe to the world's poorest people and to understanding cultural differences. By and large, however, bioethics in this country remains focused on domestic concerns, and often those that raise "interesting" but uncommon dilemmas. Even in the international context Western bioethics is still dominant. The IRB system has been established, with modifications, in all countries doing clinical research that will eventually be submitted to the Food and Drug Administration for approval.

In the 1970s and early 1980s infectious diseases were largely considered to have been controlled (except in far-off places like Africa). Medicine's successes had lulled its practitioners into complacency, and infectious diseases had never been high on the bioethics agenda. The advent of HIV/AIDS brought new and unsettling issues concerning the relationship between public health and personal liberties and the obligations of professionals to put themselves at risk by treating patients, as well as confronting their own beliefs about drug use and homosexuality. Now that effective pharmaceutical therapies are available in the United States, most but not all the bioethicists who continue to be interested in HIV/AIDS focus on the equitable allocation of antiretroviral drugs in Africa and Asia or on clinical trials in developing countries. Meanwhile, the epidemic continues at home, especially among young minority women and men. The ethical issues underlying prevention programs based on abstinence only, the pernicious role of stigma, or the power imbalance between men and women in "negotiating" safe sex are seldom discussed outside the public health world and rarely in ethics terms.

In addition to HIV/AIDS, the newest issues in bioethics concern terrorism and its threats to public health and individual liberties. The possible use of biological weapons and governmental efforts to combat terrorism have raised new questions for bioethics. Concern about medical participation in torture and interrogation of terror suspects in the Iraq war is an important related issue, one that goes to the heart of medical professional ethics. Although there is considerable continuity between the early days of bioethics and the present, the examples of HIV/AIDS and bioterrorism are reminders that the issues bioethics confronts can be new and urgent as well as old and familiar.

WHO SPEAKS FOR BIOETHICS AND IN WHAT LANGUAGE?

Even as bioethics was created as a new discipline in academia and medicine, some tensions were apparent at the outset. There was no department of bioethics to which interested people could apply for jobs or study. No one was a bioethicist; one's primary allegiance was to philosophy, medicine, nursing, theology, or law. As a consultant for the Institute on Human Values in Medicine, David Thomasma "was struck by how many philosophers were reluctant to 'leave' their own departments and disciplines and take up residency in a medical school or health sciences center" (Thomasma 2002, 335). Undoubtedly even fewer physicians were willing to leave the medical setting for a philosophy department. Veatch was probably the first person to choose the new field over his early academic training in pharmacology and his doctorate in ethics from the Harvard Divinity School to become the first staff person at the Institute of Society, Ethics, and the Life Sciences, with the title of "Associate for Medical Ethics" (Veatch 2002, 347).

From the beginning there have been tensions between clinicians and nonclinicians. Clinicians sometimes felt that their intimate knowledge of medicine, the hospital setting, and patients (as opposed to persons) privileged their views. This was particularly apparent in the development of clinical ethics, which discussed individual cases at the bedside or close to it. Nonclinicians, for their part, saw themselves as "outsiders" and believed that their perspective was more objective and brought structure to the discussion of moral dilemmas rather than letting them play out in idiosyncratic ways. Some nonclinicians took so zealously to their "white coats" that they began to sound more like doctors than doctors, some of whom learned to like the language of ethics or at least the language of autonomy and beneficence.

As Callahan points out (1999, 64), "the relationship [of bioethics] with the social sciences has always been somewhat troubled." Some of this may stem, he suggests, from the perception among social scientists that they were being replaced by ethicists on medical faculties, and that bioethicists do not take seriously enough the rigorous methods and broad perspectives of social science. And it is true, he says, that some bioethicists believe that social science knowledge is not decisive for moral judgments (the "is" is not an "ought" argument). For their part, some social scientists have been fairly caustic about bioethics. Charles Bosk, one of the most astute social science observers of medical practice and a frequent writer on ethical issues, titled one of his articles "Professional Ethicist Available: Logical, Secular, Friendly" (1999). If anything, the tension between bioethics and social sciences has not only abated, it seems to have reversed. Bioethicists today are likely to be enamored of data, and social scientists often are eager to apply their skills to bioethics issues.

Another type of dissension arose between philosophers and theologians or specialists in religious studies. Philosophers, working from a secular tradition based on texts from Locke to Rawls, sought to find grounds to justify or prohibit actions based on reason and moral arguments. The result was an appeal to principles, most influentially codified by Beauchamp and Childress (2001), as "beneficence, respect for persons, and justice." "Principlism" has been criticized since the 1980s, and autonomy, the corollary of respect for persons, is now beaten down at every turn, although there does not seem to be a movement to restore absolute authority over medical decision making to physicians. The principles approach, however, remains an important part of the bioethics canon.

For the most part theologians, whatever their denomination, looked to religious authority and traditional values for answers to modern dilemmas. This discussion did not remain a binary division for long; soon other types of value systems were suggested to fill the gaps—virtue ethics, feminist ethics, nursing ethics, narrative ethics, casuistry, for example. The earlier division between philosophers and theologians has a new incarnation in the division between bioethics as seen from a religious and politically conservative perspective (as in the President's Council on Bioethics, originally led by Leon Kass) and the academic tradition, which has been more secular and politically liberal in its interpretations.

These variations reflect, according to Belkin and Brandt (2001, 6), "a seemingly timeless tension between rules and circumstance, between an attempt at moral deliberation that derives ethics from larger theory, rules, or basic principles, or one that builds moral conclusions or consensus through responding to the particular circumstances or moral intuitions that appear in the context of a given case." Belkin and Brandt suggest a "historical ethics," one that attends to "the histories and historical assumptions that make a particular view compelling" (6–7). A historical ethics can bring more voices to the question, focus more on the process of moral deliberation rather than just the "right" answer, and can shift from abstract terms and concepts to the way in which experiences and practices are established in culture. Belkin and Brandt say: "The power of bioethical formulations is in their resonance with experience, in their consistency with how attitudes toward suffering, expectations about medicine, customs of establishing desert and entitlement, get formed, cohere, and change" (8). In giving "one cheer for bioethics," Churchill and Schenck (2005, 390) point to the importance of attending to the "moral experience of patients and practitioners" who may be "morally wise" although not "ethically learned."

In the public commission realm, Dzur and Levin (2004) see a tension between the competing visions of these groups as either "agenda-setting" or providing expertise. Agenda-setters, they say, "want to spark, guide, and learn from public debate," while experts "want answers and solutions that they can communicate to the public" (334). Critics such as Cheryl Noble (1982) argue against the idea that bioethicists have some sort of moral expertise. "Moral problems," she says, "are everybody's business" (7). Reflecting on his experience as assistant director of the President's Commission on the Protection of Human Subjects of Biomedical and Behavioral Research, Alan Weisbard concluded that staff philosophers' methods and standards were "better suited to the halls of academe than the halls of Congress" (Weisbard 1987, 783). Dzur and Levin believe that "bioethicists serving on a commission or on the staff do not have to think the same way as the average American. Instead, their pressing task is to clarify the terms of the debate" (349). "Although inevitable, the distance between the formal, small group, expert discourse of commissions and informal, widespread, public discourse must be traversed energetically and creatively" (353).

The relationship between medical humanities and bioethics is another area in which different approaches exist. Perhaps some of the tension results from differing perceptions of the definition of "medical humanities" and its place in the curriculum. For those trained in literary theory and criticism, fiction and poetry about doctors and patients comprise the core of medical humanities. Those trained in philosophy, history, and anthropology, on the other hand, see their disciplines as medical humanities as well. These fields are perhaps more easily included under the "bioethics" rubric, which tends to see literature as enrichment rather than enlightenment.

Although there is much overlap, Howard Brody, a physician, says that "the tension between bioethical and literary goals seems unavoidable . . . in the question of ambiguity" (Brody 1991, 99). Ethics seeks to strip away layers of ambiguity to find a core that can be understood in terms of agreed-upon concepts and principles. Literature, on the other hand, revels in ambiguity. "Ethics, it seems, wants us to see face to face, while literature bids us peer through a glass, darkly." Nevertheless, Brody asserts that ethics and literature can be better meshed by getting beyond an overreliance on a single approach like principles and incorporating virtues and cases. Like Belkin and Brandt, Brody says that "ethical problems do not simply have a logic—they have a history; they have narrative meaning; and they occur within a social and cultural context" (109).

Yet another tension exists between what might be called, without intending any disparagement, "elitists" and "popularizers." In the early years bioethics was clearly a forum led by and for scholars and theorists whose primary audience was their colleagues. There were a few exceptions; Callahan, for example, had been an editor and he developed the *Hastings Center Report* as an interdisciplinary publication for interested citizens. The *Report,* however, was sometimes not the first choice for writers who preferred to be published in their own disciplinary journals. "Ordinary" people, for example, individuals who had experienced the dilemmas under discussion, were not typically invited to the bioethics table. Their perspective was deemed too idiosyncratic, too biased. If it did nothing else for bioethics, the advent of HIV/AIDS made it essential to bring affected individuals to bioethics discussions. No discussion of public health or prevention measures in the mid-1980s could be effective without understanding and attending to the views of advocates from the gay community. We now have "consumers" on almost every policy group.

With the growth of media interest, including TV, radio, and op-ed columns, many bioethicists believed that it was well within their mission to use these opportunities to explain the particular dilemma to the general public. This was easier to do in the early days when almost everyone could be a generalist of sorts; today, given the way some bioethicists have specialized and the way that the media do not distinguish one specialist from another, it is harder to accomplish. It is one thing for a TV producer on deadline to recognize that a story about a new cancer drug probably requires an oncologist to comment; it is quite another for that producer to know that the bioethicist-on-call has spent years mastering the facts and issues in genetics and has only a passing knowledge of the ethics of drug research.

Some bioethicists became quite adept at translating complex arguments into short and catchy statements; others disdain such efforts as trivializing and over-simplifying serious matters. While mass media undoubtedly bring these issues home in powerful ways, they also tend to focus on extreme views and treat all points of view as equally valid. The result is that the public gets a skewed view of a particular issue and bioethics as well. The nuanced view that bioethicists may bring to an issue, with a thoughtful discussion of various alternatives, is lost in the confrontational format. Without any other source of information, it is easy to see why people may consider a bioethicist just another opinionated talking head.

The media also create a pressure to come up with a quick response for the six o'clock news before all the facts of a particular case are known and before the thoughtful analysis that is supposed to characterize bioethics can take place. This was not so in the early years, when for the most part issues could be discussed for weeks or months before any public pronouncement was made. There is a certain headiness for academics when they are pursued by the media, but it is often followed by dismay at the result. The media's lack of appreciation of the way bioethicists analyze a dilemma and their search for the snappy comeback is balanced by bioethicists' general lack of understanding of how the media work and how to fine-tune an argument to fit the format.

A final source of tension, perhaps the one most at issue today, is the relationship between funding source and independent views. Even in the early years, proposals were often tailored to the interests of the funder, whether that was the government or a private foundation. However, the initial interest in the topic usually came from the institution or scholar seeking funding, not the other way around. And there were few instances of a funder seeking to direct the results. (They could, however, withhold their support for future projects.) Whether individuals selectively censored their own thinking to satisfy what they understood as funders' goals is another question. I did not see that happen, but it is certainly a possibility.

With the growth of corporate support and the use of bioethicists as consultants by pharmaceutical companies, managed care companies, and other large for-profit enterprises, the situation has changed. In these instances bioethicists are asked to give their advice or opinion on a specific matter, or series of issues of interest to the sponsor. That places them in a difficult position but not one that is automatically a conflict of interest. Nevertheless, bioethicists, says Elliott (2005,

382), risk becoming a "branch of the advice industry" or "window dressers" (Takala 2005). This issue will be covered in more detail in other chapters and is particularly important as career paths are increasingly oriented toward the corporate sector.

THE PERSISTENCE OF CHANGE

In the relatively short history of American bioethics, there is both continuity and change. Continuity pervades most of the basic issues that bioethics addresses: care at the end of life, genetics, reproduction, and research ethics. Some new issues have been added, such as HIV/AIDS (and the potential for other new infectious diseases), and bioterrorism. There are, to conclude, some issues that have always been present but have risen to new levels of urgency. Economics is the prime example. Very few of the early discussions specifically focused on money, although it was always in the background. Now it is often the first, and sometimes the only, issue raised in, for example, discussions of new technologies and allocation of health care resources. The "elephant in the living room" of course is the existence in the most expensive health care system in the world of 45 million people without health insurance.

The growth of international bioethics, and even media attention, are important ways to expand the reach of bioethics and at the same time incorporate a range of views. By extending its reach and its audience, however, bioethics has become more politicized, and it runs the risk of becoming just another shrill voice in the cacophony of public discourse, rather than a clear and objective voice of reason. This is no reason to withdraw from political debates but a caution about keeping one's role clear, expressing one's views in ordinary (but surely precise) language, and keeping the focus on the issue, not the personalities.

What lies ahead? On one hand, there will undoubtedly be more diversity in the people who choose bioethics as a professional field and more diversity of disciplines and views among bioethicists (Fox and Swazey 2005). This trend enriches the field. On the other hand, there may be even less basic agreement on what constitutes the field and how it should carry out its goals. As Stephen Toulmin pointed out, "The problems of medical ethics are like the contents of Pandora's box. Now they are out, it will be years before they are rounded up, labeled, and properly corralled" (1988, 15). It is worth remembering that the last spirit released from Pandora's Box was Hope, sent to heal the wounds inflicted by all the evil spirits of disease and sorrow imprisoned in the box. While the early bioethicists may have begun the task of healing, it is up to current and future practitioners to continue it.

ACKNOWLEDGMENTS

I would like to thank Kathleen Powderly for advice on the structure and content of this chapter. I would also like to apologize to all those who contributed to the growth of bioethics but whose names are not mentioned. As a matter of justice, they should have been acknowledged; but expediency won out.

REFERENCES

Baker, R. 2005. Getting agreement: How bioethics got started. *Hastings Center Report* May–June: 50–51.

Beauchamp, T. L., and Childress, J. F. 2001. *Principles of Biomedical Ethics.* 5th ed. (Originally published in 1979.) New York: Simon and Schuster.

Beecher, H. K. 1966. Ethics and clinical research. *New England Journal of Medicine* 274 (June 16): 1354–60.

Belkin, G. S. 2003. Brain death and the historical understanding of bioethics. *Journal of the History of Medicine* 58(3): 325–61.

Belkin, G. S., and Brandt, A. M. 2001. Bioethics: Using its historical and social context. *International Anesthesiology Clinics* 39(3): 1–11.

Bosk, C. L. 1999. Professional bioethicist available: Logical, secular, friendly. *Daedalus* 128(4): 47–68.

Brody, H. 1991. Literature and bioethics: Different approaches? *Literature and Medicine* 10: 98–110.

Callahan, D. 1999. The Hastings Center and the early years of bioethics. *Kennedy Institute of Ethics Journal* 9(1): 53–71.

———. 2005. Bioethics and the culture wars. *Cambridge Quarterly of Healthcare Ethics* 14: 424–31.

Churchill, L. R., and Schenck, D. 2005. One cheer for bioethics: Engaging the moral experiences of patients and practitioners beyond the big decisions. *Cambridge Quarterly of Healthcare Ethics* 14: 389–403.

Dzur, A. W., and Levin, D. 2004. The "nation's conscience": Assessing bioethics commissions as public forums. *Kennedy Institute of Ethics Journal* 14(4): 333–60.

Elliott, C. 2005. The soul of a new machine: Bioethicists in the bureaucracy. *Cambridge Quarterly of Healthcare Ethics* 14: 379–84.

Engelhardt, H. T., Jr. 1996. *The Foundations of Bioethics.* 2nd ed. (Originally published in 1986.) New York: Oxford University Press.

Evans, J. H. 2002. *Playing God? Human Genetic Engineering and the Rationalization of Public Bioethical Debate.* Chicago: University of Chicago Press.

Fox, R. C., and Swazey, J. P. 2005. Examining American bioethics: Its problems and prospects. *Cambridge Quarterly of Healthcare Ethics* 14: 361–73.

Gaylin, W. 1972. The Frankenstein myth becomes a reality: We have the awful knowledge to make exact copies of human beings. *New York Times Magazine.* March 5: 12–13 ff.

Hanauske-Abel, H. M. 1996. Not a slippery slope or sudden subversion: German medicine and National Socialism in 1933. *British Medical Journal* 313(7070): 1453–63.

Jonas, H. 1984. *The Imperative of Responsibility: In Search of an Ethics for the Technological Age.* Chicago: University of Chicago Press. (Originally published in German in 1979.)

Jonsen, A. R., ed. 1993. The birth of bioethics. Special Supplement, *Hastings Center Report* 23(6): S1–S15.

———. 1998. *The Birth of Bioethics.* New York: Oxford University Press.

———. 2000. *A Short History of Medical Ethics.* New York: Oxford University Press.

Katz, J. 1994. Reflections on unethical experiments and the beginnings of bioethics in the United States. *Kennedy Institute of Ethics Journal* 4(2): 85–92.

Keenan, J. F. 2005. Developments in bioethics from the perspective of HIV/AIDS. *Cambridge Quarterly of Healthcare Ethics* 14: 416–23.

Kevles, D. 2000. The historical contingency of bioethics. *The Princeton Journal of Bioethics* 3(1): 51–58.

Kopelman, L. 2005. Are the 21-year-old Baby Doe rules misunderstood or mistaken? *Pediatrics* 115: 797–802.

Leopold, A. R. 1949. *A Sand County Almanac.* Reissued 1986. New York: Random House.

Lerner, B. H. 2001. *The Breast Cancer Wars: Hope, Fear, and the Pursuit of a Cure in Twentieth-Century America.* New York: Oxford University Press.

Martensen, R. 2001. The history of bioethics: An essay review. *Journal of the History of Medicine* 56(2): 168–75.

May, W. F. 1971. On not facing death alone: The trauma of dying need not mean the eclipse of the human. *Hastings Center Report* 1: 6–7.

Moreno, J. 2004. Bioethics imperialism. *ASBH Exchange.* Fall: 2.

Noble, C. 1982. Ethics and experts. *Hastings Center Report* 12(3): 7–9.

Potter, V. R. 1970. Bioethics: The science of survival. *Perspectives in Biology and Medicine* 14: 127–53.

———. 1971. *Bioethics: A Bridge to the Future.* Englewood Cliffs, NJ: Prentice Hall.

———. 1998. *Global Bioethics: Building on the Leopold Legacy.* East Lansing: Michigan State University Press.

Potter, V. R., and Whitehouse, P. J. 1998. Deep and global bioethics for a livable third millennium. *The Scientist* 12.1 (January 5). www.the-scientist.com/yr1998/jan/opin_980105.html.

President's Council on Bioethics. 2005. *Taking Care: Ethical Caregiving in Our Aging Society.* Washington, DC. Available at www.bioethics.gov.

Ramsey, P. 1970. *The Patient as Person.* New Haven: Yale University Press.

Reich, W. T. 1994. The word "bioethics": Its birth and the legacies who shaped it. *Kennedy Institute of Ethics Journal* 4(4): 319–55.

———. 1995. The word "bioethics": The struggle over its earliest meaning. *Kennedy Institute of Ethics Journal* 5(1): 19–34.

Rothman, D. 1992. *Strangers at the Bedside: A History of How Law and Bioethics Transformed Medical Decision Making.* New York: Basic Books.

Sass, H. M. 1983. *Reichsrundschreiben 1931:* Pre-Nuremberg German regulations concerning new therapy and human experimentation. *Journal of Medicine and Philosophy* 8: 99–111.

Short, B. W. 2003. History "lite" in modern American bioethics. *Issues in Law and Medicine* 19(1): 45–76.

Smith, W. J. 2002. *Culture of Death: The Assault on Medical Ethics in America.* San Francisco: Encounter Books.

Stevens, M. L. T. 2000. *Bioethics in America: Origins and Cultural Politics.* Baltimore: Johns Hopkins University Press.

Takala, T. 2005. Demagogues, firefighters, and window dressers: Who are we and what should we be? *Cambridge Quarterly of Healthcare Ethics* 14: 385–88.

Thomasma, D. C. 2002. Early bioethics. *Cambridge Quarterly of Healthcare Ethics* 11: 335–43.

Toulmin, S. 1982. How medicine saved the life of ethics. *Perspectives in Biology and Medicine* 25(4): 736–50.

———. 1988. Medical ethics in its American context: An historical survey. *Annals of the New York Academy of Sciences* 530: 7–15.

Turner, L. 2005. Bioethics, social class, and the sociological imagination. *Cambridge Quarterly of Healthcare Ethics* 14: 374–78.

Veatch, R. M. 2002. The birth of bioethics: Autobiographical reflections of a patient person. *Cambridge Quarterly of Healthcare Ethics* 11: 344–52.

Walter, J. K., and Klein, E. P., eds. 2003. *The Story of Bioethics: From Seminal Works to Contemporary Exploration.* Washington, DC: Georgetown University Press.

Weisbard, A. J. 1987. The role of philosophers in the public policy process: A view from the President's Commission. *Ethics* 97(4): 776–85.

Whitehouse, P. 2003. The rebirth of bioethics: Extending the original formulations of Van Rensselaer Potter. *American Journal of Bioethics* 3(4): W26–W31.

CHAPTER TWO

A History of Codes of Ethics for Bioethicists

ROBERT BAKER, PH.D.

> I see no *a priori* reason for thinking that clinical ethics is so
> complicated, confusing or delicate an enterprise that it alone
> among professions should be without a shared and public under-
> standing of the moral dimensions of its practice. Nor do I think
> that ethicists are so clear thinking and saintly a group as to be with-
> out need of such a code; nor that they are so vicious and/or close-
> minded as to render one otiose. Clinical ethics is neither above nor
> below the need for a code.
>
> —*Freedman 1989, 137–38*

Bioethicists[1] function in an environment in which most of their peers embrace codes of professional ethics.[2] Some bioethicists challenge this claim on the grounds that bioethics is really an academic discipline and such disciplines do not usually subscribe to codes of ethics (Lantos 2005). Although it is true that such humanities fields as English and philosophy lack codes of ethics, professors in these fields are protected by the American Association of University Profes- sors (AAUP) Statement on Professional Ethics, which applies in all academic fields; similarly, professors in medical colleges are protected by the American As- sociation of Medical Colleges (AAMC) Guidelines. Codes of ethics are also com- mon in the physical sciences (biochemistry and molecular biology, chemistry, ge- ology, mathematics, meteorology, nuclear science, physics) and in the social sciences (anthropology, archeology, history, political science, and sociology). More importantly, virtually every applied field, and almost all fields involved with health care, subscribe to a code of ethics.[3] Economics may be the sole major social science field lacking a code of ethics, but professional codes regulate the activities of its applied versions (financial analysis, financial planning, health care management, and health care management and information systems). Bioethics is thus unique and uniquely vulnerable. It is an applied health care field that functions without guidance from, and without the protections afforded by, a code of ethics. Yet anti-code skeptics believe that bioethics has no need for a code of ethics. A formal code of ethics seems to them unnecessary and, given the field's diversity, unachievable. Many bioethicists believe, moreover, that any effort to create a code of ethics for bioethics would not only prove divisive but, by emphasizing duties and rules, would distract from fundamental issues of character that should lie at the heart of morality.

The brief historical survey in this chapter will show that bioethics societies have been responding to situations that require professional ethics standards for a decade. It will also show that, in part because of anti-code skepticism, they have had to "make do" with ad hoc task forces' reports and preliminary or draft code-like instruments that attempt to serve as ersatz substitutes for a formal code of professional ethics. This analysis lays the foundations for the argument that the real question facing bioethics is not whether to adopt a code of ethics, but whether to continue "making do" with ad hoc code substitutes of uncertain utility and authority or to replace them with a more authoritative and effective professional code of ethics.

THE SKEPTICAL RESPONSE TO BENJAMIN FREEDMAN'S PROPOSAL (1986)

The year 1986 was important to bioethics: ELSI (Ethical, Legal, and Social Issues of the Human Genome Project) was funded; the proposed "Common Rule" regulating U.S.-government-funded human subjects research was published for comment; and the Society for Bioethics Consultation (SBC), the first formal organization dedicated to clinical ethics consultation, was founded. It was also the year in which Canadian bioethicist Benjamin Freedman (1952–97) issued what appears to be the first public call for a code of ethics for bioethicists engaged in clinical ethics consultation.[4] In his call Freedman argued that such a code would clarify the range of permissible conduct in complex contexts, create "a useful tool in professional education . . . generate discussion among professionals concerning the moral dimensions of their work," and "clarify the profession's sense of what may reasonably be expected of a competent ethical practitioner" (Freedman 1989, 129–30).

Freedman's timing was off. He was urging a fledgling field founded by reformers intent on making biomedicine more moral[5] to recognize that their expertise and personal dedication were insufficient, that clinical ethicists needed to develop a consensus on standards of conduct in morally complex contexts (such as those involving confidentiality, conflicts of interests, and so forth). The founding generation of bioethicists, still uncertain about their very raison d'être[6] but nonetheless secure in their own expertise and good intentions, treated Freedman's proposal with that overly polite condescension that decent people reserve for well-meaning but utterly impractical ideas. As Freedman cleverly anticipated in the title of his paper, his audience dismissed his proposal as "carrying codes to Newcastle."[7]

THE FIRST CODE OF ETHICS FOR CLINICAL ETHICISTS (1996–1998)

By 1996 Freedman's proposal had moved out of limbo onto the agenda of an official task force. The SBC had joined with the Society for Health and Human Values (SHHV, founded in 1970) to set up a "Task Force on Standards for Bioethics Consultation." The task force completed its report in 1998. This too was a watershed year since two major bioethics societies, SBC and SHHV, united with a third, the American Association of Bioethics (AAB, founded in 1994), to form a single consolidated national bioethics society, the American Society for Bioethics and Humanities (ASBH). It was the ASBH that issued the task force's report as *Core Competencies for Health Care Ethics Consultation* (Society for Health and Human Values—Society for Bioethics Consultation Task Force on Standards for Bioethics Consultation, 1998; hereafter referred to and cited as *CC*).

CC offered the first field-wide consensus statement on the knowledge base and skills essential to competent clinical ethics consultation. At the very end of the report is an often-overlooked section that contains the first code of ethics for clinical ethicists (*CC* §5, 28–29). The drafters justified their code on the grounds that by "virtue of their role in health care institutions" ethicists "are both granted and claim social authority to influence: the clinical care of patients; the behavior of health providers towards families of patients and towards each other; [and] the behavior of health care institutions." This authority and power, however, "can be abused" by those who may take advantage of "specialized knowledge, as well as the vulnerability of the persons they serve." To forestall any such abuse, since "existing codes are neither uniform nor do they cover the specific role of ethics consultants," *CC* offered a code of ethics specifying five "special obligations" of ethicists with respect to: confidentiality, disclosure and recusal, conflicts of interest, autonomy, and nonexploitation. (These are reproduced verbatim at the end of this chapter.)[8]

CC also states the reciprocal obligations of those employing clinical ethicists to "foster a climate [in which ethicists] can carry out their work with integrity (e.g. a climate free of concerns about job security, reprisals, undue political pressure) . . . respecting the independence of ethics consultation and ethics policy initiatives."[9] Despite this effort to assert the integrity of clinical ethics, *CC*, as the product of an "ad hoc" task force, was profoundly ambivalent about its own authority and "recommend[ed] that the content of [its] report be used as voluntary guidelines" (*CC* 1998, 31).

THE MARSHALL CASE (1998)

Even as the task force was asking institutions to "voluntarily" respect the "integrity" and "independence" of clinical ethicists in their employ, at least one institution was violating this precept. In 1998, Mary Faith Marshall, director of the Medical University of South Carolina's (MUSC) bioethics program, discovered that her promotion was stalled because MUSC's president believed that her involvement in a recent lawsuit, "the cocaine baby case," had disappointed the board. The previous year Marshall had testified in court, under subpoena, that as MUSC's "bioethicist" she believed that MUSC's "policy [on managing pregnant addicted Medicaid patients] fails to meet the institution's norms or standards that have to do with informed consent . . . [because] the risk of . . . arrest and incarceration was not made clear to the patients up front" (American Association of University Professors 1999; Antommaria 2004). MUSC's board seemed to believe that Marshall's testimony was not that of a dutiful employee. Marshall, however, acted as if her role as a bioethicist was akin to that of an internal auditor, that is, it was her duty to hold her employing institution accountable to its own standards, just as accountants and other professionals do—and just as the task force had urged clinical ethics consultants to act in its *Core Competencies* report.

Marshall's case had not arisen in the context of clinical ethics consultation; thus *CC*'s injunction to employing institutions to respect the independence of *clinical* ethicists (§ 5.2) was not applicable. Even had the injunction been relevant, its impact would have been limited, since employing institutions need not accept a voluntary code. Fortunately, Marshall was employed by an academic medical institution and was thus able to enlist the aid of the American Association of University Professors (AAUP). Upon learning that the AAUP had targeted it for investigation, MUSC approved Marshall's promotion. Within two years, however, MUSC terminated its bioethics program for "financial reasons"—and the ASBH found that, having never formally accepted the CC code, it lacked the authority to investigate, reprimand, or censure MUSC.

In October 1998, Marshall presented her case to the ASBH membership in a stirring presidential address, "Speaking Truth to Power," and several members sponsored a resolution urging the ASBH to assert the professional integrity of bioethicists.[10] That resolution ran up against an ASBH bylaw prohibiting "mak[ing] or endors[ing] positions on substantive moral policy issues." Two years later, the same bylaw publicly embarrassed the ASBH by forcing it to decline to join with the AAMC and other professional societies in publicly proclaiming that ethical research on human subjects ordinarily requires the subject's informed consent. In August 2002 the ASBH revised its bylaws to permit "adopt[ing] positions . . . relat[ing] to academic freedom and professionalism in . . . bioethics . . . upon an affirmative vote of two-thirds (2/3) of the full Board of Directors" (Antommaria 2004, W24; Nelson 2001). The ASBH was now empowered to take positions on cases like Marshall's, but it still lacked any professional code that could be cited as the basis for investigating or censuring the institution that had cut funding for her program.

THE FIRST CODE OF ETHICS FOR BIOETHICISTS (1999–2002)

The Marshall case and similar incidents were having an impact north of the U.S. border. Disturbed by this case and by other tales of bioethicists' jobs being jeopardized by conflicts with medical faculty or administrators, in 1999 several junior members of the Canadian Bioethics Society (CBS, founded in 1988) formed an Ad Hoc Working Group on Employment Standards for Bioethicists.[11] A few years later this group published *Working Conditions for Bioethics in Canada* on the CBS Web site (MacDonald et al. 2000, cited as *WC*). Drawing inspiration from several sources (*CC*; Freedman 1994), the three-page document asserted that clinical ethicists have an obligation to act as a voice of conscience for those who employ them: "The role of ethicist includes the unique obligation of speaking explicitly to moral concerns. She or he will often bear direct responsibility for speaking to concerns regarding the moral character and behavior of the organisation. Such being the case, the ethicist will often be required to offer critiques of organizational behavior and norms and to speak uncomfortable truths" (*WC* 2).

The notion that ethicists play a "special role" that generates "unique obligations" naturally raised questions about the nature of these obligations. Two years later the Working Group on Employment Standards specified these obligations in a six-page *Draft Model Code of Ethics for Bioethics*[12] (MacDonald 2003, hereafter cited as *DMC*), offering a "national standard for ethical conduct in bioethics," which may be adopted by "individuals and groups on a voluntary basis." Since this code applies to anyone who holds the title or accepts the responsibilities of a bioethicist, it is the first code of ethics for bioethicists generally, not just for clinical ethicists.

The *DMC* justifies an ethics for bioethicists on the grounds that the "social role" they play "implies" that they have "fiduciary responsibilities" as "those to whom the public looks for guidance." The body of the *DMC* is formulated as a pledge in which bioethicists commit themselves to eleven obligations (repro- duced verbatim in endnote[13]): professional integrity, humility, confidentiality, disclosure and recusal, nonauthoritarianism, nonexploitation, professional honor, advancing the field, integrity in conditions of personal employment, and integrity in positions of employment for others.

The *DMC*'s first-person oathlike format secures personal commitment, but at the price of limiting commitment to the personal, rather than the professional. By parsing bioethicists' obligations in the first-person singular—I will do so-and- so—the *DMC* had deprived itself of any conceptual or grammatical basis for as- serting the obligations of persons, or organizations, *other* than the bioethicist making the commitment.[14] As a personal commitment the *DMC* does *not* as- sert—and, by virtue of its grammar and conception, *cannot* assert—the recipro- cal obligations of employing institutions. By contrast, since the *CC* obligations are conceived as professional and reciprocal, it can and does assert that *institu- tions* have an obligation to "foster a climate in which [bioethicists] can carry out their work with integrity . . . free of concerns about job security, reprisals, [or] un- due political pressure" (*CC* § 5.2, 29).

TWENTY-FIRST-CENTURY CHALLENGES
TO THE INTEGRITY OF BIOETHICS

Fortuitously for the new field of bioethics, its conception and birth (circa 1960–70)[15] coincided with the ecumenical spirit of Vatican Council II (1962– 65), which shielded the infant field from conservative religious criticism (Baker

2005a). As the twentieth century drew to a close, however, Vatican II's influence waned and conservative Catholics were free to join with Evangelical Christians and neoconservatives in opposing bioethics, emboldening other traditionalists to disparage bioethicists as "secular priests" who abused philosophy to trespass on the traditional social authority of law, medicine, and religion (Shalit 1997; Siegler 1999; Smith 2000). With the election and reelection of the George W. Bush administration (2000–2008), this conservative Catholic-Evangelical Christian-neoconservative alliance ascended to political power, and the Bush White House began to remove prominent bioethicists who were critical of its bioethical policies from government posts.[16] Lacking a formal code that could serve as a shield for its members, the ASBH appeared powerless to respond.[17] The ASBH's inaction frustrated one of its founders so greatly that he publicly resigned from the organization to protest its inaction on protecting academic freedom and failing to develop a formal code of ethics (Board 2004; Miles 2004).[18]

Almost simultaneously, a critique emerged from the left, charging that prestige, power, and money had tempted bioethicists to abandon their watchdog role (Evans 2001; Stevens 2002). The media picked up this charge (Boyce 2001; Stolberg 2001) as some bioethicists decried the fact that major bioethicists and bioethics centers were consulting for biotech and pharmaceutical companies (Elliott 2001b; Sharpe 2002; for a reply see Coyne 2005). According to these critics, bioethics had betrayed the public's trust: "People in whom public trust is placed must not have a financial interest in violating the duties carried by their institutional role. . . . What is more they must be seen as disinterested; otherwise, the institution they represent risks falling apart. . . . If bioethicists have gained any credibility in the public eye, it rests on the perception that they have no financial interest in the objects of their scrutiny. . . . The problem with ethics consultants is that they look like watchdogs but can be used like show dogs" (Elliott 2001a).

A CODE OF ETHICS FOR CONSULTATION
IN THE PRIVATE SECTOR (2002)

Responding to concerns about the propriety of bioethicists' consulting for the biotechnological and pharmaceutical industry, the two major American bioethics societies, ASBH and the American Society for Law, Medicine, and Ethics (ASLME, founded in 1911) formed a joint task force to address the issue. In 2002 the task force issued a report, "Bioethics Consultation in the Private Sector" (Brody et al. 2002, hereafter "CPS"), offering voluntary guidelines for bioethics consultants.

The "CPS" guidelines, like the *CC*'s, are framed in terms of reciprocal obligations, in this case, the obligations of consultant and client. Consultants were said to have an obligation to provide professional consultation reports that include the following: "a review of the competing relevant positions and principles found in the literature, the reasons behind them, and their implications for the issues being examined. . . . An identification of that position, if any, which has found widespread acceptance in professional standards, regulations, and government or foundation reports, and a history of the evolution of that standard; and the position of the consultant and the reasons for holding that position, especially if the position differs from the consensus" ("CPS" 18). Clients, in turn, have an obligation to adequately compensate the consultant; however, consultants may not accept compensation in amounts, or under conditions, that would compromise their integrity.[19]

In a provision that spoke directly to the charge that bioethics consultants are merely "show dogs" for those paying their fees, "CPS" asserts that "consultants [have] obligations as an advocate and as a whistleblower" in contexts in which the "harm" from "disregarding advice may be great" ("CPS" 19). Thus if "continued advocacy within the client context is inadequate . . . public disclosure may be required, even though it may violate the terms of contract. . . . In fairness to the client and to honor the client as best as possible . . . the consultant should offer the client, at the highest level, the opportunity to respond before taking any action involving public disclosure" ("CPS" 19). "CPS" thus characterizes a consultant-client relationship of reciprocal obligations in which consultant bioethicists' obligations to prevent harm override their commitments to their clients.[20] Unfortunately, neither the ASBH nor the ASLME formally adopted the task force recommendations.

ANTI-CODE SKEPTICISM: A HISTORICAL REJOINDER

Can bioethics continue to function effectively without a code of ethics publicly proclaiming its values and standards of integrity? Like its sister fields, bioethics has matured to the point that the personal commitments of its members are insufficient to meet its needs.[21] Thus bioethics societies have been producing statements on professional standards and codelike documents since 1998. The reason for the production of these documents is clear: they speak to and for the *field*. These statements strive to articulate a field's consensus view on standards of conduct, defining them, not only for those in the field, but also for their employers, the media, and the public. No individual's statement of personal values and commitments, however expertly crafted or deeply heartfelt, can serve the same function. It is one thing, for example, for an individual to assert that he or she *personally* can act with integrity as a paid consultant to a biotechnology or pharmaceutical company. It is quite another to say that *the field of bioethics* approves of such consultations, provided that the consultant is mindful of the public interest and undertakes the responsibility to serve as a whistle-blower in certain circumstances. Similarly, protestations invoking personal standards of integrity are less likely to impress employers, the media, public officials, or the public, than are statements that a particular action—e.g., Mary Faith Marshall's testimony under subpoena or the Bush administration's firing of leading bioethicists—violates a professional code of ethics. A field can speak to issues of integrity with an authority that no individual can muster.

Bioethics, however, lacks the ability to publicly assert its own integrity or to guide and protect the integrity of its members because it lacks a code of professional ethics. As we have seen in this brief history, in attempting to assert the integrity of the field and its members bioethics societies have had to "make-do" by creating ad hoc task force reports of limited scope and no authoritative standing. Of all the reports analyzed in this chapter, all are merely advisory; *none* is considered authoritative or binding on anyone—not even by the bioethics societies that commissioned them, or by their members. Not surprisingly, the content of these draft model codes and codelike pronouncements are not well known in the field, they are not widely cited or discussed, and they have not found their way into the graduate bioethics curriculum. In a deep sense, the absence of a code of ethics deprives bioethics of a mechanism for discovering or articulating its own values and for teaching them to students.

It is often objected that the field of bioethics is too diverse to develop a code of ethics. Diversity, however, has not proved an insuperable barrier for medicine, law, or the various academic fields listed at the beginning of this chapter. Doctors embrace a code of ethics that covers employees of the Indian Health Agency, HMO medical directors, military physicians, salaried hospitalists, and solo practitioners. The lawyer's code covers a similarly diverse population, including not only solo practitioners but state prosecutors, merger and acquisition partners in big white-shoe firms, in-house counsel for insurance companies and hospitals, and salaried attorneys at corporations, federal agencies, and medical centers. Despite this diversity, practitioners' shared titles—"doctor," "lawyer"—underwrite an implicit claim that those assuming the title respond to common standards. Bioethicists also share a common title and, like practitioners of other fields, they owe themselves, their employers, and the public some explicit statement of the common standards that apply to anyone claiming the title of bioethicist. Our sister fields in academia and health care have had the ingenuity to devise codes of ethics that acknowledge common standards and responsibilities and yet are flexible enough and sufficiently detailed to cover a diverse range of roles, institutional settings, and practices. To echo the passage from Benjamin Freedman that opens this chapter, there is no reason to believe that bioethicists have less need for a code of professional ethics than those in other professions, or that bioethicists will prove less resourceful in creating a code that suits their needs.

We must overcome the decades-long intransigence that has stultified progress toward a formal code of ethics. Since bioethics societies have been producing codelike documents and draft model codes for about a decade, perhaps the first and easiest step toward developing a code of professional ethics would be to identify the overlapping consensus in current codelike documents and then formulate it as a draft code that can be discussed, debated, amended, and modified until it serves as a consensus code of ethics for bioethicists (Baker 2005b).

NOTES

I should like to thank my 2005 Union College summer research assistant, Erika Selli, for her assistance in preparing and editing this chapter. I should also like to acknowledge the helpful editorial advice of Lisa Eckenwiler and Felicia Cohn, whose helpful comments enabled me to make a stronger and more concise case for developing a code of ethics for bioethicists.

1. I take bioethics to be a multidisciplinary field whose members include administrators, clinicians, and health professionals of all sorts—historians, lawyers, literary scholars, philosophers, policy analysts and policy makers, psychologists, religion scholars, scientists, social scientists, theologians, and others united by the common purpose of analyzing, researching, studying and/or attempting to address, mediate and/or offer solutions or resolutions to *ethical* problems arising in biomedical science and health care. Clinical ethics is the branch of the field that addresses ethical problems arising in the context of the clinic and in the practice of health care delivery.

2. Professional codes of ethics are mélanges of mission statements, ideals, and practical dos and don'ts for self-regulatory fields whose practitioners conceive of themselves as dedicated to serving others and as committed to some public good.

3. The Center for the Study of Ethics in the Professions maintains a comprehensive online database of codes of professional ethics at http://ethics.iit.edu/codes.

4. Freedman's paper (Freedman 1989) was presented at the April 22–25, 1986, Conference on the Nature and Teaching of Applied Ethics in Medicine, organized and hosted by the Westminster Institute of Ethics and Human Values, the University of Western Ontario.

5. The cool reception accorded Freedman's proposal is partially explicable because early bioethicists—veterans of the Peace Corps and assorted protest movements—defined themselves in terms of their deep moral commitments. The notion that *they* would require a code of ethics to ensure *their* morality was initially unfathomable. Critics deny this, claiming that early bioethicists, especially philosophers, were drawn to the field by career opportunities. While perhaps true of later entrants, the criticism is belied by the autobiographies of early entrants. Compare the autobiographies of early philosophical bioethicists Robert Baker, Erich Loewy, and Robert Veatch with that of the later entering Laurence McCullough. 2002. *Cambridge Quarterly of Health Care Ethics* 11:4.

6. Freedman's presentation was sandwiched between Robert Veatch's challenge to the legitimacy of the role of clinical ethicist (Veatch 1989; see Baker 1989 for a response) and Arthur Caplan's critique of their moral expertise (Caplan 1989). Faced with these challenges to their very raison d'être, this audience of first-generation clinical ethicists paid scant attention to Freedman's call for a code of ethics.

7. Freedman's proposal may have had a delayed impact. Besides the author, other bioethicists attending the conference who later became involved with the ethics of bioethics were the Canadians Françoise Baylis, Michael Coughlin, Abbyann Lynch, Pat Murphy, and George Webster (the latter three served on the committee that drafted the *DMC*) and the Americans Loretta Kopelman and Robert Levine.

8. The *CC*'s "Special Obligations of Ethics Consultants" are reproduced below, verbatim.

§ 5.1 *Abuse of Power and Conflict of Interest*

a.   Ethics consultants have access to privileged information including highly personal medical, psychological, financial, legal, religious, and spiritual information. The requirements of confidentiality must be respected.

b.   If ethics consultants have significant personal or professional relationships with one or more parties that could lead to bias, that relationship should be disclosed and/or the consultants should remove themselves from the case.

c.   Individuals should never serve as ethics consultants on cases in which they have clinical and/or administrative responsibility.

d.   There is a potential conflict of interest when ethics consultants are employed by a health care institution or their jobs are dependent on the good will of an institution. Giving advice or otherwise acting against an institution's perceived financial, public relations or other interest may pose potential harms to ethics consultants' personal interests. This issue should be addressed proactively with the health care institution. If the conflict of interest in an individual case puts ethics consultants in the position of shading an opinion to avoid personal risk, they should either take the risk or withdraw from the case.

e.   Ethics consultants should never exploit those persons they serve by using their position of power. Ethics consultants, for example, should not take sexual or financial advantage of those they serve.

The above-mentioned cautions should be discussed and explained thoroughly in the training of ethics consultants (*CC* 29).

9. § 5.2 *Institutional Obligations to Patients, Providers and Consultants*

The dangers of abuse of power and conflict of interest can be mitigated if health care institutions take seriously their obligations to those who provide and utilize ethics consultation services. When patients, families, surrogates, or health care providers seek assistance in sorting through the ethical dimensions of health care they deserve assurance that those who offer that assistance are competent to do so and can offer that assistance free of undue pressure. . . . Health care institutions must be responsible to those who utilize ethics consultation services by providing support for ethics consultants in their institution. This support is needed in three areas.

Health care institutions should support a clear process by which ethics consultants are educated, trained and appointed, and provide resources . . . to ensure that [consultants] have the competencies to perform ethics consultation. This will require support for continuing education and access to core bioethics resources (such as key reference texts, journals, and on-line services).

Health care institutions should ensure that those who offer ethics consultation are given adequate time and compensation for non-remunerative activities, and resources to do ethics consultation properly.

Health care institutions should foster a climate in which [consultants] can carry out their work with integrity (e.g. a climate free of concerns about job security, reprisals, undue political pressure). This should include . . . respecting the independence of ethics consultation and ethics policy initiatives. In such a climate pressures to abuse power or give in to conflict of interest will be significantly diminished (*CC* 30).

10. The resolution was presented and seconded by the author, Kenneth Kipnis, and others.

11. Chris MacDonald chaired/co-chaired; other members were Michael Coughlin, Christine Harrison, Abbyann Lynch, Pat Murphy, Mary Rowell, and George Webster.

12. The *DMC*'s authors were prompted to use both "draft" and "model" in the code's titles, fearing that more authoritative sounding titles would prove unacceptable. Chris MacDonald, interview March 22, 2005.

13. Bioethicists commitments from the *DMC* quoted below, verbatim.

a. I will conduct myself in a professional manner, and strive for exemplary levels of honesty and integrity.

b. I will foster an awareness of the limits of my own expertise when conducting clinical consults, drafting or revising policy, educating the public or health professionals, or dealing with the media.

c. To the extent permitted by law, I will hold confidential information divulged to me by patient, patients' families, administrators, or members of health care teams.

d. I will strive to avoid conflict[s] of interest (i.e. situations in which either a personal interest conflicts with my official duties, or in which the goals of one of my institutional roles conflict with the goals of another of my institutional roles). When such conflicts arise I will take action by first divulging the conflict to the interested parties and then, if necessary, by removing myself from the decision-making process.

e. I will avoid abusing the power that my institutional role and special training give me. In particular, I will avoid conflating *expertise* in ethics with moral *authority*.

f. I will never abuse my position of power in order to exploit those I serve.

g. I will contribute, where possible, to the advancement of the field of bioethics, whether through peer-reviewed publication, teaching, mentoring, or public education.

h. I will endeavor to avoid any action or statement that is likely to bring the field of bioethics into undeserved disrepute.

i. I will strive for continuous learning, and to remain current regarding advances in bioethics, law and health care sciences to the extent required for excellent work in my field.

j. I will advocate for conditions of employment that will permit me to conduct myself according to the ethical standards outlined here.

k. Whenever my institutional position permits, I will strive to ensure that other bioethicists are subject to working conditions that are conducive to the effective and ethical pursuit of the goals of our profession.

14. When asked about the first-person-singular format that he and his colleagues chose for their code, the code's lead author, MacDonald, responded that he was attracted to it because it was "personal." "I wanted people to swear to a code. I didn't want the code to sound like a list of orders. I wanted it to be understood as—here is what I expect of myself as a professional in this role." Chris MacDonald, interview March 22, 2005.

15. Dating the conception and birth of socio-intellectual movements is essentially a constructivist activity. One can legitimately date the birth of bioethics in earlier decades of the twentieth century (see Jonsen 1998). My construction turns on the first appearance of bioethical discourse—including the term *bioethics* itself (first published uses, 1971)—in American publications during the 1970s. The new discourse, and the term *bioethics*, encapsulate a paradigm shift from an older conception and discourse, "medical ethics," which was first formally articulated by a British physician, Thomas Percival (1740–1804), in his *Medical Ethics* (1803). Percival conceived of medical ethics as the self-regulatory ethics of professional physicians and surgeons, governing their own conduct and their relations with their peers, their profession, their patients, and the public.

From Percival to the present, medical ethics and its discourses have always privileged professional perspectives. Bioethics, in contrast, is a multidisciplinary field/discourse (see note 2) addressing ethical issues in the biomedical sciences, as well as in health care, *without privileging* physicians' (or scientists') conceptions or discourses. Hence bioethicists' insistence on a nonprofessional presence on hospital ethics committees; their emphasis on concepts like autonomy and respect for persons as a counterweight to professional authority, etc. In striving to deprivilege the power and authority of physicians and other elites (and in striving to correlatively empower patients and subjects), bioethics contrasts sharply with earlier alternatives to medical ethics, such as eugenicist ethics. Those alternatives privileged the perspective of the biomedical elite over those of patients and the public, condoning the use of coercive (and sometimes covert) measures to impose the elite's conception of health on others (through forced sterilization, and—under the Nazis—through covert eugenic euthanasia programs).

In the 1960s and 1970s the efficacy of traditional medical ethics was challenged as a wave of research scandals erupted in the United States. The perceived fecklessness of traditional medical ethics in the wake of these scandals was reinforced by its seeming inability to deal with issues arising in fields of organ transplantation, critical care, and so forth. Consequently, in the 1960s and 1970s agencies of the U.S. government, private American foundations (like the Ford and Kennedy foundations), and the American media turned to the new bioethics paradigm, adopting its discourse (patients' rights, shared decision making, etc.), funding and legitimating its institutions and organizations (the Hastings Center, the Kennedy Institute, hospital ethics committees, etc.) in the hope that they would prove more efficacious than traditional medical ethics in resolving ethical issues in biomedicine. (See Baker 2005a and Evans 2001—N.B. this way of dating bioethics conflicts with the European origin narratives of Campbell 2000 and Moreno 2004).

16. In December 2002 the Bush administration removed Thomas Murray, president and CEO of the Hastings Center, from the Biological Response Modifiers Advisory Committee (Brickley 2002); in March 2004, it fired scientist Elizabeth Blackburn from the President's Council on Bioethics. Murray and Blackburn were critics of the administration's stem cell policy (Associated Press 2004; Meslin 2004; for a defense of the council see Elliott 2004).

17. Hoping to resolve tensions with the President's Council, the ASBH invited its chair, Leon Kass, to present the keynote address at its national meeting (October 2004). Kass's address was followed by a panel discussion of one of the council's reports (President's Council 2003). The atmosphere proved too charged for anything but a heated exchange and any hopes that the ASBH had for intellectual rapprochement were disappointed.

18. Among the reasons Miles lists for his resignation were the ASBH's "reluctan[ce] or [in]abil[ity] to act on behalf of the threatened academic interests of its members" and its "failure to articulate organizational positions on matters [such as] standards of conduct of bioethicists who have conflicts of interest bearing in their professional work . . . [in] sharp contrast to how other professional societies conceive of their role in society [which is] a stain on the credibility of United States bioethics and the Society" (Miles 2004; see response, Board 2004).

At the 2004 meeting the ASBH board responded to one of the issues that Miles raised by approving a proposal to devote its spring 2005 conference to the ethics of bioethics. The April 7–9, 2005, conference was co-sponsored and hosted by the Albany Medical College–Graduate College of Union University Bioethics Program (now the Alden March Bioethics Institute) and provided the occasion for which this chapter was originally written. The conference's organizing committee consisted of the author, Arthur Derse, president, ASBH; Matthew Wynia, president-elect, ASBH; and Glenn McGee, director, Alden March Bioethics Institute.

19. The Task Force states the following guidelines with respect to compensation.

a. The rate of compensation [including perks such as gifts and payment for attractive subsidized travel] must not depend on the conclusions reached. There
   should be no contingency fees. Nor should compensation involve any equity
   interest whose value might depend on the conclusions.

b. . . . [C]ompensation should not be so great as to compromise the ability of the
   consultants to drop out of the process if they are not comfortable with either
   the process or the product . . . [or] so great that the consultant would be uncomfortable if the rate became publicly known . . . [and the rate of] compensation should be commensurate with the consultant's compensation from other
   clients, and/or with the compensation offered by that client to other experts.

c. Compensation should be paid only for work actually performed, or as a re-
   tainer against work to be performed ("CPS" 18–19).

20. "CPS" did little to mollify critics of bioethics consultation in the private sector. Two
senior authors of CC, fearful that controversies over consultation in the private sector were
jeopardizing the perceived integrity of clinical ethics consultants, criticized "CPS" for "as-
sum[ing] . . . that it is a good thing for bioethicists to work as well-paid consultants to private companies." Insinuating a conflict of interest, the critics further noted that eight out
of ten of the authors of "CPS" "have chosen to adopt th[e] role" of ethics consultants in the
private sector, without disclosing the details of their relationships" (Youngner and Arnold
2002). The controversy spilled over into the October 2002 ASBH meeting, which featured
a heated panel discussion, "The Public Face of Bioethics: Watchdog or Show Dog?" At the
same meeting, the ASBH tentatively explored the subject of professional codes of ethics,
offering a workshop on the history and writing of codes of ethics (chaired by the author;
Matthew Wynia and Laurence McCullough were co-presenters).

21. For an opposing view see Carl Elliott, "The Tyranny of Expertise," in this volume.

REFERENCES

American Association of University Professors. 1999. Medical University of South Carolina administration backs down. *Academe Online* 85(4): 6.

Antommaria, A. 2004. A Gower maneuver: The American Society for Bioethics and
Humanities' resolution of the taking stands debate. *American Journal of Bioethics* 4 (1):
W24–W27.

Associated Press. 2004. Scientists rally around stem cell advocate fired by Bush. http:
//blog.bioethics.net/2005/03/elizabeth-blackburn-fired-by-president.html. March 19.

Baker, R. 1989. The skeptical critique of clinical ethics. In B. Hoffmaster, B. Freedman, and
G. Fraser, eds., *Clinical Ethics: Theory and Practice*. Pp. 27–58. Clifton, NJ: Humana
Press.

———. 2002. From metaethicist to bioethicist. *Cambridge Quarterly of Health Care Ethics*
11(4): 369–79.

———. 2005a. Getting agreement: How bioethics got started. *Hastings Center Report* 35(3):
50–51.

————. 2005b. A draft model aggregated code of ethics for bioethicists. *American Journal of Bioethics* 5(5): 33–41.

Board of Directors, American Society of Bioethics and Humanities. 2004. To members of the American Society of Bioethics and Humanities: Issues raised by Steven Miles letter of resignation from ASBH. www.asbh.org/news/Letter%20to%20Members%200504 .pdf. May 12.

Boyce, N. 2001. And now ethics for sale: Bioethicists and big bucks. *US News and World Report.* July 30: 18–19.

Brickley, P. 2002. Panel politics unresolved: Concerns continue over U.S. advisory panels' new make-up. *The Scientist.* www.biomedcentral.com/news/20021230/05. December 30.

Brody, B., Dubler, N., Caplan, A., Kahn, J., Kass, N., Lo, B., Moreno, J., Sugarman, J., and Zoloth, L. 2002. Bioethics consultation in the private sector. *Hastings Center Report* 32(3): 14–20.

Campbell, A. V. 2000. "My country 'tis of thee"—the myopia of American bioethics. *Medicine, Health Care and Philosophy* 3: 195–98.

Caplan, A. 1989. Moral experts and moral expertise. In B. Hoffmaster, B. Freedman, and G. Fraser, eds., *Clinical Ethics: Theory and Practice.* Pp. 59–99. Clifton, NJ: Humana Press.

Coyne, J. 2005. Lessons in conflict of interest: The construction of the martyrdom of David Healy and the dilemma of bioethics. *AJOB: American Journal of Bioethics* 5(1): W3–14.

Elliott, C. 2001a. Pharma buys a conscience. *The American Prospect* 12:(17).

————. 2001b. "Throwing a bone to the watchdog." *Hastings Center Report* 31(2): 19–21.

————. 2004. Beyond politics: Why have bioethicists focused on the President's Council's dismissals and ignored its remarkable work? *Slate.* March 9.

Evans, J. H. 2001. *Playing God? Human Genetic Engineering and the Rationalization of Public Bioethical Debate, 1959–1995.* Chicago: University of Chicago Press.

Freedman, B. 1989. Bringing codes to Newcastle. In B. Hoffmaster, B. Freedman, and G. Fraser, eds., *Clinical Ethics: Theory and Practice.* Pp. 125–30. Clifton, NJ: Humana Press.

————. 1994. From avocation to vocation: Working conditions for clinical bioethicists. In F. Baylis, ed., *The Health Care Ethics Consultant.* Pp. 109–32. Totawa, NJ: Humana Press.

Jonsen, A. 1998. *The Birth of Bioethics.* New York: Oxford University Press.

Lantos, J. 2005. Commentary on "A Draft Model Aggregated Code for Bioethicists." *American Journal of Bioethics* 5(5): 45–46.

Loewy, E. H. 2002. Bioethics: Past, present, and an open future. *Cambridge Quarterly of Health Care Ethics* 11(4): 388–97.

MacDonald, C. 2003. *Draft Model Code of Ethics for Bioethics.* www.bioethics.ca/publications-ang.html.

MacDonald, C., Coughlin, M., Harrison, C., Lynch, A., Murphy, P., Rowell, M., and Webster, G. 2000. *Working Conditions for Bioethics in Canada* (v. 8.0),www.bioethics.ca/publications-ang.html.

McCullough, L. B. 2002. The accidental bioethicist. *Cambridge Quarterly of Health Care Ethics* 11(4): 359–68.

Meslin, E. 2004. The President's Council: Fair and balanced? *Hastings Center Report* 34(2): 6–8.

Miles, S. 2004. To the Board and Officers of the American Society of Bioethics and Humanities: An open letter of resignation from the Society. www.asbh.org/news/Miles_letter%200304.pdf. March 31.

Moreno, J. D. 2004. Bioethics imperialism. *ASBH Exchange* 7(3): 2.

Nelson, H. L. 2001. The ASBH "taking stands" debate. *ASBH Exchange* 4(3): 1, 8.

President's Council on Bioethics. 2003. *Beyond Therapy: Biotechnology and the Pursuit of Happiness*. Washington, DC: U.S. Government Printing Office. www.bioethics.gov/reports/beyondtherapy. October.

Shalit, R. 1997. When we were philosopher kings. *New Republic* www.tnr.com/archive/04/042897/shalit042897.html. April 28.

Sharpe, V. A. 2002. Science, bioethics and the public interest: On the need for transparency. *Hastings Center Report* 32(3): 23–26.

Siegler, M. 1999. Medical ethics as a medical matter. In R. Baker, A. Caplan, L. Emanuel, and S. Latham, eds., *The American Medical Ethics Revolution*. Pp. 171–79. Baltimore: Johns Hopkins University Press.

Smith, W. J. 2000. *Culture of Death: The Assault on Medical Ethics in America*. San Francisco: Encounter Books.

Society for Health and Human Values—Society for Bioethics Consultation Task Force on Standards for Bioethics Consultation (R. Arnold, S. Youngner, and M. Aulisio co-chairs). 1998. *Core Competencies for Ethics Consultation*. Glenville, IL: American Society of Bioethics and Humanities.

Stevens, M. L. T. 2002. *Bioethics in America: Origins and Cultural Politics*. Baltimore: Johns Hopkins University Press.

Stolberg, S. G. 2001. Bioethicists fall under familiar scrutiny. *New York Times*. August 2.

Veatch, R. 1989. Clinical ethics, applied ethics, and theory. In B. Hoffmaster, B. Freedman, and G. Fraser, eds., *Clinical Ethics: Theory and Practice*. Pp. 7–26. Clifton, NJ: Humana Press.

———. 2002. The birth of bioethics: Autobiographical reflections of a patient person. *Cambridge Quarterly of Health Care Ethics* 11(4): 344–52.

Youngner, S. J., and Arnold, R. 2002. Who will watch the watchers? *Hastings Center Report* 32(3): 21–22.

PART II

Bioethics and the Problems
of Expertise

CHAPTER THREE

The Tyranny of Expertise

CARL ELLIOTT, M.D., PH.D.

When I was in medical school and first began seeing hospital patients, there was something about the way the patients behaved that embarrassed me. It was an issue of manners. In South Carolina, where I grew up, we still say "ma'am" and "sir" to our elders. It is a sign of respect. I grew up saying "yes ma'am" and "no sir" to my parents, my grandparents, and all their friends. I said it to my teachers in school, to my professors in college, and to virtually every adult in our hometown Presbyterian church. One of the ways you know you have finally become a grown-up in a small southern town is when children start to say "ma'am" or "sir" to you. What embarrassed me about seeing hospital patients in South Carolina was that older patients, often patients the age of my grandparents, would say "yes sir" and "no sir" to me. These were people to whom I would have been saying "sir" or "ma'am" outside the hospital, and who would naturally have expected it. Yet merely because I wore a white coat and carried a stethoscope, I was the one addressed as "sir." Eventually I got used to it, of course. If you wear the team colors long enough, you feel like part of the team. The white coat fits, and you feel as if you *deserve* to be called "sir" or "ma'am." The point when that happens is the point when you become really dangerous.

I wonder if bioethicists have reached this point. After so much time working on hospital consultation services, government commissions, and corporate boards, so many hours producing ethics policies, guidelines, and sound bites for the TV news, I wonder if we have started to take our own expertise for granted.

The white coat has begun to feel comfortable to us, and so has the expensive suit. Authority has become something we feel we deserve.

The growth of bioethics as an academic field has been remarked upon so often now that it seems superfluous to mention all the bioethics centers, graduate programs, professional journals, and professional societies that it has brought forth. What have received less attention are the various types of social authority that bioethicists have been granted, quite apart from their status as academics. Bioethicists now consult in hospitals, testify as expert witnesses in court, write regulatory policies, appear as expert commentators in the media, and fill positions of bureaucratic authority in pharmaceutical companies, professional bodies, and government organizations. Bioethicists are treated as experts whose judgments on ethical matters must be solicited, quoted, paid for, deferred to, and perhaps occasionally refuted or criticized, but in all cases, given the proper respect.

In some ways this is unsurprising. After all, we live in an age of expertise. By virtue of technical efficacy and a claim to truth, experts are granted a special kind of social authority that they exercise over a particular set of problems (Rose 1998, 86). As professional expertise has expanded into the domain of the self, producing experts in everything from child rearing to marital happiness, it has contributed to the public perception that problems which used to be the responsibility of the individual now fall under the authority of a professional with the proper training. Today experts advise us how to rear our children, achieve sound mental health, improve our personalities, and lose weight in the process. Bioethicists merely extend the reach of expertise even further into the self, claiming special authority over the conscience.

"People today hunger not for personal salvation, let alone for the restoration of an earlier golden age," wrote Christopher Lasch in *The Culture of Narcissism*, "but for the feeling, the momentary illusion, of personal well-being, health, and psychic security" (1979, 7). The figure of the ethicist helps to satisfy that hunger, but does it in a uniquely late-modern way. In an earlier age, a person might look to external figures for moral authority and guidance—the priest or the rabbi, say, who represented the authority of God. Those external figures of authority have faded in importance, and in modern times people (even religious people) have instead looked inward to the self—to an internal moral compass. What is unique about the ethicist as a figure of moral authority is the way that he or she reverses that inward turn. We are beginning to look outward again, but to figures who derive their moral authority not from God but from a special kind of training. The authority of ethicists comes from their claim to expertise.

What is new here is not ethics as an area of academic study, of course. Departments of philosophy, religious studies, and theology have been teaching ethics for centuries. Nor is there anything new about the figure of the public intellectual. Scholars, writers, and artists have been writing and speaking about public issues for a long time. If anything, bioethicists have played a very limited role as public intellectuals, mainly by appearing on television news programs and allowing themselves to be quoted by journalists. With a handful of exceptions, the writings of bioethicists do not appear in intellectual magazines aimed at the wider public.

What is new is ethics as a position of bureaucratic authority staffed by trained professionals. And not just ethics per se, but bioethics, the domain of which is not morality as a whole, but that subset of morality specific to biomedicine. It is worth stepping back and noting just how unusual this really is. In no other sphere of our lives has ethics been so thoroughly professionalized. There are business ethicists, but they are few in number and overlap with corporate "compliance officers," whose job description is rather different. There are environmental ethicists, but these ethicists are almost all teachers and scholars, and few hold any positions of bureaucratic authority outside universities. There are scholars studying other issues of practical and professional ethics—legal ethics, governmental ethics, engineering ethics—but in no sphere apart from biomedicine have ethicists penetrated so deeply into the bureaucratic structures which they claim to study.

Of course, many bioethicists insist that they are not moral experts and that they claim no special authority. They have no special access to truth, no pipeline to the domain of moral facts; they have simply been educated to exercise a certain set of critical skills and have become familiar with a rather specialized body of literature and regulatory policy. What such bioethicists fail to understand is that the real issue is not what skills and knowledge they claim to have. It is the position of authority that they have been given, usually by virtue of their place in a particular bureaucracy. If an ethicist occupies a position in a hospital, a pharmaceutical company, a professional body, or a regulatory organization such that their ethical judgments carry more weight than those of other people—people who do not have their particular training and bureaucratic status—they already have a kind of expertise and social authority, no matter what they happen to claim for themselves. There is something disingenuous about a bioethicist who claims to have no special expertise yet happily occupies the seat of an expert on the television news.

Experts serve a useful social purpose, of course. Many bioethicists have struggled for recognition as experts because they believe that expertise is the route to social change. But when a particular group becomes genuinely established as experts—whether they are bioethicists, surgeons, computer programmers, or economists—it is usually not merely because of their credentials and skills, but because of their links to the dominant power structures, such as industry, government, and professional bodies. These links are fixed into place through consultancies, jobs, payments, social status, and access to power. Experts are acculturated into a standard view of the world, conformity to which is rewarded through promotions, pay raises, awards, and increased status in the field. It is because of their power, not just their credentials, that experts are so difficult to challenge.

Do we really want a professional class of bioethics experts? Some people clearly do. But bioethics experts bring with them a particular kind of danger. This is not just a matter of moral conformity, nor is it a matter of serving the dominant structures of power rather than those who are subject to that power. It is a matter of individual sovereignty. Nonexperts may lose faith in their own moral judgments unless those judgments have been certified by a person with the proper credentials. They may come to believe that their own conscience is not as reliable a guide as they once thought it was. You have not described the case correctly unless an ethicist says you have; you have not made the correct moral judgment unless it has been confirmed by an ethicist; you have not produced a reliable set of ethics guidelines unless it has gotten the bioethics stamp of approval. The danger here is that bioethicists will set up an invisible barrier between you and your own moral life. And unless you pay the consultation fee, access will be denied.

REFERENCES

Lasch, C. 1979. *The Culture of Narcissism.* New York: W. W. Norton.
Rose, N. 1998. *Inventing Our Selves: Psychology, Power and Personhood.* Cambridge: Cambridge University Press.

CHAPTER FOUR

Trusting Bioethicists

JAMES LINDEMANN NELSON, PH.D.

It's spring of 1972. I'm in the basement of my college library, surer than ever that I want to become a philosopher, so I'm thinking that I should start getting to know the professional literature. A new journal catches my eye. Its cover is bright, for a start, and the title—*Philosophy and Public Affairs*—is intriguing, too. Maybe an hour later, I'm reeling, just having finished Judith Jarvis Thomson's "A Defense of Abortion" (1971). She's opened up an entirely unexpected dimension of the issue, something I had never appreciated. Could I really have been just flatly wrong about abortion?

It's spring of 1976, and now I'm *au courant* with the classic articles by Tooley (1972) and Warren (1973), too, just as sure about abortion as I was in 1972, although quite on the other side of the issue. I'm taking my first graduate level bioethics class, an exciting seminar for graduate nurses and philosophers co-taught by Mila Aroskar and Dick Hull. We see a film about a child born with Down syndrome and a blockage somewhere in his duodenum—the "Johns Hopkins Baby Doe." The parents decline to authorize low-risk, highly effective surgery, thereby ensuring the child's death; John Fletcher and Sidney Callahan, along with some others, debate the pros and cons. It seems pretty clear to me, and if anyone needed any advice about the matter, I'd be happy to provide it. It doesn't worry me at all that a few years before I'd have advised precisely the opposite course.

Now, almost thirty years later, I'm in roughly the same place about abortion as I was in 1976, but in rather a different place about kids born with Down syndrome. Nor have these been my only reversals. Now, I am starting to worry, just a bit.

Philosophers characteristically take their worries, and make them their topics. What's troublesome here is whether, in the light of the deeply contestable character of moral deliberation and decision making, and the significance attached to adults being autonomous moral agents, bioethicists can, even in principle, be trusted as wielders of some sort of moral expertise. I will argue that, granted some assumptions, the "in principle" answer is yes—or, at least, that the very concepts of "expertise" and "autonomous moral agency" do not imply that we must fail to be trustworthy. First, however, I aim to instill a sense of what we're up against, trying to make it plain that we face problems in deserving the trust of those individuals whom we try to persuade. There is, of course, a social dimension to this matter as well—why should we be trusted to exert a benign influence on the formation of social policies if we're likely to steer individuals awry—but here I will concentrate on issues in what might be called the moral psychology of bioethical persuasion that are particularly pertinent to whether we can be reliable guides to individuals.[1]

PERSUASION AND THE INFIRMITY OF PRACTICAL REASON

Bioethicists devote a large amount of effort to trying to persuade people. We write books, articles, and reviews that aim at getting our readers to accept that the positions we criticize are flawed and the positions we extol are sound. We pen editorials and op-eds, we snap off a sound bite or two on TV and radio; some of us even blog a bit. We teach classes; we lecture in pedagogical, professional, and public settings, and even if we see ourselves as exploring issues rather than arguing for specific positions, we still transmit views about what's worth thinking about and what means are useful for such thinking. We sit on committees and commissions, consult with clinicians, policy makers, and patients, suggesting how a general issue or a particular case might best be seen, how it's like or unlike cases gone before, what questions are good ones to ask, what answers might make sense, and even, sometimes, what ought to be done.

Many people with academic or professional jobs work hard at being persuasive too; it's even been known to go on in day-to-day life. Yet it is characteristic of bioethicists that we try to supply, reinforce, or dispute notions of how morality's demands ought to be understood, and that we sometimes thus attempt quite directly to alter people's convictions of how life ought to be lived, as well as to shape social policies. This is not to say that influencing what people or polities accept as the facts in, say, city planning or home plumbing is innocuous. Yet our efforts raise issues that are not so squarely on the table when the focus is on the facts. Credulity generally should be discouraged, but it's in the context of moral persuasion particularly that we talk of people being *servile* if they accept too easily what others urge upon them, and where we speak not simply of misleading people but of *corrupting* them.

We who consider moral contexts for a living ought to be paying rather more attention to what's involved in persuading people about moral matters, morally. There is, of course, a vigorous, ongoing debate about conflict of interest in bioethics. But the concerns I hope to galvanize are different. We need to think about more than what weakens our own discernment, or what will make people tend to think we're not to be trusted. We need to think about the pitfalls that we face precisely when we're doing well, thinking clearly, and seen as above reproach. The central problem is that the tools we have to wield are limited in what they can do, more so than we may let on, even to ourselves, in view of the social function we take ourselves to be fulfilling.

Others have also worried about the kind of authority we can legitimately claim,[2] but sometimes in a way that doesn't quite meet the problem head-on. For example, Erik Parens (2005) has recently written trenchantly of his discomfort with being labeled a bioethicist, largely because it connotes that we are "priggish or foolish enough to claim expert knowledge about how other people are leading and should lead their lives," and because he does not "want anybody to think that I have expertise about these things."[3] He identifies some forms of expertise to which "bioethicists" might legitimately lay claim—knowledge about the content of certain legislated rules and standards, knowledge about the history of certain debates, skills connected with mediating disagreements—but implies, as I read him, that no one has expertise with respect to "the nature of human flourishing."

This is a reasonable thing to say, but it doesn't square with what bioethicists do. We don't restrict ourselves to information about regulations and histories, or to mediation. When a bioethicist opines that Terri Schiavo ought to have her feeding tube removed, she's saying something that reflects a (contested) view of human flourishing. While it's true that this bioethicist is just another member of this moral and political community bringing her best resources to a difficult conversation, it's no accident that *she's* the community member whose view appears in the paper, on the news, or in a journal, trying to recruit others to be partisans of her take on the matter. Can she avoid being foolish or priggish? More importantly, can she sidestep prompting servility in others, and effectively guard against the dangers of corrupting them?

SERVILITY AND CORRUPTION?

Perhaps this seems a sort of rhetorical overkill. The word *servility* commonly is taken to connote obsequiousness or self-abasement, and I certainly haven't noticed anyone lately pulling his forelock as the bioethical squire passes. One of the best-known philosophical discussions of the concept, Thomas E. Hill's "Servility and Self-Respect" (1973), suggests that servile people think themselves rightfully placed behind other members of the moral community, and I can't say I've ever heard anyone report such an attitude being evoked by an encounter with a worker in this field. *Corruption* (in the sense of "corrupting someone") conveys the idea of setting out to damage something fairly central to a person's integrity with malice aforethought, and having succeeded in the attempt. I don't think many of us harbor any such Miltonic ambitions.

What's worrisome about servility, though, is not a matter of personal style or of consciously entertained attitudes of self-disrespect; the heart of the matter concerns what it is for a person to take herself with due seriousness. It's a servile thought to believe that you are not worth as much as other human beings. But one can be servile without entertaining explicitly servile thoughts, as when one defers to others about matters one ought to judge for oneself.[4] The question that should trouble us is whether we are in effect enticing others to hand over some measure of their own moral authority, and whether in so doing we're encouraging them to act as though their own moral discernment is defective.

As for corruption, it seems that the risk of degrading somebody's moral character through the installation of false beliefs about what one ought to do, promote, or think well of is a serious enough matter even if it doesn't result from malevolence. It's presumptively a bad thing to imbue someone with convictions that, at the end of the day, will stand up less well to examination than those she had prior to getting mixed up with you.

SOME FURTHER OBJECTIONS AND REPLIES

I can imagine other efforts to wiggle off this hook. Persuasion in bioethics, it will be fairly said, goes on by means of explicit, public reason—and when it doesn't we should come down hard on it. Nor do bioethicists typically offer the sort of advice that speaks directly to a person's conception of what is good; quite often, the arguments target the range of freedom a person should enjoy, or the constraints she must observe, in pursuing her own ideals. Even in my most extreme moments, I didn't think that the couple in the "Baby Doe" film had an over-riding duty to allow their child to die. Rather, I took it that such a decision was within their proper discretion.

Characteristically, as this defense will claim, bioethicists offer arguments that are disciplined by logic and by fact, and we defend the values or the rankings of values we think are pertinent by appeal to their fit with shared moral intuitions, or by showing the counterintuitive implications of alternative principles, under-standings, or rankings. Such efforts may succeed or fail, be done well or ill, but there's no call to think of them as in themselves especially morally problematic: the reasons are on the table, the mechanism is available for all to see, and, in fact, quite a number of us spend part of our professional time trying to help people develop the skills that help them assess those very mechanisms.

Yet none of these points gets us cleanly off any hooks, as I see it. Realizing that nonethical considerations can have a big role in ethical deliberation might bolster confidence in the reliability of practical reasoning, but we professional persuaders can't afford to be as sanguine as we've been simply on the plea that our arguments call on empirical data and conceptual clarification, and not just moral theory and intuition. Arguments that hinge on certain accounts of how to understand certain crucial concepts seem indefinitely contestable. Consider how the ongoing disputes about what has to be the case for something to count as a person continue un-abated despite the backdrop of virtual unanimity about applications of the term in most of day-to-day life. Too, the kinds of factual claims that figure into difficult cases of moral deliberation and disagreement are often themselves subject to lengthy dispute; this should be a well-worn point to anyone familiar with the clinic, where diagnostic and prognostic information concerns what the facts are or may be, but the information is probabilistic and contentious. We need to be more alert to the curious character of the life of the professional ethicist in a secular, plural-ist culture—to the rhetorical advantages we get from simply being recognized as a profession, with all the trappings and then some. Efforts at professionalization, disclosure statements, standards for certification, and the like can go only so far as a response to this problem; indeed, they may make it worse—we may end up looking more like other kinds of consultants than we ought. Such efforts may dis-tract us from deeper concerns about what it is to be a trustworthy bioethicist.

EXPERTISE AND DEFERENCE

The field needs a renewed discussion of the source of our authority and whether our practice stays within its limits. A start on that job is to get clearer about some of the pertinent concepts. I will try to outline a way of thinking about moral expertise that sees it as a reasonable status to aspire to, rather than as mere priggish arrogance, and a way of thinking about servility and corruption in such a way that we may hope to persuade without running afoul of either. My argument concerning servility aims to motivate a hypothetical conclusion: If bioethicists do possess any kind of moral expertise, deference to it on the part of those we attempt to persuade is not servility, so long as, while providing what reasons we can to support the specific recommendations we make, we make sure that good *second-order* reasons are available as well. Such reasons would support our general status as reliable experts. My argument concerning corruption will rely on a characterization of how moral expertise might be reasonably understood. Expertise, then, is obviously a notion important for the success of my approach, and I don't see myself as having provided an argument that we've got it; that's a horse for another, much longer, race. My hope here is to show what kind of thing moral expertise might be, why we might actually have some, and what problems it might solve for us if we did. We often defer to others when their expertise concerns matters of fact. When we're young, or when there's no time for deliberation, deferring to others' moral views makes good (or just flatly inescapable) sense, too. Apart from those circumstances, *moral* deference seems to court what Kant might have called heteronomy, and what I'm referring to here as servility. While it's no doubt rare that anyone supports her view on a bioethical issue simply by citing her favorite bioethicist, we do aim to influence how people think and act, and the arguments we do offer are in the nature of things weaker than we'd like, and weaker than we often acknowledge them to be. Our social role seems to demand that we offer something in the way of moral reasons that aren't likely to be equally available without us; unless there's reason to believe such a "metabioethical" position, our persuasive force, such as it is, draws too heavily from our social place.

Karen Jones (1999) has argued that it needn't be heteronymous to rely on another's moral judgments, even if the motivation for those judgments is not altogether available or convincing to the person persuaded. In short, her argument is that the moral domain is vast and complex, and some people know some bits of it better than others do. If we have decent reason to regard someone else as more knowledgeable about the issues in question, we don't need to be convinced via direct arguments that the position the expert advocates is the correct one. Women, to draw on one of Jones's examples, are plausibly regarded in general to be better at detecting sexist attitudes and actions than are men; deferring to a woman's judgment in a case where the sexism isn't evident to him is therefore not necessarily a servile thing for a man to do. What allows him to escape the charge of servility is precisely his well-motivated second-order belief that it is reasonable to regard women as being generally better at this sort of thing. If this is plausible in cases in which the pertinent first-order reasons are simply unavailable to the persuaded, it would seem to be even more plausible in cases in which those reasons, or some of them, anyway, are open to the scrutiny of the persuaded, even if their overall persuasive effect borrows something from the social role of the persuader.

Whether bioethicists can present themselves without a blush as having moral expertise, though, requires sorting out what might reasonably pass as requirements for the role. One clear non-starter is to mandate a special acquaintance with moral reality, of the sort attributed by Plato to his philosopher-kings. Yet Plato's ghost may still haunt us, lurking in the notion that those learned in moral theory might have something especially authoritative to add to society's conversation about problems encountered in health care.

Those of us who are optimistic about moral philosophy tend to think that it has provided ways of thinking to some purpose about the deep nature of moral normativity and moral reasons, and that the results of the best endeavors along these lines are relevant to questions concerning why we should take morality seriously and even, in broad terms, what it is to do so. Yet it's inescapable that these matters are not only open to many responsible and quite incompatible opinions, but that they typically underdetermine how to resolve practical questions. If we really mean to wean ourselves away from the notion that theories of morality place those who know them in a generally better position to determine how to act in given cases or types of cases, what do we put in its place?

Jones's nomination of women as presumptive experts about sexism is based not on theory but on experience. To my way of thinking, this is a very plausible suggestion about expertise in that domain, but it doesn't seem projectable in the way we need: bioethicists typically don't point to being medicine's lifelong victims as grounds for their authority. Still, other analogies suggest that, despite the limits to what practical reason can achieve, one can still have expert status if one can do better with it—or with some dimension of it—than most people can. Presumably Newton was a legitimate expert about the physical character of the world in his time, although from a contemporary perspective he was wrong about a great deal and not in a position to do much to detect or rectify the mistakes. If we're inclined to deny this, we'd have to deny that there were any experts about such matters in his day—and indeed, perhaps allow that there are no experts even yet—and that seems counterintuitive. Perhaps it's enough that he did about as well as could be done in his time.

If it's reasonable to understand expertise with reference to the expert's present epistemic situation rather than an ideal one, perhaps the more accurate way of understanding corruption is similarly contextual: not flatly as a matter of instilling false moral beliefs and dispositions but as a matter of instilling beliefs and dispositions whose falsity should be apparent, not at "the end of inquiry" but now. We corrupt someone, on this view, if we persuade her into sexist or racist beliefs, for example. If at the end of the day, it turns out we were wrong about Schiavo, and encouraged others to similarly false beliefs, that's deeply regrettable. Yet on this view, our current practice would, even so, not necessarily be incompatible with some form of expertise, nor would we necessarily be corrupting those we may have convinced.

So much for my effort to open up the conceptual side of the argument; we still need to provide reason for people to think that bioethicists can improve the quality of thought and action, and here one might still quail. We disagree about a good bit among ourselves, and the general lines of agreement we do tend to share are far from infallible. The questions of whether and why we can make a claim to expertise, and of what its limits might be, need a good deal more in the way of pondering. But as a start we might point out that we are acquainted with some of the best that our culture has thought and said, on both general matters of moral reasoning and specific questions of bioethics, and that our discussions and disagreements have played a role in making manifest just how complicated the issues are, laying the groundwork for what might be more satisfying answers in the future. This sort of thought can only take us so far: there is plenty of reason to think that the moral traditions we draw from have, for example, slighted the insights of women and other marginalized people. Such deficits have to be remedied *tout de suite,* if we're serious about the claim to expertise. Still, if there is any comfort for philosophers to take from Derek Parfit's (1983) observation that secular moral philosophy is historically a very new endeavor whose best days may be ahead, surely bioethicists—mere infants in comparison—can help themselves to some of it as well.[5]

NOTES

1. I'm grateful to Lisa Eckenwiler for underscoring the social, policy-formation features of the general issue of whether bioethicists ought to be trusted.

2. For a very interesting example, see Walker (1993).

3. Parens (2005), inside front cover.

4. I'm not suggesting that Hill thinks otherwise.

5. I'm grateful to Hilde Lindemann and to Lisa Eckenwiler, both of whom read earlier drafts, and helped me make the present one clearer and more cogent.

REFERENCES

Hill, T. E. 1973. Servility and self respect. *Monist* 57: 87–104.

Jones, K. 1999. Second hand moral knowledge. *Journal of Philosophy* 96: 57–78.

Parens, E. 2005. A good label is hard to find. *Hastings Center Report* 35: inside front cover.

Parfit, D. 1983. *Reasons and Persons*. Oxford: Oxford University Press.

Thomson, J. J. 1971. A defense of abortion. *Philosophy and Public Affairs* 1: 47–66.

Tooley, M. 1972. Abortion and infanticide. *Philosophy and Public Affairs* 2: 37–65.

Walker, M. U. 1993. Keeping moral spaces open. *Hastings Center Report* 23: 33–40.

Warren, M. A. 1973. On the moral and legal status of abortion. *Monist* 57: 43–61.

PART III

Contributions and Conflicts

Policy and Politics

CHAPTER FIVE

Intellectual Capital and Voting Booth Bioethics

A Contemporary Historical Critique

M. L. TINA STEVENS, PH.D.

The age that gave birth to bioethics fairly teemed with public intellectuals offering every manner of sometimes incendiary critique of science, medicine, technology, and society (Stevens 2003). Do bioethicists today serve the public as did these intellectual predecessors? Considering the sheer tonnage of paper dedicated to the bioethics of biotechnologies, is the public more aware, more educated, more impassioned for the effort? Sun Microsystems co-founder Bill Joy implied an answer when in 2000 he mused over unintended consequences of robotics, genetic engineering, and nanotechnology. Why, he wondered, were so many colleagues, though aware of the dangers, "strangely silent"? When pressed, they replied in part that "there are universities filled with bioethicists who study this stuff all day long." "Your worries and your arguments," colleagues told Joy, "are already old hat" (Joy 2000). The proliferation of bioethics, it seems, has induced quiescence among those who produce the technologies of bioethical concern—an ironic legacy for the era that seeded bioethics' florescence. No need to stall, choking on biotechnological controversies—ethics experts will grasp those nettles and so allow production to stay on course. Micro choices bioethicists make concerning where to create, invest, or spend their intellectual capital (to teach, consult, sit on commissions, etc.) end up serving—or failing to serve—macro, public functions (e.g., informing the public of ethical quandaries or sustaining intense, policy-relevant dialogue). Does the micro-macro dynamic of bioethics foster quiescence in the public more generally as it seems to among biotech producers more specifically?

To help answer this, imagine a world without bioethicists. Imagine that, as biotechnology becomes big business, citizens are called upon to vote on complicated, highly technical, and controversial ballot initiatives that would divert billions of tax dollars from public services such as schools, hospitals, and emergency rooms to speculative lines of research that could offer long-term benefits. Who would be there to help voters understand the impenetrable fine print of the proposed legislation and distinguish it from advertisements representing the perspective of partisans? Who would explain obscure scientific terms, marshal scientific evidence to assess the likelihood of promised cures, encourage examination of possible unintended consequences, and provide tools for an objective analysis? What kind of public policy would emerge in such a world?

Californians, of course, scarcely need imagine. In 2004, we passed Proposition 71 making stem cell research a constitutionally guaranteed right—including the right to create human embryos using cloning technology; and the California Institute of Regenerative Medicine (CIRM)—Prop. 71's bureaucratic incarnation—is slated to receive $3 billion over ten years ($6 billion total cost to taxpayers including interest) to see that the research gets done. Of the several areas of stem cell research in existence, the initiative seems to have prioritized research for which the Bush administration had placed funding restrictions—embryonic stem cell research.[1] CIRM research will include research cloning, known also as embryonic cloning, therapeutic cloning, cloning for biomedical research, and "somatic cell nuclear transfer."[2] Who helped explain to Californians, in accessible language, what a stem cell is, or clarified the meaning of words like *pluripotent* and *totipotent* and the phrase "somatic cell nuclear transfer"? Who offered citizens an account of the various sources for and methods of retrieving stem cells, illuminated the ethical controversies surrounding such research, and reported on the success and failure rates of experiments so far? Who opened discussion about connections between stem cell research, cloning, and its function as the technological gateway to inheritable genetic modification? Who helped voters assess the seriousness of the state's budget crisis and consider which research and health care services would not get funding with vanishing state resources? Who helped sort through all the weighty questions surrounding this monumental decision? Well, there was media personality Ron Reagan. He helped us fantasize about how we can have our own (costless?) personalized cure kits one day; and there were armies of paid signature gatherers who stopped shoppers at supermarkets and malls and told them that their children would be cured of diabetes; and, of course, there were Nobel laureate science-entrepreneurs with vested commercial interests who saturated radio waves and TV broadcasts asking listeners, simply, to believe. For the vast majority of California voters, bioethicists seemed not to exist.[3]

It is a good idea to reflect on California's world-without-bioethicists because this state's experience with voting booth bioethics is part of a trend. As of this writing, other states that either have tried or are trying to make stem cell research a state concern include Connecticut, Delaware, Florida, Illinois, Maryland, Massachusetts, Pennsylvania, New Jersey, New York, Washington, and Wisconsin (Mansnerus 2005).[4] With controversial biomedical research being evaluated at the state level, either by legislatures or at the polls, it is clear that the cultural politics surrounding science and medicine has shifted from the earliest days of bioethics. What is the changed nature of these politics? In these altered environs, where do bioethicists spend their intellectual capital?

The impulses that led to the emergence of bioethics as a social institution arose in the late 1950s and early 1960s. Part of those impulses were the brewing anxieties among leading geneticists that reached public attention after those scientists aired their hopes and concerns at a number of conferences. Some of these scientists saw themselves, explicitly, as falling within the historic wake of the responsible science movement that had emerged after the atomic detonations at Hiroshima and Nagasaki. Biology, once a docile, descriptive science, was, they believed, poised to unveil the mystery of the gene in much the same way that atomic scientists had unleashed the power of the atom. Would the consequences of genetic research be as far-reaching, or as troubling, as those from atomic research? They thought so, and they thought that people should know as much.

Some geneticists wanted to garner support for their favorite eugenic programs. Nobel Laureate Hermann Muller floated his idea of "germinal choice," which would increase opportunities to use artificial insemination with vetted semen. Nobel Laureate Joshua Lederberg urged the merits of "euphenics," a desire to improve the human race, in part by regulating brain size. Nobel Laureate Francis Crick proposed a procreation licensing program designed to prevent the "genetically unfavorable" from reproducing. Other geneticists, however, wanted to alert the public about the eugenic proclivities of their colleagues and inform people about the transforming potential of "human engineering." For Dr. Guido Pontecorvo, for example, "biologists, and in general all scientists . . . have learned from the experience of nuclear energy and are conscious that it is their duty to inform society of the implications of the advances in their own fields" (Stevens 2003, 12–19). Bioethics' clarion call—the need to safeguard public interest by providing interdisciplinary ethical examination of scientific and medical developments—rose, in part, as a response to these and similar concerns over what contemporaries interpreted as an unprecedented "biological revolution."

Now, forty-plus years later, Nobel laureates and other distinguished molecular cell biologists again have felt an urgency to reach out to the public. But today the politics of scientific research is laid out on a landscape wholly altered from the postwar era, and scientists traverse the shifting terrain in a way different from their predecessors. For one thing, as referenced repeatedly in print media, scientists have felt compelled to hit the pavement and take to the states after George W. Bush, motivated by the pro-life sensibility that human embryos should not be sacrificed for research, placed major funding restrictions on embryonic stem cell research in 2001. It is hard to identify a more immediate trigger for targeting a pro-choice, biotech-friendly state like California as a source of research dollars. But other factors (of concern whether pro-life or pro-choice) already had loaded the gun.

In 1980 the U.S. Supreme Court recognized a right to patent genetically engineered living organisms, which, as the Court decreed, constituted "compositions of matter" (*Chakrabarty v. Diamond* 1980). That same year Congress passed legislation allowing universities and their researchers to patent research products funded by the federal government, legitimating the use of public money for private gain.[5] These twin enabling developments transformed biotechnological research into a multi-billion-dollar commercial enterprise. Many scientists morphed into commercial entrepreneurs along the way (Press and Washburn 2000; Munro 2002). The rails of commerce connecting the university and the business sector came to run in both directions more sleekly than ever before in history. Increasingly, pharmaceutical and chemical companies invest lavish sums directly into university research departments, and scientific researchers stretch one foot out of the ivory tower to start up their own biotech companies.[6] For science-entrepreneurs refocusing with an eye toward profit, the blurry line between basic and applied research can become nearly invisible.

Proposition 71 promoters broadcast commercials and distributed brochures that never revealed how richly science-entrepreneurs stood to gain from stock options, shares, and biotech patents—even if cures are never found. Television ads featuring Stanford University science-entrepreneur Irving Weissman, for example, introduced him as a cancer researcher and as the "California Scientist of the Year" for 2002.[7] They failed to mention that he was also a major stock and options holder of Stem Cells, Inc., a biotech company that he had helped start up. The Monday after California's governor, Arnold Schwarzenegger, endorsed Prop. 71, the volume of trading in Stem Cells, Inc., stock rose sharply; it was the fourth biggest gainer on the NASDAQ, climbing 51 percent (Elias 2004; Mecoy 2004). At the time, Weissman owned approximately 1.7 million shares. Another biotech company, Geron, saw its stock go up 16 percent. Science-entrepreneurs also stand to profit through patenting.[8] In the area of genetic screening, patenting has been a sweet monopoly deal that in some cases has made genetic testing prohibitively expensive for many consumers (Paradise 2004). There is nothing in the text of Prop. 71 to prevent this from happening for promised cures derived from stem cell research. Moreover, partisans wrote the initiative to ensure that the state of California would not have discretion on how royalties from patents would be shared.[9] For biotech investors, targeting the state as a source of venture capital would provide a fresh infusion of riskless cash into a market gone bearish after sequencing the human genome brought scant immediate payoff and gene therapy failed to live up to promoters' promises (Tansey 2004; Pollack 2004; "FDA . . . " 2005; Begley 2005; Regalado 2005).

Does having conflicts of interest mean that those scientists lose all credibility when asking voters to authorize $3 billion to fund their favorite research projects? Maybe it does. Sheldon Krimsky reports that "most scientists view conflicts of interest as a public perception problem. . . . [I]t is widely accepted among members of the scientific community that the 'state of mind' of the scientist is not prone to the same influences that are known to corrupt the behavior of public officials" (Krimsky 2003, 130). Bioethicists could counsel voters on how to think about this and other ethical nettles surrounding policy making for stem cell research. It could be countered, of course, that making policy on issues as complex as stem cell research at the ballot box is a misuse of the initiative process—that consideration of such issues belongs in the legislature, where the merits of democracy can be balanced against the need for expertise. Why then, it could be argued, should any bioethicist validate such misuse of the democratic process by participating in it? But, if the initiative process is an inappropriate venue for science and medical research policy making, surely *that* is something to share with those being tasked to become citizen science policy makers.

The commercialization of biotechnological research and the new habit of setting a research agenda by fracturing it throughout the states presents bioethicists with an urgent historic challenge and novel options: will they spend their intellectual capital on the one entity who cannot afford to pay for it—the public—and, if so, how will they do it? Instead of responding, as a number did, to journalists seeking snappy sound bites and becoming part of the journalist's "frame," will they proactively offer citizens full engagement on crucial issues: sponsor high-profile public debates, write pro/con newspaper columns and op-eds, circulate petitions, launch signature drives, call press conferences (Lakoff 2004)? But to address voters credibly in direct and candid ways bioethicists would have to publicly parse the political nature of issues deemed "bioethical," rather than declaring the day's work done after parlaying abstract philosophical principles in the classroom, boardroom, hospital corridor, or professional journal. Moreover, they would, themselves, have to be unfettered by bio-corporate influence and conflicts of interest. As compared to selling intellectual capital to biotech corporations, as many have done, there is little to gain financially by donating it at the town square.[10] And, too, there is the risk that donations of candid critique to the public could leave a bioethicist unmarketable at the corporate exchange where a willingness to create enabling assessments of research agendas is key to fetching top dollar.[11]

Perhaps it is for such reasons that Californians heard so little either from researchers who, in the tradition of the responsible scientist, wanted to educate people about the ethically dicey aspects of their research, or from their proxy holders: the truly independent bioethicist or bioethical partisans engaged in critical, public debate.[12] Instead, frustrated by Bush science and enticed by the opportunity to refresh biotech's flagging commercial prospects, science-entrepreneurs targeted Californians as impressionable and deep-pocketed bioethical decision makers. Relentlessly, voters were inundated with pleas to invest in promises.

A September 2004 edition of *Science* quotes science-entrepreneur Irving Weissman urging modesty when making claims for cures. "Don't expect any cures from this in the next 5 years," he cautioned. "Every time a public relations sort of person tries to talk about cures," he said, "I tell them you can't say that without qualifications. It's just not right" (Vogel 2004, 1544–45). But in the more popular media during the campaign, science-entrepreneurs were not selling caution. They saturated airwaves with advertisements suggesting that their vanguard of biological research would find cures for just about everything, from cancer to Parkinson's disease to spinal cord injuries. Weissman himself told television viewers, "The chances for diseases to be cured by stem cell research are high, but only if we start" (Milloy 2004). Advertising told Californians, repeatedly, that over twenty Nobel laureates backed the initiative. Nobel Laureate Paul Berg, for example, quoted on thousands of glossy color advertising handbills for Prop. 71, encouraged citizens to vote for the initiative because it would "energize vitally needed research . . . for the use of stem cells to cure millions of children and adults." The YES on 71 campaign featured a "countdown to cures" graphic on its Web site. "Voting Yes on 71," the Nobel-laureate-endorsed brochures assured, "could save the life of someone you love" ("Support . . . " 2004). But *why* scientists were so optimistic about the promise for cures was harder to discern. Did embryonic stem cells have an encouraging record in animal studies? (In fact, the research was in its infancy and animal studies were showing clearly that embryonic stem cells were causing tumors. None of the cures touted for stem cells generally was owing to embryonic stem cells specifically—although no high-profile expert sought to publicly correct for voters that widely shared misapprehension.)[13] Had human trials been conducted? (No.) Scientists were not telling us much about any of that. What did bioethicists think? There was scarcely any evidence of their whereabouts at all. With ethics experts pretty much publicly silent on the subject (in nonprofessional media venues anyway) perhaps no news was good news. Maybe voters should foot the bill and follow the laureates to Lourdes. And so the voters of California did just that.[14]

While the campaign was under way, the huckstering effort of science-entrepreneurs betrayed no bioethical concerns regarding how embryonic stem cell research opens the door to human cloning or techno-eugenics.[15] Is it ironic or merely predictable that while we were considering supporting a research agenda that would move us significantly closer to intervening in human evolution in ways reminiscent of those that troubled postwar geneticists we were hearing less about it? In fact, science-entrepreneurs and Prop. 71 backers deftly concealed the fact that questing for cures by cloning embryonic stem cells also carries us to the threshold of human reproductive cloning—and there was scarcely a bioethicist around to put these concerns before the public.[16]

Proposition 71 advertisements consistently referred generically to "stem cell research" and did not clarify adequately the different sources of stem cells or their track record for realizing cures so far: adult, cord blood, and two sources of embryonic stem cells—from donated surplus embryos created for in vitro fertilization (IVF) and from clonal embryos created by scientists in the lab. As for the text of the actual initiative, only those rare voters who read, extremely carefully, through the eight pages of the proposition's dense, single-spaced, double-columned, small-type text would have had even a chance at discerning that the bulk of Prop. 71 funds designated for actual research could be headed for embryonic stem cell research.[17] The word *embryo* is never used. IVF surplus embryos are referred to as "surplus products of in vitro fertilization treatments." Clonal embryos (those to be created by scientists in the lab for the purpose of deriving stem cells) are nowhere visible in the text even as a conceptual entity.[18] The initiative nowhere makes reference to research cloning. It refers to the cells it seeks: "pluripotent stem cells and progenitor stem cells," and to the technology by which pluripotent cells may be derived: "somatic cell nuclear transfer."

In the year before Proposition 71 was placed on the ballot, science-entrepreneurs associated with Stanford University (an institution that stood to be one of Prop. 71's major beneficiaries) urged broader use of the abstruse term "somatic cell nuclear transfer" (SCNT) (Novak 2003; Siegel-Itzkovich 2004). These researchers promulgated this semantic preference despite the fact that scientists in the field more generally were almost exclusively using the original terminology referencing cloning (Newman 2004). Such linguistic artistry aimed to signify that there was no intent, on the part of the researchers, to implant clonal embryos in order to reproduce human beings—only to derive stem cells from the early stage embryos and then destroy them. The researchers, from Stanford's Institute for Cancer/Stem Cell Biology and Medicine, discouraged continued use of the cloning nomenclature by characterizing such use as inaccurate on the part of the press.[19] But, in fact, a Medline search conducted in August 2004 revealed that the terms *embryo cloning* and *cloned embryo* were in wide use within the scientific profession itself.[20] The text of Proposition 71 mentions cloning only to proclaim that no funds would be spent on human reproductive cloning.[21] The initiative otherwise does such a good job hiding the fact that the proposition concerned cloning of any kind that the proclamation appears as an odd denial of something its authors seem to have no reason to be thinking about.

Backers of the proposition were so keen on their desire to occlude any connection to cloning that they initiated legal action to muzzle the opposition's reference to it in their rebuttal as it appeared in the *Official Voter Information Guide*. Attorneys for several of the proposition's chief promoters petitioned the superior court to block information from appearing in the voter guide that they argued was "false and/or misleading." Several areas of contested claims concerned SCNT: (1) that the research constituted human embryo cloning; (2) that to do the research, which required eggs, thousands of women would have to undergo substantial risks associated with high-dose hormones and egg extraction procedures solely for research purposes;[22] and (3) that perfecting research cloning (a.k.a. SCNT, a.k.a. embryo cloning) would, at one and the same time, be perfecting the means for producing cloned human beings.[23] (The initiative took pains to reiterate California's ban on human reproductive cloning. But as Prop. 71 provided no program to prevent the dissemination of the technology and since there is no federal ban, the SCNT technology perfected in California could be used to produce a possibly genetically enhanced cloned human in any of the many states without a prohibition [Beeson 2004]). The court roundly rejected this outrageous partisan effort and, with only slight alteration, all three pieces of information concerning SCNT appeared in the voter information guide.[24] Losing this legal battle, however, was no barrier to winning a war fueled by over $34 million.[25]

It may be that, offered all the arguments pro and con and a chance to consider them, the public would have chosen to fund biotechnologies that could alter human biological development, including reproductive cloning, inheritable genetic modification, and chimerism.[26]   But hiding the truth that such a technological bundle is tied together by a partisan promise of cures may have resulted in citizens' acceptance of this package without ever recognizing its contents. Countering the cliché that history repeats itself, the chronicles of science and society offer this stark contrast: on the one hand, postwar geneticists fretting over the need to inform the public about highly consequential implications of genetic research and, on the other, twenty-first-century science-entrepreneurs bringing legal action to prevent it.[27] How will bioethicists position themselves under the altered light this contrast casts? Will bioethicists (those of them not burdened by their own conflicts of interest) donate their intellectual capital to a public now targeted as uninformed bioethical decision makers?

In retrospect, Proposition 71 was for California a historically unprecedented game of voting booth bioethics with a lopsided set of "we'll-hide, you-seek" rules. Commercial biotechnology did all the hiding: hide the conflicts of interest, hide the early-stage nature of the research, hide the cloning, hide the techno-eugenic threshold, hide the embryo, hide the women needed for eggs. But the hardest thing to find was a bioethicist prepared to help seek. Having no intellectual capital of their own to spend, voters had to do that largely on their own. Even a stacked game should have a set of rules fairer than that.

ACKNOWLEDGMENTS

For their comments or encouragement I offer thanks to Joan Ryan, Gloria Jeanne Stevens, James E. Stevens, and especially, Diane Beeson, Rosann Greenspan, Stephen Shmanske, and this volume's editors. I am grateful also to UC Berkeley's Center for the Study of Law and Society, where I was a visiting scholar while writing this chapter.

NOTES

1. See "Voter Information Guide, California General Election, Text of Proposed Laws, Proposition 71," Section C, p. 152.

2. For a discussion of terminology regarding cloning see Kass 2002.

3. The presidential bioethics commissions can be seen as attempts to generate public bioethical discussion of controversial biotechnologies, including stem cell technologies. Arguably, however, the commissions are less the instrument of effective public dialogue (i.e., a dialogue that reaches/enlightens a broad spectrum of voting Americans) than an administrative process, by and for elites, that functions to move forward controversial technologies—their specific criticisms of biotechnologies notwithstanding. For a consideration of how private bioethics centers may function to advance larger biotechnological agendas in a context outside the stem cell controversy, see Stevens 2003.

4. "Confusion in the states over stem cells, federal action expected," *Genetic Crossroads: Newsletter of the Center for Genetics and Society,* March 31, 2005, online at, www.genetics_and_society.org/r.asp?s=gc20050331&t=http://msnbc.msn.com/id/7253997.

5. For the Bayh-Dole legislation see, Government Patent Policy Act of 1980, Pub. L. No. 96-517, 94 Stat.3019.

6. From 1980 to 1981, DuPont invested $23 million in Harvard Medical School (12-year contract), Monsanto invested $4 million in Rockefeller University (5-year contract), Monsanto invested $4 million in Washington University Medical School (5-year contract), Allied Chemical Corp invested $2.5 million in UC Davis (5-year contract), Celanese invested $1.1 million in Yale University (3-year contract) (Wright 1986).

7. See, Milloy, "Stumping for stem cells," October 18, 2004, online at www.foxnews.com/story/0,2933,135697,00.html.

8. See, "Live forever: Stem cell science drives ethical controversy," *Pharmaceutical Business Review,* April 11, 2005, online at: www.pharmaceutical_business_review.com/article_feature.asp?guid=C75FB80A_75D3_4948_8854_2B50AB8742BF.

9. See section B(h), "Patent Royalties and License Revenues Paid to the State of California," in "Text of Proposed Laws, Proposition 71," Voter Information Guide, California General Election, November 2, 2004, p. 149.

10. This discussion does not mean to suggest that all bioethicists have financial ties to biotech commercial interests. Rather, the intention is to indicate that those bioethicists most inclined to speak out in favor of pursuing research agendas despite unresolved controversy about those agendas seem to have such ties (Elliott 2001, 2003; Stolberg 2001; Brower 1999).

11. For a cautionary tale see Gilbert 2001.

12. See www.allianceagainstprop71.org for a list of pro-choice signatories on a Web site declaration against the proposition that included some scientists and bioethicists. Unfortunately, this effort to blip the media radar screen, initiated by a small group of pro-choice feminists (including myself) was unsustainable due, in part, to lack of funds and to the unwillingness of most journalists at the time to valorize any criticism of the proposition other

than that which denounced the destruction of human embryos for research. This journalistic bias buttressed the uninformed but oft-encountered default position of many liberals: "If Bush is for it, I'm against it." An important early exception to this journalistic bias was Woodward 2004.

13. See citations listed on "Fact Sheet on Embryonic Stem Cells," online at www .allianceagainstprop71.org.

14. Proposition 71 passed in California's November 2004 election by a margin of 59 percent to 41 percent.

15. On techno-eugenics see Hayes 2000. Stuart Newman discusses cloning, stem cell research, embryo gene modification, and chimerism (Newman 2003).

16. In California newspapers, a notable exception was the jointly authored op-ed by Cameron and Lahl (2004), which explicitly discussed Prop. 71 as an initiative about human cloning. David Winickoff (2004) penned an op-ed which referenced the connection to cloning. To my knowledge, no other bioethicist clarified in a California newspaper that Prop. 71 had implications for human cloning. None discussed how somatic cell nuclear transfer (also known as human embryonic cloning or research cloning) was the gateway technology to inheritable genetic modification. Although he did not reference cloning or inheritable genetic modification, Daniel Callahan (2004) offered Californians an op-ed critical of Prop. 71.

17. "In order to ensure that institute funding does not duplicate or supplant existing funding, a high priority shall be placed on funding pluripotent stem cell and progenitor cell research that cannot, or is unlikely to, receive timely or sufficient federal funding, unencumbered by limitation that would impede the research. In this regard other research categories funded by the National Institutes of Health shall not be funded by the institute" (*Official* . . . 2004, 152). See also page 147: "Pluripotent stem cells may be derived from somatic cell nuclear transfer or from surplus products of in vitro fertilization treatment when such products are donated under appropriate informed consent procedures. Progenitor cells are multipotent or precursor cells that are partially differentiated, but retain the ability to divide and give rise to differentiated cells" (*Official* . . . 2004). (Note that it is highly unlikely that the average reader could have had even an inkling that these passages were making any reference at all to anything involving an embryo or cloning.)

18. Pun acknowledged if not intended.

19. "Clearly, what will occur at Stanford's Institute for Cancer/Stem Cell Biology and Medicine does not involve cloning human embryos, that is, placing nuclear transplant pseudo-blastocysts into a woman's uterus. . . . Hopefully, the press will portray further scientific research in a more accurate light. Dr. [Irving] Weissman is not taking any more chances, however. In the future he will work much harder to ensure the press understands the issues by spelling out exactly what is planned and why, including any tricky issues such as nomenclature" (Beverly 2003, 30). Note: presumably a "pseudo-blastocyst" is one they do not intend to implant, whereas an "authentic blastocyst"—also referred to in the article—is one that would be intended for transplantation. But compare: "Whether or not a scientist or physician intends to implant a cluster of cells does not determine whether or not it is an embryo. If it is a cluster of liver cells, for example, the intention to implant it does not make it an embryo. Correspondingly, if it is a blastocyst capable of giving rise to

embryo stem cells, the lack of intention to implant it does not cause it not to be an embryo" (Newman 2004, 2).

20. As Newman puts it, "Until Stanford University decided in the last year to stop using the terms 'embryo cloning' and 'cloned embryos' to describe the technique of producing human embryos by nuclear transfer and the products of this technique, these were the terms used virtually exclusively by scientists for these items. The term 'cloned embryo' is still the term of art in this field of research for the products of nuclear transfer." A Medline search using this phrase turned up forty-two uses of this term in article titles or abstracts during 2003–2004. In 2003, Ian Wilmut, the first scientist to clone a mammal, published an editorial in the journal *Cloning and Stem Cells* titled "Human Cells from Cloned Embryos in Research and Therapy" (Newman 2004, 2).

21. Proposition 71 defines "human reproductive cloning" as "the practice of creating or attempting to create a human being by transferring the nucleus from a human cell into an egg cell from which the nucleus has been removed for the purpose of implanting the resulting product in a uterus to initiate a pregnancy" (*Official* . . . 2004, 154). By contrast, the term "research cloning" is meant to suggest that clonal embryos will be created for research purposes only and not for the purpose of implanting them in a woman's uterus. The initiative, however, never uses the term "research cloning" anywhere, preferring instead to describe the processes used to derive pluripotent stem cells.

22. Stem cells may be extracted from unused IVF (in vitro fertilization) embryos. To extract stem cells from clonal embryos, however, eggs are required first in order create the clone from which the cells may be derived. These eggs typically are extracted from women after placing them on leuprolide acetate (more commonly known as Lupron). Because the long-term health effects associated with use of this powerful hormone are unknown, it is not possible to give women a satisfactory informed consent. "More careful and long term research is needed, especially regarding the risks of . . . Lupron . . . commonly used to shut down a woman's ovaries before using super-ovulating drugs for hyperstimulation. As of the spring of 1999, the FDA had already received 4228 reports of adverse drug events from women using Lupron. Of these reports, 325 involved hospitalization . . . 25 deaths were reported" (Beeson 2004). Additionally, Proposition 71 allows for egg "donors" to be "reimbursed of expenses." At IVF clinics payments run $5,000 to $10,000, leading critics to refer to egg donation as "egg buying" and presenting the ethical quagmire that Prop. 71 will lead to a largely rich man's war but a poor woman's fight. For more information see Norsigian 2005.

23. The relevant section in the "Rebuttal against the Argument in Favor of Proposition 71" in the November 2, 2004, *Official Voter Information Guide* reads: "Stem Cell Research? YES! Human Embryo Cloning? NO! Here are just some of the many problems with Proposition 71: It specifically supports 'embryo cloning' research also called 'somatic cell nuclear transfer' which poses risks to women and unique ethical problems. To provide scientists with eggs for embryo cloning, at least initially, thousands of women may be subjected to the substantial risks of high dose hormones and egg extraction procedures just for the purposes of research. In addition, the perfection of embryo cloning technology—even if initially for medical therapies only—will increase the likelihood that human clones will be produced" (*Official* . . . 2004, 72). (Although I was one of three signatories on this state-

ment, the text was the joint effort of a larger number of pro-choice feminists. The other two signatories were Judy Norsigian, executive director, Our Bodies Ourselves, and Francine Coeytaux, founder, Pacific Institute for Women's Health.)

24. The court demanded of the rebuttal only that one change be made, from "thousands of women *will* be subjected to substantial risks" to "thousands of women *may* be subjected to substantial risks." See Berg et al. 2004.

25. See California secretary of state Web site: http://cal-access.ss.ca.gov/Campaign/ Measures.

26. Chimerism is the creation of organisms by combining genes from two different animals, or from a human and another animal. On stem cell research and chimerism see Newman 2003; Shreeve 2005.

27. This is not to suggest that there is, today, no glimmer of a responsible science movement; only that the legal, political, and economic developments spurring the growth of biotechnology as a commercial enterprise have created an environment much more hostile to its efforts. For examples of scientists operating within the tradition of the responsible science movement consider the efforts of New York Medical College cell biologist Stuart Newman (Weiss 2005), and microbial ecologist Ignacio Chapela (online at www .tenurejustice.org/Index.html).

REFERENCES

Beeson, D. 2004. Statement to the California State Senate Health Committee hearing on Proposition 71. San Diego, CA, September 15, on behalf of ProChoice Alliance against Prop. 71. www.allianceagainstprop71.org/articles.htm#DianeBeeson.

Begley, S. 2005. Why gene therapy hasn't produced forecast breakthroughs. *Wall Street Journal,* February 18. www.wsj.com.

Berg, P., Klein, R. N., and Goldstein, L. 2004. *Petitioners v. Kevin Shelly, Secretary of State of California, Respondent,* Case No. 04CS01015, Peremptory Writ of Mandate (Proposition 71), August 4.

Beverly, B. 2003. Stemming controversy. *The Stanford Scientific,* Spring: 28–30.

Brower, V. 1999. Biotechs embrace bioethics, June 14. www.biospace.com.

Callahan, D. 2004. Combining hope, hype and hucksterism. *San Diego Union Tribune,* October 22. www.signonsandiego.com.

Cameron, N. M., and Lahl, J. 2004. Legislating medicine: California's bizarre cloning proposition. *San Francisco Chronicle,* July 11. www.sfgate.com.

Chakrabarty v. Diamond, 447 U.S. 303 (1980).

Confusion in the States over stem cells, federal action expected. 2005. *Genetic Crossroads: Newsletter of the Center for Genetics and Society,* March 31. www.genetics_and_society.org/ r.asp?s=gc20050331&t=http://msnbc.msn.com/id/7253997.

Elias, P. 2004. Biotech prices surge ahead of stem cell vote. *San Francisco Chronicle,* October 26: D3.

Elliott, C. 2001. Pharma buys a conscience. September 24. www.prospect.org/print/V12/ 17/elliott_c.html.

―――. 2003. Not-so-public relations: How the drug industry is branding itself with bio-ethics. December 15. http://slate.msn.com.

FDA shuts down three gene therapy experiments; Two in Los Angeles. March 4, 2005, on-line at www.sfgate.com.

Gilbert, A. 2001. Bioethics professor loses his job, only to find his philosophy. *Daily Penn-sylvanian.* August 9. www.dailypennsylvanian.com/vnews/display.v/ART/2001/08/ 09/3b7346754b8bf.

Government Patent Policy Act of 1980, Pub. L. No. 96-517, 94 Stat.3019.

Hayes, R. 2000. Interview: Human genetic engineering. In Casey Walker, ed., *Made Not Born: The Troubling World of Biotechnology.* Pp. 80–95. San Francisco: Sierra Club Books.

Joy, B. 2000. Why the future doesn't need us. *Wired Magazine* April (8.0). www.wired.com/ wired/archive/8.04/joy.html.

Kass, L., et al. 2002. *Human Cloning and Human Dignity: The Report of the President's Coun-cil on Bioethics.* New York: Public Affairs.

Krimsky, S. 2003. *Science in the Private Interest.* New York: Rowman and Littlefield.

Lakoff, G. 2004. *Don't Think of an Elephant: Know Your Values and Frame the Debate.* White River Junction, VT: Chelsea Green Publishing.

Live forever: Stem cell science drives ethical controversy... April 11, 2005. www .pharmaceutical_business_review.com/article_feature.asp?guid=C75FB80A_75D3_ 4948_8854_2B50AB8742BF.

Mansnerus, L. 2005. New Jersey faces tough competition for stem cell scientists. *New York Times,* January 17: A16.

Mecoy, L. 2004. Rivals charge Prop 71 conflict: Stem cell researcher in 'Yes' ads could get rich, they contend." *Sacramento Bee,* October 20. Online at sacbee@newsbank.com.

Milloy, S. 2004. Stumping for stem cells. October 18. www.foxnews.com/story/0,2933, 135697,00.html.

Munro, N. 2002. Dr. Who: Scientists are treated as objective arbiters in the cloning debate. But most have serious skin in the game. *Washington Monthly,* November. www.wash ingtonmonthly.com/features/2001/0211.munro.html.

Newman, S. 2003. Averting the clone age: Prospects and perils of human developmental manipulation. *Journal of Contemporary Health Law and Policy* 19: 1.

―――. 2004. Declaration of Dr. Stuart A. Newman, Ph.D., in Opposition to Petition for Writ of Mandate and Alternative Writ of Mandate/Order to show Cause. Paul Berg, Robert N. Klein, and Larry Goldstein. 2004. *Petitioners v. Kevin Shelly, Secretary of State of California, Respondent,* Case No. 04CS01015, Superior Court of the State of Califor-nia, August 4, p. 2.

Norsigian, J. 2005. Egg donation for IVF and stem cell research: Time to weigh the risks to women's health. *Different Takes,* Population and Development Program at Hampshire College, No. 33, Spring.

Novak, K. 2003. New Stanford Institute sparks cloning quarrel. *Nature Medicine* 9(2): 156– 57. www.nature.com/nm/journal/v9/n2/pdf/nm0203–156b.pdf.

Official Voter Information Guide, California General Election. 2004. Text of Proposed Laws, Proposition 71.

Paradise, J. 2004. European opposition to exclusive control over predictive breast cancer testing and the inherent implications of U.S. patent law and public policy: A case study of the myriad genetic BRCA patent controversy. *Food and Drug Law Journal* 59(1): 133– 49.

Pollack, A. 2004. Is biotechnology losing its nerve? *New York Times,* February 29: B1.

Press, E., and Washburn, J. 2000. The kept university. *Atlantic Monthly.* www.theatlantic .com/issues/2000/03/press.html.

Regalado, A. 2005. Big companies quietly pursue research on embryonic stem cells. *Wall Street Journal,* April 12: A1.

Shreeve, J. 2005. The other stem cell debate. *New York Times Magazine,* April 10: 42–47.

Siegel-Itzkovich, J. 2004. Cloning, it's not. *Jerusalem Post,* February 16.

Stevens, M. L. T. 2003. *Bioethics in America: Origins and Cultural Politics.* Baltimore: Johns Hopkins University Press.

Stolberg, C. G. 2001. Bioethicists fall under familiar scrutiny. *New York Times,* August 2.

Support Stem Cell Research, YES on 71. 2004. Brochure, the California Stem Cell Research and Cures Initiative, 11271 Ventura Blvd. #509, Studio City, CA.

Tansey, B. 2004. So many paths to pursue: Human genome opened myriad possibilities, but medical payoff has been slight. *San Francisco Chronicle,* June 9: C1.

Vogel, G. 2004. California debates whether to become stem cell heavyweight. *Science,* September 10: 1544–45.

Weiss, R. 2005. U.S. denies patent for a too-human hybrid. *Washington Post,* February 13. www.washingtonpost.com.

Winickoff, D. 2004. Prop. 71 a risky experiment in squandering public monies. *San Francisco Chronicle,* October 17. www.sfgate.com/cgi-bin/article.cgi?file=/chronicle/archive/ 2004/10/17/ING9T995C41.DTL.

Woodward, T. 2004. Cell divide. *San Francisco Bay Guardian,* September 29. www.sfbg.com/ 38/53/cover_stem_cell.html.

Wright, S. 1986. Recombinant DNA technology and its social transformation. *Osiris,* 2nd ser., 2: 303–60.

CHAPTER SIX

Bioethics and Society

From the Ivory Tower to the State House

DAVID ORENTLICHER, M.D., J.D.

Controversies in bioethics routinely land in legislatures, before governors and presidents, or in court. The question whether to withdraw artificial nutrition and hydration from Terri Schiavo was an extreme example—it generated statutes by the Florida legislature and by Congress, intervention by Governor Jeb Bush and President George Bush, and more than a dozen opinions by state and federal courts between 2000 and 2005.[1]

But many other bioethical dilemmas also capture the attention of government. Cases involving abortion,[2] the withdrawal of life-sustaining treatment (Meisel and Cerminara, 2004), drug testing of pregnant women,[3] denial of health care on grounds of medical futility,[4] and disputes over frozen embryos[5] pepper the judicial landscape. Similarly, Congress and state legislatures regularly pass laws regulating end-of-life care,[6] reproductive decisions,[7] and other matters in bioethics, including access to care,[8] genetic testing,[9] and public health practices (Gostin 2000).

Lawmakers can have a profound effect on the evolution of issues in medical ethics. President Bush's decision to limit federal funding for embryonic stem cell research slowed the progress of medical discovery in the United States (Stolberg 2002), Congress's enactment of Medicare increased the percentage of older Americans with health care insurance from about 50 percent to nearly 100 percent (Moon 2001), and the Supreme Court's decision in *Roe v. Wade* gave every American woman the freedom to terminate her pregnancy before viability.

Because lawmakers greatly shape the outcome of dilemmas in bioethics, it is important for bioethicists to become active in the legal process. As judges decide cases, governors or presidents implement policies, and legislatures pass laws, they may adopt rules that raise serious moral concerns. When the Florida legislature and Congress ventured into the Terri Schiavo case, they enacted legislation that did not reflect good bioethical analysis (and that was also unconstitutional).[10]

Bioethicists can particularly influence the law through legislatures. Whereas courts must wait for disputes to come before them, legislators can anticipate problems and develop laws to prevent or limit harm. A bioethicist can persuade legislators to take up an issue and respond to it in a morally desirable way. In addition, the legislative process is typically more open to public input than is a judicial proceeding or the policy making of a president or governor. Finally, in the absence of constitutional constraints, legislatures can override decisions by courts or executive branch officials. Thus, when the Illinois Supreme Court erected unduly stringent procedural safeguards for withdrawing artificial nutrition and hydration, bioethicists could work with the Illinois legislature to adopt more reasonable guidelines (Hall et al. 2003, 542).

Bioethicists can extend their involvement in the legislative process by becoming legislators. I have had the privilege of doing so. First elected in November 2002 to the Indiana House of Representatives, I write this piece in my third year in office, almost midway through my second two-year term. Like most state legislatures, the Indiana General Assembly operates on a part-time basis, so I also continue, at reduced time, as a professor at the Indiana University Schools of Law and Medicine. As a legislator, I have come to a better understanding of the contributions that bioethicists can make in the legislative process.

SHARING EXPERTISE ON IMPORTANT ISSUES

Legislatures regularly grapple with issues on which bioethicists can bring their expertise to bear. With Medicaid costs rising rapidly and state budgets being squeezed, access to—and rationing of—health care are key concerns. In states across the country, legislators have had to reduce Medicaid funding and then choose among cutting back on the range of health services covered, decreasing the number of indigent persons eligible for Medicaid coverage, or implementing both kinds of reductions (see Dewan 2005, A8). Devising a just system for rationing health care requires difficult choices, and bioethicists can help ensure that the choices take account of all the relevant moral considerations.

Legislators address many other issues in bioethics as well. As scientists probe into promising but ethically controversial areas like stem cell research or genetic technology, legislators entertain proposals for regulation that must be carefully drafted before enactment. It is all too easy for a statute to blur the line between ethically acceptable and unacceptable practices. In the Indiana General Assembly's 2005 session, for example, a bill to ban cloning included a ban on trafficking in human eggs, in order to deprive scientists of an essential element of the cloning process.[11] However, the bill also would have prohibited compensation (other than reimbursement of expenses) to women who donate their eggs for procreation by infertile women. While the question of compensation for egg donors is an important one, the proposed ban had elicited no discussion when the bill was considered in the Indiana Senate. Because of my background in bioethics, I was able to highlight the problem when the bill came to the House and broker a compromise that will allow infertile couples to continue to use the services of egg donors in Indiana.[12]

Several aspects of the nature of a state legislature increase the importance of a bioethicist's expertise in the legislative process. Most legislators come to bioethical matters with a rudimentary understanding, and their part-time role leaves them little opportunity to delve deeply into issues. The operation of the Medicaid system is complicated enough for health care experts, but it can be especially daunting for officeholders who may have spent their careers mining coal, raising soybeans, or teaching high school English. Similarly, most legislators have not spent much time considering the differences between reproductive and therapeutic cloning and how those differences should affect cloning legislation. A bioethicist can much more easily identify the strengths and weaknesses of a health care bill and suggest ways to improve the proposal.

In addition to coming to the legislature without much background in health care, state lawmakers generally have minimal staff assistance. Members of the Indiana General Assembly, for example, share a legislative assistant with two or three other legislators. Unlike members of Congress, they cannot assign an aide to study particular issues on their behalf. As a result, state legislators routinely look for guidance to others, whether legislative colleagues, faculty from local universities, or representatives of interest groups.[13] Legislators often introduce bills drafted by interest groups rather than by themselves. Hence, it is common to hear bills described as being "carried" by Representative X or Senator Y. It is also common to see legislators rely on interest group advocates to explain their bills when the bills are considered in committee. Knowing the background on a particular health care issue—or at least knowing where and how to look for information— puts the bioethicist in an especially good position to advocate for health care legislation.

A third important factor is the brevity of the legislative session. Indiana's session lasts either two and a half months (nonbudget year) or four months (budget year). Some state legislatures meet for shorter periods. With hundreds of bills to consider, on topics from methamphetamine regulation to school funding to prescription drug costs—along with other matters competing for a legislator's time—a legislator cannot devote much time to any but a small percentage of the bills that will be debated. The professional expertise of a bioethicist helps compensate for the time limits of a brief legislative session.

MEDIATING CONFLICT

The legislative process regularly involves highly charged issues that can divide the parties involved. Sometimes the divisions among legislators or representatives of advocacy groups are unbridgeable, but consensus often can be accomplished by sitting down with the different sides and understanding their concerns. Frequently people do not articulate their concerns accurately, and it may take time to tease out the source of the conflict. For example, I introduced a health care insurance bill that included a small employer mandate, but a tax credit would have more than covered the costs of the mandate. I was surprised when some lobbyists objected to the mandate, and it eventually became clear that they were really worried that the mandate would expand over time such that its costs would not be covered by the tax credits—a funded mandate would evolve into an unfunded mandate. By identifying the true source of the conflict, it was possible to find a good avenue for resolution. In this way, the legislative process had much in common with ethics consultation. There too, extended discussion with the involved parties (e.g., families and physicians) can be necessary to understand where the difficulties lie and how to resolve them. The mediating skills of a bioethicist can be a valuable asset at the state house.

ELEVATING THE LEVEL OF ETHICS

Legislators generally are not viewed as having good ethical standards. In a November 2004 Gallup Poll, for example, fewer than one-fourth of those surveyed rated state officeholders as "high" or "very high" on honesty and ethical standards (Hitti 2004, 1). Whether a bioethicist can create a more ethical atmosphere in a state's legislature is a difficult question to answer. Electoral politics drive much of what happens in a legislature, and voters tend not to reward candidates for ethical purity or punish them for ethical perfidy unless the violations are egregious (e.g., sexual misconduct or financial fraud) or the candidate has alienated constituents in other ways (e.g., a legislator has not done a good job of communicating with constituents and appears uninterested in their concerns).

Unethical behavior not only may go unpunished; it may be advantageous. Misleading statements by legislators can directly sway their colleagues' votes or do so indirectly by influencing public opinion. Political advertising that violates ethical standards for accuracy often is effective. Many candidates have been damaged when attacked with half-truths and/or total falsehoods. Consider in this regard the inaccurate Swift Boat Veterans for Truth ads (Kristof 2004, A15) challenging Senator John Kerry's Vietnam War record during the 2004 presidential campaign (Wilgoren 2004, A24). If voters do not police ethical misconduct effectively, bioethicists might urge legislators to adopt internal ethical standards, and to some extent that has happened. Congress limits the ability of its members to accept gifts and political contributions from lobbyists,[14] and most state legislatures do as well.[15]

However, professionals typically do not do a good job of self-regulation. Members of a profession may be able to adopt reasonable standards, but effective enforcement usually must come from outside the profession (Orentlicher 1994). Consider, for example, how the enactment of the federal Health Insurance Portability and Accountability Act of 1996 (HIPAA) has resulted in much greater attention by physicians and hospitals to their obligations to respect patient privacy. At the Indiana University School of Medicine, HIPAA resulted in mandatory training for health care providers regarding their duties to protect patient confidentiality, and stricter privacy practices have been adopted throughout the medical center's clinics and other patient-care settings. The confidentiality rules of HIPAA may simply track the confidentiality obligations that already existed by virtue of ethical principles and state laws, but physicians take them much more seriously because of the federal government's decision to enforce the obligations.

The need for outside enforcement can particularly undermine observance of ethical standards in the legislature. The U.S. Constitution and state constitutions include a principle of separation of powers among the different branches of government. While the separation-of-powers principle includes checks and balances by which each branch of government can restrain the other two branches, the principle also limits the ability of one branch of government to regulate the practices of another branch. Thus, although the U.S. Senate must approve certain presidential appointments, Congress cannot require the president to seek its approval before firing those same appointees.[16] Because of the separation-of-powers principle, it is difficult for the executive or judicial branch to subject legislators to the dictates of an ethics enforcement mechanism that lies outside the legislature. In short, the public generally does not give legislators sufficient incentive to adopt strong ethical standards, and constitutional considerations may prevent such standards from being imposed by others.

MAINTAINING ONE'S INTEGRITY

Politics, it is said, is the art of compromise, and many people choose not to run for elective office or advocate in the political process out of concern that they will be forced to sacrifice their integrity by compromising their principles. My own sense is that the need for officeholders to vote against their principles is exaggerated. In fact, it is not clear that legislators face substantially greater pressures than other professionals to compromise their principles. First, constituents often do not apply much pressure. This is partly because legislators tend to have views that are consistent with those of their constituents. It is very difficult for a liberal to win election in a conservative district or for a conservative to prevail in a liberal district. Moreover, voters can be quite forgiving. Legislators who cultivate close relationships with their constituents will be given a good deal of leeway on their voting because they have built up a reservoir of trust. Indeed, I have found that constituents who like their legislators may refuse to believe it when told that their legislator cast a vote at odds with the constituents' preferences.

Second, the reelection rate of incumbents is very high. In 2002 and 2004, 99 percent of incumbent U.S. Representatives won their reelection bids (Abramowitz et al. 2005). In Indiana State House races in 2004, 89 out of 95 incumbents (94 percent) won their reelection bids, and 43 incumbents ran unopposed or with opposition only from a Libertarian candidate.[17] With such high reelection rates, it is unlikely that legislators will lose because they voted their conscience rather than what the majority of their constituents wanted.

To the extent that legislators vote against their constituency for reasons of conscience, they probably are overestimating the risk of an unpopular vote. Indeed, I have found that legislators can be quite risk averse when it comes to casting their ballots. A number of factors contribute to this. Elections are winner-take-all affairs. If an incumbent loses by only one vote, it is still a total loss of the legislative position. In addition, most election cycles include at least one unexpected loss by an incumbent, leading other incumbents to worry that they may be next. Finally, many members of part-time legislatures obtain more lucrative employment outside the legislature by virtue of their public office. Those legislators face the loss not only of their state house office but also of their other employment if they do not prevail on election day. For members of full-time legislatures, there is even more at stake. They will have resigned their previous positions and may have trouble relaunching a career in the private sector, or they may view private employment as far less desirable after holding public office (Rosenthal 1998, 71).

Perhaps the greater pressure on legislators to vote against their conscience comes from colleagues in their party caucus. On many key issues, party leaders may push for a party-line vote as a way to create leverage on other issues, and it can be difficult for legislators to break from the party. They may want the leverage for their own issues, or they may worry that deviating from the party line will affect their committee assignments, the chance that their bills will receive committee hearings, or other aspects of their legislative role.

This pressure to align with the party is analogous to the pressure that a bioethicist may face when speaking as an advocate before the legislature. Often a bioethicist will come before a legislative committee as a representative of the bioethicist's hospital, medical school, or other institution. For example, the legislature may be considering a proposal to regulate stem cell research in the state, and a bioethicist may speak to the ethical concerns of stem cell research on behalf of the state university. As the bioethicist works with other university officials to shape the testimony, he or she may be influenced by the institution's other interests before the legislature. The legislature will determine the state budget's allocation for the university, and university officials may believe that they will lose funding if they take a position at odds with the views of legislators who play a key role in the budget process.

Participation in the political process is an important civic obligation for all citizens. It is a special obligation for citizens with special expertise. Just as farmers can help legislators understand agricultural issues and urban planners can help legislators understand zoning issues, bioethicists can help legislators understand the moral aspects of issues in health care. Active involvement by bioethicists can help ensure that public policy on bioethical issues properly reflects sound ethical analysis.

NOTES

1. The University of Miami Ethics Programs have compiled a timeline of the Schiavo case at www.miami.edu/ethics/schiavo/timeline.htm.

2. *Roe v. Wade*, 410 U.S. 113 (1973); *Planned Parenthood of Southeastern Pennsylvania v. Casey*, 505 U.S. 833 (1992).

3. *Whitner v. South Carolina*, 492 S.E.2d 777 (S.C. 1997); *Johnson v. State*, 602 So. 2d 1288 (Fla. 1992).

4. *In re Baby K*, 16 F.3d 590 (4th Cir. 1994); *Causey v. St. Francis Medical Center*, 719 So. 2d 1072 (La. Ct. App. 1998).

5. *J.B. v. M.B. & C.C.*, 783 A.2d 707 (N.J. 2001); *Davis v. Davis*, 842 S.W.2d 588 (Tenn. 1992).

6. All states have statutes for living wills and/or powers of attorney for health care, and Congress passed the Patient Self-Determination Act in 1990 to facilitate end-of-life decision making.

7. Laws regulating abortion and artificial insemination, for example, are common.

8. The Emergency Medical Treatment and Active Labor Act requires hospital emergency departments to provide care to all individuals who have a need for emergency care. *Roberts v. Galen of Virginia*, 525 U.S. 249 (1999).

9. The National Conference of State Legislatures tracks state legislation on genetic testing and other genetics issues at www.ncsl.org/programs/health/Genetics/charts.htm.

10. *Bush v. Schiavo*, 885 So. 2d 321 (Fla. 2004).

11. Senate Bill 268, Indiana General Assembly (2005).

12. The legislation allows reimbursement of lost wages, travel costs, and medical expenses, and up to $3,000 for recovery time. Ind. Code § 35-46-5-3.

13. Of course, members of Congress also look to lobbyists for guidance. See Graziano 2001, 22.

14. 2 U.S.C. § 31-2 (2005).

15. For a state-by-state compilation of restrictions on gifts to legislators, see the Web site of the National Conference of State Legislatures, at www.ncsl.org/programs/ethics/e_gift.htm.

16. *Myers v. United States*, 272 U.S. 52 (1926).

17. Calculations were based on data compiled from the Web site of the Elections Division, Indiana Secretary of State.

REFERENCES

Abramowitz, A. I., Alexander, B., Gunning, M. 2005. Incumbency, redistricting, and the decline of competition in U.S. House elections. www.emergingdemocraticmajorityweblog.com/spsa/spsa.html.

Bush v. Schiavo, 885 So. 2d 321 (Fla. 2004).

Causey v. St. Francis Medical Center, 719 So. 2d 1072 (La. Ct. App. 1998).

Cerminara, K., and Goodman, K. 2006. Key events in the case of Theresa Marie Schiavo. www.miami.edu/ethics/schiavo/timeline.htm.

Davis v. Davis, 842 S.W.2d 588 (Tenn. 1992).

Dewan, S. 2005. In Mississippi, soaring costs force deep Medicaid cuts. *New York Times,* July 2: A8.

Gostin, L. O. 2000. Public health law in a new century: Part III: Public health regulation: A systematic evaluation. *JAMA* 283: 3118–22.

Graziano, L. 2001. *Lobbying, Pluralism, and Democracy.* New York: Palgrave.

Hall, M. A., Bobinski, M. A., and Orentlicher, D. 2003. *Health Care Law and Ethics.* 6th ed. New York: Aspen Law and Business.

Hitti, M. 2004. Nurses top list for honesty. WebMD Health, at http://my.webmd.com/content/article/98/104677.htm?z=1674_00000_5022_pe_01. December 8.

In re Baby K, 16F.3d 590 (4th Circuit 1994).

J.B. v. M.B. & C.C., 783 A.2d 707 (N.J. 2001).

Johnson v. State, 602 So. 2d 1288 (Fla. 1992).

Kristof, N. D. 2004. A war hero or a phony? *New York Times,* September 18: A15.

Meisel, A., and Cerminara, K. L. 2004. *The Right to Die.* 3rd ed. New York: Aspen Publishers.

Moon, M. 2001. Medicare. *New England Journal of Medicine* 344: 928–31.

Myers v. United States, 272 U.S. 52 (1926).

National Conference of State Legislatures Website. 2004. Legislator gift restrictions overview. www.ncsl.org/programs/ethics/e_gift.htm.

———. 2006. Genetic laws and legislative activity. www.ncsl.org/programs/health/Genetics/charts.htm.

Orentlicher, D. 1994. The influence of a professional organization on physician behavior. *Albany Law Review* 57: 583–605, 603–4.

Planned Parenthood of Southeastern Pennsylvania v. Casey, 505 U.S. 833 (1992).

Roberts v. Galen of Virginia, 525 U.S. 249 (1999).

Roe v. Wade, 410 U.S. 113 (1973).

Rosenthal, A. 1998. *The Decline of Representative Democracy: Process, Participation, and Power in State Legislatures.* Washington, DC: CQ Press.

Senate Bill 268, Indiana General Assembly (2005).

Stolberg, S. G. 2000. Stem cell research is slowed by restrictions, scientists say. *New York Times,* September 26: A27.

Whitner v. South Carolina, 492 S.E.2d 777 (S.C. 1997).

Wilgoren, J. 2004. Truth be told, the Vietnam crossfire hurts Kerry more. *New York Times,* September 24: A24.

CHAPTER SEVEN

Democratic Ideals and Bioethics Commissions

The Problem of Expertise in an Egalitarian Society

MARK G. KUCZEWSKI, PH.D.

Being a bioethicist is a funny thing. It makes one welcome in polite social conversation in a way that being called a philosopher does not. "Bioethics" immediately suggests some familiar issues to the news-savvy public. Names such as Quinlan, Cruzan, Kevorkian, and Schiavo have each been familiar to many Americans at some time. Issues such as abortion, withdrawing life-sustaining treatment, assisted suicide, cloning, stem cell research, and many others also come and go and come around again. So, when bioethics comes up in conversation, people feel like they know *what* to talk about, that is, what subjects my job deals with. Of course, shortly thereafter, the conversation is often abruptly interrupted.

The enthusiasm for talking about intriguing issues often gives way to a sudden surge of self-consciousness as our interlocutor feels he may have said a bit too much to an expert. He becomes worried that we may be judging him as none-too-bright since he is not so sure how his opinions sound to someone who works in the field. Nevertheless, such stumbling blocks in the conversation are generally easily set aside. One simply explains that these are matters that should concern everyone and that it is important that thinking individuals consider the subjects thoughtfully. Of course, as the discussion progresses, the question of what I actually know and do is invariably at issue. That is, the impetus for much of the discussion becomes finding out whether I am not only more familiar with these widely discussed issues but am someone who knows something different from my interlocutor, even if this is explored in indirect terms and questions.

This cocktail-party-like dialogue is a microcosm of a discussion that has been going on between citizens and experts at least since the time of Attic Greece. Moral matters are interesting and attract our attention. However, moral matters can also be surprisingly complicated and can lead to a desire to enlist the aid of experts. No sooner do we consider enlisting such guidance than we become concerned about losing control over matters that deeply concern us. Worse still, we fear losing this control to people who are merely "seeming" experts. After all, is there really any genuine expertise in morality?

This fictional conversation mirrors the tension between society and the bioethics community. Namely, the general public can vacillate between a sense that everyone can solve moral matters and a respect for expert solutions. While bioethical issues are of widespread general interest, their complexity can inspire humility in the general public, who would like to see the problems taken care of by experts working in the public interest. At the same time, when it comes to moral matters, Americans have a faith in the common sense of everyman and a suspicion of experts. It is not surprising, therefore, that there should be an ambiguity with respect to the role of ethicists in general, and more specifically, ethicists who work with government, such as bioethics commissions.

In general, bioethics commissions in a democracy like the United States raise several kinds of questions: Is there a role for some kind of expertise in regard to what seem to be moral matters? If there is a role for expertise, what might this role be? But the first question is why are these considered collective matters at all? That is, is not morality in health care simply an individual matter?

I will attempt to outline answers to these questions. Contemporary biomedicine is a collective enterprise in which the public has invested so heavily that it is difficult to separate a private sphere from the public sphere. Furthermore, the choices made within the biomedical-industrial complex frame the choices for individuals and their options for achieving the good life. As a result, bioethics must also be a public matter, facilitating public deliberation. Entities such as bioethics commissions assist this process by clarifying policy options and pointing the way to potential consensus solutions that respect the competing values at stake. In this way, bioethics commissions can aspire to perform a public service.

BIOETHICS AS A PUBLIC ENTERPRISE

One way to think about all moral issues, one that is unrealistic in the modern world, is that there should be no community or government involvement with such matters. On this approach, all moral questions are similar to matters of free speech or freedom of religion. The liberties accorded in these domains should be maximized and restricted only by clear threats they pose to similar freedoms for others or by posing imminent dangers to the good of the community. However, it is unlikely that all health care or biomedical questions with moral overtones can or should be treated as if they are matters of fundamental and inalienable personal liberties, for two reasons.

First, individual choice often presupposes a prior process of collective decision making in health care. For instance, before you decide whether to utilize a service or not, that service must have been developed through research and testing and is likely to have been assessed and deemed worthy of insurance reimbursement. This process takes place within an intertwined web of public and private funding for medicine. This web has many interlocking threads, including tax exemptions for nonprofit health care facilities, direct government subsidies to medical and residency education, federal funding of biomedical research, and a host of other collective decisions. As a result, the citizenry will have already participated in and subsidized the creation of this treatment option before each citizen considers whether this treatment is appropriate for him or her.

Second, the decision of a society to develop or decline to pursue various technologies may have an impact on the options for happiness of many regardless of how those persons exercise their individual liberties. For instance, no one must consent to prenatal testing for Down syndrome. However, once such a test is developed and becomes a routine part of care, it has implications for women who would not desire to avail themselves of the test or to terminate a pregnancy. As a consequence, the percentage of children who are born with Down syndrome has been much reduced (Vassey 2005). Thus any such children who are born will probably live in a world with fewer accommodations and services routinely available and will likely suffer through more misunderstanding and discrimination than their predecessors have, in that they will be very rare beings. Furthermore, their parents, in exercising their right to bring this child into the world, may be seen by others as having done something immoral. That is, when the vast majority of persons in a situation do one thing, to do another may be seen as a violation of a social norm and a failure to do one's duty (Zuckoff 2002). Social norms and expectations exert a strong influence.

Biomedicine is an enterprise in which the public has a large monetary investment and an even larger investment in directing the manner in which it affects our lives. While our democratic ideals ask that we let each person be free to pursue his or her vision of the good life, we must acknowledge that the development of a certain common biomedical infrastructure will shape the kinds of lives available to us and our possible paths to fulfillment and happiness. Our society is not simply a collection of moral strangers. We are morally acquainted through the public infrastructure. The challenge is to be a moral community that shapes these options through respectful and informed dialogue and deliberation rather than through mere self-interested politics. It is this aspiration that calls forth the possibility of bioethicists and bioethics commissions playing a public role within the democracy.

BIOETHICS COMMISSIONS OR THE BALLOT BOX?

As health care has become more sophisticated, the ethical issues involved often require a fair amount of knowledge. Of course, this creates a tension between the interest of the individual citizen in the biomedical enterprise and the need for expertise from others in order to resolve dilemmas. The appropriate method of institutionalizing approaches to such issues will depend partly on the degree to which one believes the public wishes to deal directly with such matters and partly on the degree to which expertise is seen to be essential in these matters.

One may prefer that all such matters be dealt with through an expert body, on the assumption that difficult choices about life and death matters, especially those that admit of no good solution, are things that most people do not like to deal with directly and in fact cannot deal with well (Calabresi and Bobbitt 1978). As a result, some may argue that these matters are best managed for the public by agents who actually hide the nature of the tragic choice from general public view. While it is important that we acknowledge this position because the public may seem to avoid making difficult choices from time to time, it is incumbent on those who hold this opinion to provide evidence that the public genuinely would not prefer to be involved in matters that shape their lives to such a large extent.

The mainstream position that runs from Kant through John Rawls and Norman Daniels takes a very different approach and argues that the very nature of a liberal democracy requires a "publicity condition" in all decisions, that is to say transparency regarding decisions made in the public realm. Some argue further that decision makers must be publicly accountable and that it is preferable to allow as many decisions as possible to be made by health care consumers in developing localized health plans (Emanuel 1991). These community-oriented approaches are premised on the idea that while the public may not be adept at handling these matters, citizens actually get better at it through hands-on decision making and develop their civic virtue. Bioethics commissions are based on combining elements of each of these strands of thought.

Health care can involve tragic choices, value conflicts, and a certain amount of technical knowledge. As a result, those who argue against having the populace directly make most of these choices have a strong case. The tragic element of biomedical decisions is clear, as when trade-offs that seem unacceptable but are inevitable must be made, and even assuming ample resources, human life will always inevitably end in death. Clearly cherished values such as the value of human life can come into conflict with personal autonomy, the need to advance research can conflict with the interests of individual patients, and the list of potential conflicts can be continued. While this need not lead to a lack of transparency on the part of those who design institutions and solutions to address these concerns, it does suggest that mere voting by the citizenry may be too blunt an instrument to capture the subtlety that stable solutions will require.

If we examine two issues in which direct referenda have been utilized reasonably well in the past, namely, insurance coverage for in-hospital stays after labor and delivery and legalization of assisted suicide, we see why direct democracy may prove overmatched by a plethora of such issues. Referenda are generally "up or down" questions and will be most effective when questions are easily framed in such terms. A question such as whether an insurer is required to provide forty-eight hours of coverage after delivery or whether assisted suicide should be legal would seem to be good candidates for a yes or no vote. But, even here, we encounter the need for expertise. That is, a referendum on postpartum hospital stays must be framed in terms that make medical claims concerning how long is appropriate and in what circumstances, as in cases of vaginal delivery versus delivery by caesarean section (American Academy of Pediatrics . . . 2004). A referendum concerning assisted suicide is still more complicated. Many persons will immediately support being able to make decisions regarding one's care when near death. However, they will want to know what their current rights are and how this practice might affect current ways of doing things. Questions about the appropriate scope of application of the practice and appropriate safeguards will likely occur to the concerned citizen. What at first seemed a simple issue can turn out to be rather complicated.

This is not to say that bioethics commissions should settle issues because questions are usually too complicated for the average citizen. I am suggesting that bioethics commissions can be and have been quite useful because they can help to bring the kind of expertise to bear on an issue that helps to frame the questions appropriately for public deliberation. The questions and options for the public can be sharpened so that the options posed are as good and realistic as may be possible. This surely enhances public discourse. We also see that an argument can follow from this approach that expert input can lead directly to legislation without violating any democratic ideals.

THE TASK OF A BIOETHICS COMMISSION IN A DEMOCRACY

Bioethics commissions have legitimate roles in a democracy. They consider complex issues and bring to bear the resources of various kinds of expertise. They may also make recommendations for ways to address the ethical concerns that arise in biomedical research and treatment. These recommendations receive their legitimation by reflecting the values of the public (Kuczewski 2001). This has generally been the aspiration of most of the bioethics commissions from the 1970s through approximately the turn of the century.

Clarifying Options: The President's Council on Bioethics

In contrast to the consensus-building approach, the most recent high-profile commission, the President's Council on Bioethics (PCB), has generally set a less ambitious agenda for itself. Following a contemporary popular trend that denies that there are shared values in a nation that sometimes seems deeply divided and in the midst of ongoing "culture wars," the PCB began by aiming only to clarify the options for the public. The immediate past chairman, Leon Kass, affirmed in his vision statement: "Because reasonable and morally serious people can differ about fundamental matters, it is fortunate that we have been liberated from an overriding concern to reach consensus. As the Executive Order indicates [Sec. 2(c)], in pursuit of our goal of comprehensive and deep understanding, 'the Council shall be guided by the need to articulate fully the complex and often competing moral positions on any given issue . . . [and] may therefore choose to proceed by offering a variety of views on a particular issue, rather than attempt to reach a single *consensus position*'" (Kass 2002). Obviously, this position has a prima facie appeal. After all, people disagree on moral issues all the time and it can be notoriously difficult to persuade or be persuaded by those with whom we disagree. Alasdair MacIntyre pointed out long ago that many such issues result in "shrill and interminable" debates rather than reasoned discourse (MacIntyre 1981).

The most striking example of using the clarification of options as the telos of the PCB's work is manifest in the report *Beyond Therapy: Biotechnology and the Pursuit of Happiness* (PCB 2003). This report considers the traditional but rapidly collapsing moral prohibition on human enhancement technologies. The distinction between treatment and enhancement has become more difficult to sustain with recent developments in biomedicine, and simply using the label of "enhancement" to prohibit various technologies would seem inadequate to the questions posed by biomedicine. This report outlines a variety of enhancement technologies for various life stages and provides ethical analysis of each. But the report makes no definitive recommendations. The final paragraph of the report states: "We must first understand what is at stake, and we must begin to imagine what the age of biotechnology might bring, and what human life in that age might look like. In these pages, we have sought to begin that vital project, in the hope that these first steps might spark and inform a public debate, so that however the nation proceeds, it will do so with its eyes wide open" (PCB 2003, 310).

The report demonstrates, however, that clarification is not simply explaining technologies and listing options. The descriptions and analyses it offers are noteworthy because they consider a variety of goods, including the effects of technologies on relationships and somewhat more vague categories such as "medicalization." As with any attempt to explicate somewhat elusive values, such analyses are easy targets for criticism. Nevertheless, these discussions demonstrate that "clarifying options" may include attempting to articulate categories that might capture important public sentiments that are typically undervalued by academic bioethicists and members of the biomedical industrial complex (Lysaught 2004). If so, this is not mere clarification but important work that is preparatory to the method of balancing considerations in an attempt at consensus (Cohen 2005).

Producing Consensus: The Mainstream View of Bioethics Commissions

Bioethics as an academic discipline has grown by leaps and bounds precisely because it has often found consensus on seemingly intractable issues. The birth of contemporary bioethics is sometimes traced to the National Commission for the Protection of Human Subjects of Biomedical and Behavioral Research in the mid-1970s. It was feared that "matters of eternal principle would be decided by a 5 to 4 vote" (Jonsen and Toulmin 1988, 17) because the scientist members of the committee might value scientific progress highly while the nonscientists would be far more concerned with the rights of, and prevention of harm to, human participants in research. But the commission never fractured along these lines. Instead, they produced consensus reports that made recommendations to balance the principles of respect for persons, of beneficence, and of justice. These reports formed the basis of the federal regulations, the "Common Rule" (HHS 45 CFR 46), which governs federally funded biomedical and behavioral research.

Similarly, the National Commission's successor body, the President's Commission for the Study of Ethical Problems in Medicine and Biomedical and Behavioral Research, authored a significant number of reports that laid the foundation for the development of a broad consensus on end-of-life decision making in the United States. This consensus has proven remarkably stable. The President's Commission thoroughly explored informed consent as the foundation of medical decision making and then built upon this foundation dealing with end-of-life decision making. In their subtle analyses and recommendations, the commission balanced the patient's right of self-determination with considerations regarding the integrity of the medical profession and its duty to benefit patients. As a result, the commission's work has influenced court decisions and state legislatures and helped to frame the debates concerning end-of-life care. It has genuinely established a consensus (Meisel 1992).

Consensus is not mere compromise. Compromises are typically agreements arranged by particular parties that are minimally acceptable to those parties. Compromises can reflect idiosyncratic preferences and fail to be reflective of the choices that many or most persons would make. In contrast, a consensus position is one that reflects and builds upon the values of each party such that those values are respected. A consensus position is one that is a win for each party rather than a choice between competing principles (Kuczewski 2002).

The particulars of a consensus may seem obscure to those who have not gone through the reasoning process. The consensus on forgoing life-sustaining treatment respects self-determination by insisting on the right of a competent patient to refuse unwanted medical treatment. It also safeguards the profession's duty to promote the patient's well-being by setting more cautious standards of decision making for patients who lack decision-making capacity and suggesting conflict resolution mechanisms at the bedside and through the courts. While these particulars may be obscure to the uninitiated, they tend to make sense to people when they are explained in detail, especially to people facing such situations.

A well-constructed consensus can be said to reflect what-I-would-think-if-I-thought-about-it (Moreno 1995). As a result, a consensus may seem shaky when a high-profile case emerges and causes the public to turn its attention to the issue. But, as the public becomes more educated through media reports and debate, a stable consensus may reassert itself, even if some details are amended. The case of Theresa Marie Schindler Schiavo ("Terri Schiavo") illustrated this nicely. The case pitted the patient's husband, her duly recognized surrogate decision maker, against the patient's parents. The patient's husband requested the removal of artificial nutrition and hydration from her, as she had been unresponsive for a number of years and had virtually no hope of recovery. Her parents wished to continue the feeding tube.

Public sentiment was influenced by initial visual images and news reports that suggested that Ms. Schiavo had more cognitive awareness than the best scientific knowledge, and ultimately her autopsy, would indicate. This public sentiment led to political opportunism by the Florida legislature and governor, who enacted laws to govern this one case. The United States Congress followed suit in using legal subterfuges such as its subpoena power to undermine due process. Although these politicians felt confident that they had a "wedge issue" that would work in their favor, public opinion ultimately swung against such violations of the appropriate rights of the patient and her husband to make medical decisions. It seemed that the consensus was reasserted and Congress was effectively told it was not welcome at the bedside (ABC News Poll 2005; CBS News Poll 2005).

This view of the work of bioethics commissions in creating consensus clearly shows that their work is not to dictate the "right" or "correct" solution to the public. Their work is to attempt to respect the legitimate values and concerns of the public and help to craft approaches that respect those values. While we have gotten used to thinking of our nation as deeply divided, social science research has long indicated that Americans coalesce around moderate views on most values and issues (Wolfe 1998; Baker 2005). The perceptive bioethics commission will combine its expertise on the particulars of issues with the values of the citizenry.

The examples of the National Commission and the President's Commission indicate that the work of such bodies may be directly implemented through regulatory mechanisms, as in the case of the former, or they may have more of a role in influencing court opinions and legislators, as in the case of the latter. But this wide influence and the stability of the resulting products follows from their moderate consenses. Obviously such a role is compatible with democratic ideals. When a bioethics commission fails to have such influence, it can be very difficult to discern whether it has failed in producing such a moderate consensus or whether other factors that are at work have undermined it (Eiseman 2003).

HOW BIOETHICS COMMISSIONS CAN GO WRONG

Given this description of bioethics commissions, it is worth thinking for a moment about how such a group can fall short of its reason for being. This will usually involve becoming partisan by failing to sufficiently balance values that the public believes are important. As a result, personal preferences and commitments, however acquired, can come to dominate the reasoning of the group.

First, bioethics commissions obviously fail the public if they do not accurately represent the aspects of a question that are the province of "experts," such as the scientific dimensions of issues. Good ethics requires a sound factual basis. For instance, recent controversy has swirled around whether the cell lines derived from embryos are adequate for research purposes and whether there are reasonable alternative sources of suitable material for research (President's Council 2005). Clearly, the claim of the present policy to balance research concerns with respect for human life would have to rest on a good faith effort to provide the opportunity for research advancement. Similarly, those who argue that the advancement of research can be balanced with respect for human life through use of cells derived from embryos that would ordinarily be discarded must accurately describe whether this is likely to satisfy researchers who wish to do such work, or whether conceptual difficulties are already apparent that would quickly lead to less morally acceptable forms of research, such as the creation of embryos for use as subjects. While I make no judgment on how accurately these matters are currently represented by bioethicists, it is important to note that it would not be acceptable for a bioethics commission to advance an argument that is based on faulty facts because it moves public policy in the direction the members find desirable.

Second, bioethics commissions should not allow the values of their members to lead them to delegitimize the values of sizable portions of the citizenry. That is, as professional academics, bioethicists may be more inclined to value the advancement of science than the average person and to value sanctity of life considerations less than much of the general public. (Of course, some sectarian bioethicists may have the opposite inclinations.) However, to craft solutions to public issues by arguing against the importance of one of these values rather than attempting to balance the considerations does a disservice to the public and to the purpose of bioethics commissions.

Although there is no clear rule for the composition of a commission, finding commissioners who are able to accurately appreciate the positions and values of the array of common positions within a culture is important. Commissions are unlikely to be successful if all of their members come from a narrow spectrum of viewpoints. Despite their best efforts to represent the views of others in their deliberations, they may be unlikely to see those positions "from the inside out," as those who hold those positions do. As a result, the commissioners might gloss over important subtleties and produce a false consensus, or they may fail to see genuine possibilities for common ground. Diversity, in a broad sense of that term, will be important for bioethics commissions. The consensus must be built by a diverse group of persons, for such persons.

Conversely, the commission will fail if it chooses persons who absolutize particular solutions and refuse to seek ways of accommodating the fundamental values behind their position. While this kind of person is easily found in society, a commission of such people will likely not find the kind of consensus that can engage the vast majority of citizens. Such persons can only be accommodated by actually embracing their position. Of course, because most Americans do not usually embrace the particular vantage point of these people, it forces a trade-off between the views of the majority and those of a small but vocal minority. Such either/or choices are the foundation of a "shrill and interminable" debate and cannot be the work of a representative bioethics commission.

Third, in general, bioethics commissions (and bioethicists) must not allow themselves to become one more tool of the "culture wars." For instance, when the commission is closely tied to a particular elected official such as the president of the United States, it can easily fall into the trap of providing "cover" for the president's partisan views by providing a "blue ribbon" seal of approval. The positive aspect of a close working relationship with a particular chief executive might be that it allows the defusing of an emerging issue by referral to the commission for study and the crafting of a balanced solution.

The measure of the work of a bioethics commission is the casual social-gathering conversation we imagined at the beginning of this chapter. Our interlocutor felt his values were relevant but vacillated between thinking his opinion mattered as much as any and reticence in the face of seeming expertise. A commission is successful if its work reinforces each of these tendencies. That is, he should feel that, as he is a human being and citizen, his values and opinions count. As consensus solutions to the issues are explained, he is likely to admire the technical issues, nuances, and additional concerns that have been taken into account. And ultimately if, as these things are explained clearly, he should nod in agreement and say "that makes good sense," the commission has hit the mark.

REFERENCES

ABC News poll of March 21, 2005, www.abcnews.go.com/images/Politics/978a1Schiavo .pdf.

American Academy of Pediatrics Committee on the Fetus and Newborn. 2004. Hospital stay for healthy term newborns. *Pediatrics* 113(5): 1434–36.

Baker, W. 2005. *America's Crisis of Values: Reality and Perception*. Princeton, NJ: Princeton University Press.

Calabresi, G., and Bobbitt, P. 1978. *Tragic Choices*. New York: W. W. Norton.

CBS News poll of March 23, 2005 (report of), www.cbsnews.com/stories/2005/03/23/politics/main682619.shtml.

Cohen, C. B. 2005. Promises and perils of public deliberation: Contrasting two national bioethics commissions on embryonic stem cell research. *Kennedy Institute of Ethics Journal* 15(3): 269–88.

Eiseman, E. 2003. *The National Bioethics Advisory Commission: Contributing to Public Policy*. Santa Monica, CA: Rand Science and Technology Policy Institute.

Emanuel, E. J. 1991. *The Ends of Human Life: Medical Ethics in a Liberal Polity*. Cambridge, MA: Harvard University Press.

Jonsen, A. R., and Toulmin, S. 1988. *The Abuse of Casuistry: A History of Moral Reasoning*. Berkeley, CA: University of California Press.

Kass, L. R. 2002. Chairman's vision. Adapted from the Chairman's opening remarks at the first meeting of the Council, January 17, 2002.www.bioethics.gov/about/chairman.html.

Kuczewski, M. G. 2001. The epistemology of communitarian bioethics: Traditions in the public debates. *Theoretical Medicine and Bioethics* 22(2): 135–50.

———. 2002. Two models of ethical consensus, or what good is a bunch of bioethicists? *Cambridge Quarterly of Healthcare Ethics* 11(1): 27–36.

Lysaught, M. T. 2004. Keywords in bioethics: RESPECT, or How respect for persons became respect for autonomy. *Journal of Medicine and Philosophy* 29: 665–80.

MacIntyre, A. 1981. *After Virtue*. Notre Dame, IN: University of Notre Dame Press.

Meisel, A. 1992. The consensus about forgoing life-sustaining treatment: Its status and prospects. *Kennedy Institute of Ethics Journal* 2(4): 309–45.

Moreno, J. D. 1995. *Deciding Together: Bioethics and Moral Consensus*. New York: Oxford University Press.

President's Council on Bioethics. 2003. *Beyond Therapy: Biotechnology and the Pursuit of Happiness*. New York: HarperCollins.

———. 2005. *Alternative Sources of Human Pluripotent Stem Cells*. Washington, DC: President's Council on Bioethics.

U.S. Department of Health and Human Services, Code of Federal Regulations, Title 45 Public Welfare, Part 46 Protection of Human Subjects.

Vassey, C. 2005. How prenatal diagnosis became acceptable in France. *Trends in Biotechnology* 23(5): 246–49.

Wolfe, A. 1998. *One Nation, After All*. New York: Penguin Books.

Zuckoff, M. 2002. *Choosing Naia: A Family's Journey*. Boston, MA: Beacon Press.

CHAPTER EIGHT

The Endarkenment

R. ALTA CHARO, J.D.

In March 2005, the *Washington Post* broke the news that then-chairman Leon Kass and others appointed by George W. Bush to his "President's Council on Bioethics" (PCB), purportedly acting as private citizens and not as members and staff of the council, had been meeting privately for months to develop and circulate a memorandum with a conservative bioethics agenda for the second term of the Bush administration (Weiss 2005), one broader and more ambitious than ongoing congressional efforts because, as the memorandum stated, "We have today an administration and a Congress as friendly to human life and human dignity as we are likely to have for many years to come. It would be tragic if we failed to take advantage of this rare opportunity to enact significant bans on some of the most egregious biotechnical practices" (http://blog.bioethics.net). But of course this was not really news. Many of the specifics outlined in the memorandum had already appeared in print, in the new conservative bioethics journal *The New Atlantis*. And William Saletan, a regular on *Slate*, had been reporting repeatedly on the Bush bioethics council's efforts to build political coalitions to undermine support for embryonic stem cell research (Saletan 2005).

As an intellectual movement, bioethics constantly transforms itself. Long a creature of theologians, it was snatched away by secular philosophers in the 1970s, swallowed up by physicians and lawyers in the 1980s, and infused with humanists in the 1990s. Now it is being balkanized into its liberal and conservative wings, and has come into its own as a public policy player. No longer restricted to academic conferences and advisory boards, it has even come to develop organs of aspiring power, such as the "bioethics defense fund" (www.bdfund.org), which offers white papers, policy briefings, and legal briefs on "any human life issue." Its board includes the founder of the Becket Fund, which is dedicated to things like school prayer and government support for religious schools. The Becket Fund board of directors, in turn, features a snake-swallowing-its-tail pattern of interlocking boards of conservative religious/bioethics/public policy groups that, increasingly, is a hallmark of the conservative bioethics movement.

It would be absurd of course to imagine that bioethics discussions aimed at influencing public policy can ever be free of actual politics. Such "public bioethics" discussions take place on major governmental and nongovernmental advisory boards, such as the Department of Health and Human Services Secretary's Advisory Committee on Human Research Protections (SACHRP) or the various National Academy of Sciences committees that have issued reports on stem cell research and cloning policy. And the appointment of members to such committees is certainly the focus of political interest from time to time, for example, when one person appointed to the SACHRP declined to serve (*Chronicle* 2003) or when embryo research opponents complained that a National Institutes of Health panel set up to develop funding guidelines failed to include firm opponents of all such funding (Marshall 1994; Irving undated). But the Bush bioethics council has been dogged by allegations of bias, litmus tests, and undue involvement with partisan politics (Siegal 2005; Caplan 2004; Cook 2004; Smith 2004; Holden 2004; Stolberg 2002; Bottum 2002). And very importantly, though often overlooked in public commentary, the staffs of presidential commissions were not selected with political agendas in mind.

POLITICAL AGENDAS AND PUBLIC BIOETHICS COMMISSIONS

Aggressively political agendas in public bioethics commissions are associated with failure, whether measured in terms of public policy influence or simply public credibility. As one congressional study put it: "Successful commissions were relatively free of political interference, had flexibility in addressing issues, were open in their process and dissemination of findings, and were comprised of a diverse group of individuals who were generally free of ideology and had wide ranging expertise" (U.S. Congress 1993).

The overtly conservative agenda outlined by the former executive director of President Bush's bioethics council, Yuval Levin, and implemented in many of the council's reports, has been pursued in a manner that is different not only in its political dimensions but in its organizational dimensions as well. Unlike all the

presidential bioethics bodies before it, this council's charter eschews appointment of "public members," that is, of persons without academic or technical credentials but simply of good character and great intelligence. But eschewing public participation as an approach is consistent with the attitudes associated with
neoconservative Leo Strauss, who followed a Platonic philosophy that emphasized the importance of elites as leaders of both discussion and society: "Something of a cult developed around Strauss. The cult is appropriate because Strauss
believed that the essential truths about human society and history should be held
by an elite, and . . . [h]e held that philosophy is dangerous because it brings into
question the conventions on which civil order and the morality of society depend.
This risks promoting a destructive nihilism. According to Strauss, the relativism
of modern American society is a moral disorder. . . . 'Moral clarity' is essential"
(Pfaff 2003, 6).

Another distinguishing characteristic of this council is the degree to which,
unlike its predecessors, it has become associated with the views of its chair. Even
its Web site is unusual, featuring a picture of Kass, some of his statements, and
a lengthy "vision" statement which sets out the council's agenda, an agenda that
includes rejection of moral relativism, recognition of evil, attention to curtailing
"runaway scientism" and "unbridled technological advance," and incorporation
of religious values in discussions aimed at shaping biological research and modern health care in ways that avoid "dehumanization" (PCB). Further, these views,
once developed into reports and recommendations by the council in the elitist atmosphere of limited opportunity for uninvited presentations and public participation, are packaged with an eye toward the general public, which is invited to be
educated by this group of academics and intellectuals.

The most profound dimension of all this, for this presidential group and for
all who came before and will come after, is the enduring question of the relationship between ethical analysis and public policy. Moral angst is one thing; federal criminalization of research or medical practice is another. While the PCB's
work features much discussion on the subject of human dignity, scant attention
is paid to what political philosophy teaches is the significant difference between
arguing something is unethical and arguing that it is (or ought to be) prohibited
by federal law. Its report on assisted reproductive technologies, for example, han-
dles these issues in twelve paragraphs in the introductory chapter (PCB 2004).

But attention to political philosophy is precisely what is needed to make bioethics analysis relevant to public policy. The debate, in large part, is joined not
over whether a particular technology is absolutely good or absolutely bad. Most
bioethicists would agree that nearly all technologies are fundamentally disruptive

to society, because they make possible new choices and new interpersonal relationships. The question is not whether they promote change but whether the government can and should halt or curtail such changes. Indeed, while it would be
foolish to suggest that bioethicists, both left and right, have consistently eschewed
offering personal opinions, it is worth noting that the field as a whole gained some
of its credibility because it was thought to offer something distinctive: knowledge
of ethical and political theory, as well as relevant law, and a commitment to analytical reasoning that helps others to articulate their assumptions and fundamental values and challenges others to develop positions that logically flow from
those assumptions and values.

THE BUSH BIOETHICS COUNCIL

An intriguing aspect of the Bush bioethics council is the wealth of deep connections many of its staff and members have to the neoconservative movement,
which may account for its generally worried tone about science altering our perceptions of ourselves, our relationships, and our gods, a tone that has been a hallmark of its meetings since its first session in January 2002, which Leon Kass devoted to a discussion of science run amok through the lens of Nathaniel
Hawthorne's short story "The Birth Mark." As one critic of the PCB leadership
put it: "One of Kass's primary intellectual influences is . . . Hans Jonas, . . . one
of the first bioethicists, who advocated a 'heuristics of fear' to help stave off biomedical advance. . . . While at times he quotes Plato and Aristotle, Kass has more
frequently argued on the basis of *Brave New World*" (Mooney 2001, 10).
This strain of thinking has long characterized both Kass and the bioethics
council he leads, a kind of dystopianism strongly linked to a suspicion of anything
that tinkers with the "natural" world: "In 1962, political philosopher Leo Strauss,
guru of many neoconservatives like Kass (and an influence on other bioethics
commission members like Francis Fukuyama), wrote . . . that science risked up-
setting the 'natural order.' . . . Strauss and Kass argue that we can know our place
through a device Kass calls the 'wisdom of repugnance,' the gut instinct that tells
us right from wrong" (Hall 2002, 323). This wisdom of repugnance has some of
its roots in the work of other notable bioethicists, such as the aforementioned
Hans Jonas (Jonas 1982), who worried about the future of humanity in an age of
scientific discovery. Kass has said that he has been deeply influenced by Jonas,
and scholars describe both Jonas and Kass as skeptics leery of unforeseen ills in
technological gains, especially concerning biomedicine (Kukis 2001).
The membership and the reports of the PCB not only demonstrate a widely

shared vision about the perils of scientific advances, but a wide array of personal connections into the neoconservative movement. While "neocon" is a label without precise description, one of its hallmarks is a wariness born of pessimistic views of human nature and a "resulting worldview [that] tends to Manicheanism—the notion that the world consists of a permanent struggle between the forces of good and evil, light and dark (an idea that also accords very well both with the thinking of the Christian Right, not to mention, of Bush himself)" (Lobe 2003).

Of course, political philosophies are hardly ever so simple, and even within the neoconservative movement, there are shifts and currents that allow members both to reinvent themselves and to propose plans that seemingly conflict with founding principles. For example, PCB member Francis Fukuyama, a leading and long-standing member of the neocon movement, points out that neoconservatism was founded on skepticism about social engineering—the conviction that grand schemes like Lyndon Johnson's Great Society program produce unintended, uncontrollable consequences—and thus he criticizes the neocon enthusiasm for democracy building in Iraq (*The Economist* 2004). But at the same time, Fukuyama is the loudest proponent of a grand social engineering scheme in which all biotechnological innovation in the realms of human health and reproduction would be banned or heavily regulated by federal law in the name of protecting society's morality (Fukuyama 2002). In the end, it seems at times as if neoconservative is more a label of membership in a club than it is a description of a coherent worldview. But even limiting it to club membership has its implications for the development of a bioethics more attentive to fear than hope.

THE NEW NEOCONSERVATIVE BIOETHICS CLUB

This new neoconservative bioethics club is an interlocking network of conservative and neoconservative figures, appearing together at fora, writing for and editing the same journals, and working with one another as members or staff within a small circle that orbits former PCB chair Leon Kass. The Project for the New American Century (PNAC) is a neoconservative think tank closely affiliated with the New Citizenship Project, founded by one of the most prominent neoconservatives, William Kristol, who chairs its "bioethics project." PNAC also has strong ties to the conservative American Enterprise Institute. Leon Kass, along with Newt Gingrich, Irving Kristol, and Charles Murray (of *The Bell Curve* fame), are all listed as scholars and fellows of the American Enterprise Institute (Charo 2004). One of PNAC's members, the aforementioned Francis Fukuyama, best known in bioethics circles for his book *Our Posthuman Future* (Fukuyama 2002), has collaborated under the auspices of the conservative (Christian) Center for Bioethics and Human Dignity (CBHD) to undermine support for basic science research with William Kristol, J. Bottum (founder of the neocon publication *The Weekly Standard*), and Wesley Smith (frequent defender of the PCB in columns for *The Weekly Standard* and himself affiliated with the creationist Discovery Institute) (Charo 2004).

Among CBHD's most prominent members and advisers is Nigel Cameron, another creationist who is himself affiliated with the Biotechnology Project of the Wilberforce Forum, whose goal is to "shape culture from a biblical perspective" (Charo 2004). Cameron was recently featured at a bioethics training session for the Statesmanship Institute, which gathers congressional aides and members for instruction in how to merge evangelical theology with lawmaking (Simon 2005). Other CBHD members include PCB member Gilbert Meilaender, who is a board member of *First Things*, a journal on religion, edited by the neoconservative Richard John Neuhaus, and which has featured articles by Wesley Smith and PCB member Mary Ann Glendon, member of the anti-gay Alliance for Marriage and head of the Pontifical Academy of Social Sciences, thus making her the Roman Catholic Church's highest-ranking lay woman. PCB member Robert George serves on the boards of directors of a series of conservative groups: the Ethics and Public Policy Center, the Institute for American Values, the Institute on Religion and Democracy, the National Association of Scholars, and the Catholic League for Religious and Civil Rights. George is also on the board of the Alliance for Marriage and the editorial board of *First Things* magazine. And PCB member James Q. Wilson has served as chairman of the board of academic advisers of the American Enterprise Institute (Charo 2004).

The ideas linking these people and institutions lie at the heart of both bioethics and more general discussions of political philosophy. Beyond the shared dark vision of science and the fear of social change wrought by technological innovation is a shared belief in the permissibility, nay, imperative of governmentally enforced morals regulation. Whether it is parental choice about whether to embrace or avoid the birth of a child with genetic disease or individual choice to hasten or delay death or the intimate choice of homosexual couples to marry or not, a basic divide exists between those who call for the government, based on pure majoritarian will (often itself driven by majoritarian theology) to limit or ban such choices and those who take a more liberal (in the libertarian sense of the word) approach to morality, with its concomitant reticence on the part of government to interfere except to protect vulnerable third parties from concrete harms.

Another area of overlap within the membership of the neocon bioethics entities extends into the staff. Unlike presidential commissions before it, whose staff
were drawn from academe without necessarily having any prior connections,
PCB's first executive director, Dean Clancy, is a former staffer for Dick Armey,
who, among his many conservative credentials, is a signatory for Americans
United for Separation of School and State, which calls for an end to public education and a return to home (often religious) schooling (Charo 2004). In another
example of hiring conservative staff, the PCB's senior research consultant, Eric
Cohen, runs the Biotechnology and American Democracy project at the Ethics
and Public Policy Center (EPPC), which promotes the infusion of religious values into public policy. He was also managing editor of *The Public Interest,* a recently defunct neoconservative publication that has published some of Kass's
most provocatively conservative writing, including his late 1970s condemnations
of in vitro fertilization (Kass 1979a, 1979b, 1979c) and his more recent condem-
nation of premarital sexual activity among "careerist" women (Kass 1997). (Indeed, *The Public Interest* publication committee read almost like a Who's Who of
the PCB. It included PCB members Kass, Fukuyama, and Wilson, as well as
Charles Krauthammer, James Q. Wilson, and newly appointed PCB member Di-
ana Schaub.) And PCB senior consultant, Peter Berkowitz of George Mason Law
School, was himself a frequent contributor to *The Public Interest,* the *Weekly Standard,* and *First Things,* venues in which, among other things, he has reviewed
work by Leon Kass (see Berkowitz).

Interestingly, this effort is hardly limited to the Bush bioethics council, or to
debates surrounding embryonic stem cell research, or even abortion. For example, in the now famous case of Terri Schiavo, a woman in a persistent vegetative
state for fifteen years whose husband's efforts to discontinue futile artificial support for nutrition and hydration were met with years of litigation and political interference (*Bush v. Schiavo,* 125 S. Ct. 1086 [2005]), Attorney Jon Eisenberg published the following account of interlocking conservative organizations that
provided the funding for the opposition:

> Many of the attorneys, activists and organizations working to keep Schiavo on
> life support all these years have been funded by members of the Philanthropy
> Roundtable . . . a collection of foundations that have funded conservative causes
> ranging from abolition of Social Security to anti-tax crusades and United Nations
> conspiracy theories. The Roundtable members' founders include scions of Amer-
> ica's wealthiest families, including Richard Mellon Scaife, . . . Harry Bradley, . . .
> Joseph Coors, . . . and the Smith Richardson family. . . . Lawyer Pat Anderson was

paid directly by the anti-abortion Life Legal Defense Foundation. . . . Much of the support for [this] Life Legal Defense Foundation, in turn, comes from the Alliance Defense Fund, an anti-gay-rights group. . . . [T]he Alliance Defense Fund received [money] from Philanthropy Roundtable members that include the Lynde and Harry Bradley Foundation and the Richard and Helen DeVos Foundation. [Anti-euthanasia activists] Wesley Smith and Rita Marker also work for organizations that get funding from Roundtable members. Smith is a paid senior fellow with the Discovery Institute, a Seattle-based [creationist] think tank that . . . received [money] from the Bradley Foundation. Marker is executive director of the International Task Force on Euthanasia [which] received [money from] an affiliate of the Smith Richardson family. . . . The Family Research Council, which [lobbies] for prayer in public schools and against gay marriage, filed an amicus curiae brief . . . [and received money] from the Bradley Foundation. Another amicus brief . . . was filed by a coalition of disability rights organizations [that] received [funding from] the Scaife Family Foundations, the Richard and Helen DeVos Foundation, and the JM Foundation. (Eisenberg 2005, 4)

Certainly if one were to look at the boards of directors and editorial staffs of prominent liberal advocacy organizations one might expect to emerge with similar kinds of overlapping interests and affiliations. What is unusual about the recitation above, however, is that it documents a tight-knit circle of conservative and neoconservative organizations, many of which are tightly linked to figures on what was heralded as a balanced presidential council designed to reflect the range of opinions in the public, and capable of considering all points of view. Instead, it more strongly resembles organizations with an openly partisan agenda. Thus, the point is not solely whether previous commissions were liberal or conservative but whether there was a concerted effort to use them to develop and advance a political agenda. During the time of the prior commissions, specifically dedicated institutions, such as the EPPC and *The New Atlantis,* did not exist. Nor were previous commission members on the boards of standard liberal organizations such as the ACLU.

THE NEOCONSERVATIVE BIOETHICS AGENDA

The existence of such an interlocking network is not in and of itself a matter of ethical concern; political movements will often devolve into such incestuous forms. Rather, the depth and breadth of the pattern is a signal that a new universe of neoconservative bioethics has now emerged as a strong, disciplined voice that has special access to all three branches of government and can serve as a coherent think tank for the neoconservative policy makers throughout government.

Yuval Levin, former acting executive director of the PCB, is now the associate director of the White House's Domestic Policy Council. He is also a senior editor of *The New Atlantis* (a creation of the Ethics and Public Policy Center [EPPC]). In the inaugural issue he wrote that "among the more prominent peculiarities of our politics in recent years is that something called 'bioethics' has become a key conservative priority." After describing the general angst experienced by some as they witness science uncovering the origins of life, behavior, and even consciousness, he notes that "the resulting intellectual and political activity has melded some of the interests of the pro-life movement with those of conservatives more concerned with the general culture and its institutions, and it has formed, through that combination, an altogether plausible conservative program. . . . The present task of a conservative bioethics, therefore, must be to develop and articulate a coherent worldview—to put meat on the bones of loosely defined terms like 'human dignity' and 'Brave New World' and turn ethical disquiet into public arguments" (Levin 2003, 64).

It is in this most fundamental of culture divides that the special characteristics of this bioethics council emerge. In the widespread attachment to a neoconservative worldview that is suspicious of technological advance, opposed to moral relativism and moral pluralism, determined to identify moral absolutes, and open to an increased permeation of religious values into public policy and bioethics analysis, this council and its leadership appear to reflexively endorse the view that science is a threat to both society and government. Indeed, the PCB chair himself wrote that "science essentially endangers society by endangering the supremacy of its ruling beliefs. . . . Science—however much it contributes to health, wealth and safety—is neither in spirit nor in manner friendly to the concerns of governance or the moral and civic education of human beings and citizens. Science fosters and encourages novelty; political society, governed by the rule of law, cannot do without stability. Science rejects all authority save the truth, and prefers skepticism to truth . . . ; the political community requires trust in, submission to, and even reverence for its ruling beliefs and practices" (Kass 1985, 4).

Perhaps this is merely the first and best articulation of a cultural divide in the bioethics world that has been brewing for years. This divide, between those who celebrate the transformative power of science and those who fear it, is both broad and profound. It is broad because it reaches into many other areas of national debate. It is hardly a leap to move from asserting that each child has a human right to be conceived by both a man and a woman (as the PCB does in its recent call for a legislative prohibition on any form of conception other than fertilization by sperm and egg) to asserting that each child has a human right to a father and a mother, a statement with obvious implications for debates on the structure of the family and access to state-sanctioned marriage contracts. And it is profound because it is a divide that reflects competing fears, with one group most fearful of the social change wrought by technology and the other most fearful of the oppressive overreaching of a government bent on controlling those changes.

More fundamentally, the conservative and neoconservative bioethics is yet the latest attack on the Enlightenment, the movement grounded in seventeenth-century Europe, the movement that was the very basis for the American experiment of the eighteenth century. Enlightenment thinkers believed that human reason could be used to combat ignorance, superstition, and tyranny and to build a better world. Their principal targets were the entanglement of state and religion, and the domination of society by a hereditary aristocracy or other elites. The PCB, developed by the George W. Bush administration, and its interlocking journals, conferences, and funders represent an effort to reintroduce religion as the basis for public policy, pessimism and fear as the basis of technology assessment, and elitist discussion and morals regulation as the basis of governance. It is a movement perhaps best dubbed the "endarkenment."

AN ENLIGHTENMENT PROJECT FOR BIOETHICS?

Perhaps it is the time, then, for liberal bioethics to take up this challenge, and create parallel structures devoted explicitly to public bioethics, that is, bioethics as a basis for public policy formation rather than academic debate, and bioethics focused on the role of government rather than the morality of individual choices. American jurisprudence and the Bill of Rights favor the individual over the collective, the dissenter over the majority, and the eccentric over the conformist, at least with respect to such things as free speech, reproductive choice, and other fundamental rights (Charo 2000). In a sense, this is an approach that favors intergenerational concerns, such as the long-term viability of peaceful regime change, over intragenerational concerns, such as the most efficient or popular legal ordering for this time. Indeed, in 2003 the Supreme Court declared that the fact that a state's governing majority has traditionally viewed a particular practice as immoral is not a sufficient reason for upholding a law prohibiting the practice.

In a sense, in many cases, regardless of the technology or human choices at issue, it is overarching politics that is being debated more often than the bioethics, and it may well be that it is sweeping political forces that will determine the policy outcomes more than the merits of the individual arguments. Although this is acknowledged from time to time (Bowman 2004; Feder 2004; Marshall and Koenig 2004; Somerville 2004), rarely is it the primary means of argumentation. And bioethics dilemmas are answered by reference to political philosophy as well as politics. The Enlightenment tolerance for moral relativism is also a call for government restraint in morals regulation. And the Enlightenment highlighted other core values: logic versus faith in resolving dilemmas; optimism versus pessimism regarding the improvability (though not perfectibility) of the human condition; and acceptance versus resistance regarding the changes wrought by economics, technology, and science (Charo 2004). Perhaps it is time to develop an enlightenment agenda for progressive bioethics, to counter the neoconservative "endarkenment."

NOTE

Portions of this essay first appeared in 2004 as "Passing on the right: Conservative bioethics is closer than it appears," in *Journal of Law, Medicine, and Ethics* 32(4): 307–12.

REFERENCES

Bdfund.org. www.bdfund.org.

Berkowitz, P. http://mason.gmu.edu/%7Eberkowit/bio.htm.

Blog.bioethics.net. http://blog.bioethics.net/2005/03/kass-agenda-bioethics-for-second-term.html.

Bottum, J. 2002. Journalism at the *Post:* The *Washington Post* confuses an editorial with a news story, and takes a shot at the president's new bioethics council. *Weekly Standard,* January 18.

Bowman, K. 2004. What are the limits of bioethics in a culturally pluralistic society? *Journal of Law, Medicine, and Ethics* 32(4): 664–68.

Jeb Bush, Governor of Florida, Petitioner, v. Michael Schiavo, Guardian of Theresa Schiavo. No. 04-757. Supreme Court of the United States. 543 U.S. 1121; 125 S. Ct. 1086; 160 L. Ed. 2d 1069; U.S. Lexis 810; 73 U.S.L.W. 3448.

Caplan, A. 2004. Council lacks balance. *OB GYN News* 11(39): 9.

Charo, R. A. 2000. Principe de precaution, bioethique, et role des conseils publics d'ethique [The precautionary principle, bioethics, and the role of public ethics commissions], in *Les Cahiers du Comite Consultatif National d'Ethique pour les Sciences de la Vie et de la Sante.* Pp. 27–29. Paris, Editions La Documentation Française.

———. 2004. Passing on the right: Conservative bioethics is closer than it appears. *Journal of Law, Medicine, and Ethics* 32(4): 307–12.

————. 2005. Realbioethik. *Hastings Center Report* (July/August): 6–7.

Chronicle of Higher Education. 2003. Bush appoints new advisory committee on human subjects (January 17).

Cook, M. 2004. Embryo-centrism and other sins: The unceasing, unfair complaints of the Kass council's critics. *The Weekly Standard* 10(2).

The Economist. 2004. Yesterday's men, and tomorrow's. *The Economist* (September 18).

Eisenberg, J. B. 2005. The Terri Schiavo case: Following the money. *The Recorder* 129(43): 4.

Feder J. 2004. Crowd-out and the politics of health reform. *Journal of Law, Medicine, and Ethics* 32(3): 464–68.

Fukuyama, F. 2002. *Our Posthuman Future: Consequences of the Biotechnology Revolution.* New York: Farrar, Straus, and Giroux.

Gazzaniga, M. 2003. Session 6: Biotechnology and Public Policy: Proposed Interim Recommendations, II, Discussion of Section III of Staff Working Paper, *U.S. Public Policy and the Biotechnologies That Touch the Beginnings of Human Life: Draft Recommendations.* www.bioethics.gov/transcripts/sep03/session6.html. Friday, September 5.

Hall, S. 2002. President's bioethics council delivers: The deeply divided panel last week recommended a moratorium on all human cloning, yet a majority of the members had expressed support in principle for cloning for biomedical research. *Science* 297(5580): 322.

Holden, C. 2004. Researchers blast U.S. bioethics panel shuffle. *Science* 303(5663): 1447.

Irving, D. What is wrong with this picture? www.all.org/issues/dni002.htm.

Jonas, H. 1982. *The Phenomenon of Life: Toward a Philosophical Biology.* Chicago: University of Chicago Press.

Kass, L. R. 1979a. Ethical issues in human in vitro fertilization, embryo culture and research, and embryo transfer. *In Vitro Fertilization,* appendix, Ethics Advisory Board, U.S. Department of Health, Education, and Welfare. May 4, 1979.

————. 1979b. "Making babies" revisited. *Public Interest* 54: 32–60.

————. 1979c. A conversation with Dr. Leon Kass: The ethical dimensions of in vitro fertilization. An occasional paper published by the American Enterprise Institute for Public Policy Research. Washington, DC: AEI Studies.

————. 1985. *Toward a More Natural Science: Biology and Human Affairs.* New York: Free Press.

————. 1997. The end of courtship. *Public Interest* 126: 39–63.

Kukis, M. 2001. White House bioethicist a cautious skeptic. *United Press International,* August 20.

Levin, Y. 2003. The paradox of conservative bioethics. *New Atlantis* 1 (Spring): 53–65.

Lobe, J. 2003. What is a neo-conservative anyway? Inter Press News Agency, 2003. www.ipsnews.net/interna.asp?idnews=19618.

Marshall, E. 1994. Rules on embryo research due out. *Science* 265(5175): 1024.

Marshall, P., and Koenig, B. 2004. Accounting for culture in a globalized bioethics. *Journal of Law, Medicine, and Ethics* 32(2): 252–59.

Mooney, C. 2001. Irrationalist in chief: The real problem with Leon Kass. *American Prospect* 12(17): 10.

PCB. www.bioethics.gov/about/chairman.html.

Pfaff, W. 2003. The long reach of Leo Strauss. *International Herald Tribune*, May 15. www
.iht.com/articles/96307.html.

President's Council on Bioethics. 2003. *Being Human: Readings from the President's Council on Bioethics*. Washington, DC: Government Printing Office.

———. 2004. Reproduction and responsibility: The regulation of new biotechnologies,
chap. 1, sec. 5. Washington, DC: Government Printing Office.

Saletan, W. 2005. Oy Vitae. Posted Friday, March 11, 2005, at 10:01 p.m., http://slate.msn
.com/id/2114733/.

Siegal, N. 2005. Bioethics, Bush style: Research on embryonic stem cells. *The Progressive*
5(69): 24.

Simon, S. 2005. Grooming politicians for Christ: Evangelical programs on Capitol Hill seek
to mold a new generation of leaders who will answer not to voters, but to God. *Los Angeles Times*, August 23: A1.

Smith, W. 2004. Staying human. *National Review* (June 14).

Somerville, M. 2004. Social-ethical values issues in the political public square: Principles
vs. packages. *Journal of Law, Medicine, and Ethics* 32(4): 731–39.

Stolberg, S. 2002. Bush's advisers on ethics discuss human cloning. *New York Times*, January 22: A18.

U.S. Congress, Office of Technology Assessment. 1993. Biomedical Ethics in U.S. Public
Policy. OTA-BP-BBS-105, GPO stock #052-003-01325-8 NTIS order #PB93-203768.
(1993). Available on the Web at www.wws.princeton.edu/~ota/ns20/year_f.html.

Weiss, R., 2005. Conservatives draft a "bioethics agenda" for president. *Washington Post*,
March 8: A06.

CHAPTER NINE

Left Bias in Academic Bioethics

Three Dogmas

GRIFFIN TROTTER, M.D., PH.D.

In what follows, I argue: (1) that there is left bias in academic bioethics, and (2) that academic bioethics' left bias is a problem that warrants remediation. I use the term *left bias* to designate systematic favoritism toward political positions and ideas that characterize the "left" in the United States—i.e., the side occupied primarily by Democrats in what amounts to a two-party system.

It may be the case that leftward drift in the academy has been accentuated during the Bush era, with even right-leaning scholars recoiling at President Bush's conspicuous failure to exhibit scholarly virtues (such as excellence in argument formation). If so, this trend is countered to some degree by the sudden permissibility of conservatism in government bioethics under the Bush administration. For instance, the current President's Council on Bioethics is right leaning, though it has a better mix of political viewpoints than any of the previous, uniformly leftward national panels. Conservative think tanks are also increasingly addressing bioethics issues—and employing conservative "bioethicists." The conservative leanings of the President's Council and the appearance of independent conservative bioethicists hardly undermines the thesis of this chapter, however, as for the most part they feature political operatives or scholars from primary fields other than bioethics. The American Society of Bioethics and Humanities (ASBH) is the largest and most important society of academic bioethicists. Though there is a small contingent of libertarian bioethicists in ASBH, most of the country's prominent social-conservative bioethicists do not belong to this organization.

Regardless of the shifting patterns, my concern is not merely with the present slice in time. I claim that left bias in academic bioethics is sustained and stubborn. The usual way to exhibit bias, at least in the academy, is to exhibit inequalities; and the most creditable way to exhibit inequalities is by reference to empirical data. But, for reasons clearly evident, there is not much data about the political convictions of academic bioethicists—bioethicists having little to gain by conducting a study exhibiting their own monolithic political orientation. We know, courtesy of a recent study by the American Council for Trustees and Alumni, that, across the spectrum from sciences to humanities, academic departments in America's elite universities tend to be dominated by political liberals. By implication, bioethicists, who live mostly in the academy, are also probably liberals.

My approach here is to dispense with opinion polls, data on political donations and party affiliations, and anecdotes about teachers kicking conservative students or applauding Al Qaeda. The anecdotes prove nothing, and the polling and demographics prove only what everyone with a whiff of objectivity already knows. Of course most bioethicists are political liberals. We know this in the same way we know that children prefer candy over brussels sprouts—we learn it from experience, without the benefit of formal empirical studies. Just pick up a scholarly bioethics journal and observe the claims that academic bioethicists think they can presume, without argument. These include dubious normative claims such as "justice requires universal access to a basic package of healthcare benefits," "health inequalities in the United States reflect rampant social injustice," and "abortion is a matter of conscience that individual women have a right to decide for themselves." *not just liberal*

The mere fact that a majority of bioethicists fall to the left on the political spectrum does not demonstrate, however, that there is left bias in bioethics. That datum is consistent, for instance, with bioethicists being an extraordinarily impartial bunch going out of their way to give right-wing ideas a fair hearing—yet still tentatively concluding, in the majority of cases, that leftward ideas are better supported.

My allegations of left bias imply that the left-liberalism in bioethics runs deeper than a mere coalescence of opinion around good arguments. I am concerned with forms of left bias that consist in deeply ingrained habits of feeling and thought that bioethicists rarely scrutinize critically. These constitutive psychological patterns are deeply at odds with the sentiments, ideals, and opinions that frame various forms of conservative, libertarian, or other right-wing discourse; and as a result serious dialogue between right and left rarely occurs in bioethics. Of course, right-wing thinkers are occasionally invited to speak at academic bioethics meetings or contribute to scholarly bioethics volumes. But their arguments are rarely given a serious or charitable reading and the reply (if there is one) often consists in changing the subject.[1]

One way of exhibiting such ingrained left bias, and of arguing that this bias is problematic, is through an analysis of the ethical and political premises that undergird various methodologies in bioethics. For instance, I have argued elsewhere that pragmatic bioethics, in its typical manifestations, is rife with dysfunctional left-liberal presumptions (Trotter 2003, 2001). For present purposes, however, I will pursue a similar but more modest strategy. After briefly unpacking the phenomenon of left bias by explaining ways in which it implies, and does not imply, anti-conservative bias, I will examine several prominent, unsubstantiated dogmas that shape bioethical discourse. In the process, I will try to shed light on some of the ways in which these dogmas beg the question in favor of left-liberalism. If you want to know people's biases, find out what they take for granted.

THE NATURE OF LEFT BIAS IN BIOETHICS

The claim that there is left bias in bioethics implies reciprocally that bioethics exhibits an anti-right bias, which might be taken to imply that it is anti-conservative. But that is only half true. I wish to distinguish two senses of conservatism. First, there is conservatism as the disposition to honor timeworn traditions and adhere to established practices. Conservatism of this variety—let's call it stasis conservatism—is the contrary of radicalism (radicalism being advocacy for sweeping changes). Bioethics is not biased against stasis conservatism. In the academy, left-liberalism has become a timeworn tradition, dating back to the 1960s. Bioethics' fidelity to this tradition is a manifestation of stasis conservatism. As an academic bioethicist, or someone trained in the academy, moderate left-liberalism is the path of least resistance. Further, there is an element of stasis conservatism arising from bioethics' sponsorship by established health care institutions such as hospitals, pharmaceutical companies, and governments. Bioethics arose in recent decades as a response to public anxiety and perceived ethical tensions caused by the increasing intrusiveness and expense of technological medicine. As ethical pluralism (or at least our acknowledgment and acceptance of it) became more pronounced, and as institutions of public morality (state, church, professions) dwindled in authority, a need arose for some means of navigating the anxiety about technological medicine and the perception of excessive paternalism in the medical profession. Hence, bioethics garnered social legitimacy from its ostensibly critical stance toward the medical profession and toward other established powers in health care—even as it relied heavily on these powers for access and sponsorship. The influence of the established medical power structure keeps bioethics close to medicine's sociopolitical mainstream.[2] Consequently it also frustrates potential radical elements—on both the left and on the right—by diligently keeping them at the margins (Stevens 2000).

The second sense of conservatism is as a wastebasket category for differing, sometimes antagonistic positions that share one overriding family resemblance—their tendency to beget rightward political loyalties. We'll call it partisan conservatism. Included among the ranks of partisan conservatives are representatives from such disparate groups as competitive market libertarians, free market libertarians, social conservatives, contemporary Whigs, neoconservatives, and Christian fundamentalists. There is a second family resemblance between the various perspectives that contribute to partisan conservatism, of concern in this essay. None of them is well represented on bioethics faculties or at national scholarly bioethics meetings (such as the annual meeting of ASBH). One obvious reason for the paucity of partisan conservative bioethicists is that partisan conservatives, like most ordinary human beings, are uneasy about paying homage to ideas that countervail their deepest moral sentiments. Yet that is what they experience under the aegis of the academy, where left-wing ideas provide the context for discourse on health, health care, bioethics—and just about everything else. Let us briefly examine just a few of the explicit and implicit dogmas that political conservatives would view as prominent myths nurtured in the field of bioethics.

FIRST DOGMA

First, let us consider the dogma that terminological clarification is a relatively value-neutral strategy employed by bioethicists to mediate moral controversies. As the tendency to spin off comprehensive ethical theories dissipated around the beginning of the twentieth century, moral philosophers—especially tough-minded scientific sorts—began to refashion their vocation on the analytic model, where the focus was on working out logical implications of substantive moral premises. Substantive moral claims themselves came to be regarded as essentially subjective or contingent—and hence largely beyond the pale of objective moral philosophy. Much of the activity in this new version of moral philosophy consisted in clarifying definitions and working out their implications.

Though contemporary bioethics attempts to reengage the world of substantive ethics, with newfound hopes of resolving some of its intractable controversies, bioethics borrows from analytic ethics its penchant for making distinctions and clarifying terms. Like the analytic ethicists, bioethicists tend to believe they can execute meaning-clarification activities without introducing their own, particular ethical biases. Thus, for instance, bioethicists Willard Gaylin and Bruce Jennings assume the posture of neutral interpreters imparting a vocabulary lesson, writing: "The generalized misconception of coercion as involving physical force must be laid to rest. Coercion must be perceived as the psychological phenomenon it inevitably is" (2003, 148). Later (176), they opine that "carrots are as coercive as sticks."

In the above-quoted passages, Gaylin and Jennings faithfully impart the meaning of *coercion* as it is used by many contemporary bioethicists. Several characteristics of this conception warrant scrutiny. First, it is not the conception of *coercion* that holds sway in the natural language employed by the general public. If it were, then Gaylin and Jennings would not have to address a "generalized misconception" that coercion involves the use or threat of physical force. Second, it is not the original or traditional conception of *coercion*. Gaylin and Jennings acknowledge this, at least indirectly, in the passages in which they treat Latin roots, quote *Black's Law Dictionary*, and acknowledge that physical force "is the prototypical case of coercion" (143, 147). Third, the newfangled conception of *coercion* employed by bioethicists has allowed them to use this emotionally charged word to condemn practices that bioethicists, as a group harboring relatively congruent, leftist moral intuitions, find objectionable.

One example is bioethicists' use of this term *coercion* in research ethics. Bioethicists (wielding a canon they established during meetings sanctioned by the Carter administration at the Smithsonian's Belmont Center) have succeeded in institutionalizing their disapproval of practices such as, say, offering substantial financial rewards for participating in Phase I clinical trials or donating kidneys, by calling the incentives coercive. Gaylin and Jennings recognize and lament the fact that liberal understandings of *coercion* have been exploited to heap disfavor on all manner of human activity. Their response, however, is to retain bioethics' expansive conception of coercion as psychological manipulation while urging that coercion should not always be viewed negatively. Perhaps that is wise counsel—though my own sympathy lies with libertarians who complain that they have been deprived of the only word that succinctly imparts the notion of an infringement of liberty through the use or threat of physical force. For the purposes of this essay, the important point is that bioethicists have effected leftward reforms in part by exploiting the supposedly value-neutral strategy of meaning clarification. *Coercion* is, of course, only one example. The meanings of symbolic and emotion-laden terms such as *justice, freedom, consensus, death, killing,* and *hunger* have also significantly transmogrified as academic specialists, including bioethicists, have undertaken to clarify them.

SECOND DOGMA

Second, consider the dogma that professes that most academic bioethicists avoid moralizing about unhealthy lifestyle choices and habits, preferring instead to remain open to various moral worldviews. For the contemporary bioethicist, it is better in some instances to eliminate terms rather than clarify them. Hence, words like *promiscuity* and *sloth* have been replaced in bioethical discourse by expressions such as "partner changing" and "misfortune in the natural and social lotteries." An important class of terms that bioethicists seek to eliminate are those that express traditional forms of moral disapproval. *Promiscuity,* on this view, imposes the Judeo-Christian preoccupation with sexual fidelity and marriage. *Sloth* imposes Judeo-Christian notions of industriousness and personal responsibility. Should conservative social commentators use terms like *promiscuity* and *sloth* to characterize presumably unhealthy lifestyles that also offend traditional moral norms, bioethicists will accuse them of moralism. In this vein, Dan Beauchamp holds that whenever laws are "based on reforming the moral character" of a suspect population, there is moralism at work. For the sake of completeness, his statement should have added a proviso: moralism occurs whenever laws are passed (or practices publicly condemned) on the basis of reforming moral character *in the direction of traditional morality.*

After all, Beauchamp and others in the liberal reform camp do not hesitate to advocate for public health laws that would reform the moral character of those who offend their own, presumably liberated moral sensibilities (boxers, concealed weapons carriers, smokers, bikers, etc.). For instance, Beauchamp supports motorcycle helmet laws on the basis of his disapproval of some bikers' belief that the good life reaches *fortissimo* only through hugging the saddle of a Harley as the wind blows wildly through one's hair. These bikers' objections to helmet laws are regarded as "in the end, rather silly" (Beauchamp 1988). No doubt, Beauchamp would object that he is not being moralistic, since his beef against non-helmet-use is based on concern about bikers' safety rather than a desire to reform their moral character. But that is merely a charade. The moral character of the bikers in question tangibly manifests differing intuitions about acceptable risk and individuality, as well as their opinion that certain particular goods are more important than safety. Views on moral character proceed, after all, largely from notions of the good life. Beauchamp insists not only that the bikers are wrong, but that they are silly as well. And he bases this opinion on his conception of republican community—where citizens are expected to exhibit "shared sentiments and attachments" (1988, 15). To me, that sounds like moralism.

THIRD DOGMA

A third dogma of liberal bioethicists is that when bioethicists reach consensus, their opinion should guide health policy formation. In his book *Deciding Together: Bioethics and Moral Consensus* (1995, 12), Jonathan Moreno opines that bioethics "is widely seen as a more or less neutral space" in which moral controversies can be mediated. Consensus formation, in his view, is bioethics' fundamental methodology. And when bioethicists reach consensus—as for example in their work on national commissions, at consensus conferences, or through discourse in the scholarly literature—then the consensus carries a kind of moral authority and democratic authenticity that lends legitimacy to health policy decisions. Moreno, I submit, is certainly right about one thing. Consensus formation has indeed become bioethics' modus operandi. But he is wrong—as the recent Schiavo case so tangibly demonstrates—about the public perception of bioethics' neutrality. And he is wrong to think that a consensus of bioethicists is authoritative in any important, political sense (Trotter 2002). At best, academic bioethics can be viewed as the health-conscience of the Democratic Party.

For a consensus of bioethicists to bear authority for public policy decisions in a pluralistic democracy like the United States, it would need to be connected in some demonstrable way to the moral intuitions and considered judgments of the general population. Such a connection is not manifest when selected samples of uniformly leftward bioethicists convene on panels such as the National Bioethics Advisory Commission.

A REMEDY?

Academic bioethics' aforementioned three dogmas are strategically familiar. Left-liberal academics have long recognized and denounced the strategic basis for the first dogma in non-lefties (e.g., by showing that vocabularies enshrine values, that privilege for a given vocabulary begets privilege for the underlying values, and that conservative rhetoric exploits the manner in which traditional values have embedded themselves in a popular vocabulary). The second dogma exhibits a related strategy that has been recognized by left-liberals and partisan conservatives alike—for instance in the denunciation of corporate euphemisms and campus speech codes. The third dogma appropriates the social power of expertise— a strategy, again, that liberals have been keen to recognize and condemn when it is used to promote conservative ideology. It should not be much of a stretch, then, to call the three dogmas into question.

These dogmas warrant remedy because they thwart the spirit of inquiry, and academic bioethics should be pro-inquiry even before it is pro-health, or pro-choice, or pro–social justice—or whatever other advocacy position it takes based on confidence that it has things right and that further inquiry is hardly needed. If inquiry is no longer necessary on a certain topic, then that topic is no longer a matter of concern to academic bioethics, which presumably inquires into matters that are not settled.

The remedy cannot be merely including more conservatives in our discussions, or hiring more conservative bioethics faculty. After all, none of the problematic strategies that underlie left-bias in bioethics is unique to the political left or even particularly concentrated there. What we need is a way for people with differing political convictions to approach one another constructively in debate, and to cooperate in inquiry.

These objectives might be advanced if we viewed bioethics as an academic field in which: (1) the primary concerns are with knowledge claims and with the implications of bioethical knowledge for public policy; (2) immediate prospects are dim for authoritative knowledge claims based solely on reason, common moral intuitions, or moral consensus; and (3) relevance to public policy is limited (given item 2) to helping trace the meaning and consequences of various, diverging moral outlooks and suggesting a modus vivendi or a procedure for attaining one. Each of these suggestions requires far more argument than I can offer here. But the basic spirit is not difficult to capture, since it is, after all, the spirit that animates many in the academy. Knowledge is a worthy pursuit, but difficult—especially when hypotheses (such as claims about the good life) must be believed and lived to be tested. Our chances of accumulating knowledge increase if we can learn from those with differing perspectives (even though these differing perspectives may be incongruent with the spirit of inquiry and have no ultimate value other than exposing truth through folly). It is understandable—even imperative—that the liberal mind be wary of conservatism, and alert to its tactics. This imperative derives not from the need to eradicate right-wing ideas; but rather from the need to encounter, consider, and confront them in fruitful ways.

NOTES

1. A classic case of subject changing (tinged with sarcasm) is Laurie Zoloth's response to a plenary presentation by Leon Kass, the chairman of the President's Council on Bioethics (PCB), at the 2004 annual meeting of the American Society for Bioethics and Humanities. Zoloth's main point seemed to be that from the standpoint of bioethics, Kass's discussion of the potential moral pitfalls of medical enhancements lacked legitimacy because it failed to focus on foundational bioethical concerns—such as the redistribution of income and resources from rich to poor. Much outrage was voiced among ASBH members that the meeting featured a speaker who was also a Bush appointee—a curious response, given the lack of protest when members of Clinton's National Bioethics Advisory Commission (NBAC) were invited to speak at earlier ASBH meetings (or, in a somewhat different venue, the lack of protest when John Kerry was invited to speak at the 2005 American Public Health Association annual meeting). For her part, Zoloth claimed pleasure at learning that Bush's President's Council featured members who "despite being actual Republicans, unlike any single person on Clinton's NBAC, were surely interesting thinkers." In the end, however, Zoloth took exception to the fact that the council's mixed Republican-Democratic membership expressed ideas that were too Republican. In a recent essay, Alta Charo makes essentially the same point (Charo 2004). Though Charo's argument is itself biased (e.g., in its use of personal communications from a disgruntled former council member), her basic point seems correct: the PCB does exhibit rightward, especially neoconservative, tendencies. Note, however, that hardly anyone in academic bioethics was concerned when previous government bioethics panels exhibited leftward leanings.

2. Note that even the traditionally right-wing medical profession has drifted toward the political left on a number of key issues such as health care entitlements and government sponsorship of health care and medical research.

REFERENCES

Beauchamp, D. E. 1988. *The Health of the Republic: Epidemics, Medicine, and Moralism as Challenges to Democracy.* Philadelphia: Temple University Press.

Charo, R. A. 2004. Passing on the right: Conservative bioethics is closer than it appears. *Journal of Law, Medicine, and Ethics* 32 (2): 307–14.

Gaylin, W., and Jennings, B. 2003. *The Perversion of Autonomy: Coercion and Constraint in Liberal Society.* Rev. ed. Washington, DC: Georgetown University Press.

Moreno, J. 1995. *Deciding Together: Bioethics and Moral Consensus*. New York: Oxford University Press.

Stevens, M. L. T. 2000. *Bioethics in America: Origins and Cultural Politics*. Baltimore: Johns Hopkins University Press.

Trotter, G. 2001. Pragmatism, bioethics, and the grand American social experiment. *American Journal of Bioethics* [online] 2 (1).

———. 2002. Bioethics and healthcare reform: A Whig response to weak consensus. *Cambridge Quarterly of Healthcare Ethics* 11(1): 37–51.

———. 2003. Pragmatic bioethics and the big fat moral community. *Journal of Medicine and Philosophy* 28 (5–6): 655–71.

CHAPTER TEN

Bioethics as Politics

A Critical Reassessment

H. TRISTRAM ENGELHARDT JR., M.D., PH.D.

AUTHORITY, POWER, AND POLITICS: EXPLORING
THE THIRD SPATIALIZATION OF DISEASE

Bioethics is biopolitics, although it is surely not only politics, because it is a medical morality that has been understood in terms of the political agendas it can serve. It is impossible to appreciate the rapid emergence of bioethics at the end of the twentieth century apart from its roles in authorizing health care policy and law. It is not just that bioethics received an important impetus to its development through explicitly political establishments such as the National Commission for the Protection of Human Subjects of Biomedical and Behavioral Research. More significantly, that commission, and subsequent analogues such as the President's Commission for the Study of Ethical Problems in Medicine and Biomedical and Behavioral Research, the National Bioethics Advisory Commission, and the President's Council on Bioethics, employed bioethicists and engaged bioethical reflection in ways that presupposed that bioethics is able morally to authorize particular appropriate health care policies and laws. This was the case, although bioethical disagreement was early apparent.[1] Bioethics was regarded as a source of secular, political authority. Its practice became integral to what Michel Foucault characterized as the third spatialization of disease: the nesting of medicine, its descriptions, and its diagnoses, as well as therapeutic interventions, within social structures of authority and power (Foucault 1973, 16).

Bioethics took shape as a way of directing clinical choice, the governance of health care institutions, and the formation of health care law. It was engaged in the service of shaping social reality. Or to put matters in a different idiom, politics offered the higher social truth within which the interminable disputes of moral theorists and proponents of different ethical viewpoints could be set aside in what appeared to be a single, normative approach to health policy and law. A Hegelian *Sittlichkeit*, a socially authorized morality, could be created and established at law as normative, within which a particular account of a proper bioethics would be rendered officially normative and authoritative for the governance of health care institutions and the shaping of health care policy.[2] If this could be accomplished, bioethics' troubling pluralism could be set aside (indeed *aufgehoben*) in a legally established morality (i.e., the higher truth of the moral domain where pluralism reigns).

In this discussion, I first offer a brief account of the appearance of bioethics and the constitution of dominant expectations regarding the field, expectations that bioethics could not in principle fulfill. In the course of giving this account, I then indicate why we confront a robust, irresolvable, moral pluralism that brings into question many of the promises made on behalf of bioethics. In advancing this account, I do not endorse a moral relativism, but rather I indicate why a moral pluralism is unavoidable, given the limits of secular moral epistemology. We are confronted with a plurality of moral understandings among which one cannot conclusively choose on the basis of a sound rational argument. Having given this account of the emergence of bioethics and of the unjustifiable expectations regarding its abilities, I advance a brief account of why, though bioethics could not accomplish what it promised as a normative endeavor, it nevertheless appeared to do so anyway, in both the clinic and for public policy, by serving goals of governance and political order. I conclude with a set of warnings for the future: the predicament of our moral context requires recognizing the unavoidability of moral pluralism and the need to rethink the character of bioethics' role as biogovernance and biopolitics.

WHY BIOETHICS GAINED AUTHORITY SO QUICKLY

An indication of the power of the social forces shaping the emergence of bioethics is the rapidity with which the field took shape. No sooner had the term, originally coined by Van Rensselaer Potter,[3] been recast by André Hellegers and Sargent Shriver,[4] than an entire scholarly field, along with a cadre of practitioners, came into existence. By 1978 the field could claim not just a body of publications and an influence on the National Commission for the Protection of Human

Subjects of Biomedical and Behavioral Research (National Commission 1978), but it could also support an encyclopedia (Reich 1978). In addition, the Center for Bioethics of Georgetown University had through its summer total-immersion/ intensive courses come to produce numerous individuals claiming an expertise in bioethics that allowed them to function as clinical consultants and public policy advisers. Within less than a decade, a scholarly field was established, along with practitioners who were purported to have important moral expertise.

The remarkably rapid appearance of bioethics as a widely recognized secular field of moral expertise can be explained in terms of five significant changes in the character of American society that produced a medical-moral vacuum which bioethics came to fill as if by spontaneous generation.

First, the dominant culture of American society, which had been both de facto and de jure religious, indeed Christian, more precisely generically Protestant, became de jure even if not de facto secular,[5] leading to the marginalization of moral-theological reflections and the taken-for-granted place of religious moral advisers.[6]

Second, previously legally established norms of Christian morality were brought into question, as for example by the Supreme Court decision in *Roe v. Wade,*[7] which fueled much bioethical controversy and reflection, as well as occasioning the first report produced by the National Commission (National Commission 1975).

Third, American medicine was transformed from a de facto guild (Krause 1996) into a trade so that it became controlled by the usual legal and moral expectations of other trades,[8] leading to the need for a medical morality to be elaborated within a moral framework accessible to and appreciable by society as a whole.

Fourth, the civil rights movements of the 1960s, along with their various accents on individual choice, engendered suspicions regarding established authority figures and institutions, which underlay a shift from a professional standard for the disclosure of information in the process of informed consent, to the objective or reasonable-and-prudent-person standard,[9] all of which led to the need to develop medical-moral reflections to flesh out the newly established paradigm of individually oriented medical decision making.

Last but not least, American society became saliently medicalized, in that health care and the biomedical sciences were appreciated as dramatically influencing the character of ordinary life through medicine having become:

1. effective in successfully treating numerous diseases and alleviating numerous disabilities;
2. expensive in consuming by 1970 7.6 percent of the gross domestic product—and by 1980 9.4 percent (Levit 1985);

3. provocative in occasioning numerous medical-moral puzzles, questions ranging from the nature of the proper criteria for the allocation of scarce medical resources (Rescher 1969), the allowable circumstances under which to withdraw life-sustaining treatment (Cantor 1973), and the appropriate criteria for determination of death (Ad Hoc Committee 1968), to the determination of the moral norms that should guide such new technologies as genetic engineering.[10]

The result of all of this was the production of a moral and public policy vacuum. Just as medicine had become powerful, expensive, and provocative of moral questions, the usual resources for guidance had been brought into question.[11]

The result was an attempt to authorize a new discipline supposedly able to disclose the appropriate norms for health care and the biomedical sciences, as well as to train practitioners who could apply those norms in the clinic and in the development of biopolitics and law. Bioethics came into existence, promising to be the equivalent of a secular moral theology *cum* secular moral priesthood and chaplaincy able to speak beyond the professional confines of medical ethics. Bioethics emerged, seeming to offer a basis for a consensus grounded in a common, secularly accessible morality (Engelhardt 2002). Once established, this bioethics was in various forms exported worldwide.

WHY BIOETHICS COULD NOT DELIVER WHAT IT PROMISED; OR, WHY BIOETHICS IS AT THE HEART OF THE CULTURE WARS

The expectation was that bioethics could deliver a set of moral norms that would be in accord with the general commitments of moral rationality. In this, bioethics reflected strong Enlightenment presuppositions regarding the moral, content-establishing character of discursive analysis and philosophical reflection.[12] Had these expectations been well-founded,

1. there would have been a robust accord between morality and rationality,
2. the authority of health care policy and biolaw could have been derived from and grounded in this rationality, such that those who demurred from compliance could be characterized as irrational, so that biopolitics would in essence be the politics of enlightenment (i.e., a political commitment to disabusing persons of their parochial and "fundamentalist,"[13] merely religious, moral commitments), and therefore
3. the legitimacy of societal coercion could be understood as the establish-

ment of rightly ordered social relationships and the restoration of appropriate autonomous action (i.e., through a rationally warranted attitude readjustment),

4. while at the same time demonstrating the existence of an implicit community of all rational persons, that is, of all moral agents, despite seemingly profound moral, religious, and cultural differences and disagreements, which were considered remnants of a pre-enlightened past, even apart from religiously grounded differences.

The difficulty is that bioethics, biopolitics, and biolaw show not consensus but dispute and controversy, because the participants are separated by incompatible basic moral and metaphysical premises and rules of evidence. Moreover, religiously grounded differences have not evanesced and, if anything, fundamentalist positions have hardened. Controversialists find themselves to be moral strangers, separated by different substantive moral rationalities, or at least disparate understandings of the morally reasonable (Engelhardt 1986). Nevertheless, this foundational failure of consensus is widely denied (MacIntyre 1981).

For instance, there was an attempt to employ strong readings of John Rawls's *Theory of Justice* (Rawls 1971) in the service of normatively directing health care policy (Daniels 1985). Though his account was invoked as a moral basis for proposals for health care reform (White House Domestic Policy Council 1993, 11–13), Rawls recognized that his account is sustained not within a canonical moral rationality but within a particular sense of reasonableness nested in a freestanding view of social-democratic, constitutional polity.[14] Relying at best on a contingency, Rawls claims his view as authoritative and likely to endure stably over time.[15] The point is that bioethicists entertained expansive claims, just as arguably the most influential twentieth-century moral theorist, Rawls, was reducing his moral-theoretical account of justice to a political account.[16] The crisis in general moral justification went largely unnoticed in bioethics, given the apparent success of the National Commission in articulating the three principles of the *Belmont Report*,[17] subsequently recast into four principles by Beauchamp and Childress (Beauchamp and Childress 1979). Such events were taken as demonstrating the ability of bioethicists to articulate a canonical morality that could be shown to be normative for all. There was a general failure to appreciate both the impossibility of this task as well as the grounds for it nevertheless seeming to have succeeded: namely, it served goals of governance and public order.

The impossibility of establishing through sound rational argument a particular account of bioethics as canonical lies in the circumstance that one cannot justify a particular ordering of values or of right-making conditions without begging the question, arguing in a circle, or engaging in an infinite regress. Any particular ordering always presupposes a background guiding normative account. Yet this is precisely what is at issue. The difficulty, as the early skeptic Agrippa appreciated,[18] is that one should not expect that philosophy, or more generally discursive rationality, which failed to establish a normative moral account after eight hundred years of sustained dispute, as for Agrippa, or after two and a half millennia of dispute, as for us, would finally succeed. Moreover, not only is each account with its arguments nested within a particular perspective or interpretive framework, which both shapes and separates it from competing accounts, but many of the crucial terms and premises are incommensurable in the sense of being in their foundations highly theoretically laden. As already noted, because one must always at the beginning concede particular premises and rules of evidence, all such arguments beg the question, go in a circle, or engage in an infinite regress.

A difficulty often overlooked lies in the circumstance that there is no common morality. Even if all participants in bioethical or moral controversies affirm the same values and moral principles, different sets of guiding judgments as to how one ought to rank values and moral principles will constitute different moralities. Persons will not share settled moral judgments that can reliably lead to similar decisions in similar circumstances. For example, it may be the case that all humans in their various moralities are concerned with the moral significance of killing of humans, telling of lies, and taking of property. However, moralities are distinguished by the conditions under which it is held to be forbidden, allowed, or praiseworthy to kill, lie, and transfer property, as expressed in our deep divisions regarding the proper approach to allocating scarce medical resources, terminating human fetal life, and assisting patients in suicide. The controversialists are separated by different ontologies, if not metaphysics, as well as by different moral premises and rules of evidence (Engelhardt 1996, chap. 4). All that we know of the contemporary debates in bioethics, and of what they presuppose, shows Agrippa to be justified.

In the face of such difficulties, why would persons have embraced such inflated expectations regarding bioethics? In part, this state of affairs can be accounted for by the initial success of the National Commission. Persons with different theoretical accounts or apparently different appreciations of morality, when placed on committees and commissions, came to similar conclusions regarding issues of health care policy and law. What few noticed was that those in authority tend to appoint as members of ethics committees and commissions persons who share their own background moral commitments. If one wants to secure practical recommendations in order to establish public policy and law, rather than to create a forum for an extended philosophical debate, one is best advised to appoint those who can deliver the desired recommendations. If one carefully appoints those who share one's own views, one will in general secure the conclusions one seeks—as is demonstrated by the differences in approaches, commitments, and conclusions of Bill Clinton's National Bioethics Advisory Commission and George Bush's President's Council for Bioethics: one can at least determine the range and character of the disagreement. Unjustified expectations regarding the capacity of bioethics to produce a rationally warranted consensus[19] were supported as well by the circumstance that Beauchamp and Childress's *Principles of Biomedical Ethics* (which served as the initial textbook for the field and as a background for much of the Kennedy Center summer total-immersion courses) appeared to enjoy success in securing agreement among a wide range of individuals. It was scarcely noticed that these individuals were generally like-minded in their political/moral ideology and generally voted for the same political party. That is, few noticed that the middle-level principles endorsed could be used to achieve common conclusions only if the parties shared common understandings of such cardinal notions as autonomy, beneficence, nonmaleficence, and justice. When, for example, the parties engaging such principles embraced contrary understandings of justice, appeals to the principle of justice only helped to outline the differences between moralities—the disparate senses of justice and fairness.

WITH SUCH DEEP MORAL DISAGREEMENT, HOW CAN BIOETHICISTS SUCCEED IN SELLING THEIR SERVICES?

If the culture wars[20] reach so deeply into our moral understandings, how then could bioethicists have succeeded so well in establishing themselves in the clinic and in the production of public policy? The answer is complex. In addition to the false impression generated by the political success of bioethics commissions and committees, as well as the broad popularity of middle-level principles, it is important to notice that most of what bioethicists do, strictly speaking, is not to provide normative direction. To begin with, bioethicists engage in a form of value-clarification that is core to, and a staple of, much instruction in philosophy. That is, bioethicists:

1. analyze cardinal concepts,
2. assess the soundness of arguments,

3. lay out the assumptions of different positions, and

4. display the geography of those positions in terms of their relationship to various views of right conduct and human flourishing.

All of this can be undertaken without embracing a particular, normative, moral view. In addition, bioethicists provide a cluster of social services that support institutional governance.[21] In particular, bioethicists:

1. give inexpensive legal advice without the benefit of being admitted to the bar,

2. offer risk management through aiding in the careful documentation of the apparent reasonableness, or at least the care taken in reaching particular health care decisions,

3. provide conflict mediation among disputing parties (e.g., physicians, nurses, family members),

4. all without actually offering concrete, normative guidance, save for

5. articulating, in committees, policy recommendations and guidelines for care within the boundaries set by law and the value commitments of the authorizing institution.

Where bioethicists are in authority to make decisions, this occurs often without bioethicists acting as normative authorities about a particular moral view taken as governing.[22] Thus, for example, when bioethics committees are employed at law to certify the justification of the refusal by physicians to provide a particular treatment as being inappropriate, they need not do so in terms of particular established content-full principles or criteria, but instead in terms of a procedural mechanism. In short, bioethicists have done well in establishing themselves in the clinic while all along claiming an intellectual, moral authority for their activities and for their services (i.e., as being bioethicists or ethicists), all without necessarily offering content-full, normative, moral guidance.

So, too, one might observe that the primary function of policy-guiding ethics committees, commissions, or councils has been:

1. to offer an official forum for institutional or public moral reflection and debate,

2. to constitute a body able to forward recommendations addressing pressing governance or policy needs,

3. to ensure that such recommendations fall within the parameters set by the authorizing power, insofar as this can be indirectly accomplished,

4. to preordain the general character of the recommendations that will be pro-

duced through the authorizing power's establishing membership and setting the agenda.

Bioethicists, when assembled in committees, commissions, and councils, thus help to clarify, articulate, and apply a normative agenda for political purposes *as if* the body in which they participate were not just in authority (i.e., officially appointed and given authority to make a decision), but had collected together persons who are moral authorities about the moral content of appropriate action (i.e., as experts who know what persons as such should do in the circumstances under consideration). Bioethics, as a consequence, is an instrument of governance and political power, as well as a vehicle for unpacking the particular implications of a more general political vision or agenda.

HUMAN RIGHTS: THE POLITICS OF DECEPTION

Just as voices in the Pacific Rim are being raised against the purportedly established American–Western European bioethical account of the moral basis of appropriate health care policy,[23] there is a move to enshrine lists of basic human rights as foundations that can guide, among other things, institutional governance, biopolitics, and biolaw.[24] One might think of the United Nations Universal Declaration of Human Rights, and in particular Articles 12 and 25, which bear on the required standard of health care. The difficulty is that the establishment of any particular, purportedly normative basic list of human rights always requires a political decision and cannot be grounded in an unambiguous, uncontroversial, moral-theoretical conclusion, in that no particular content-full conclusion can be warranted by sound rational argument without begging the question, arguing in a circle, or engaging in an infinite regress. Because there are always grounds for different orderings of basic human values and right-making conditions that would justify one in framing different understandings of the content of such rights, the choice is one guided by its implications for governance and public policy. But then the issue arises of whose politics and which political vision should (i.e., will) guide. This state of affairs is usually hidden because there is an advantage to advancing a list of human rights as a moral-intellectual discovery, rather than as a particular policy choice or political agenda. However, advancing particular lists of human rights inevitably constitutes a political manifesto toward the end of establishing a particular list of basic human rights that can serve to justify a particular approach to institutional governance, biopolitics, and biolaw.

In short, the purported claim by those in political authority that through a bioethics committee, commission, or council they have made a general moral disclosure rather than a political choice serves the political agenda of controlling public discourse. It sets limits to moral and political debates by confining them within bounds defined by an authorized consensus. For example, by claiming to speak in the name of a set of basic human rights that are advanced as being self-evident, clearly rationally justified, etc., one may remove such claims from serious moral/political discussion. After all, although it is considered appropriate to negotiate particular policies, it may not seem as appropriate to negotiate the nature of justice, fairness, and basic human rights. Yet, insofar as there are contrary views and substantive disputes regarding the nature of justice, fairness, and basic human rights, among which a final choice cannot be uncontroversially made by sound rational argument, then the public establishment of any particular account is not only a political choice, but one subject to negotiation. If this circumstance is not recognized, the bioethics established in biolaw becomes an ideology, as Marx and Engels recognized. Such moral claims become equivalent to "the ruling ideas of an epoch . . . the relationships which make the one class the ruling one," and bioethicists become merely "conceptive ideologists, who make the perfecting of the illusion of the [ruling] class . . . their chief source of livelihood" (Marx and Engels 1969, 39, 40).

TOWARD A BIOPOLITICS THAT TAKES MORAL DIVERSITY SERIOUSLY

Given this state of affairs, rather than searching for consensus, one would be better advised to search for the political structures that will allow us to live in the face of an apparently irresolvable moral pluralism. In this fashion, we may be able to avoid a political zero-sum, winner-take-all biopolitics, which if anything may be an invitation to violence, and instead attempt to come to terms with the enduring moral plurality and difference that confronts us. The claims of those holding contrary views can be adequately appreciated only if one acknowledges that moral pluralism characterizes our fallen human condition and if one does not attempt to establish in a totalizing fashion any particular bioethics, understanding of human rights, or other form of secular fundamentalism. This recognition requires recognizing the limits of moral rationality and the political nature of the forceful imposition of any one particular view of justice, fairness, and basic human rights. The recognition of the controversial character of the foundations of biopolitics and biolaw is by default an argument in favor of the priority of forbearance rights, procedural approaches, and formal-right constitutions such as that of the United States over against the material-right constitutional approaches of Europe. Limited democratic constitutional frameworks that give space for competing visions of human vision and the human good take seriously moral diversity and the finitude of secular moral knowledge.

NOTES

An ancestral version of this chapter was presented as a part of the conference Playing God or Playing Politics?, Northwestern University, Chicago, Illinois, October 22, 2004.

1. The Ethics Advisory Board of the Department of Health, Education, and Welfare, which addressed moral issues involved in the then-emerging technology of in vitro fertilization, produced an indication of the deep disagreements in bioethics (Ethics Advisory Board 1979).

2. Unlike Kant, who relies on an as-if appeal to God and immortality to secure a harmony of the right and the good, as well as of the justification of morality and the motivation to act morally (not to mention to secure a single account of morality—a point never clear to Kant), Hegel appeals to the state. The state for Hegel is the equivalent of Kant's God, in that the state can impose, *inter alia*, a structure harmonizing the good and the right, while giving a motivation through its coercive power to conform to an established morality. "The state consists in the march of God in the world" (Hegel 1998, 279).

3. The term *bioethics* evidently appeared for the first time in 1970 in V. R. Potter, "Bioethics, the science of survival," *Perspectives in Biology and Medicine* 14: 127–53, and "Biocybernetics and survival," *Zygon* 5: 229–46. See also Potter, *Bioethics, Bridge to the Future* (Englewood Cliffs, NJ: Prentice-Hall, 1971).

4. Sargent Shriver claims an independent coinage of the term *bioethics* as we now use it. Letter to the author, January 26, 2001. See Reich 1994.

5. To appreciate the secular recasting of America's public culture, one must note that the mid-twentieth-century public forum was de facto religious; indeed Protestant Christianity defined the context for law and public policy. See *Church of the Holy Trinity v. United States*, 143 US 457 (1892) at 470; and *United States v. Macintosh*, 283 US 605 (1931) at 625. The established culture was recast by a number of American Supreme Court holdings. See *Roy R. Torcaso v. Clayton K. Watkins*, 367 US 488, 6 L ed 2d 982, 81 S Ct 1680 (1961); and *School District of Abington Township v. Edward L. Schempp, William J. Murray et al. v. John N. Curlett et al.*, 374 US 203, 10 L ed 2d 844, 83 S Ct 1560 (1963).

6. Prior to the 1970s, Roman Catholic medical-moral-theological reflections were extensive and well-developed. In the twentieth century, Roman Catholic medical-moral reflections had sought to define and maintain a Roman Catholic medical morality in part expressed in ecclesial directives to American Roman Catholic hospitals. For an overview of this history, see Griese 1987, 1–19. These developments in Roman Catholic medical-moral theology were located within a more than three-hundred-year tradition of producing manuals to guide moral decisions. In the late 1960s and early 1970s, this academic and pas-

toral practice rapidly fell into chaos. Before its collapse, it produced an extensive literature. The marginalization of religious advisers occurred not simply through the secularization of American society, but also in consequence of the moral-theological chaos that followed in the wake of Roman Catholicism's Second Vatican Council.

7. America's established Christian morality was disestablished through a number of court decisions: *Griswold v. Connecticut*, 381 US 479, 85 S Ct 1678, 14 L Ed 2d 510 (1965); *Eisenstadt v. Baird*, 405 US 438, 92 S Ct 1029, 31 L Ed 2d 349 (1972); and *Roe v. Wade*, 410 US 113 (1973); and *In re Cruzan* 58 LW 4916 (June 25, 1990).

8. A number of court holdings placed American medicine and its morality within a larger socio-moral context. See, for example, *The United States of America, Appellants, v. The American Medical Association, A Corporation; The Medical Society of the District of Columbia, A Corporation; et al.*, 317 U.S. 519 (1943); and *American Medical Assoc. v. Federal Trade Comm'n*, 638 F.2d 443 (2d Cir. 1980).

9. Decisive were such decisions as *Canterbury v. Spence*, 464 F. 2d 772, 789 (D.C. Cir. 1972); *Cobbs v. Grant*, 8 Cal. 3.d 229, 246; 502 P.2d 1, 12; 104 Cal. Rptr. 505, 516 (Calif. 1972); and *Sard v. Hardy*, 397 A. 2d 1014, 1020 (Md. 1977).

10. For example, concerns regarding the dangers associated with recombinant DNA research led to *Recombinant DNA Research*, vol. 1: *Document Relating to "NIH Guidelines for Research Involving Recombinant DNA Molecules," Feb. 1975–June 1976*, Publ. no. (NIH) 76-136. Washington, DC: H.E.W., 1976; vol. 2: *Document Relating to "NIH Guidelines for Research Involving Recombinant DNA Molecules,"* Publ. no. (NIH) 781139. Washington, DC: H.E.W., 1976.

11. The perceived need for guidance in morally freighted clinical decisions led *inter alia* to a call for the establishment of ethics committees. The existence of such committees required members who were ethicists, whatever that might eventually mean. The emergence of this phenomenon was influenced by an article cited in the Karen Quinlan decision (*In the Matter of Karen Quinlan* 70 NJ 10 [1976]). See Teel 1975. This decision suggested falsely that ethics committees were widespread. Though the Quinlan decision did not endorse ethics committees as we now know them, the decision gave impetus to their development. From this grew an official affirmation of the need for bioethical guidance. Such committees have provided various procedures for decision making, even when they have failed to disclose a canonical basis for moral guidance.

12. As bioethics emerged, the claims of medical ethics were brought to a critical examination and assessment that nested bioethics in general philosophical/analytic concerns. See Clouser 1974, 1975, and 1977.

13. The term *fundamentalist* was introduced to identify those individuals who defended points of doctrine they took to be essential to Christian belief over against a movement out of the nineteenth century to reshape Christian commitments in "more modern" terms. According to the *Oxford English Dictionary*, the term first identified "a religious movement which became active among various Protestant bodies in the United States after the war of 1914–18, based on strict adherence to traditional orthodox tenets (e.g. the literal inerrancy of Scripture) held to be fundamental to the Christian faith; opposed to *liberalism* and *modernism*" (Oxford: Clarendon Press, 1933), Supplement, p. 399. The usage of *fundamentalist* predates that recorded in the *Oxford English Dictionary*. It is grounded in twelve pamphlets

entitled "The Fundamentals," which were published beginning in 1909. See Torrey 1990. A second sense of fundamentalism has developed to identify those who would follow truths that fall outside of the established secular-democratic understanding of proper political deportment. John Rawls, for example, defines *fundamentalism* as the rejection of the dominant secular social-democratic understanding of the politically rational, in favor of some other basis for proper conduct. For Rawls, a fundamentalist is one who holds that "the religiously true, or the philosophically true, overrides the politically reasonable" (Rawls 1997, 806).

14. Rawls attempted to avoid having to establish a particular view of moral rationality by granting that his account was not grounded in reason or anchored in being (Rawls 1985) but in a freestanding view (Rawls 1993, xxx).

15. "Such a consensus consists of all the reasonable opposing religious, philosophical, and moral doctrines likely to persist over generations and to gain a sizable body of adherents in a more or less just constitutional regime, a regime in which the criterion of justice is that political conception itself" (Rawls 1993, 15).

16. "Thus, political liberalism looks for a political conception of justice that we hope can gain the support of an overlapping consensus of reasonable religious, philosophical, and moral doctrines in a society regulated by it. . . . Political liberalism, then, aims for a political conception of justice as a freestanding view. It offers no specific metaphysical or epistemological doctrine beyond what is implied by the political conception itself" (Rawls 1993, 10).

17. The National Commission for the Protection of Human Subjects of Biomedical and Behavioral Research in The Belmont Report was initially received by many as disclosing a common framework for bioethics, especially through its three principles of Respect for Persons, Beneficence, and Justice (National Commission . . . 1978, DHEW [OS] 78-0012, pp. 4–6, 8–9). The strategic ambiguity of the principles is important: they identify family resemblances among quite different sets of moral considerations. Moralities will have a very different character, depending on the extent to which autonomy involves a particular account of an inviolable right-making condition, the nature of the good, and the character of property rights, to identify only a few cardinal issues.

18. The third-century A.D. philosopher Agrippa, a Greek skeptic and member of the late Academy, recognized that philosophy could not uncontroversially establish its truth claims. See Sextus Empiricus, *Outlines of Pyrrhonism*, I.164, and Diogenes Laertius, *Lives of Eminent Philosophers*, IX.88. The reader should not conclude from this endorsement of Agrippa's contention that the author is a moral relativist, or that he is skeptical about the existence of moral truth. Rather, the position is one of secular moral epistemological skepticism that recognizes that the only way free from these problems that Agrippa lays out, as Orthodox Christianity knows, lies in the restoration of communion with God, the healing of the nous through achieving purity of heart (i.e., catharsis, photisis, and theosis). See Romanides 2002 and Dragas, 2004. Veridical knowledge requires a union of the knower and the known. True knowledge is always at its root theological, for God is the root and standard of all true knowledge.

19. No consensus exists about what it would mean to have a bioethical consensus. See Bayertz 1994 and ten Have and Sass 1998.

20. James Davison Hunter introduced the term *culture wars* to indicate how in the face of robust moral difference there is a struggle to define and establish a particular morality for public policy and law. See Hunter 1991 and Huntington 1998.

21. My reflections bear a very special indebtedness to years of conversations and reflection with Lisa Rasmussen on this issue. See Rasmussen 2003. For a more extensive account of my position on these matters, see Engelhardt 2003.

22. A counter-example may seem to lie in the role of bioethics as court-recognized ethics experts. For disputes regarding this function, see Wildes 1997 and Kipnis 1997.

23. Since at least the 1990s, a reaction against the hegemony of an American–Western European account of bioethics has developed, especially in Asia, with the goal of framing a bioethics that is not grounded in the presuppositions of the standard American account. See, for example, Alora and Lumitao 2001; Fan 2002; Fan and Li 2004; Hoshino 1997; and Qiu 2004.

24. The last two decades have witnessed a groundswell of interest in producing international declarations on bioethics and on global ethics generally. See, for example, Council of Europe 1997; International Bioethics Committee of UNESCO 2003; Schmidt 2000; Universal Declaration on the Human Genome and Human Rights 1997.

REFERENCES

Ad Hoc Committee of the Harvard Medical School to Examine the Definition of Brain Death. 1968. A definition of irreversible coma. *Journal of the American Medical Association* 205 (August 5): 337–40.

Alora, A.T., and Lumitao, J. M., eds. 2001. *Beyond a Western Bioethics: Voices from the Developing World*. Washington, DC: Georgetown University Press.

Bayertz, K., ed. 1994. *The Concept of Moral Consensus: The Case of Technological Interventions into Human Reproduction*. Dordrecht: Kluwer.

Beauchamp, T. L., and Childress, J. F. 1979. *Principles of Biomedical Ethics*. New York: Oxford University Press.

Cantor, N. 1973. A patient's decision to decline life-saving medical treatment: Bodily integrity versus the preservation of life. *Rutgers Law Review* 26: 228–64.

Clouser, K. D. 1974. What is medical ethics? *Annals of Internal Medicine* 80: 657–60.

———. 1975. Medical ethics: Uses, abuses, and limitations. *New England Journal of Medicine* 293: 384–87.

———. 1977. Biomedical ethics: Some reflections and exhortations. *The Monist* 60: 47–61.

Council of Europe. 1997. Convention for the protection of human rights and dignity of the human being with regard to the application of biology and medicine: Convention on human rights and biomedicine, Oviedo: April 4 (http://conventions.coe.int/Treaty/en/Treaties/Html/164.htm).

Daniels, N. 1985. *Just Health Care*. New York: Cambridge University Press.

Dragas, G., ed. and trans. 2004. *An Outline of Orthodox Patristic Dogmatics*. Orthodox Research Institute.

Engelhardt, Jr., H. T. 1986. *The Foundations of Bioethics*. New York: Oxford University Press.
———. 1996. *The Foundations of Bioethics*. 2nd ed. New York, Oxford University Press.
———. 2002. The ordination of bioethicists as secular moral experts. *Social Philosophy and Policy* 19 (Summer): 59–82.
———. 2003. The bioethics consultant: Giving moral advice in the midst of moral controversy. *Healthcare Ethics Committee Forum* 15 (December): 362–82.
Ethics Advisory Board. 1979. *HEW Support of Research Involving Human In Vitro Fertilization and Embryo Transfer with Appendix*. Washington, DC: U.S. Government Printing Office, May 4.
Fan, R. 2002. Reconstructionist Confucianism and health care: An Asian moral account of health care resource allocation. *Journal of Medicine and Philosophy* 27(6): 675–82.
Fan, R., and Li, B. 2004. Truthtelling in medicine: The Confucian view. *Journal of Medicine and Philosophy* 29(2): 179–93.
Foucault, M. 1973. *The Birth of the Clinic*. Trans. A. M. Sheridan Smith. New York: Pantheon Books.
Griese, O. N. 1987. *Catholic Identity in Health Care: Principles and Practice*. Braintree, MA: Pope John Center.
Hegel, G. W. F. 1998. *Elements of the Philosophy of Right*. Ed. Allen W. Wood, trans. H. B. Nisbet. New York: Cambridge University Press.
Hoshino, K., ed. 1997. *Japanese and Western Bioethics*. Dordrecht: Kluwer.
Hunter, J. D. 1991. *Culture Wars: The Struggle to Define America*. New York: Basic Books.
Huntington, S. P. 1998. *The Clash of Civilizations and the Remaking of World Order*. New York: Simon and Schuster.
International Bioethics Committee of UNESCO. 2003. Report of the IBC on the possibility of elaborating a universal instrument on bioethics. Paris, June 13.
Kipnis, K. 1997. Confessions of an expert ethics witness. *Journal of Medicine and Philosophy* 22(4): 325–43.
Krause, E. A. 1996. *Death of the Guilds*. New Haven: Yale University Press.
Levit, K. R. 1985. National health expenditures, 1984. *Health Care Financing* 7: 3.
MacIntyre, A. 1981. *After Virtue*. Notre Dame, IN: University of Notre Dame Press.
Marx, K., and Engels, F. 1969. *The German Ideology*. New York: International Publishers.
National Commission for the Protection of Human Subjects of Biomedical and Behavioral Research. 1975. *Research on the Fetus*. Washington, DC: H.E.W., DHEW [OS] 76-127, 128.
———. 1978. *The Belmont Report*. Washington, DC: U.S. Government Printing Office, DHEW [OS] 78-0012.
Qiu, R. Z., ed. 2004. *Bioethics: Asian Perspectives, A Quest for Moral Diversity*. Dordrecht: Kluwer.
Rasmussen, L. 2003. Clinical Bioethics: Analysis of a Practice. Ph.D. dissertation, Rice University, Houston, Texas.
Rawls, J. 1971. *A Theory of Justice*. Cambridge, MA: Belknap Press.
———. 1985. Justice as fairness: Political not metaphysical. *Philosophy and Public Affairs* 14(5) (Summer): 223–51.
———. 1993. *Political Liberalism*. New York: Columbia University Press.

————. 1997. The idea of public reason revisited. *University of Chicago Law Review* 64 (Summer): 765–807.

Reich, W., ed. 1978. *The Encyclopedia of Bioethics*. New York: Macmillan Free Press. A second edition appeared in 1995.

————. 1994. The word "bioethics": Its birth and the legacies of those who shaped its meaning. *Kennedy Institute of Ethics Journal* 4: 319–36.

Rescher, N. 1969. The allocation of exotic medical lifesaving therapy. *Ethics* 79: 173–86.

Romanides, J. 2002. *The Ancestral Sin*. Trans. George S. Gabriel. Ridgewood, NJ: Zephyr Publishing.

Schmidt, K., ed. 2000. *Journal of Medicine and Philosophy* 25(2): 123–266.

Teel, K. 1975. The physician's dilemma: A doctor's view: What the law should be. *Baylor Law Review* 27: 6–9.

ten Have, H., and Sass, H. M., eds. 1998. Consensus Formation in Healthcare Ethics. Dordrecht: Kluwer; and *Cambridge Quarterly of Healthcare Ethics* 11 (Winter 2002): 1–108.

Torrey, R. A., ed. 1990. *The Fundamentals*. Grand Rapids, MI: Kregel.

Universal Declaration on the Human Genome and Human Rights. 1997. Adopted on November 11, 1997, by UNESCO, endorsed by the U.N. General Assembly on December 9, 1998, Res. No. A/RES/53/152.

White House Domestic Policy Council. 1993. *The President's Health Security Plan*. New York: Times Books.

Wildes, K. W. 1997. Healthy skepticism: The emperor has very few clothes. *Journal of Medicine and Philosophy* 22(4): 365–71.

CHAPTER ELEVEN

ASBH and Moral Tolerance

MARY FAITH MARSHALL, PH.D.

> The purpose of action is to allow philosophy to continue, for if
> men are reduced to the material alone they become no more than
> beasts.
>
> *Sophia,* The Dream of Scipio *(Pears 2002)*

I just got off the phone with my colleague Steve Miles. He's helping me with a poetry compilation on the downside of war. We're designing the cover. He said, "I've got a good picture of a guy with a severed ear I could send you." And I thought, Hmm . . . Do I want to use the photo of the guy sans ear? Or, instead, the one of a pile of severed ears? I think I'll go with the pile. Maybe juxtapose it with a picture of a woman filing her nails. Play up the indifference angle. Play off the Carolyn Fourché poem, "The Colonel." Re: the Salvadoran colonel who emptied a bag of ears on the dining room table while his daughter sat by and plied her emery board. He said to Fourché, "Something for your poetry, no? As for the rights of anyone, tell your people they can go f—— themselves" (Fourché 1981). All of this is prefatory to Steve's upcoming Abu Ghraib talk on campus (Miles 2004). Not that they severed any ears at Abu Ghraib. They favored interrogatories like smothering, electric prods, rape, beatings, attack dogs, pretzeling, sexual humiliation, bodily suspensions, and feces smearing—some of which resulted in death. Not, of course, that we didn't sever ears in Iraq. And Vietnam. That's part of war's basic horror show. Standard issue psycho-warrior stuff.

Consider this Milesean thought exercise:

Place yourself in a room. It is cold. A naked man is there. He is a prisoner. His back is arched at an awkward angle in a stress position. His wrists are cuffed, crucifixion-style, to the top bunk. His feet brush the floor. A pair of underwear covers his head and face. He has been suspended like this for a long time.

Place yourself in a room. A man lies on the floor. He is a prisoner. He has not slept or eaten for several days. His wrists are tightly bound behind him with flexi-cuffs. His jailer beats him with a chemical light wand, then smashes it and pours the phosphoric liquid over his naked body.

Place yourself in a room. A man lies on the floor, his hands chained to the door. He is a prisoner. He wears a hood. It obstructs his vision and breathing. He is beaten with a chair and a broomstick. Then sodomized with a light wand. And with the broomstick.

Place yourself in a hallway. A man inches toward his cell. He is a prisoner. He has just been released from the hospital where his gunshot wounds and broken leg have been treated. He cannot walk, so he crawls. His captors beat his injured leg.

Place yourself in a room. A man is placed head first into a sleeping bag, his hands cuffed behind him. He is a prisoner. One of his captors sits on his chest. The prisoner dies. He has been asphyxiated. By his captors. Who subsequently lie and report that he has suffered a heart attack.

Place yourself in a hallway. A medic is there, attending to a wounded prisoner. The man has been severely beaten. He has collapsed on the floor; his nose is broken and lacerated. The medic begins suturing the prisoner's nose. The chief interrogator, the man who administered the beating, asks to learn how to suture. The medic shows him, and the interrogator finishes the procedure (Strasser 2004; Danner 2004).

Place yourself in these rooms. You are a nurse, or a physician. You are a witness. You do nothing. You are complicit.

Or you aren't in the room, but you know of these things. The dead bodies bear the evidence. The wounded prisoners bear the evidence. You do not report these abuses up the chain of command. You might even falsify death certificates. Either way, you are an accessory to torture. You are an accessory to murder.

Or, you write the truth. You record the cause of death, "Asphyxia due to smothering and chest compression." A Pentagon spokesperson maintains that the prisoner died of natural causes. Does your honesty suffice? Is honesty the minimum moral requirement for maintaining your oath as a healer? Is honesty the minimum moral obligation owed to your patients?

Place yourself in a room. It is your office. You are a nurse, physician, historian, anthropologist, a professor of literature. You are a medical humanist. Or a bioethicist. Or both. You learn that these things have happened at Abu Ghraib. That some have happened in the presence of nurses and doctors and medics. On the Internet you see photographic evidence of torture and abuse. Or on television.

You remain silent. Why? You are, perhaps, indifferent. Or cautious. Torture-at-a-distance is unpleasant to consider, inconvenient to act on. Perhaps the subject doesn't fit your research portfolio. The NIH doesn't fund it. Nor, for that matter, does the Department of Justice.

You lose your claim, then, to humanism. You lose your claim to applied ethics. Because you have done nothing. Even if you claim to abhor torture. Or murder. Or to espouse patriotism.

Conversely, you choose, when solicited, to endorse a protest. Perhaps the Call to Prevent Torture and Abuse of Detainees in U.S. Custody by Physicians for Human Rights. Or a similar call from Amnesty International. One admonishing the complicity of doctors and nurses who bore silent witness at Abu Ghraib. Or did worse than nothing. Is this the minimum moral requirement for you as a medical humanist? A bioethicist?

> The crab, more than any of God's creatures, has formulated the
> perfect philosophy of life. Whenever he is confronted by a great
> moral crisis, he first makes up his mind what is right, and then
> goes sideways as fast as he can.
>
> *Oliver Herford*

Place yourself in a room. At a meeting of the American Society for Bioethics and Humanities board of directors. The board wishes to speak out about Abu Ghraib. It composes a letter to President George W. Bush. The letter invokes Nuremberg, the Tokyo Declaration, the American Medical Association (AMA) and American Nurses Association (ANA) Codes of Ethics, the World Medical Association's Declaration of Hamburg. The letter speaks to the obligations of health professionals, civilian and military, not to participate in or aid in the abuse of prisoners. And of their duties to report such abuses. The letter exhorts the administration to "issue a clear directive affirming the primacy of ethical principles for military medical professionals during wartime." A directive that, in theory, will protect medical professionals from orders to participate in the abuse of prisoners, will clarify the expectation that abuses by others are to be reported up the chain of command. It will safeguard prisoners, ours and theirs. It will "clarify that our society will not condone or tolerate the inhumane treatment of any person." The letter is posted on the ASBH Web site.

This letter is not an absolution for ASBH. It is hypocritical. As were Telford Taylor's opening remarks at Nuremberg. Taylor presumed to speak for the United States of America in *U.S. v. Brandt,* a uniquely American tribunal. He proffered the United States as "the voice of humanity," stating, "We stamp these acts, and the ideas which engendered them, as barbarous and criminal" (Annas and Grodin 1992). Powerful prose. The foundation of the Nuremberg Code. Taylor failed to mention, of course, concomitant and similar barbarous and criminal acts perpetrated by the U.S. government against its own citizens. And that the United States declined to prosecute Japanese physicians who tested biological warfare on prisoners who were subsequently dissected alive.

The ASBH board opined on the duties of clinicians to report abuses against military detainees, while concomitantly maintaining its own silence about human rights in general, and while failing to articulate its own "clear directive affirming the primacy of ethical principles." Our bylaws prevent it: "The Society shall not issue positions on substantive moral and policy issues" (ASBH bylaws, section 4.1). And, as was evidenced at the 1995 annual meeting in Washington, D.C., we can't even agree, as a society, on whether or not to have our own code of ethics. We are silent on fundamental and global issues such as lack of access to basic health care, nutrition, and education. Silent about human rights violations perpetrated by big pharma, or by members of the health care community. The letter to the president was a step forward for an organization whose position had formerly been "no position." But it was nonetheless hypocritical; a single stand by an organization whose fundamental policy is silence.

Let us be honest, and acknowledge then that our professional society explicitly tolerates the inhumane treatment of persons. By choosing silence in the arena of policy and politics, it has chosen moral neutrality over moral agency.

Why the conspiracy of silence? Because the membership is afraid. Afraid that it might one day make a huge, collective error. Take a wrong position. Afraid that it might alienate a portion of its own, that some might abandon the collective. The fallback position being: it is all right if you, as an individual want to decry an injustice, an abuse, a travesty, should you so choose, but we're not taking any collective risk. We might get it wrong. Embarrass ourselves publicly. We are worried, too, about the tyranny of the majority; of doing violence to our secular pluralist foundation. We worry about objective versus subjective values. Or about the telos versus deon debate and what moral agency requires (or doesn't). We worry about moral truths (or the lack thereof). We are certain that there are few, if any, things on which we can agree. *Res ipsa loquitur.* If we cannot agree we must have nothing to say.

Except for this. We have managed to pass one resolution that allows us to speak collectively. We have amended the ASBH bylaws (section 4.2) to protect ourselves from incursions against academic freedom, and to allow position statements on issues of professionalism. We have looked after our own voices, our own rights as scholars, our own academic freedoms. These things, out of collective self-interest, we have agreed upon. But we can't imagine agreeing on the interests of others. Thus, we have agreed on the background conditions for moral advocacy, but not on moral advocacy itself. The narrow exception being advocacy for those in our club who have been wronged by virtue of their work; wronged by a mentor in England, let go in Brazil, or denied the freedom to travel to Cuba for a professional meeting. An exception that is inherently praiseworthy, but embarrassingly insufficient.

We have remained silent, collectively, on the issue of adequate health care for the uninsured. Silent on the criminalization of addiction. Silent on issues of human rights. We presume to advocate, on our Web site, support for victims of Hurricane Katrina, many of whom are poor and black. But we were silent before the deluge, before the disaster and destruction. ASBH jumped the bandwagon way after the horse had left the barn, and remains silent about the sorts of conditions that obtained in New Orleans prior to Katrina. About, for example, poverty, racism, violence, health disparities, inadequate education, and inadequate infrastructure.

> We may uphold tolerance because we believe we should not stand
> for one moral vision rather than another, but the idea of a tolerant
> society, protecting individual freedom, is as substantive a moral
> position as one could wish. . . . The idea of total moral neutrality
> must always be an illusion, since it itself embodies a view of what
> a good society should value most.
>
> *Trigg 2005*

There are moral truths for the conduct of a free society. These are embedded in the aspirations of our nation, its constitution, and in international law. They include respect for free speech, academic freedom, and freedom from retribution for those who fairly disclose injustice or professional misconduct. There are moral truths in the healing professions. These include the primacy of the patient, the patient's dignity and rights, the provision of compassionate and competent care, and the caregiver's responsibility and accountability for individual judgments and actions. There are moral truths that inhere in the medical humanities and bioethics. We ascribe to the truth that the examination of the good life is a worthwhile endeavor. And that what we learn from this examination can be applied for the good of others. This allows us to give advice. To, on occasion, exhort others to do the right thing. To advocate a position, if you will.

It is morally relevant that I am a citizen of a democracy. It is morally relevant that I am a health care professional. And it should be morally relevant that I am a member of the American Society for Bioethics and Humanities. But, paradoxically, it is not. Because its members have explicitly chosen a position of moral neutrality on issues of substance.

Inherent in the moral truths for a free society, for the healing professions, for bioethicists and medical humanists are truths about human rights. What, after all, do the medical humanities entail if not the human condition? Bioethicists and those involved in the medical humanities are perhaps even more fundamentally beholden to such governing principles than are members of other professions; just as we are beholden to our own core competencies for ethics consultants, because these values are the foundation for the entire conduct of our professions. The character traits, for example, identified by our organization in its *Core Competencies for Health Care Ethics Consultation, 1998* include:

1. Tolerance, patience and compassion
2. Honesty, forthrightness, and self-knowledge
3. Courage
4. Prudence and humility
5. Integrity

These competencies, required of each of us as individuals, beg the question of what the ASBH, as our professional organization, owes to its members and to its larger constituency—patients, research subjects, health care providers, the public, our government, the world's populations and environment. To those who are treated inhumanely. To those whose human rights are abrogated. To refrain from upholding our standards in a clear and public fashion, not to condemn, collectively, injustices that violate those standards, is to engage in the conspiracy of silence. Which, for a purported ethics organization, is morally reprehensible.

Patria es humanidad (Humanity is the only country).

José Martí 1946

The controversy over ASBH taking substantive positions on issues of substance began in 1989. The backstory begins in a room . . .

It is a jail cell. There is a woman there. She is pregnant. She is a prisoner. She stays in the cell until the time of her parturition, when she is transported to the state hospital in shackles and handcuffs. Her head is hooded by a towel.

At the hospital she is handcuffed to the bed. A policeman guards her room. She returns to the cell twenty-four hours after delivering her infant, wearing hospital slippers and ankle chains, clutching a box of maxipads in her cuffed hands. She has seen her child only briefly, and will not see him again for months, or perhaps longer.

She is in the cell because nurses and doctors at the state hospital have turned her over to the police and the local prosecutor. The nurses and doctors have screened her urine for illegal drugs without her knowledge or permission. She has tested positive for cocaine. Because she is pregnant, she is now a criminal.

The nurses and doctors are white; she is black. And poor. She has exchanged sexual favors for drugs. A Magdalene, of sorts. She is alone in her cell. She is afraid. She despairs at being separated from her newborn, the very newborn for whom she sought prenatal care. She is separated from her other children, too. Children for whom she is the sole caretaker. They are lost to foster care.

The nurses and doctors who judged and betrayed her are complicit in her arrest and incarceration. They are complicit in the disintegration of her family. They are complicit in similar scenarios involving thirty-eight other patients, all but one of whom are black. The sole Caucasian woman has a black boyfriend. This is noted in her medical record: "boyfriend is a Negro." Written in the patient's chart by the high-risk obstetrics clinical nurse specialist, who was an architect of the criminalization policy. Written in 1989, in the United States of America. In Charleston, South Carolina, where the civil war began. Written at the Medical University of South Carolina, the hospital that provides indigent care to the region and the state. The nurses and doctors who judged and betrayed her are complicit in the evolution of the Tuskegee legacy.

The hospital ethics committee claims to abhor this betrayal by their colleagues, but it has done nothing. Because it hasn't been "invited" into the case. By their silence, the ethics committee's members, too, are complicit. They are silent even though the case has garnered national and international attention. The BBC has made a documentary. *60 Minutes* has aired a segment. The *New York Times* and the *L.A. Times* have written it up. The Office for Protection from Research Risks has sanctioned the university. A lawsuit has been filed in federal district court. The case ultimately makes its way to the U.S. Supreme Court. And finally, years after the inception of the criminalization program, the ethics committee complains to the university administration.

South Carolina is the first state to establish that a viable fetus is considered a person under the child abuse and neglect statute. Today, a pregnant woman may be held criminally liable for any action (legal or illegal) during her pregnancy that would "endanger the life, health or comfort" of her fetus. Statutory mandatory reporters (health care professionals, teachers, others) are required under state policy to report pregnant women whom they suspect of substance abuse to state authorities, to law enforcement. Noncompliance on the part of clinicians could result in legal sanctions against them. The attorney general of South Carolina has made that explicit threat to the South Carolina health care community. The very same attorney general who was an architect of the criminalization scheme, and, as Charleston's former solicitor, prosecuted pregnant substance abusers.

Let us be clear—this policy is about abortion politics in the Deep South. It is not about healthy pregnancies with felicitous outcomes. It is not about the welfare of children and their families. It is about political expediency. Does that make it off-limits to ASBH? Because it is political? Because it is of moral substance?

> Just dropped in to see what position my position was in.
> *With gratitude to Mickey Newbury ("Just Dropped In*
> *[To See What Condition My Condition Was In]" by singer/*
> *songwriter Mickey Newbury, Acuff/Rose Music, 1968)*

Through their professional associations and their amicus briefs for the plaintiffs, physicians and nurses in South Carolina have performed their collective professional duty. Their voices were raised by their professional associations: the South Carolina Medical Association and the South Carolina Nurses Association. Collective voices were heard, too, on a national scale, the American Medical Association, the American Nurses Association, and the American Academy of Pediatrics, all of which filed amicus briefs for the plaintiffs, as did scores of other professional organizations.

But no voices were raised by the ASBH. It did not speak for patients, or their families, or for clinicians who opposed the policy, or for the institutional bioethicist who critiqued the policy (Jos, Marshall, and Perlmutter 2003; Marshall, Menikoff, and Paltrow 2003; Marshall 1999; Nelson and Marshall 1998; Jos, Marshall, and Perlmutter 1995). The same bioethicist whose promotion was denied and whose program was dissolved by the university's president as punishment for "leaving the reservation." It offered no opinion to this president or the university's board of trustees. It couldn't. In 1999, the ASBH board was hamstrung by the organization's bylaws. The board could not issue position statements, not even on issues of academic freedom or professionalism, much less on "substantive moral or policy issues."

This case fostered a rancorous debate within ASBH (Nelson 1991). Debate that was further inflamed when the Society could not sign on to a national statement endorsing the responsible conduct of research and asserting research participants' right to informed consent. The ASBH held a spring forum on the issue of "issues." Letters and e-mail flew—among members, and between members and the board. A task force comprising past ASBH presidents was formed to propose altered bylaws. In October 2002, after three years of deliberation, the membership amended the bylaws, allowing the Society to voice opinions on professional issues and issues of academic freedom.

More recently, the ASBH board has formed the Advisory Committee on Ethics Standards to survey the membership on the need for an organizational code of ethics. The advisory committee evolved from the ASBH Ethics Standards Task Force (the ex-presidents), a group convened by former president Art Derse to consider the issue of ethical standards for its members—the notion being that any positions on academic freedom or professionalism taken by the board on behalf of the Society should be based on professional norms endorsed or promulgated by the organization. There is, of course, ongoing debate among the membership regarding the need for and purpose of such a code.

ASBH can now speak out against unprofessional conduct, against infringements of academic and professional freedom. But it cannot speak for patients or research participants. It cannot address injustice. It can speak only for its own, within the narrow context of unprofessional behavior.

Most of the physicians and nurses in South Carolina continue to advocate for their patients. They individually and collectively commit overt civil disobedience—they ignore the criminalization policy, take care of their patients, and hope for the best. They talk the talk, and walk the walk—forward, not crabwise. They take a risk in the interests of their patients and in the interest of professional integrity.

In October 2005, UNESCO's General Conference adopted the Universal Declaration on Bioethics and Human Rights. The declaration advocates universal access to health care, essential medicines, nutrition, and water. It advocates reproductive health and the alleviation of poverty and illiteracy. It espouses the sharing of benefits. It speaks to human dignity—to the well-being of individuals and humanity. It explicitly names social responsibility as a guiding principle. A moral truth, of sorts (Yesley 2005, 8).

UNESCO has accomplished what ASBH has not. A failure of which ASBH, collectively, should be ashamed.

REFERENCES

Annas, G., and Grodin, M. 1992. *The Nazi Doctors and the Nuremberg Code: Human Rights in Human Experimentation*. New York: Oxford University Press.

Danner, M. 2004. *Torture and Truth: America, Abu Ghraib, and the War on Terror*. New York: New York Review Books.

Fourché, C. 1981. *The Country between Us*. New York: Harper and Row.

Jos, P. H., Marshall, M. F., and Perlmutter, M. 1995. The Charleston policy on cocaine use during pregnancy: A cautionary tale. *Journal of Law, Medicine, and Ethics* 23(2): 5–13.

———. 2003. Substance abuse during pregnancy: Clinical and public health approaches. *Journal of Law, Medicine, and Ethics* 31(3): 340–50.

Marshall, M. F. 1999. Mal-intentioned illiteracy, willful ignorance, and fetal protection laws: Is there a lexicologist in the house? *Journal of Law, Medicine, and Ethics* 27(4): 343–46.

Marshall, M. F., Menikoff, J., and Paltrow, L. M. 2003. Perinatal substance abuse and human subjects research: Are privacy protections adequate? *Mental Retardation and Developmental Disability Research Review* 9: 54–58.

Martí, José. 1946. *Obras Completas*. Vol. 1. Havana: Editorial Lex.

Miles, S. 2004. Abu Ghraib: Its legacy for military medicine. *The Lancet* 364: 725–28.

Nelson, H. L. 1991. The ASBH Taking Stands Debate. www.asbh.org.

Nelson, L. J., and Marshall, M. F. 1998. An ethical and legal policy analysis of state-compelled loss of liberty as an intervention to manage the harm of prenatal substance abuse and drug addiction. *Robert Wood Johnson Foundation Substance Abuse Policy Research Program Report*. July.

Pears, I. 2002. *The Dream of Scipio*. New York: Riverhead.

Society for Health and Human Values—Society for Bioethics Consultation Task Force on Standards for Bioethics (co-chairs). 1998. *Core Competencies for Ethics Consultation*. Glenville, IL: American Society for Bioethics and Humanities.

Strasser, S., ed. 2004. *The Abu Ghraib Investigations: The Official Reports of the Independent Panel and the Pentagon on the Shocking Prisoner Abuse in Iraq*. New York: Public Affairs.

Trigg, R. 2005. *Morality Matters*. Malden, MA: Blackwell Publishing.

UNESCO Declaration of Bioethics and Human Rights. http://portal.unesco.org.

Yesley, M. 2005. What's in a name: Bioethics—and human rights—at UNESCO. *Hastings Center Report*, March–April: 8.

CHAPTER TWELVE

Bioethics as Activism

LISA S. PARKER, PH.D.

In recent years, discussions of bioethics and activism have often devolved into debate about whether bioethicists, and especially bioethical organizations (like the American Society for Bioethics and Humanities, ASBH), ought to adopt substantive moral positions on particular issues (Nelson 2001a; Antommaria 2004). That the discussion of "taking to the streets" is refocused onto the appropriateness of "taking stands" may strike observers of the field as disappointing, even disingenuous. Some within bioethics share this disappointment and become rather dispirited, even cynical, about the immense energies expended on internal debate that may effect little more social change than the "navel gazing" indulged in by so-called academic elites.

In this chapter, I explore the relationship between bioethics and activism. It would seem that, while bioethics shares with social activism the goal of social justice, bioethics' methods and normative framework have greater affinity with the methods and norms of deliberative democracy to which activism is often contrasted.[1] Nevertheless, I shall try to support the perhaps surprising conclusion that in its goals, methods, and outcomes bioethics should be regarded, and practiced, as a form of activism. Bioethics both contributes to deliberative democratic processes and embraces the norms of rational deliberation and deliberative democracy, but when practiced well, bioethics also illuminates the genealogy of these norms and seeks the inclusion of parties historically excluded from deliberative processes. Even while participating in deliberative democratic processes and rational discourse, bioethics should serve as a corrective to their deficiencies, and thus serve an activist role.

Of course, even quintessential cases of activism are susceptible to multilayered ethical and political critique. Criticisms of Live 8,[2] for example, were reported in a *New York Times* article flanked by advertisements for earrings from Tiffany & Co. and a Bulgari pendant (each retailing for $1,850), as well as a photograph of Sri Lankan fishermen returning to their primitive wooden fishing posts six months after the 2004 tsunami. The juxtaposition of these images prompts as much thoughtful reflection on the value of the musicians' activist efforts as the critics' comments quoted in the article. The irony of rich celebrities' pushing for African aid, while Madison Avenue pushes baubles and the impoverished recipients of the last aid effort return to business as usual, hardly constitutes an argument against well-intentioned, albeit "drop in the ocean" activism.[3] Irony and insinuation are tools of activism, not of argument; yet they are often effective in drawing attention to problems and possibilities that the usual terms of argument obscure. This is, however, to get ahead of this essay's argument, even while illustrating its conclusion. The first task, however, is to consider what is meant by activism.

ACTIVISM'S AIMS, METHODS, AND JUSTIFICATION

This is not the place to explore fully the concept of activism and its justification, methods, and goals. Nevertheless, some attention to these may be helpful, as discussions in bioethics seem implicitly informed by different conceptions. While one goal here is to illuminate, interrogate, and complicate understanding of activism, much of the discussion assumes a popular understanding of the term *activism* such as: "intentional action to bring about social or political change . . . in support of, or opposition to, one side of an often controversial argument."[4]

Some believe bioethics to have embraced activism (e.g., Kelly 2002) or urge it to do so (e.g., Stone 2002), while others analyze why bioethics has turned its back on its activist roots and aspirations (Wolf 1996). Another view holds that bioethics has the potential to blaze a "middle way between activism and 'informing the debate'" (Andre 2002; Parsi and Geraghty 2004).

From the perspective of our colleagues in the academy, bioethicists may appear to be quintessential activists; many of us entered bioethics from our home disciplines seeking to work "where the action is" and to have practical, not "merely academic," effect in the "real world." While ethical theorist C. D. Broad argued that "it is no part of the professional business of moral philosophers to tell people what they ought or ought not to do or to exhort them to do their duty" (1952, 244), bioethicists—admittedly, only some of them moral philosophers— have participated in policy making and clinical decision making since the "birth" of the interdisciplinary field (Jonsen 1998). The roles of bioethicists on public commissions, as expert witnesses, and at the bedside have been documented (e.g., Rothman 1991), prescribed (e.g., ASBH 1998), and criticized (e.g., Scofield 1994; Stevens 2000). Debate continues about whether there is such a thing as ethical expertise and, if so, whether bioethicists possess it (Parker 2005; Rasmussen 2005). Yet most no longer worry, as Broad did about moral philosophers, that we "have no special information not available to the general public, about what is right and what is wrong; nor . . . any call to undertake those hortatory functions which are so adequately performed by clergy-men, politicians, leader-writers, and wireless loudspeakers" (1952, 244). Most agree that it is not just inevitable but appropriate for bioethicists to articulate and argue for particular ethical positions when they provide conceptual clarity regarding the moral terrain (Crosthwaite 1995; Tong 1991).

But even when our arguments are in support of social justice, generally considered to be activism's goal, this taking of a stand and arguing in its support is not what we have in mind when we inquire about an activist role for bioethics and bioethicists. Instead, such transparent ethical reasoning is the business as usual of the field. In any domain—ethics, medicine, politics—activist activity is intended to disrupt "business as usual," to cause a rupture that draws attention to systemic flaws, particularly injustices. This essay contrasts activism with the usual methods both of theorizing and of deliberative democracy, as bioethics obviously involves theorizing, and because there is a strong parallel between many methods and activities of bioethicists and those of deliberative democracies.[5]

Public debate, open discussion, and the norms of rational deliberation characterize the structures and processes of deliberative democracy: "The deliberative democrat thinks that the best way to limit political domination and the naked imposition of partisan interest and to promote greater social justice through public policy is to foster the creation of sites and processes of deliberation among diverse and disagreeing elements of the polity" (Young 2001, 672). This articulation of deliberative democracy serves as both a "normative account of the bases of democratic legitimacy and a prescription for how citizens ought to be politically engaged."

Bioethicists *contribute to* the practical workings of deliberative democracy both as contributors of expert opinion in policy debates and as public intellectuals who help people appreciate the effect of the debate on their own lives (Parsi and Geraghty 2004, W21–22). Moreover, many bioethical activities strongly resemble those of deliberative democracy; to engage in bioethics is to engage in reason-giving in support of ethical positions. In clinical consultation and policy development contexts, for example, bioethicists seek to create a site in which parties to ethical conflict or inquiry can share reasoned arguments in support of their differing positions, within a climate of value pluralism and competing belief systems, and with the goal of achieving resolution or consensus. In scholarship and policy making, bioethicists argue in support of particular ethical positions to inform and sway debate. A methodological goal for both bioethics and deliberative democracy is to "bracket the influence of power differentials" by reaching agreement on the "basis of argument, rather than as a result of threat or force" (Young 2001, 672).

Nevertheless, bioethics _differs_ from deliberative democracy; the two have substantively different constraints on their deliberative operations (Kelly 2003, 349–51): "Extant normative considerations regarding the nature, 'quality,' and moral authority of consensus prefigure the characteristics of public [bioethics'] participation in debate, placing public bioethics work on a distinctly different plane from ideals of deliberative democratic engagement" (Kelly 2003, 346). In particular, bioethics' goal of consensus and its methods of achieving it may serve to "exclude some [potential participants[6]] and to define the legitimate form of participation and voice of publics and experts" (Kelly 2003, 346).[7] As some critics have recognized, some parties are better equipped to participate in the activities of rational discourse than others. Differences in social power—for example, differences that construct some parties as male/Western/dominant and others as female/non-western/subordinate or dependent—may be responsible for parties' different abilities to participate effectively in reasoned discourse and deliberative democratic processes. This has led some critics to question the norms and structure of these processes themselves. Sally Haslanger, for example, articulates two "underlying suspicions" about reason at the outset of her exploration of its relationship to oppressive social roles: "The first is that those situated in certain oppressive or problematic roles succeed (for example, their activities are furthered and sustained) by satisfying the ideals of reason. The second is that those who satisfy the ideals of reason thereby function in a problematic or oppressive social role; that is, simply satisfying the ideals of reason is enough to situate you in the role of oppressor. Plausibly, in both cases we would have grounds to question the value of reason if we are concerned to promote social change" (Haslanger 1993, 94).

Most bioethicists (it is tempting to say all) are invested in preserving the value

of reason and using it in service of social justice to combat dogmatism and oppressive ideology. Moreover, like Haslanger, bioethicists would generally be skeptical of engaging in "reasoned debate over the value, or legitimacy, or reality, of
reason and rationality" (Haslanger 1993, 87). Nevertheless, like Haslanger, bioethics can and should explicitly recognize how the norms and venues of rational
discourse, as it has traditionally been practiced, may disproportionately serve the
interests of the powerful.[8] In exercising this critical capacity, I suggest, bioethics
serves an activist role without embracing wholesale rejection of reasoned argument.

Concern about injustice resulting from exclusion and from the (de)legitima-
tion of norms of participation suggests a need for activism, which is grounded in
this skepticism about the possibility of bracketing the influence of power in either deliberation or deliberative democracy. In this warranted skepticism lies the
justification for (traditional) activism's departure from reasoned argument and
recourse to its (un?)traditional activities (e.g., demonstrations, sit-ins, boycotts)
and methods (e.g., emotional appeals, disruptive tactics, and use of irony, humor,
or drama). Like the (ideal) deliberative democrat, the activist is committed to social justice; however, the activist also "believes that the normal workings of the
social economic and political institutions in which he dwells enact or reproduce
deep wrongs. . . . Since the ordinary rules and practices of these institutions tend
to perpetuate these wrongs, we cannot redress them within those rules" (Young
2001, 673). Activism seeks to redress structural inequalities and injustices by
challenging the dominant conceptual frameworks and terms of discourse through
which issues are framed, discussion is conducted, and consensus is achieved.

Activism (as it is traditionally conceived) and theory (social, political, and ethical) may share social justice as an ultimate goal, but they necessarily diverge in
both their methods and interim aims. Ironically, activism may be in particular
tension with modes of theorizing—for example, feminist and queer theories—
that recognize the potential of theory itself to replicate and further entrench
power differentials. To counter this entrenchment, such theorizing seeks to de-
construct identity categories and modes of binary thought (found in more traditional theories). In contrast, activist activities and methods rely on what such
theorizing deconstructs and destabilizes. Where such theorizing proceeds by
"holding in tension" opposing ideas ("competing truths"), traditional activism
may regard such a strategy as fence-sitting, a failure to take a stand. Theory explores concepts and situations that are simultaneously p and $\sim p$ (e.g., people who
are simultaneously powerful and vulnerable, actions that appear both justified
and unjust, or lesbians who are and are not real women). Traditional activism de-

mands that one be for-it or agin-it; half measures give quarter to the status quo. Nuanced explanations do not fit on posters; consciousness-raising humor and irony may rely on stereotype.

The theorist may dismiss the activist for acting with too blunt an instrument. Activists may accuse theorists of failing to act instrumentally at all, and—worse— of creating a "postmodern argumentarium" that may be used to undermine the possibility of pointing to harms and injustices as real (Mann 2002), and of build- ing coalitions to alleviate them. When queer theory critically investigates the meaning of *lesbian,* it may simultaneously undermine lesbians' ability to militate for health care attentive to their needs or for health insurance benefits for their partners. Bioethical arguments for the reduction of race-associated disparities in health and health care may be undermined when other arguments are seen to "question the reality" of racial categories. The activist claims that "there remains a political imperative to use these necessary errors or category mistakes"—these debunked concepts and deconstructed categories—"to rally and represent an op- pressed political constituency" (Butler 1991, 16). While the need to carry placards remains, absorption in signs and signifieds may prove distracting, even destruc- tive.

Thus bioethics and activism simultaneously have a natural affinity and an am- bivalent relationship. On one hand, bioethics has "the sensibilities of a popular social movement" (Parsi and Geraghty 2004, W21). It is, writes Daniel Wikler, "one of the numerous movements on behalf of the ignored and dispossessed that arose in the wake of the civil rights struggle" and as such has had a dual charac- ter as "a field of inquiry . . . and also a particular kind of advocacy": "A bioethicist- scholar who does not believe in informed consent, or who thinks it proper to sacrifice the well-being of unconsenting research subjects in the interests of fu- ture patients, would be a colleague in full standing (however unpopular) with those holding the opposite, more conventional points of view. In the role of ad- vocate, however, it is understood that bioethicists are attached to a certain set of positions on these issues. . . . In this sense, the point of bioethics was not to study the morality of clinical practice, but rather to change it" (Wikler 1991, 236).[9] More- over, the authority of the field stems, in part, from its being viewed as "distinct from, and a corrective . . . to the unbridled authority and privilege of, science," al- though in reality the domains of science, policy, and bioethics are "fluid and co- productive" (Kelly 2003, 345; see also Brock 1993). Bioethics' outsider status helped to constitute it as a field with norms, practices, and structures—a discur- sive site within which one could be an insider.

On the other hand, in making itself useful to medicine and science, bioethics has failed to maintain sufficient independence and distance to consistently fulfill its critical, corrective role. By taking as given various medico-scientific agendas, practices, and technological innovations, bioethics has chipped away at the edges of science's authority and found means to render more ethical what some suggest should have been rejected wholesale for not serving appropriately vetted ends (Evans 2002). Furthermore, by adopting the individualistic perspective of both clinical medicine and Western ethical theory, bioethics has tended to neglect issues better analyzed through the lenses of population-based approaches, group identities, and socially constructed vulnerability/power.

Perhaps because contemporary bioethics owes such an intellectual debt to academic philosophy, rather than, say, to cultural studies—and also to academic medicine and the sociology of the professions, not to social work and the history of social movements—most bioethicists qua bioethicists have been reluctant to engage in traditional forms of activism. Perhaps because, like me, most bioethicists are quite comfortable—materially and socially—within the admittedly non-ideal political structures of the United States, most of us are unaccustomed to needing to achieve our aims by operating outside the norms of rational deliberation and consensus building. To the extent that we remain outsiders within the institutions where we work, especially as the poor cousins of the "real" faculty in medical centers (i.e., clinicians and scientists), perhaps we experience our subordination more by means of seduction than outright rejection. This is a distinction Patricia Hill Collins utilizes in her reflections on the different conditions of subordination of white women and women of color. Collins observes that as a group black women hold few delusions of sharing in white male power and enjoying the privileges that attach to it.

> In contrast, white women have been offered a share of white male power, but only if they agree to be subordinate. "Sometimes I really feel more sorrier for the white woman than I feel for ourselves because she been caught up in this thing, caught up feeling very special," observes Fannie Lou Hamer (Lerner 1972, 610). Thus "white women, as a group, are subordinated through seduction, women of Color, as a group, through rejection" (Hurtado 1989, 610). (Collins 1991, 189)

Because we have a fair amount to lose—insider status in the health care hierarchy, marks of respectability within the academy, our jobs (and access to be able to do them)—we may be both reluctant and ill-equipped to engage in activist activities. Guerrilla warriors travel light. They also rely on solidarity in their ranks and have an infrastructure that supports them in the countryside. Bioethicists have a lot of baggage, tolerate and invite dissent within the field, and have tended to collaborate less with the truly vulnerable than with those in power.

If we have been seduced and have thereby allowed our status as social critics to be somewhat undercut, we have not, however, been rendered powerless. In our baggage we carry a variety of methods we use to work for social justice.

BIOETHICS' TRADITIONAL ACTIVIST METHODS

I have argued that bioethics reflects elements of both deliberative democracy and activism. In its theorizing and its clinical and public practice, bioethics not only relies on the norms of reason and the process of rational deliberation, but also interrogates those norms and appeals to considerations and constituencies outside the traditional deliberative space. If the "Georgetown mantra," first published in 1979, reflects bioethics' embrace of social justice and individual rights, Virginia Warren's urging ten years later that attention be paid to "housekeeping issues" may be seen as an activist refocusing of the principlist justice agenda (Beauchamp and Childress 1979; Warren 1989). Bioethical scholarship has taken up many of the key prescriptions of its feminist theorists: attend to structural inequities; include diverse perspectives, especially those of the less powerful; advocate for the material conditions necessary for autonomous choice to be effective and valuable; and recognize the import of people's dependence and relatedness. Combining activist methods of engaging an audience at an emotional level with activist goals of questioning the dominant discursive frame, we offer counternarratives as well as counterarguments. While we are mindful of the problems of representation and the pitfalls of presuming to speak on behalf of others, we give voice to perspectives of those who lack the standing or strength to present their own stories and advocate for their own interests (Nelson 2001b). We offer counternarratives for professionals, too; for example, we suggest that giving bad news sensitively is heroic and that following simple rules of etiquette *directly* expresses recognition of another's moral value (Buss 1999).

Although we seldom directly disrupt the health-care/research system ourselves, when it is obvious that the system is not working, we seek structural causes and solutions. In the interest of justice and beneficence, for example, we can endorse the aim of requiring that investigators set and achieve realistic targets for recruiting subjects into research studies. But we can point out undesirable ethical consequences of funding agencies' enforcing such targets by penalizing investigators who make reasonable recruitment efforts but fall short of enrolling the promised number of subjects. One consequence of such a punitive strategy is that investigators will soon learn to set their sights lower, be satisfied with slightly less powerful statistical results, and perhaps avoid trying to oversample in hard-to-recruit minority populations. A punitive regulatory approach does not address the underlying reasons for difficulty in recruiting psychiatric in-patients or people of color—namely, nonresearch clinicians lack incentives to take the time to refer to research protocols, and a legacy of mistrust and other more pressing concerns trump minority members' interest in participation.

In our theorizing, we do seek to disrupt dominant conceptual schemes and normative frames.[10] We suggest that "fragility" and dependence are not enemy states to be vanquished but preconditions for many forms of human flourishing (Parens 1995; Tronto 1993). We explore whose interests are neglected by such ostensible goods as evidence-based medicine or community consultation in research. Autonomy is not merely a capacity of individuals or the basis for their being ends in themselves, we argue, but an achievement that implicates others in our ends. We embody, employ, and directly argue for this "both/and" reasoning. In our theorizing, we are both scholarly and activist, and we struggle to use concepts while acknowledging their contingency and what they exclude (Butler 1991). Some might argue that to be true activists we need to reject forums of deliberation and the norms of reason. Yet most of us do not find institutional and political structures or the system of rational discourse so corrupted by the influence of power that we are willing to reject them wholesale, or perhaps we simply find it too hopeless to envision the intellectual and political realms following such wholesale rejection. Moreover, to the extent that as bioethicists we have power or celebrity to use to agitate for social change, much of that power and celebrity is drawn from our association with reasoned discourse and its ability to influence democratic process. So, in our attempt to effect social change, we simultaneously employ and interrogate norms. We use concepts and modes of argument while acknowledging their contingency and what (and who) they exclude. We engage in theory, reasoning, and activism.

Through the success of our clinical teaching and consultation services, we hope to render ourselves largely unnecessary. Except for teaching each new crop of students and assisting with the rare novel cases that arise, we try to equip clinicians to address ethical concerns without turfing the questions to us.[11] We try to teach them how to "fish" for ethical resolutions, rather than giving right answers, in hope that they will have ethical sustenance for a lifetime, not merely for as long as we are on rounds.

In our clinical ethics teaching, we not only transmit a body of bioethical information and model skills of ethical reasoning, but also attempt to develop our students' capacities for moral discernment and empathy. Some of us employ art and literature for the same reasons that Theodor Adorno urged attending to unfamiliar and difficult music: because it is valuable to learn to withhold facile understanding and thereby "resist the allure of false clarity in the world beyond the concert hall" (Eichler 2005). We provide tools not only to argue and analyze, but also to wonder and question (Young 2001), and we seek to focus that questioning on prevailing social practices and structures, including those within which we and they are engaged. We raise students' consciousness of inequities and reaffirm the moral sensibilities often numbed by the process of medical education. We suggest how our students can harness their passions, anger, frustrations, and grief to effect positive change in the lives of their patients (and the patients' families) and within the health care system and society. If we have evidence that harassment creates a hostile environment on one of the services through which our students rotate, we need to seek a resolution, thereby modeling the possibility, and responsibility, of protecting the vulnerable. In one sense, pursuing such evidence would be mere business-as-usual ethical action, even a case of following institutional policy. In another sense, investigating the stories of the vulnerable, using one's position and institutional policy to protect the weaker and pursue justice, would be a classic instance of activism.[12]

We also do well to acknowledge our own vulnerability and ethical failings in order to demonstrate the empowering effects of both giving voice to the imperfect and weak and illuminating the wrong. From my own failure to pursue evidence of sexual harassment—my failure to capitalize on the teachable moment, to pursue structural change, to do the right thing—I have gained the opportunity and responsibility to advance justice differently with a different audience (and to do the right thing next time). Like the ironically juxtaposed images in the *Times*, my combination of good intentions, power, vulnerability, lack of courage, and limited efficacy can serve to prompt reflection on the responsibility to try to create more just institutions.

If we think clearly about the substantive aims and specific methods associated with activism, it seems that bioethicists do engage in activism. Though we don't take to the streets, we take substantive moral positions and also seek to create tolerant venues in a pluralistic society in which others may do the same. We need to remain critical of the norms that construct such sites for debate and that constrain the conversations that result, and we need to take steps—in our theorizing and in sociopolitical practice—to expand access to such domains of discourse.

We need to be transparent about our own limitations and to illuminate the limitations, as well as the value, of deliberative processes. If we do this and teach others to do the same, bioethicists have the opportunity to storm barricades and strike down barriers in powerful yet, some would say, modest ways. This analysis is not novel, nor are the prescriptions radical; yet the claims and suggestions are neither conservative nor lacking in courage. It isn't easy to do well what bioethicists ought to do. When done well, bioethical work—especially bioethics teaching—is activist in its approach, method, and effect.

NOTES

1. This examination draws upon the analysis of Iris Marion Young (2001).

2. Live 8 was a series of rock concerts and protests mounted in July 2005 in an effort to pressure the Group of Eight nations to address African poverty through debt relief and direct aid. The article was Alan Cowell's "Celebrities' Embrace of Africa Has Critics," *New York Times*, July 1, 2005, A3.

3. Providing evidence that activist efforts may disappear in both the metaphorical and literal ocean, five pages later in the same issue of the *Times*, Marc Lacey's news brief, "Somalia: Pirates Seize Tsunami Aid Ship," reported on the diversion of 850 metric tons of rice donated by Japan and Germany intended for Somali tsunami victims. Of course, whether provision of direct aid, especially on the part of a foreign government, should be considered an act of activism may be debated, further suggesting the difficulty of characterizing activism.

4. By citing the collaboratively authored *Wikipedia: The Free Encyclopedia* (2005), I quite explicitly introduce a *popular* understanding of the word *activism*, which in avoiding ties to any particular substantive normative view or conception of justice, risks being too broad and vague to be useful. Moreover, in recent years, the meaning of the term has been complicated by its employ in political rhetoric, usually as a pejorative term, and especially with respect to so-called judicial activism. (See, for example, Gewirtz and Golder 2005.) In this rhetoric, the label of being "activist" has become largely meaningless beyond indicating the labeler's disapproval.

5. "Deliberative democracy" describes a system of political decision making that contends that the legitimacy of political decisions and lawmaking derives from the public deliberation of the citizens. To a greater extent than other democratic political theories, deliberative democracy emphasizes the development of coalitions and the importance of reflecting minority perspectives and interests in the outcome of democratic decision making.

6. Among the potential participants who may be excluded from public debate and consensus building are, problematically, those who lack the means to make their positions and interests known and those whose voices are intentionally ignored because they lack the power to make such neglect have consequences for those in power. Stone (2002) discusses

how emotionality, physical appearance, and modes of persuasion departing from traditional argumentative forms can lead some potential participants to be excluded from discourse in public policy and health care settings; see also Young (1996). These illegitimately excluded parties must be distinguished from those who are necessarily and appropriately excluded—at least from the substantive outcome of public debate, if not from the process—because they are "unreasonable" in Rawls's sense of being intolerant of others' incompatible substantive moral points of view and because their intolerance motivates activities undermining achievement of an overlapping consensus of reasonable positions and doctrines (Rawls 1996).

7. Bioethics panels and commissions are frequently criticized for failing to represent relevant normative positions. For example, on the Human Embryo Research Panel see Green (1995) and Kelly (2003); on the National Bioethics Advisory Commission see Pence (1998); and for his insider perspective on the Recombinant DNA Advisory Committee and criticisms of the President's Council on Bioethics, though not for his argument concerning political applications of behavioral genetic research, see Carmen (2004).

8. This observation is not incompatible with recognizing that reasoned discourse may also serve as a barrier to the exercise of raw power by the powerful over the vulnerable. Institutions and social practices that are structured by those in power are likely to disproportionately serve their interests, but they may also substantially benefit the less well-off.

9. In the first line quoted resides a primary reason that a substantial portion of the ASBH membership has been loath to amend the society's bylaws to permit the taking of stands on "substantive moral or policy issues." Some pragmatists within the organization oppose such bylaw change because of the energy that would likely be expended trying to achieve intraorganizational consensus on such issues, energy that could be applied directly to addressing the issue at hand.

10. Recognizing and pursuing this activist aspect of bioethics returns the field to epistemological and philosophy of science questions—i.e., to some of bioethics' academic origins—but with attention to the practical, political, or social import of the answers to those questions.

11. I develop this argument more fully and, I trust, convincingly in Parker (2005).

12. Here I intentionally use the phrase "*classic* instance of activism" and have in mind the *Oxford English Dictionary*'s definition of *activism:* "a doctrine or policy of advocating energetic action." Sometimes a just policy is in place, but activist energies must be exerted to pursue its application.

REFERENCES

American Society for Bioethics and Humanities (ASBH) Task Force on Standards for Bioethics Consultation. 1998. *Core Competencies for Health Care Ethics Consultation.* Glenview, IL: American Society for Bioethics and Humanities.

Andre, J. 2002. *Bioethics as Practice.* Chapel Hill: University of North Carolina Press.

Antommaria, A. H. M. 2004. A Gower maneuver: The American Society for Bioethics and

Humanities' resolution of the "taking stands" debate. *American Journal of Bioethics* 4 (1): W24–W27.

Beauchamp, T. L., and Childress, J. F. 1979. *The Principles of Biomedical Ethics.* New York: Oxford University Press.

Broad, C. D. 1952. *Ethics and the History of Philosophy.* London: Routledge and Kegan Paul.

Brock, D. W. 1993. *Life and Death: Philosophical Essays in Biomedical Ethics.* New York: Cambridge University Press. 55–79.

Buss, S. 1999. Appearing respectful: The moral significance of manners. *Ethics* 109: 795–826.

Butler, J. 1991. Imitation and gender insubordination. In D. Fuss, ed., *Inside/Out: Lesbian Theories, Gay Theories.* New York: Routledge.

Carmen, I. H. 2004. *Politics in the Laboratory: The Constitution of Human Genomics.* Madison: University of Wisconsin Press.

Collins, P. H. 1991. *Black Feminist Thought: Knowledge, Consciousness, and the Politics of Empowerment.* New York: Routledge.

Cowell, A. 2005. Celebrities' embrace of Africa has critics. *New York Times,* July 1: A3.

Crosthwaite, J. 1995. Moral expertise: A problem in the professional ethics of professional ethicists. *Bioethics* 9 (5): 361–79.

Eichler, J. 2005. A secular messiah gets his own opera. *New York Times,* July 17: AR24–25.

Evans, J. H. 2002. *Playing God: Human Genetic Engineering and the Rationalization of Public Bioethical Debate.* Chicago: University of Chicago Press.

Gewirtz, P., and Golder, C. 2005. So who are the activists? *New York Times,* July 6: A23.

Green, R. 1995. The human embryo research panel: Lessons for public ethics. *Cambridge Quarterly of Health Care Ethics* 4: 502–515.

Haslanger, S. 1993. On being objective and being objectified. In L. Antony and C. Witt, eds., *A Mind of One's Own: Feminist Essays on Reason and Objectivity.* Boulder, CO: Westview Press.

Hurtado, A. 1989. Relating to privilege: Seduction and rejection in the subordination of white women and women of color. *Signs* 14 (4): 833–55.

Jonsen, A. R. 1998. *The Birth of Bioethics.* New York: Oxford University Press.

Kelly, M. 2002. The meanings of professional life: Teaching across the health professions. *Journal of Medicine and Philosophy* 27 (4): 475–91.

Kelly, S. E. 2003. Public bioethics and publics: Consensus, boundaries, and participation in biomedical and science policy. *Science, Technology, and Human Values* 28 (3): 339–64.

Lerner, G. 1972. *Black Women in White America: A Documentary History.* New York: Vintage.

Mann, B. 2002. Talking back to feminist postmodernism: Toward a new radical feminist interpretation of the body. In R. Fiore and H. Nelson, eds., *Recognition, Responsibility and Rights: Feminist Ethics and Social Theory.* Lanham, MD: Rowman and Littlefield.

Nelson, H. L. 2001a. The ASBH "taking stands" debate. *ASBH Exchange* 4 (3): 1, 8.

———. 2001b. *Damaged Identities, Narrative Repair.* Ithaca, NY: Cornell University Press.

Parens, E. 1995. The goodness of fragility: On the prospect of technologies aimed at the enhancement of human capacities. *Kennedy Institute of Ethics Journal* 5 (2): 141–53.

Parker, L. S. 2005. Ethical expertise, maternal thinking, and the work of clinical ethicists.

In L. M. Rasmussen, ed., *Ethics Expertise: History, Contemporary Perspectives, and Applications*. Philosophy and Medicine Book Series. Dordrecht, The Netherlands: Springer.

Parsi, K. P., and Geraghty, K. E. 2004. The bioethicist as public intellectual. *American Journal of Bioethics* 4 (1): W17–W23.

Pence, G. E. 1998. *Who's Afraid of Human Cloning?* Lanham, MD: Rowman and Littlefield.

Rasmussen, L. M. 2005. *Ethics Expertise: History, Contemporary Perspectives, and Applications*. Philosophy and Medicine Book Series. Dordrecht, The Netherlands: Springer.

Rawls, J. 1996. *Political Liberalism*. New York: Columbia University Press.

Rothman, D. J. 1991. *Strangers at the Bedside: A History of How Law and Bioethics Transformed Medical Decision Making*. New York: Basic Books.

Scofield, G. R. 1994. Is the medical ethicist an "expert"? *Bioethics Bulletin* 3 (1): 1–2, 9–11.

Stevens, M. L. T. 2000. *Bioethics in America: Origins and Cultural Politics*. Baltimore: Johns Hopkins University Press.

Stone, J. 2002. Race and healthcare disparities: Overcoming vulnerability. *Theoretical Medicine* 23: 499–518.

Tong, R. 1991. The epistemology and ethics of consensus: Uses and misuses of "ethical" expertise. *Journal of Medicine and Philosophy* 16: 409–26.

Tronto, J. C. 1993. *Moral Boundaries: A Political Argument for an Ethic of Care*. New York: Routledge.

Warren, V. L. 1989. Feminist directions in medical ethics. In H. B. Holmes and L. M. Purdy, eds., *Feminist Perspectives in Medical Ethics*. Pp. 32–45. Bloomington: Indiana University Press.

Wikipedia. 2005. *Wikipedia: The Free Encyclopedia*, http://en.wikipedia.org/wiki/Activism.

Wikler, D. 1991. What has bioethics to offer health policy? *Milbank Quarterly* 69 (2): 233–51.

Wolf, S. M. 1996. Introduction: gender and feminism bioethics. In S. M. Wolf, ed., *Feminism and Bioethics: Beyond Reproduction*. Pp. 3–43. New York: Oxford University Press.

Young, I. M. 1996. Communication and the other: Beyond deliberative democracy. In S. Benhabib, ed., *Democracy and Difference: Contesting the Boundaries of the Political*. Pp. 120–35. Princeton: Princeton University Press.

———. 2001. Activist challenges to deliberate democracy. *Political Theory* 29 (5): 670–90.

PART IV

Contributions and Conflicts

Consultation in the Clinic and the Corporate World

CHAPTER THIRTEEN

Ethics on the Inside?

DEBRA A. DEBRUIN, PH.D.

It is, in practice, simply not possible to adopt such a critical attitude
towards an employer and at the same time provide good service.

(*Kazuo Ishiguro*, The Remains of the Day)

Bioethics has become "an accommodating handmaiden" (Callahan 1996, 3) to
the biomedical sciences, and in so doing, has "sold out" (Loewy 2002, 388). So
goes the concern, raised by a number (albeit a small one) of passionate voices in
the field. It is a very troubling worry, one that merits serious consideration. In this
chapter, I shall describe this criticism and assess its legitimacy. I shall address the
responsibility of individual bioethicists for responding to this concern. However,
I shall also insist that the institutions within which we work must share this responsibility.

THE CHARGE: BIOETHICS HAS "SOLD OUT"

Erich Loewy argues that bioethicists tend to cater to privilege:

The development of bioethics has been mainly focused on those who had good access to healthcare. Those with a lack of access have been given short shrift. Basic
healthcare provided to all within a given society has been the case in virtually all industrialized countries except for the United States since at least World War II, and
even longer in most cultures. Here in the United States, our main bioethics soci-

eties, and bioethicists as individuals, have tended to concentrate on individualistic ethics and its problems (euthanasia, abortion, termination of care, IVF, etc.) and have, to a large measure, practiced "rich man's ethics." The lack of access to health-care as well as many other faults have been labeled "system errors" and are in gen-eral considered to be beyond the responsibility of the bioethical profession. (Loewy 2002, 396)

Steven Miles agrees, and suggests a parallel between bioethicists' relative neglect of social justice concerns and the failure of Kitty Genovese's neighbors to raise the alarm despite their knowledge that she was being brutally murdered on the street outside their homes (Miles 1997, 97). Indeed, one of the most striking crit-icisms of bioethics that I have ever seen is currently displayed on Miles's office door. The display includes a poster captioned "One Week of U.S. Gun Deaths (ex-cluding nine not reported when poster was made)" that includes the photos of more than 450 victims of gun violence, along with a list compiled by Miles of all of the articles written by bioethicists on gun deaths in the past decade. The list is three items long.

These critics admit that some work in bioethics attends to issues of social jus-tice. Their complaint concerns the degree of attention paid to certain types of top-ics rather than others. As Miles explains, "This selectivity suggests a partial moral vision" (Miles 2002, 5). To protest the partiality of our vision is not to deny the importance of what we do see; it is to affirm the importance of the things we tend to overlook. A simple review of the bioethics literature reveals that it does, indeed, selectively attend to topics in individualistic ethics that tend to presume access to care rather than to social justice issues (Miles 2002, 2).

Daniel Callahan suggests bioethicists should be chastised not only for their ne-glect of certain types of topics, but also for the commentary they provide on the topics they do address:

> While bioethics creates problems now and then for mainstream, right-thinking trends, it mainly serves to legitimate them, adding the imprimatur of ethical exper-tise to what somebody or other wants to do. It is hardly likely that the National In-stitutes of Health (NIH) Human Genome Project would have set aside 5 percent of its annual budget for the Ethical, Legal, and Social Implications program if there had been even the faintest likelihood it would turn into a source of trouble and op-position; and it indeed hasn't. (Callahan 1996, 3)

Pandering constitutes a sell-out, indeed. Yet it is also difficult to establish that such pandering occurs; no simple literature search will suffice here, it seems. I shall not attempt to establish the charge in this chapter. Even Callahan admits that his generalization about the field is not entirely fair (Callahan 1996, 3), and it has certainly met with some resistance (Jonsen 1996, 4–5; Fox 1996, 5–7). Still, it should not be smugly disregarded, and I shall return to it shortly.

SEEKING THE ROOT OF THE PROBLEM

Bioethics' harshest critics tend to agree that the problems they cite have developed as the field has matured. It is standardly acknowledged that bioethics began as a reformist enterprise, and its commitment to the individualistic values of respect and liberty has fostered valuable changes in policy and the practice of biomedicine.

> Bioethics really started as an inquiry into the largely uncontrolled practices, habits, and proceedings of the medical structure and profession. In doing this inquiry it had to adopt a position of being neither inside nor outside the activity itself—that is, bioethicists required a basic understanding of what medicine and the practice of medicine were all about in addition to having enough distance from medicine to ask sometimes troubling and often very troubling and vexing questions. . . . Today . . . the problem is that ethicists have begun to be identified with (and, more disastrously, have begun to identify themselves with) the establishment instead of remaining fence-straddlers who understand but are not integral parts of regular medical institutions and maintain their independence to question and to criticize. (Loewy 2002, 392–93)

That is, Loewy contends that bioethicists have come to hold insider status, and thus have become accommodating handmaidens rather than reformers.

Perhaps Loewy's generalization is a bit too broad. Does it apply equally to those who work within the context of biomedical institutions (academic health centers, for example) and those who work outside that context (in departments of philosophy, for example)? I personally do not (any longer) live in that latter sort of institutional context, and so do not feel qualified to speak about it. Some bioethicists of my acquaintance who do work in such contexts have privately confessed to feeling like outsiders. I do come from such a context, however—a philosopher by training and previous employment—though I now work in a biomedical setting. Much to my surprise, since I arrived here I have never felt as though my colleagues in medicine—where my tenure home is located—have treated me as an outsider. Of course, issues of my own sense of my identity are somewhat separate from those of how I am treated. Am I an insider if others define me as such, or only if I (also?) so define myself?

On the other hand, working within a biomedical context does not seem to automatically grant one insider status, since some individuals of my acquaintance who do work in such contexts feel relegated to the outside (nurses, for example, or allied health professionals, whose work may be subordinated within the hierarchy of biomedicine). Thus it appears that one's status as an insider or outsider relates not only to where one works but to other factors as well. Admittedly, limited accounts of personal experience hardly justify the drawing of any robust general inferences. Still, the matter of whether bioethicists count as insiders or outsiders—and why that may be so—appears to be a complicated one.

Still, some bioethicists have acknowledged that they not only have become identified with the biomedical establishment, but that they have actively pursued such status.

> I do not by any means exclude myself or the Hastings Center from this observation. We courted legitimacy, sought money from the big foundations, tried to make it in the higher reaches of academia, and endlessly worked to persuade physicians and biomedical researchers that we should be seen as allies and not as opponents. That was not a pose. We felt that way and worked to convey that feeling. We succeeded. . . . We became insiders by default, without ever resolving in any full way the question of whether those who pursue bioethics should be insiders or outsiders. (Callahan 1996, 3)

This question cuts to the core of bioethics' identity as a field, and to its moral legitimacy. It admits of no simple answer.

MORAL IMPLICATIONS OF OUR
INSTITUTIONAL SITUATEDNESS

As Callahan's account of the growth of the Hastings Center (quoted above) suggests, much good can come from insider status. Close familiarity with the work of biomedicine allows our work to be informed and relevant in a way that a more distant perspective might not. An alliance with health professionals can help our work to be more effective, since they may be more open to our message if they view us as partners rather than opponents. Institutional acceptance may assist in providing needed support for our work. We needn't be sycophants to appreciate the value of insider status.

However, we must recognize that our work is in some ways shaped by the biomedical context in which we (at least some of us) function. If our promotion and tenure depends upon our record of NIH funding and publication in respected biomedical journals, then the topics that we address will be shaped, in part, by this requirement. If the NIH is more likely to fund projects on best practices for research ethics education than projects on gun violence, then those funding priorities will shape our work. If prestigious medical journals are more likely to publish work on stem cells than on disaster relief, then those publication priorities will shape our work. If our institution views the mission of bioethics as being one of service to biomedicine, then our time and attention will be devoted to matters of clinical ethics consultation, or training in the responsible conduct of research, or teaching medical students about informed consent. Institutional forces shape our work. To some extent, that is inevitable; it is simply the nature of institutions that they affect the work that is done within them.

Yet to some extent, in the case of bioethics and its institutions, it is also morally troubling. Our work may be compromised if we become too beholden to the institutions of biomedicine for our support. No ethicist worth her salt would condone the sentiment expressed by the fictional Mr. Stevens in the epigraph to this chapter. We should be troubled by his vision that professionals achieve dignity through unquestioning loyalty to their employers. Such a suspension of critical thinking cannot be consistent with the work of bioethics. But wherein lies the dignity of our profession, when, as I have argued, our institutions influence the topics we take up? This is not a morally neutral description of our work. Our partial moral vision results in neglect of topics of great moral importance.

And the worry is more complicated than simple neglect. Miles suggests that, in part, bioethics' partial moral vision reflects the emphasis in Western (especially American) culture on individualism: "American Bioethics partly reflects a national culture in which respect for liberty often eclipses a sense of social justice. Bioethicists' substantial focus on issues like genetics or new reproductive technologies over issues like unaffordable health care reflects this culture" (Miles 2002, 5). However apt this observation, as Miles acknowledges, it alone cannot account for the partiality of bioethics' vision. For example, it cannot explain why bioethicists ignore the assault on our culturally cherished individualistic values of life, health, and liberty caused by gun violence, while we champion those values in the discussion of new technologies in health care. Or why we are eager to discuss some issues of justice, such as the allocation of organs for transplant, while we give scant attention to others, such as lack of access to care or the affirmation by the Universal Declaration of Human Rights that persons have a right to a standard of living adequate to promote health. Or why it was "politicians, not bioethicists, ensconced in health care centers, [who] condemned the practice of dumping patients from hospitals" (Miles 2002, 5; cf. Loewy 2002, 390). Western bioethics may be born of its culture, but we must say more than that to explain the partiality of its vision, and thus its neglect of vital topics.

Bioethicists' neglect reflects the interests of our patrons. We are responsible for scrutinizing the practices and structures of biomedicine, but the institutions of biomedicine set our agenda. Admittedly, this overstates the case somewhat (to make a point). But this sort of inherent conflict should give us all pause. Of course, this does not necessarily mean that we say simply what these institutions would like to hear, that our analysis of the topics we address reflects their interests. But caution is warranted here, too. If our livelihood depends on the support of biomedical institutions, then we may feel pressure to please our patrons. If we accept corporate money for our work (corporate consulting, seats on corporate boards, industry-funded honoraria for talks, etc.), we may compromise our judgment and betray the trust that others have in our work. As Carl Elliott puts the point,

> it is a rare corporation that will continue to fund bioethicists who are constantly and publicly criticizing corporate policy. This does not mean that corporations are morally suspect. It means that it is not good business to give money to the very people who are criticizing your marketing practices in the developing world, who are calling for a halt to your stem cell research, who are lobbying to place limits on the life of your drug patents, or who are attempting to block your clinical trials. The fact that this is not good business is exactly why bioethicists should be wary. . . . I worry that each corporate check cashed takes us one step closer to the notion of ethics as a commodity, a series of canned lectures, white papers, and consultation services to be purchased by the highest bidder and itemized on an annual budget report. (Elliott 2001, 11)

While we may vehemently deny that we pander to our patrons, we nevertheless should be wary of possible—or even perceived—institutional influences on our judgment. Thus institutional forces may influence not only the topics we take up but also the analyses we provide of them. Although we reject the unquestioning loyalty of the misguided Mr. Stevens, these institutional forces may compromise our ability to speak critically, and so undermine the dignity—the moral legitimacy—of our profession.

HOW SHOULD BIOETHICISTS NAVIGATE THESE PERILS?

Thus far, bioethicists appear to be damned if we do embrace insider status, and damned if we don't. Yet Erich Loewy rejects Callahan's suggestion that bioethicists must make this choice. He contends that there is a middle ground between the inside and the outside, and it is on this middle ground that we ought to locate ourselves. In his view, we ought to be fence-straddlers (Loewy 2002, 393). We need to be near enough to the institutions of biomedicine to truly understand them, but detached and independent enough to avoid problematic influences on our work.

Renée Fox and Judith Swazey suggest still another model for our work. They describe their work on organ transplantation as a sort of field work, and cite Margaret Mead's characterization of field work as involving the "cumulative experience of immersing oneself in the ongoing life of another people, suspending for the time both one's beliefs and disbeliefs, and of simultaneously attempting to understand mentally and physically this other version of reality. . . . Immersing oneself in the field is good, but one must be careful not to drown. One must somehow maintain the delicate balance between empathic participation and self-awareness, on which the whole research process depends" (Mead 1977, 1, 7; as cited by Fox and Swazey 1992, 9). Fox and Swazey did, indeed, immerse themselves in another culture, albeit not one to be found in "geographically and culturally isolated primitive villages" (Fox and Swazey 1992, 9). They acknowledge that the people involved in transplantation that they studied were both their teachers and their research subjects. They insist that their association with these individuals was not the academic detachment of Loewy's fence-straddler but an empathic sharing of their reality. They were, they contend, insiders (Fox and Swazey 1992, 9). Yet they never lost their own perspectives, and what they learned left them extremely troubled by the implications of such heroic medicine for both those who have and those who lack access to it.

I leave it to others to assess the relative epistemological merits of these two models of knowledge-seeking: that of the detached fence-straddler and that of the empathic insider. It is most relevant to the work of this chapter to note that neither model completely resolves the moral issues that concern us here. That is, neither model removes the day-to-day tensions and perils posed by our work within our institutions. Both require moral vigilance—the straddler's vigilance that he does not fall off the fence, the field worker's vigilance that she does not drown in the culture in which she is immersed. Such vigilance may be especially difficult to maintain in the face of institutional pressures, but it is necessary nevertheless.

INSTITUTIONAL RESPONSIBILITIES

But the burden should not rest completely on individual bioethicists. Indeed, given the effect of institutions on our work, it cannot. Miles is right when he declares, "Some say that we respond to the issues demanded by our 'market' of donors, sponsors, students, and institutions. This passive definition of the content of teaching demeans us" (Miles draft, 6). We cannot simply pass the buck and attribute responsibility for our failures to the institutions within which we work. However, we must also recognize that we do not work as isolated individuals, but as members of communities, in the context of institutions. It is far too simplistic, and quite unfair, to place full blame for the failures of bioethics on individual bioethicists themselves. We have, indeed, become the handmaidens of biomedicine. It does not follow that we have sold out.

Our institutions bear responsibility as well. They should guarantee our freedom to speak, to conduct our work responsibly. Our institutions fail to satisfy this requirement if they simply refrain from overtly pressuring us to take up certain topics or advocate particular views. As we have seen, institutional priorities and requirements concerning funding, publication, service, and promotion and tenure all can exert problematic influence on our work. Systems can and should be designed (or redesigned) to help avoid these difficulties. Our institutions' obligations follow from their commitment to pursue excellence, to foster the free exchange of ideas, and to promote responsibility in the biosciences (as well as other disciplines). In addition, institutions have an instrumental reason to enable our work, if they wish to attract and retain talented bioethicists.

The center that employs me celebrated its twentieth anniversary last year. We chose to meet this milestone by not only honoring our past but also by explicitly pondering what our future ought to be. An open dialogue on these issues is sorely needed. Our departments and centers of bioethics, as well as our professional organizations, bear special responsibility for promoting such dialogue. How should we understand our identity, our work as bioethicists? How should that work be enabled? These organizations are best situated to include the diversity of individual voices in this dialogue. They are also best placed to advocate for the needs of bioethicists in the broader institutional contexts within which we work (academic health centers, departments of philosophy, etc.).

Should departments and centers of bioethics be administratively independent to ensure their intellectual and moral independence (as opposed to housed within departments of medicine, for instance)? Should they accept or refuse corporate

funding? How can we help (re)direct NIH funding priorities and biomedical journal publication practices? How can the importance of our service be recognized,
and its place in our overall duties be calculated to enable our work as scholars and
activists with moral visions of our own? How can promotion and tenure requirements be revised to acknowledge that bioethicists do not fit the molds of standard
disciplines? Bioethicists who work within philosophy may conduct empirical research, and so deviate from their discipline's norms. Bioethicists who work
within biomedicine will face similar difficulties, in conducting research, securing funding, and producing publications that may depart from biomedicine's
standards. Our work may be quite unpopular, and safeguards may need to be built
into the review process to ensure fairness.

I have tried, in this chapter, to explicate some of bioethics' most fundamental
challenges. I have argued that both individual bioethicists and the institutions
within which we work bear responsibility for meeting these challenges. There are,
I fear, no easy answers to the questions that these reflections raise. But that is true
of many of the most important questions we confront. It would be a pity indeed
if these challenges were to create such a crisis of confidence that we despair and
so fail to meet them. Since these are not purely issues of individual responsibility, there will be limits to what individuals can accomplish working alone. However, recognition of the challenges presents an opportunity for further dialogue
about how to understand them and work together to meet them. We must seize
this opportunity if we are to reclaim the dignity of our profession.

REFERENCES

Callahan, D. 1996. Bioethics, our crowd, and ideology. *Hastings Center Report* 26(6): 3.
Elliott, C. 2001. Throwing a bone to the watchdog. *Hastings Center Report* 31(2): 9–12.
Fox, R. C. 1996. More than bioethics. *Hastings Center Report* 26(6): 5–7.
Fox, R. C., and Swazey, J. P. 1992. Leaving the field. *Hastings Center Report* 22(5): 9–15.
Ishiguro, K. 1988. *The Remains of the Day.* New York: Vintage International.
Jonsen, A. R. 1996. Bioethics, whose crowd, and what ideology? *Hastings Center Report* 26(6): 4–5.
Loewy, E. H. 2002. Bioethics: past, present, and an open future. *Cambridge Quarterly of Healthcare Ethics* 11(4): 388–97.
Mead, M. 1977. *Letters from the Field, 1925–1975.* New York: Harper and Row.
Miles, S. 1997. Is bioethics one of Kitty Genovese's neighbors? *APA Newsletter on Philosophy and Medicine* 97(1): 11–13.
———. 2002. Does American bioethics have a soul? *Bioethics Examiner* 6(2): 1, 2, 5.
———. Draft manuscript. Medical ethics on the Richter scale.

CHAPTER FOURTEEN

Strategic Disclosure Requirements and the Ethics of Bioethics

VIRGINIA A. SHARPE, PH.D.

"NO CONFLICT, NO INTEREST": THE COMMERCIALIZATION OF SCIENCE AND ACADEMIA

Although there are historical, conceptual, and economic obstacles that make it difficult to address the ethics of bioethics, the need for such reflection is made more urgent by the growing commercialization of science and academia. Over the last twenty-five years, a number of forces have spurred this commercialization. One was the passage of the 1980 Bayh-Dole Act (Patent and Trademark Act 1980) authorizing licensing and patenting of results from U.S. federally sponsored research. That law has given rise to technology transfer programs at the nation's private and public institutions, creating new incentives for academic entrepreneurialism and partnerships with industry. Many legislatures, hoping to spur economic growth in their states, have championed the development of research corridors anchored to partnerships between corporations and public research universities. Entrepreneurial faculty members with the blessing and sometimes the backing of their universities are starting their own companies as a sideline to their university appointments. Between 1992 and 1999 industry-funded research and development at public and private universities grew exponentially, with up to a 725 percent increase at some of the largest state universities (Lawler 2003). Since 1980 more than 4,300 start-up companies have been formed based on a license from an academic institution. These institutions received an equity interest in close to 70 percent of their start-ups and collected over $1 billion in royalties from patent licensing (Stevens and Toneguzzo 2003).

Bart Chernow, the vice dean for research at the Johns Hopkins University medical school has even gone so far as to trumpet Hopkins as "one of the biggest biotech companies in the world" (Birch and Cohn 2001, 1A). Like this university leader, many have enthusiastically embraced business development within academia, pointing to the potential for important scientific advances and to the benefits of this new revenue to the competitiveness of universities and to the states and regions in which they are located. It is also generally acknowledged, however, that such arrangements introduce significant conflicts of interest—placing researchers' and academic institutions' proprietary or sponsorship interests in conflict with their responsibility to maintain integrity in research and teaching (Washburn 2005). On this subject, the Hopkins vice dean has argued that the school's new partnerships with industry are essential to the school's success and competitiveness. "To move your research forward, you've got to do partnerships with industry. . . . No conflict, no interest" (Birch and Cohn 2001, 1A).

WHO IS BUYING BIOETHICS?

As Carl Elliott has so ably described (2003), commercial affiliations are also increasingly common in the world of bioethics. The AMA Ethics Institute receives funding from the drug industry to develop a code of ethics for the drug industry, Pfizer funds bioethicists at the University of Pennsylvania to write on the ethics of pharmaceutical gift-giving, and Dow, DuPont, and Monsanto have funded that center's development of an ethics code for the biotechnology industry. Individual bioethicists receive funding as consultants on industry advisory boards or as speakers at industry-sponsored conferences.

As in industry-funded science, industry funding to bioethicists has the potential to bias the particular funded work in favor of the sponsor's interests—the usual focus of concerns about conflicts of interest. It also, and more importantly, has the potential to set the agenda of the field by influencing the scope and focus of bioethical work. Imagine, for example, that bioethics as a field of inquiry has developed primarily in response to issues concerning the biosphere and human activity. The focal issues for bioethicists in this scenario are the role of human activities and our responsibilities regarding the health of global, regional, and local ecosystems and human communities. Bioethicists weigh in on issues such as land use, environmental justice, air and water quality, agricultural biotechnology, habitat and species management, and global warming. Imagine that bioethicists have become key players in the area of environmental policy and it has become common to include a bioethicist on environmental task forces. The higher profile that bioethicists have gained outside of academia has been accompanied by an increase in centers focusing on bioethics degree-granting programs for aspiring bioethicists and also an increase in funding to those programs from environmentally interested parties.

Now imagine a few funding scenarios. On the issue of land use, prominent bioethicists and their bioethics center have received grant funding from property developers and property-rights associations to address the ethical implications of a ballot initiative to financially compensate landowners for restrictive land-use regulations. The funding, which comes with "no strings attached," is to be used to convene a group of stakeholders to address "property rights and unconstitutional takings." The products of the grant are expected to be a "white paper," a few op-eds, and a survey on property rights. In this "no strings attached" grant, the money, in fact, comes with a predefined research agenda that privileges the question of property rights. The fundamental question of what effects the new land-use provisions will have on streams, forests, and soils is not on the table—and not likely to be if funding comes from sources that are principally interested in preserving property rights. The research products, scheduled to be presented in the month leading up to the election on which the initiative appears, are likely to have an impact on the vote.

On the issue of environmental justice, a chemical company, previously involved in a massive and harmful spill, would like to understand its corporate responsibilities with regard to compensation of largely minority homeowners near a current polluting facility. It engages a bioethicist to serve as a consultant both to meet with homeowners and to advise the company regarding what is owed to homeowners in fair compensation. In this scenario, the consultation is designed to focus strictly on compensatory justice as a response to industrial hazards. Broader conceptions of social justice, including power differentials between communities and hazardous industries as well as decision-making processes and the disproportionate distribution of risk in minority communities, are not on the consultant's agenda because these are not the immediate concerns of the funder. As an emissary of the company, the bioethicist engaged with community members will have a hard time looking beyond the immediate issue of compensation to broader questions of procedural and social justice.

Suppose that on the issue of genetically modified organisms, a number of agricultural bioethicists have been invited to attend a symposium called "Feeding the

World" sponsored by a major agricultural biotechnology company. At the symposium, a $10,000 prize is announced for the best paper submitted to the company on "An Ethical Argument for GMOs." A symposium on "Feeding the World" with GMOs is not likely to mention that, as Nobel laureate Amartya Sen has demonstrated, inefficient food distribution and poverty, rather than an absolute shortage of food, are the causes of famine (Sen 1981). And certainly, the winning paper on "An Ethical Argument for GMOs" could become an important part of GMO marketing, especially as authorship rights would belong to the company.

Of course the work of bioethicists doesn't focus principally on environmental matters. Instead, as is well known, the field of bioethics evolved to favor bio*medical* matters emphasizing human research, death and dying, genetics, and reproduction as foundational issues. So, although none of the examples in the thought experiment are strictly true, if you change the research focus slightly and substitute "scientist" or "bio*medical* ethicist" in each example, you have a picture of the background conditions that increasingly accompany the practice of science, clinical medicine, and bioethics in the United States.

Recently, for example, pharmaceutical company Eli Lilly initiated a public relations campaign called "The Ethics, the Urgency, the Potential" to promote its $6,800-per-treatment drug Xigris for severe sepsis. As the public relations company president put it, "the premise [of the campaign] was that it was unethical *not* to use the drug" (Regalado 2003, 1A). As part of the effort, Lilly funded a $1.8 million project called "Values, Ethics, and Rationing in Critical Care Task Force." The task force, which included a number of prominent bioethicists, received an "unrestricted" eighteen-month educational grant to study "Intensive Care Unit (ICU) rationing practices, attitudes and behaviors among U.S. critical care physicians, nurses and hospital administrators." In keeping with its funder's interests, the task force Web site lists Xigris, commonly known as protein C, as a "life-saving medication ranking high on the 'to-be-rationed' list" (VERICC Taskforce 2003). Independent studies of Xigris have not found the drug to be appreciably more effective than the standard $50 treatment.

Carl Elliott has pointed out the dangers of an uncritical embrace of such relationships. In a recent paper, he provides a detailed account of the ghost writing and publication strategies used by pharmaceutical companies to influence medical education, practice, and the medical literature. Bioethicists who take industry money, he warns, are also part of these strategies. "Still," he says, "we cling to the vast collective delusion that because we cannot see a provable causal link between funding and our own individual behavior, no real influence has been exerted" (Elliott 2004, 22).

WHY IS IT SO HARD TO THINK ABOUT
THE ETHICS OF BIOETHICS?

Industry funding constitutes only one (growing) source of support for bioethicists. Historically, external funding and, often, salary support in bioethics has been tied to the medical profession and mostly nonprofit health care institutions. As Tina Stevens has argued, American bioethics' historical focus on the products of biomedicine and on the professional goals of medicine has, ever since the emergence of the discipline over thirty years ago, largely displaced broader reflection on social critiques of the role of science in society (Stevens 2000, 28). For example, argues Stevens, the early commitment by the Hastings Center, the world's first independent bioethics institute, to a nonactivist, "apolitical" mission has resulted in a methodology that emphasizes "ethics management" rather than social critique. As Hastings Center co-founder Dan Callahan observed, the premise of this approach was "Tell us what you want to do and we'll tell you how to do it ethically" (Stevens 2000, 66). Stevens's historical analysis is a good reminder of how the early allegiances of bioethics—and the tendency of its funders to reward moderate positions—helped to constitute the field as more conciliatory than critical, more enabling than challenging.

A similar point has been made by John Evans in his book on the role of bioethics in human genetic experimentation (Evans 2002). According to Evans, the model of consensus decision making common in public bioethics has resulted in the dominance of means-ends reasoning, over more substantive discussions about the appropriate ends of scientific research. The formal rationality that came to characterize bioethics was especially suited to determining the most efficacious means for achieving predetermined ends. If Stevens and Evans are right in their analyses, then it is no wonder that bioethicists have difficulty talking about the ethics of bioethics: *it is impossible to talk adequately about the ethics of bioethics without talking about the ends or substantive commitments of the field.*

The field has also been substantially shaped by its close connection to clinical medicine—with its normative focus on duties to the individual. This connection has produced a field that, in general, has placed secondary importance on population health issues and the investigation of the political and economic factors that produce ill health and health disparities. Also the field, especially as it has developed in North America and western Europe, has been shaped by its grounding in liberal democratic political and philosophical traditions that give paramount importance to individual autonomy. These traditions, which regard the self as essentially prior to and independent of its "ends," tend to emphasize individual agency at the expense of insights about how agency is actually influenced by, indeed constituted by, social factors and relationships. Importantly, each of these influences predisposes the field to the individualistic orientation of the market.

Apart from political and philosophical influences that steer the field away from substantive normative commitments and toward individual autonomy, there is another obvious obstacle to reflection on the ethics of bioethics: the range of disciplines that make up the field and the variation in training and bioethical work. Bioethicists constitute a motley crew. We come from disciplines in the humanities, social sciences, business and health administration, and professional disciplines such as public health, medicine, nursing, chaplaincy, law, and education. Some who have had only the minimal one- or two-week training offered in intensive courses are identified as ethicists within their institutions, while some people who are recognized as leaders in the field do not refer to themselves as bioethicists at all.

The norms that *do* explicitly inform bioethics practice often come from the individual's foundational discipline. Clinicians are guided by a primary obligation to patients, lawyers to clients, educators to students. The importance of these professional moorings is one reason why people have objected to bioethics as a freestanding discipline. The underlying question again is what does it mean, in terms of one's normative commitments, to have a degree in "bioethics"? And if the resources that sustain bioethics education and bioethics institutions increasingly come from the commercial sector, will the norms of the marketplace—competition, self-interest, secrecy, caveat emptor—also become the norms of bioethics?

Even without particular professional or disciplinary norms, bioethicists employed within institutions are, still, as with any employee, bound by institutional requirements regarding conflicts of interest, outside activities, and the use of proprietary information. Absent an "ethics of bioethics," that is, absent substantive norms to guide bioethical practice, however, it is not clear how competing obligations in these contexts are to be resolved, or, for that matter, recognized. For example, in the recent report of the Task Force on Bioethics Consultation in the Private Sector (Brody et al. 2002), the problem of conflicts of interest figures most prominently as conflicts one might have in addressing similar issues with two competing corporate clients, *not* as conflicts between obligations one might have first as a bioethicist and, second, as a corporate consultant. Likewise, as champions of private-sector consultation, the Task Force emphasizes the need to *balance* openness and client confidentiality, going so far as to say that a bioethicist who feels an obligation to be a whistleblower "should offer the client, at the highest level, the opportunity to respond before and in place of public disclosure" (Brody et al. 2002, 19). This only makes sense if respecting the contractual agreement with the client is regarded as one's highest duty.

DISCLOSURE AS A STRATEGIC REQUIREMENT
FOR BIOETHICS IN THE PUBLIC INTEREST

In an earlier piece I argued that bioethicists should serve public not private interests (Sharpe 2002). Although one could make any number of arguments about exactly what constitutes the "public interest," there is general agreement that it is served by a commitment to transparency: the provision of clear, relevant, and comprehensible information to the public enabling people to make informed decisions. I argued that, at the very least, an ethics of bioethics requires bioethicists to provide information on their funding sources to colleagues, students, and the public. There are two responses to this call for disclosure that are worth noting. One, by Lynn Jansen and Dan Sulmasy, is that disclosure requirements go too far, the other, by Carl Elliott, that disclosure does not go far enough.

In a response to my article calling for disclosure as a *minimum* requirement for bioethicists, Jansen and Sulmasy argued that disclosure requirements go too far when they supplant critical appraisal of an argument with information that is prejudicial—either favorably or unfavorably—to the author. Disclosure of conflict-of-interest information, they argue, invites the same sort of biased reading that may follow from learning of an author's race, gender, sexual preference, or other arbitrary characteristic. Normative arguments, they say, should speak for themselves. If they aren't allowed to, we risk undermining the value of reasoned argument (Jansen and Sulmasy 2003).

What is missing from this argument is the insight from feminist epistemology that all knowledge is situated—socially, psychologically, and politically (Harding 1991). This does not mean that knowledge claims are pernicious in their biases but that we need to be up front about the way our own situated knowledge presupposes, expresses, and reinforces our commitments to a particular distribution of power (Rorty 1988, 21). Disclosure of the financing behind bioethical work is a marker of the political and social projects that constitute that work and that are constituted by it. As such, disclosure is an essential component of bioethics in the public interest.

In Carl Elliott's view, "disclosure is an empty ritual designed to ease the consciences of academics unable to wean themselves from the industry payroll" (Elliott 2004, 22). Although Elliott may be right that disclosure is a salve for some, from a public-interest point of view disclosure is a strategic requirement that can be used to reveal the political alignment of a field and to connect the dots that reveal an otherwise obscure picture of industry influence. As we know from the documents from the Master Settlement Agreement in the litigation against tobacco companies, the knowledge gained from the (in these cases, *forced*) disclosure of information has been vital in revealing the pervasive influence of these companies on academics, academic institutions, and the published literature (Legacy Tobacco Documents Library; Glanz et al. 1996; Freedman and Cohen 1993).

In line with Elliott's skepticism, it is also important to point out that disclosure can be frankly counterproductive. As I have pointed out elsewhere (Sharpe 2003), disclosure (via warning labels or statements) can be a stratagem to shift responsibility from the producers of risk or known harms to the individual, who may not understand what he or she is being told. As we know from the literature about tobacco companies and lead paint manufacturers (Markowitz and Rosner 2002) who continue(d) to aggressively market products that they know to be deadly, warning labels can be a cynical strategy adopted in order to protect the discloser from liability. Likewise, disclosure of potentially biasing financial ties by bioethicists, clinicians, or researchers can also be a way of shifting responsibility to the person who "chooses" to assume a risk and away from the one who imposes it. This is the "informed consumer" model of responsibility that is the basis for caveat emptor. On the other hand, disclosure can be understood as a way of empowering participation and supporting an individual's or a community's "right to know."

If we accept that disclosure is not the best or even a good way of fulfilling one's moral obligations (for example, few would argue that the disclosure "Honey, I'm cheating on you" is a satisfactory way of fulfilling one's obligation of fidelity), the question then becomes whether disclosure requirements can be used as an effective *strategic* mechanism, especially in circumstances in which the nature of moral obligation is contested, as is increasingly the case in science, academia, and bioethics. I believe we have come to that point. The influence of commercial interests is so pervasive and commercial marketing is itself so strategic that in order to grasp this influence we need to be able to "connect the dots." Information about who gets money from where and for what purposes is essential to constructing this picture.

So, although disclosure has clear deficiencies as a mechanism of substantive moral accountability, disclosure requirements serve an essential strategic purpose, allowing us to understand how funding might influence findings and entire research agendas on matters of importance to public policy, public health, and public safety. Yes, the demand for disclosure implies distrust, but it also helps us to determine what the basis for trust is, that is, what the appropriate normative behaviors *should* be. The Toxic Release Inventory (TRI) provides an example. As part of the Emergency Planning and Community Right-to-Know Act of 1986, the TRI required companies to disclose their annual releases of toxic chemicals into the environment so that local, state, and federal governments could get a sense of existing practice. Despite the limitations of the TRI, it turned out that the disclosure requirement itself was a sufficient prompt for industries to reduce their toxic emissions over 45 percent between 1988 and 1995 (Graham 2002, 24). So, the disclosure requirement, and the sense of public shame that it seems to have produced, prompted a commitment to otherwise neglected normative behaviors.

CONCLUSIONS AND RECOMMENDATIONS

The ethics of bioethics is a hard subject not simply because it makes us hold ourselves up to moral scrutiny, but also because there are so many features of the discipline—conceptual, historical, and political—that stand as obstacles to this line of inquiry. It's also an especially hard subject because of economic interests and the growing commercialism of all fields of knowledge. Some bioethicists, like many academics, scientists, and academic institutions, are embracing support from commercial entities, thinking somehow that this will not adversely affect their work or the norms that guide it. Some see these affiliations as an economic necessity, some see them as an essential part of practical ethics, some see them as impossible to avoid given the institutional commitments over which they have no direct control. In the absence of collective refusal, I have argued that robust disclosure of financial ties should be a *minimum* requirement of all bioethicists in all venues where they teach, write, or make statements to the public. Given that money tends to encourage conformity and to obscure moral obligations, silence about the sources of our funding assures that we will make little headway on the ethics of bioethics.

As some modest recommendations on the task of an ethics of bioethics, I would suggest that there be no degrees granted in an independent field of bioethics, but rather that degrees be granted in professional fields that have articulated guiding norms; that curricula in bioethics include courses on the politics and sociology of science, as well as on the politics and sociology of bioethics, the commercialization of science and bioethics, and conflicts of interest; and that all of us work hard to strengthen both conflict-of-interest standards and institutional protections for academic freedom. But as we do this, we should keep in mind George Bernard Shaw's admonition that "all professions are a conspiracy against the laity" (Shaw 1946). We should guard against concentrating power among ourselves, rather than transferring it to the public.

NOTE

This work is not intended to represent the views of the Department of Veterans Affairs, where I work as a medical ethicist, or of the U.S. government.

REFERENCES

Birch, D. M., and Cohn, G. 2001. The changing creed of Hopkins science. *Baltimore Sun,* June 25.

Brody, B., Dubler, N., Blustein, J., Caplan, A., Kahn, J. P., Kass, N., Lo, B., Moreno, J., Sugarman, J., and Zoloth, L. 2002. Bioethics consultation in the private sector. *Hastings Center Report* 32(3): 14–20.

Elliott, C. 2003. Not-so-public relations: How the drug industry is branding itself with bioethics. *Slate,* December 15. http://slate.msn.com/id/2092442.

———. 2004. Pharma goes to the laundry: Public relations and the business of medical education. *Hastings Center Report* 34(5): 18–23.

Evans, J. H. 2002. *Playing God?: Human Genetic Engineering and the Rationalization of Public Bioethical Debate.* Chicago: University of Chicago Press.

Freedman, A. M., and Cohen, L. 1993. Smoke and mirrors: How cigarette makers keep health question "open" year after year. *Wall Street Journal,* February 11.

Glanz, S., Slade, J., Bero, L. A., et al. 1996. *The Cigarette Papers.* Berkeley: University of California Press.

Graham, M. 2002. *Democracy by Disclosure: The Rise of Technopopulism.* Washington, DC: Brookings.

Harding, S. 1991. *Whose Science? Whose Knowledge? Thinking from Women's Lives.* Ithaca: Cornell University Press.

Jansen, L. A., and Sulmasy, D. P. 2003. Bioethics, conflicts of interest, and the limits of transparency. *Hastings Center Report* 33(4): 40–43.

Lawler, A. 2003. Last of the big-time spenders? *Science* 299(5605): 330–33. Available at www.sciencemag.org/cgi/content/full/299/5605/330.

Legacy Tobacco Documents Library at http://legacy.library.ucsf.edu.

Markowitz, G., and Rosner, D. 2002. *Deceit and Denial: The Deadly Politics of Industrial Pollution.* Berkeley, CA: University of California Press.

Patent and Trademark Act Amendments of 1980. (Bayh-Dole Act) 1982. Pub. L. No. 96-517, 94 Stat. 3019 (codified at 35 U.S.C. §§200-11 [1982]).

Regalado, A. 2003.To sell pricey drug, Lilly fuels a debate over rationing. *Wall Street Journal,* September 18, 1A.

Rorty, A. O. 1988. *Mind in Action: Essays in the Philosophy of Mind.* Boston: Beacon Press.

Sen, A. 1981. *Poverty and Famines.* Oxford: Clarendon Press.

Sharpe, V. A. 2002. Science, bioethics, and the public interest: On the need for transparency. *Hastings Center Report* 32(3): 23–26.

———. 2003. Letter: Disclosure—Is it enough? *Hastings Center Report* 33(3): 4–5.

Shaw, G. B. 1946. *The Doctor's Dilemma.* New York: Penguin.

Stevens, A., and Toneguzzo, F., eds. 2003. *AUTM Licensing Survey, FY 2002.* Northbrook, IL: Association of University Technology Managers. www.ipal.de/cmsupload/2002% 20Licensing%20Survey%20Summary.pdf.

Stevens, M. L. T. 2000. *Bioethics in America: Origins and Cultural Politics.* Baltimore: Johns Hopkins University Press.

Values, Ethics, and Rationing in Critical Care Task Force. 2003. http://vericc.org/03_ rationing/common.htm.

Washburn, J. 2005. *University, Inc.* New York: Basic Books.

CHAPTER FIFTEEN

Ties without Tethers

Bioethics Corporate Relations in the AbioCor Artificial Heart Trial

E. HAAVI MORREIM, PH.D.

My objective in this essay is not to argue the broader question whether bioethicists should become involved with corporations or, if so, under what conditions. Rather, I describe one arrangement in which a corporation-bioethics relationship seemed to work well, with minimal opportunities for the kinds of potential corruption about which many bioethicists have expressed concern.

BACKGROUND

The AbioCor artificial heart is a totally implantable biventricular replacement device. Eligibility for the initial trial of fifteen patients[1] was limited to people in biventricular failure who were on maximal medical support, ineligible for cardiac transplantation, and very close to death. The AbioCor's goal is to promote quality as well as duration of life (ABIOMED 2006). Prior to the first human implants in 2001, executives at ABIOMED, the small Massachusetts corporation that created the device and sponsored the trial, initiated an advisory group to serve two purposes: assisting patients and families both during the informed consent process and following implantation, and advising the corporation concerning ethical issues of the trial. The company deemed it imperative that such a group be independent. This was reflected in the structure of the IPAC (independent patient advocacy council), of which I became chair.

The IPAC needed independence not only from the company but also from the hospitals and clinical staffs at the six cities across the country at which the initial implants would take place. Several elements were important.

Financial Structure

Funding for the IPAC was in the form of a lump-sum, irrevocable trust fund. By contract with the fund's trustee (a Boston area bank), once the money went into the trust, it could never revert to the company. If the trial somehow ended early, any residual funds would go to a charity. The trustee was instructed to pay any bill it received from IPAC members within ten business days, no questions asked. No substantive criteria delineating what would be legitimate bills were provided, leaving the IPAC itself to determine how best to use the money.

Only two specific constraints were placed on the trust. One, a written agreement between IPAC members and ABIOMED, stated that the funds were to be used to provide advocacy services to patients in the AbioCor trial. However, none of the formative documents defined "patient advocacy services," thereby permitting the IPAC to define this pivotal concept. Neither the company nor the trustee could deny payment on the grounds that IPAC activities did not fit some preconceived definition of patient advocacy. The other specification was that IPAC members would receive a modest annual honorarium, plus per diem payment designed to replace any monies forgone because the member was providing services during the trial. To fit more closely the nature of our activities, the IPAC transformed the per-diem sum into a per-hour remuneration. To avoid financial conflicts of interest, IPAC members were required to sign an agreement promising that we and our families would not own shares of ABIOMED stock for the duration of the trial. The same agreement was also signed by the trial's surgeons and other people in positions of key clinical decision making.

By implication of this structure, ABIOMED had no financial leverage to influence IPAC activities. It could not withdraw or reduce our funding if displeased, nor reciprocally would IPAC spending decisions affect the company or its finances in any way. Once transferred to the trust fund, the money was permanently out of the company's hands. Quite literally, the company would have had no recourse had the group decided to spend the majority of the funds on meetings at exotic resorts, discussing the nuances of patient advocacy. A few months after the first implant, the IPAC evaluated its spending patterns and developed in-house criteria to govern what sorts of expenditures would be covered, so that we could live within our means and achieve reasonable consistency across the members' expenditures. Several months thereafter, these criteria were tightened further to ensure the funds would last throughout the trial.

Selection of Members

Member selection poses a challenge in any such effort. On one hand, if the company chooses the entire group, it might be accused of "stacking the deck" with people favorable to its views. On the other hand, in the absence of any preexisting entity to make such selections or to provide the services described, the company has no alternative but to choose at least the first few members. Accordingly, ABIOMED selected the IPAC's first four members, who then chose the rest of the group. The final composition required that at least six members be site-based—that is, that there be at least one person based in each of the six cities where the initial implants would occur, so that these members would be readily available to provide direct services to patients and families. Other members could be at-large, to help address broader issues.

Of the initial four ABIOMED selections, two people were site-based while the other two were at-large, one being the chair. Both site-based members were physicians specializing in hospice and palliative care, as the company felt this would figure importantly in their ability to assist these dying patients. The two at-large members, including the chair, were probably chosen for our specialization in bioethics. These four chose the other members. In a few instances where competing commitments prompted a member to resign during the multiyear duration of the trial, the IPAC chose replacement members. Indeed, one of the original four resigned a short time after the trial began, due to changes in responsibilities at his home institution. ABIOMED had no authority to influence member selection, nor to remove any member if it were displeased. The IPAC simply informed the company, after the fact, of selections and changes.

The initial few of us looked for several characteristics. Because we would be involved in the informed consent process, each patient advocate (PA) needed to be clinically knowledgeable. If one is to help explain what a stroke is, one must know what a stroke is. As it happens, nearly everyone in the group is an M.D. This was not mandatory, since other kinds of clinically qualified people might also have done well. It was more a matter of identifying people whom we knew and believed could serve well in the role. Second, we sought people with experience conducting difficult end-of-life conversations. Eligibility for the AbioCor trial required that the candidate be within thirty days of death, and it was clear that PAs would be required to engage patients and families in clear, if also compassionate, discussions about difficult topics. Hence some IPAC members specialize in hospice/palliative care and some others are psychiatrists. Additionally, we wanted people who were adept at the collaborative problem solving that is often essential in the clinical setting.

Mission and Responsibilities

As indicated, the written documents that created the IPAC did not specifically define the group's mission, other than "patient advocacy services" and a corporate advisory role. The group was left to fill in the details. How we did so evolved considerably throughout the trial.

In sum, the IPAC's structure precluded any material opportunity for the company to control or substantially influence the group's operations. The company could not remove, replace, or add members. It could not change funding or influence disbursement, nor was any other material form of leverage available.

The major remaining form of influence was the kind present in virtually all human interactions: people who respect each other may be inclined to listen to one another and take each other's views very seriously, while people who disrespect each other may be disinclined to listen. As discussed below, this sort of influence can be far more powerful than more conventional kinds of leverage. Yet in most cases this influence cannot be removed if the interaction is to be effective.

CORPORATE ADVISORY FUNCTION

Although direct services to patients and families were the most obvious IPAC function, its corporate advisory role was also important, and is the focus of this essay. ABIOMED executives indicated that ethical concerns were important to them throughout the development of this device. For instance, the company intends the AbioCor to be a "destination device" (one with which the person would live for the rest of his life) rather than a bridge to transplant. This is at least partly for ethical reasons. A bridge does not help more people; it only rearranges the list of those receiving a donated heart. A destination device could increase the number of people who are helped. As another example, the company regarded quality of life to be at least as important as extension of life. Their interviews with sur-

viving family members of the Jarvik-7 patients indicated that the device would
need to be very quiet in its day-to-day operation. This directly affected the engineering of components such as the heart's four valves.

Accordingly, ABIOMED executives emphasized that they wanted us to alert
them to any issues we deemed important to the ethical conduct of the trial. Adequate description of our corporate advisory services requires briefly summariz-
ing our on-site clinical functions. The IPAC's site-based patient advocates participated actively in the informed consent process, supplementing though not
supplanting the principal investigators' efforts. Thereafter, PAs visited frequently,
at least weekly and, during the first weeks post-implant, often daily to help patients and families understand ongoing developments and to address emerging
issues, such as whether to reveal one's identity to the media.

The chair, in turn, maintained frequent telephone contact with PAs at each
site, exchanging information about the latest developments and passing these
along to the other PAs. The IPAC also held periodic telephone conferences at
which each member updated the group on local events, after which the group as
a whole discussed a variety of issues. In this way, developments and challenges
arising at one site could flag issues that might arise elsewhere. The chair also held
frequent phone conversations with the IPAC's primary ABIOMED contact, a vice
president in the company, to exchange information and ideas. The chair also attended periodic meetings at which company executives, principal investigators
(PIs), and other physicians and surgeons discussed the trial's ongoing developments and potential solutions to emerging challenges.

These multiple sources of information proved important. Because the PAs
were on site, learning directly about patients' experiences and the trial's ongoing
developments, the IPAC was not excessively dependent on the company, the hospitals, or the PIs for our information. Indeed, occasionally, albeit rarely, the IPAC
knew of a new development before the company did. This broad information base
permitted the IPAC to identify emerging ethical issues. Since a problem that
cropped up at one site might well appear at other sites, the ongoing communication permitted the IPAC members to alert each other and the company, as
needed, about emerging ethical issues.

The IPAC's corporate advisory was thus tuned to the particulars of the trial.
This contrasts markedly with most cases in which corporations ask for ethical advisory. Typically, the company chooses a group of ethicists and poses to them one
or more questions. The group might then discuss, deliberate, perhaps write background papers for further discussion, and then write a report (Brody et al. 2002;
Green et al. 2002). The IPAC's corporate advisory function for ABIOMED was

very different. This was an ongoing, on-the-fly "curbside consult." Occasionally ABIOMED asked us to evaluate a specific question. More commonly, the IPAC brought issues and ideas to the company. In some instances we described the issue and proposed concrete solutions, while in other cases we simply outlined various possible approaches the company might take, offering reasons for and against each.

Two examples may illustrate. Prior to the first implant ABIOMED, resolving to avoid the media frenzy that swirled around the Jarvik-7 implants during the 1980s, adopted a "quiet" media policy in which only limited information would be released publicly. The press responded very critically, and a controversy ensued in which some commentators argued that the company was "gagging" free discussion of a project that had earlier received taxpayer support (Morreim 2004). In response, I as IPAC chair drafted a summary of the controversy, posed several questions, and e-mailed it to IPAC members. Two ABIOMED executives were invited to "listen" in. A variety of ideas emerged in the ensuing e-mail discussion, both pro and con, which helped the company to reflect on the issues and develop its response to the controversy. In this instance the IPAC did not recommend any particular resolution, but rather brought to light as many of the important considerations as possible. ABIOMED considered these ideas as it formulated its public response.

In a second example, as the trial progressed and postimplant patients experienced both good and bad results, PAs felt it would be helpful if the consent form were revised to include a summary of the trial's events to date. Such a change was not mandatory by regulatory standards, and indeed few if any trials change their consent forms midstream. Many cannot because results are blinded until the trial is over, and even in small unblinded trials where such updates would be possible, they are not required.[2] Nevertheless, in a high-profile trial involving dying patients and significant uncertainties, the IPAC felt that it would be ethically preferable to include a factual update in the consent form. Following the first seven implants the trial entered a temporary hiatus, which provided an opportunity to undertake such a revision. The company agreed and disseminated a modified consent form to the trial sites. Local institutional review boards then inserted whatever further modifications they thought appropriate.

Independence and Corporate Advisory

No matter how carefully a company such as ABIOMED might try to ensure independence for an advisory group, the bare fact of its corporate origins may trigger caution. Ideally, some free-standing entity might be a preferable source of financing, member selection, and the like. Given the absence of any such entity, however, and with a desire to provide such assistance for patients and families, the corporation in this case had no alternative but to create the group itself, promoting its independence via insulating the group's finances, minimizing its own voice in selecting members, and building into the relevant documents a vagueness that would permit the group to define the scope and content of its own mission.

However, whatever the structure, "independence" can be a challenging issue. On one hand, it is possible to create structures that remove many if not all of the most obvious forms of leverage—opportunities for direct or indirect coercion— that might be exerted by a company over such a group. But leverage is not the only form of influence. When people work together closely, as they must to be effective in such a project, the personal relationships they develop can become more powerful than conventional leverage. If mutual respect develops, the parties may go to significant lengths to earn and retain each another's esteem. If antagonism or disrespect develops, the result obviously can go the other direction.

Though not without hazard, mutual respect would seem distinctly preferable. Independence without effectiveness is essentially worthless. And effectiveness is not often achieved by standing at a distance, pointing the moral finger of blame— particularly in the setting of a constantly evolving clinical research trial. Effectiveness is better achieved when various parties listen to each other carefully because they respect each other and trust that the other is acting in good faith (providing, of course, that persons on both sides are indeed acting in good faith— arguably a prerequisite for ethics consultation to corporations) (Brody et al. 2002; Youngner et al. 2002; Sharpe 2002; Green et al. 2002). Where confrontation is necessary, it is arguably more useful when done in the spirit of "be my best of friends by being my sharpest of critics." Nevertheless, those more positive relationships pose important challenges. One must be vigilant to avoid becoming overly enthused, or identifying too closely with the company or, in the case of a multisite clinical trial, with the trial sites, the clinical teams, or others closely involved in the project.

BROADER APPLICATIONS

It would be vain and very likely incorrect to suppose that this group's structure is the only or even best way to provide bioethics advisory services to a corporation, even in the context of a clinical trial. It is costly and labor intensive, and for those reasons alone unlikely to be replicated frequently. Nevertheless, I believe it has provided at least one example of a structure in which bioethicists can provide real assistance to a corporation while maintaining a level of integrity essential to good bioethics consultation. We were able to assemble a group of people who, as I look back, were extraordinarily effective both in their clinical services and in collectively thinking through issues that were difficult and sometimes very unusual. We felt genuinely free to speak our minds to the company, including the fact that sometimes our perspectives within the group differed. Our ideas were taken very seriously and in a number of instances shaped changes in the trial.

Several potentially useful insights might be gleaned for those wishing to adapt the IPAC's approach for other kinds of corporate advisory projects, particularly in the context of clinical research. First, a diversified, firsthand information base seems important. I doubt that the IPAC would have been nearly as cogent in its ability to identify incipient ethical issues and advise the corporation, or to help patients, had we not had constant, unfiltered access to the ongoing developments in the trial. Good ethics begins with good facts. Much of this information came through our direct, ongoing contact with patients, families, PIs, and other clinical team members in the various local medical centers. While the company was willingly forthcoming with information we requested, the diversity of our information sources enriched our database in ways that no single source could have. For others interested in adapting this model, it might be noted that much clinical research takes place in an outpatient setting. Yet even here it might be possible to forge direct, ongoing contact with patients, PIs, corporate executives. One might establish regular telephone follow-up, for instance, or periodic gatherings in which the research subjects are invited to share their experiences and questions. Myriad adaptations can be imagined.

Second, the IPAC's thick communication patterns, both among ourselves and between us and ABIOMED, also seem to have been important. The cross-fertilization that came from diverse minds sharing information and evaluating issues was remarkably fruitful for the IPAC's own thinking and, thereby, for the quality of our advisory role to ABIOMED.

Third, it was very important for the IPAC to have one senior ABIOMED executive whose recognized job responsibilities included communicating with the IPAC. While I as chair would have been free to speak to anyone in the corporation (another important requirement, I think), I found it very helpful to know that my communications with the designated executive were explicitly invited, and not an unexpected intrusion on his time. At the same time, his vice-president position within the corporation had sufficiently high stature that he was usually able to answer my questions directly, on the basis of his own knowledge. When he did not have the necessary information at hand, he was usually able expeditiously to find the answers within the company.

As noted, I make no claim that the IPAC's approach to corporate-bioethics relationships was flawless. Nevertheless, it represents a promising approach that I hope can serve as a springboard for a variety of fruitful adaptations.

NOTES

1. The term *patient* is often abjured in the clinical research context, in favor of alternatives like *subject* or *volunteer*, which are less susceptible to the therapeutic misconception (i.e., a conflation between research and treatment). In this chapter I will primarily use *patient*. Although the people enrolled in this trial were indeed research subjects who received an experimental device, they were also patients. Most of their care was not protocol-governed "research." Rather, it was largely postoperative clinical care, some of which was innovative (e.g., as clinicians attempted to discern optimal management for anticoagulation and nutrition), and much of which was the fairly routine clinical care that follows any major surgery. Thus this selection of terms is by stipulation, with acknowledgment that it is not without controversy.

2. In *Goodman v. United States*, 298 F.3d 1048 (9th Cir 2002), the Ninth Circuit expressly held that in an NIH trial for cancer with metastases to liver, providing isolated liver perfusion [ILP] with direct drug injection, the investigators were not required to inform prospective enrollees about prior patients' course: "As the district court recognized, 'there is no legal requirement that the consent form developed for [the ILP] study must be amended as each group of patients proceeds through the study.' To hold that the signed consent form was inadequate would require the NIH to update its already detailed consent form every time a patient experiences any sort of complication from an experimental procedure. The NIH was not required to update the consent form under these circumstances. The consent form and procedures were medically reasonable and legally adequate" (at 1059).

REFERENCES

ABIOMED Web site. 2006. www.abiomed.com.

Brody, B., Dubler, N., Blustein, J., Caplan, A., Kahn, J. P., Kass, N., Lo, B., Moreno, J., Sugarman, J., and Zoloth, L. 2002. Bioethics consultation in the private sector. *Hastings Center Report* 32(3): 14–20.

Goodman v. United States, 298 F.3d 1048 (9th Cir 2002).

Green, R. M., DeVries, K. O., Bernstein, J., Goodman, K. W., Kaufmann, R., Kiessling, A. A., Levin, S. R., Moss, S. L., and Tauer, C. A. 2002. Overseeing research on therapeutic cloning: A private ethics board responds to its critics. *Hastings Center Report* 32(3): 27–33.

Morreim, E. H. 2004. High-profile research and the media: The case of the AbioCor artificial heart. *Hastings Center Report* 34(1): 11–24.

Sharpe, V. A. 2002. Science, bioethics, and the public interest: On the need for transparency. *Hastings Center Report* 32(3): 23–26.

Youngner, S. J., and Arnold, R. 2002. Who will watch the watchers? *Hastings Center Report* 32(3): 21–22.

PART V

Defining Values and Obligations

CHAPTER SIXTEEN

Of Courage, Honor, and Integrity

FRANÇOISE BAYLIS, PH.D.

Courage is the price we pay for justice.

I have, for some time, written about the importance of character for the work of health care ethics consultation in the clinical setting (e.g., Baylis 1989, 1994, 1999, 2004; Baylis and Brody 2003; Webster and Baylis 2000). In these writings I have asked and answered the questions: "What kind of person should the health care ethics consultant be? What traits of character should she have to be effective in the clinical setting?" Following Aristotle, I originally suggested that the health care ethics consultant needs *"wisdom* to reason through the stages of deliberation and judgment toward ethically defensible options, recommendations, and actions . . . *justice* in order to secure the cooperation of, and mutual trust among, health care professionals, patients, patients' families, and others . . . *courage* to take a stand in the face of serious wrong, and . . . to persevere in the face of seemingly constant 'setbacks, weariness, difficulties and danger' [and] . . . *temperance* to avoid being distracted from worthy long-term goals by short-term pleasures" (Baylis 1989, 37–38; italics added). In addition, I have suggested that the ethics consultant needs compassion, humility and integrity (Baylis 1989, 39).

More recently, in my work on the heroes of bioethics—ethics consultants of extraordinary talent who excel in strength, courage, or ability—I have focused narrowly on the virtue of courage (Baylis 2000, 2004). This virtue is described in the ethics consultation literature by Jonathan Moreno as "the strength of will not to take the easy way out" (Moreno 1991, 47), and by me as the strength of will to take a principled stand in the face of serious wrong or injustice (Baylis 1994, 2000). More generally, I think of the morally courageous person as someone with strong moral convictions, a strong will, and boundless moral energy (Bird 1996).

In writing about heroism and health care ethics consultation, I have sought to understand why it is that, despite the many opportunities for heroism, ethics consultants have hardly shown themselves to be a courageous lot. To be sure, some ethics consultants, "uncowed by the immoral and amoral forces" around them (Bird 1996, 8), have exhibited tremendous courage (without tremendous fanfare), and there are others who no doubt would do the same should the circumstances warrant. Still others, however, have been confronted with situations that called for what might be termed "ordinary courage" and have failed to so act. Also, among those who have not yet been challenged to act courageously (because the opportunity simply has not yet arisen), there are many who would fail to do so.

Failure to act courageously in the context of ethics consultation may be due to cowardice or overwhelming fear—fear of being ethically inarticulate, fear of being ignored, fear of alienating others and being labeled disloyal, fear of isolation and marginalization, fear of loss of reputation, fear of retribution, fear of job loss, fear of litigation, and so on. An interest in self-protection or self-preservation, however, cannot fully explain the silence, inaction, or even complicity with evil among those of us who work as ethics consultants. Indeed, my recent experience in national policy consultation (as individual consultant and committee member) has helped me to understand that, on occasion, failure to act courageously may not be due to fear so much as uncertainty, doubt, undue deference, or guilt. And, sometimes, failure to act courageously may be due to unwilled and not-easily-changed contextual factors (Bird 1996, 8).

In this chapter, I want to look beyond the ethics consultant and whether she has (or should have) strong convictions, a strong will, and boundless moral energy. I am less interested in explaining the apparent absence of courage among ethics consultants as a result of weak convictions, weak will, and limited moral energy and more interested in the (mis)perceptions and (mis)interpretations of others who witness courageous acts of integrity and dismiss them as acts of arrogance. Indeed, I now think that the apparent failure of ethics consultants to act courageously may not simply be due to the fact that they sometimes (perhaps often) fail to display courage; it may also be due to the fact that sometimes others with the power to recognize and honor the courage of ethics consultants fail to do so. They mistake or misrepresent courageous acts of integrity as acts of arrogance.

I have long known that moral courage is at the mercy of power and politics (e.g., cultural politics, organizational politics, corporate politics, and national politics). What I have only recently witnessed and understood is that moral courage is also at the mercy of identifiable individuals in positions of authority and responsibility who, owing to a lack of understanding or a lack of trust, unwittingly or willfully, mischaracterize discernment, moral achievement, and integrity as arrogance. The courageous person whom they label "arrogant" is thereby effectively marginalized as her words and deeds are now all interpreted through this disparaging lens. In important respects, this practice of disempowerment is similar to what happens to patients and families when they are labeled "problem patients" or "problem families" by their health care providers and everything they say or do thereafter is interpreted through this lens.

IN THE WORKPLACE

In the clinical setting and the policy arena, the health care ethics consultant is often called upon to offer insight, if not advice. When she does so, it is not as a disinterested, morally neutral observer, nor as an interested bystander with her own idiosyncratic moral views and values. As Susan Sherwin and I have argued elsewhere (Sherwin and Baylis 2003), the ethics consultant is an engaged participant with her own set of value commitments. In itself, this is not problematic unless the consultant is corrupt or otherwise compromised (for example, by financial interests). Furthermore, in a policy context, the ethics consultant has a "responsibility to take clear moral positions on matters of injustice and to work towards making health care institutions, practices, and policies more just in their impact on individuals and groups" (Sherwin and Baylis 2003, 142). The ethics consultant does so as someone who has mastered certain analytical skills and is able to use her knowledge of ethical principles, concepts, and theories to contribute in innovative ways to the just resolution of ethical problems. Now some will deny this description and insist that, at most, the ethics consultant uses her technical expertise to promote conceptual clarity, theoretical consistency, and comprehensive discussion of foundational assumptions (Brock 1996). Moral neutrality is neither possible nor desirable, however, and the imposition of idiosyncratic views and values is clearly unjustifiable. Between these extremes, there is a place for the ethics consultant to make substantive contributions to value formation in pursuit of social justice.

To be sure, when the ethics consultant offers advice, it will not always be consistent with the interests of those in positions of authority and responsibility. Indeed, at times there will be serious conflict. The challenge in these situations is for the consultant to negotiate an integrity-preserving compromise—a compromise whereby those in conflict modify their original positions, without compromising their fundamental values or principles (Benjamin 1990). The goal is to reach a mutually satisfactory decision based not only on what the parties in conflict think should be done, given their core values, but also based on what they think should be done given their conflict and given other values they have in common such as "mutual respect, acknowledgment of reasonable differences, not settling matters by force or rank, and so on" (Benjamin and Curtis 1992, 115).

It follows that a critical question for the ethics consultant in situations of moral conflict is: What does one do when integrity-preserving compromise is not possible, as when, for example, this option is blocked by those in positions of authority who prefer to settle the matter by force or rank, using propaganda or censorship? The short answer to this question is that the consultant must take a moral stance consistent with her deeply held (and publicly professed) values and principles (Webster and Baylis 2000, 220). This is not to say that the path chosen by the ethics consultant is the "right" path or the "one true" path, but that under the circumstances—when she has exhausted options for an integrity-preserving compromise—it is the only one she can defend in good conscience. The ethics consultant cannot tolerate or cooperate with what she sincerely believes to be unjust, without embracing serious moral compromise and violating the trust of those who depend upon her to act justly. For these reasons, she cannot accede to views she does not hold, abandon or compromise views she does hold, or retreat in silence on matters of ethical principle in order to placate others. Rather, she must speak and act in a manner consistent with her deeply held and cherished principles—principles that concern how we, as beings interested in living justly and well, can do so (Baylis and Brody 2003). Only in this way, by showing proper regard for her own best judgment, can she affirm her integrity (Calhoun 1995).

Paradoxically, this approach risks being mistaken, misinterpreted, or misrepresented as arrogance. Irrespective of what the ethics consultant says, others hear: "I have privileged access to the right, the good, the truth; others should defer to my wisdom." This characterization is flawed, however, insofar as integrity, unlike arrogance, is not self-serving or self-congratulatory. Integrity is not to be confused with sanctimoniousness or self-righteousness. Nor is it to be confused with dogmatism, obstructionism, uncooperativeness, obstreperousness, or closed-mindedness. With integrity there is compassion and humility as the consultant struggles to face conflicting obligations with cooperation and collaboration.

ARROGANCE

In an excellent article on arrogance, Valerie Tiberius and John Walker helpfully expand our understanding of this complex vice (1998). They carefully distinguish arrogance from vanity and pride, and in so doing highlight the highly interpersonal nature of arrogance. By all accounts, arrogant people are necessarily full of themselves. Not so, according to Tiberius and Walker, who maintain that high self-esteem is neither necessary nor sufficient for arrogance. There are people with considerable talents and abilities who, aware of this fact, exhibit tremendous self-confidence. This self-confidence, however, does not in and of itself make for arrogance. Further, high self-esteem may not even be a necessary condition for arrogance. Consider, for example, those who present an arrogant persona but who are known to be deeply insecure and plagued with feelings of inferiority. Perhaps, then, arrogance is not so much about high self-confidence but rather about unwarranted self-confidence. On this view, arrogance involves having too high an estimation of oneself, based on false beliefs about one's talents, abilities, or accomplishments. This is also an insufficient account of arrogance, however, as it fails to explain why arrogance is a vice. Delusions of grandeur do not distinguish the virtuous from the vicious.

The problem with either of these accounts of arrogance, as Tiberius and Walker explain, is that they wrongly remain focused on the individual ego, when arrogance is essentially an interpersonal matter. Arrogance "consists in a particular way of regarding and engaging in relations with others" (Tiberius and Walker 1998, 381). Arrogant people—the "high and mighty" among us—are not only (truly or falsely) self-confident, but they are also self-important. They not only know better and do better than others, they intend that others should know this about them. They exude pride, conceit, and a sense of superiority not only in relation to specific aspects of their lives (e.g., intellectual, economic, or other successes), but also in relation to their person—their excellence as human beings. As Tiberius and Walker summarize it, "the arrogant person has a high opinion of himself. He differs from the self-confident person in drawing certain *conclusions* from that belief, conclusions about his normative status in relation to others. What he concludes about his normative status is not (necessarily) that he has more intrinsic moral worth, or more numerous and stronger moral rights, but rather that he is a better person according to the general standards governing what counts as a successful human specimen" (Tiberius and Walker 1998, 382). This self-perception leads one to expect deference from others while displaying disdainful and dismissive attitudes toward them. For this reason, arrogance is a vicious character trait—bad for the arrogant person and for those with whom she interacts in both hurtful and disrespectful ways.

INTEGRITY

Just as arrogance can helpfully be distinguished from vanity and pride, so too can integrity be usefully distinguished from honesty and sincerity—closely related but distinct virtues. As James Gutmann reminds us: "What was once an inclusive, and controlling ideal, comprehensive of the whole of life—the *integer vitae* of the poet—has come to be a synonym of honesty or sincerity. However important and admirable these virtues are, they are surely less complete than what integrity in its root meaning implies" (Gutmann 1945, 210). Following Gutmann, a person—a human life—has integrity "when it attains, first, a measure of wholeness, and second, when it achieves a degree of recognizable individuality" (Gutmann 1945, 211).

Integrity, so defined, presumes a certain coherence, but significantly does not presuppose a lack of "inward division" or an "absence of inner opposition." A person of integrity is one who recognizes, and by choice struggles to overcome, the disintegrating elements of the self so as to achieve harmony and wholeness. Indeed, on this view, inner struggle may well be the basis of personal integrity, as one seeks coherence between one's inclinations (inner dispositions, beliefs, and desires) and one's outward conduct (Gutmann 1945, 216).

Writing some thirty years later, Stanley Hauerwas rekindles the idea of integrity as agency and wholeness in his writings on the difference between "having a character trait" and "having character." Hauerwas equates integrity with "having character" insofar as this refers to the moral continuity of the person. Character, according to Hauerwas, is what allows others to predict with confidence how one will act. "By the idea of character I mean the qualification of man's [sic] self-agency through his beliefs, intentions, and actions, by which a man acquires a moral history befitting his nature as a self-determining being" (Hauerwas 1975, 11). A person of character (i.e., of integrity) "can be relied upon and trusted even under duress" to act in a manner that is true to oneself—a manner that evidences self-control and consistency (Hauerwas 1975, 15).

Martin Benjamin also writes about personal integrity in terms of wholeness and a certain "fit" between one's beliefs and actions. Integrity consists of: "(1) a reasonably coherent and relatively stable set of highly cherished values and principles, (2) verbal behavior expressing these values and principles, and (3) conduct embodying one's values and principles and consistent with what one says" (Benjamin 1990, 51).

In this same vein, Michael Yeo and Ann Ford identify four constituent features of integrity: moral autonomy, fidelity to promise, steadfastness, and wholeness (Yeo and Ford 1996). As regards the first of these features, moral autonomy, Yeo and Ford explain that integrity "develops as we assume greater control over and accountability for our moral life" in choosing the moral values and principles to which we will adhere. With this choice comes the implicit promise to act consistently with the values and principles professed: "We project ourselves into the future as the sort of person whose actions will be guided by that to which we now promise ourselves." There may be coercion or temptation, but "people of integrity have a certain incorruptibility, an unwillingness to yield their values and principles even when the pressures to do so are great." This incorruptibility appears because people of integrity aspire to wholeness—"consistency and continuity across the various dimensions of their lives" and most particularly between their ideals and practices (Yeo and Ford 1996, 269).

The problem with each of these accounts of integrity is that they mask the interpersonal nature of this virtue in failing to recognize that integrity is not just about internal consistency and maintaining a coherent, undivided, uncorrupted true self. If integrity were only about this, then evil persons who consistently adhered to morally suspect values and principles would count as persons of integrity. Integrity is about principled consistency, but it is also very much about the self in community. As Cheshire Calhoun argues persuasively, integrity is an interpersonal virtue "fitting us for proper social relations" (Calhoun 1995, 253).

Consistent with this view, Margaret Urban Walker develops and defends the notion of integrity as a kind of reliable accountability: "Its point is not for us to will one thing nor to be it, but to maintain—or reestablish—our reliability in matters involving important commitments and goods. This view exchanges global wholeness for more local dependability, and inexorable consistency for responsiveness to the moral costs of error and change. . . . This view of integrity takes utterly seriously to what and to whom a person is true, but looks with suspicion upon true selves" (Walker 1998, 106).

What matters on this feminist account of integrity is not adherence to a set of ordered values and principles but rather adherence, in a particular instance, to a rule-set that promotes social justice and maintains or, as needs be, reestablishes reliability. On this view, coherence and continuity are not important in themselves. Rather, these qualities are important for what they make possible, namely reliable accountability in relation to a chosen set of values and principles that promote justice. Persons of integrity can be relied upon to act justly in an unjust situation. They can also be counted on to repair or compensate for damage when they are responsible for harm or injury: "A central use of 'integrity' then is to describe not only people who act well from, as it were, a standing position but also people who own up to and clean up messes, their own and others" (Walker 1998, 118).

With this conception of integrity there is principled consistency, but the focus is on other-regarding commitments. There is not "maximal evaluative integration, unconditional commitment, or uncorrupted fidelity to a true self" but there is reliability and responsiveness in one's relations with others (Walker 1998, 106). On this view, flexible resilience takes precedence over internal coherence (inward solidarity). Flexible resilience requires of the ethics consultant that she stand firm in defense of her moral convictions, but at the same time that she be willing to reevaluate her fundamental principles and commitments. She must be neither inflexible nor too flexible.

INTEGRITY AND ETHICS CONSULTATION

Taking all of this into consideration, it would appear that integrity requires of the ethics consultant principled consistency, reliable accountability, and flexible resilience. The ethics consultant must strive for coherence between her inner and outer life. Insofar as she succeeds in establishing coherence and consistency between her values, principles, and actions, she can be relied upon to act in a manner that honors her moral convictions. Further, she can be counted upon to respectfully consider the views and values of others, in that she is prepared to be flexible in her pursuit of integrity-preserving compromise, though not prepared to compromise the values and principles that promote justice. In this context, the ethics consultant values responsibility, self-discipline, respect, and cooperation (Women's Encampment n.d.).

Responsibility requires the ethics consultant to actively participate in efforts to achieve integrity-preserving compromise by appropriately voicing her opinions and contributing to relevant discussions. In this process, self-discipline inclines the consultant away from self-interested attempts to preclude legitimate compromise. The difference between being compromised and being willing to compromise is well understood by the ethics consultant who shuns the former but embraces the latter. Integrity-preserving compromise is pursued in a cooperative manner that evidences both respect for and trust in others who are equally committed to the mutual project of achieving a morally legitimate compromise. At all times, however, the ethics consultant remains vigilant: she must be neither inflexible nor too flexible with respect to her value commitments, and she must be responsive to the moral costs of error and make changes with regard to these commitments. Only in this way can she hope to avoid the problem with integrity (for both medicine and bioethics) so aptly described by Carl Elliott:

> There is a problem with the idea of integrity. Integrity involves, among other things, the notion of being true to your own ideals or moral convictions, of not allowing coercion or temptation to lead you away from what you believe is right. It is a matter of being true to yourself. The problem is that you change; or rather, you are changed, by what you do, where you live, whom you associate with and so on. So your ideals and convictions change. And integrity then becomes a matter of being true to those convictions and ideals. The problem comes if you and your convictions are changed in the wrong ways; if you—as a result of what you do and where you work and whom you associate with and so on—become the kind of person who no longer perceives the moral world in the way you once did. The problem then is not betraying your ideals but being true to the wrong ones, and wrong ones that you can no longer even see as wrong. (Elliott 1999, 18)

OF ARROGANCE AND INTEGRITY

In sum, what makes arrogance vicious and integrity virtuous is a key difference in their other-regarding features. The arrogant person is self-aggrandizing, judgmental, and typically dismissive of others; she acts with disdain toward those she considers her inferior (most everyone). Paradigmatically, the arrogant person is a moral braggart: "I don't care what you think—I am right." The ethics consultant acting with arrogance is primarily concerned with self, with power, and with personal advantage.

In sharp contrast, a person of integrity does not presume superiority, though she too believes herself to be right: "I think I am right, but I care what you think and I'm open to the possibility of morally legitimate compromise." A person of integrity is capable of self-critical humility—an "awareness of [her] own limitations and need for others . . . that ultimately results in a sense of equality with others" (Lebacqz 1992, 299–300). She believes that the values and principles to which she is deeply committed are morally sound, but she recognizes (indeed, is attentive to) the possibility of error (both in terms of her original convictions as well as those convictions that are in transition or have been transformed). The ethics consultant acting with integrity will voice her moral commitments in relation to her work, and when courage is called for she will act with principled consistency. She does so aware of her own fallibility, however. Thus, trusting others to also act with integrity, she remains open to the possibility that her moral convictions may need to be revised in response to moral insights offered by others. There is no dogmatism associated with this sort of commitment to act with principled consistency in relation to oneself and to others.

On this understanding of arrogance and integrity, it is not possible for persons of integrity to also be arrogant persons. This is not to deny, however, that individuals acting with integrity may nonetheless sometimes appear arrogant. To be sure, not all persons of integrity are equally skilled in interpersonal relations, and on occasion some no doubt will exhibit arrogant mannerisms in their patterns of communication and forms of argumentation. In challenging situations, when frustration grows and opposition mounts, the ethics consultant may become weary and discouraged. This, in turn, may negatively affect her orientation toward others, particularly if she now finds herself calling their integrity into question.

In closing, I continue to believe that the ethics consultant requires courage "to take a stand in the face of serious wrong, and . . . to persevere in the face of seemingly constant 'setbacks, weariness, difficulties and danger'" (Baylis 1989, 37–38). In addition to strong convictions, a strong will, and considerable moral energy, however, the ethics consultant also needs integrity, which, in turn, requires principled consistency, reliable accountability, and flexible resilience. The courageous ethics consultant needs to act conscientiously and with humility, in a manner that accurately reflects her moral convictions and evidences consistency and coherence in her other-regarding commitments. In this way, the ethics consultant remains overtly committed to the project of identifying the moral issues, exploring alternative ways of moving forward, and, where possible, negotiating an integrity-preserving compromise.

Sadly, however, none of this guarantees that others (including ethics colleagues) will recognize and honor the courageous acts of persons of integrity. Unwitting or willful misperception and misinterpretation, which can seriously undermine the work of the ethics consultant, is always a risk.

ACKNOWLEDGMENTS

This chapter is in part a public apology to my colleague Nuala Kenny for my own arrogance in believing that I could succeed where she had once failed. It is also in part a sad commentary on what I have observed in my national committee work over the past several years, where too often I have watched principles give way to pragmatics and politics. To be sure, I have also witnessed persons of integrity persevere in pursuit of the good, and I dedicate this essay to them.

Helpful comments on an earlier draft of this chapter were provided by the Novel Tech Ethics research team at Dalhousie University (www.noveltechethics.ca), as well as Judy Johnson, Nuala Kenny, Christy Simpson, and George Webster. Thanks are owed to Caroline McInnes for her invaluable research assistance.

NOTE

The epigraph is inspired by Amelia Earhart: "Courage is the price that life extracts for granting peace. The soul that knows it not, knows no release from little things; knows not the livid loneliness of fear."

REFERENCES

Baylis, F. 1989. Persons with moral expertise and moral experts: Wherein lies the difference? In B. Hoffmaster, B. Freedman, and G. Fraser, eds., *Clinical Ethics: Theory and Practice*. Pp. 89–99. Clifton, NJ: Humana.

———. 1994. The profile of a health care ethics consultant. In F. Baylis, ed., *The Health Care Ethics Consultant*. Pp. 25–44. Totowa, NJ: Humana.

———. 1999. Health care ethics consultation: "Training in virtue." *Human Studies* 22(1): 25–41.

———. 2000. Heroes in bioethics. *Hastings Center Report* 30(3): 34–39.

———. 2004. The Olivieri débâcle: Where were the heroes of bioethics? *Journal of Medical Ethics* 30: 44–49.

Baylis, F., and Brody, H. 2003. The importance of character for ethics consultants. In M. Aulisio, R. M. Arnold, and S. J. Youngner, eds., *Doing Ethics Consultation: From Theory to Practice*. Pp. 37–44. Baltimore, MD: Johns Hopkins University Press.

Benjamin, M. 1990. *Splitting the Difference: Compromise and Integrity in Ethics and Politics*. Lawrence, KS: University Press of Kansas.

Benjamin, M., and Curtis, J. 1992. *Ethics in Nursing*. 3rd ed. New York: Oxford University Press.

Bird, F. B. 1996. *The Muted Conscience: Moral Silence and the Practice of Ethics in Business*. London: Quorum Books.

Brock, D. 1996. Public moral discourse. In L. W. Sumner and J. Boyle, eds., *Philosophical Perspectives on Bioethics*. Pp. 271–96. Toronto: University of Toronto Press.

Calhoun, C. 1995. Standing for something. *Journal of Philosophy* 92: 235–60.

Elliott, C. 1999. *Bioethics, Culture and Identity: A Philosophical Disease*. London: Routledge.

Gutmann, J. 1945. Integrity as a standard of valuation. *Journal of Philosophy* 42: 210–16.

Hauerwas, S. 1975. The idea of character: A theological and philosophical overview. In *Character and the Christian Life: A Study in Theological Ethics*. Pp. 11–18. San Antonio: Trinity University Press.

Lebacqz, K. 1992. Humility in health care. *Journal of Medicine and Philosophy* 17(3): 291–307.

Moreno, J. D. 1991. Ethics consultation as moral engagement. *Bioethics* 5(1): 44–56.

Sherwin, S., and Baylis, F. 2003. The feminist health care ethics consultant as architect and advocate. *Public Affairs Quarterly* 17(2): 141–58.

Tiberius, V., and Walker, J. D. 1998. Arrogance. *American Philosophical Quarterly* 35(4): 379–90.

Walker, M. U. 1998. *Moral Understanding: A Feminist Study in Ethics*. New York: Routledge.

Webster, G., and Baylis, F. 2000. Moral residue. In S. Rubin and L. Zoloth, eds., *Margin of Error: The Ethics of Mistakes in the Practice of Medicine*. Pp. 217–30. Hagerstown, MD: University Publishing Group.

Women's Encampment for a Future of Peace and Justice, Seneca Army Depot, NY, n.d. *Resource Handbook:* 42.

Yeo, M., and Ford, A. 1996. Integrity. In M. Yeo and A. Moorhouse, eds., *Cases and Concepts in Nursing Ethics*. 2nd ed. Pp. 267–91. Peterborough, ON: Broadview Press.

CHAPTER SEVENTEEN

I Want You

Notes toward a Theory of Hospitality

LAURIE ZOLOTH, PH.D.

> But we are in the world.
> *Emmanuel Levinas (in answer to Heidegger's "True life is in absence").*

Here we all are, in the room of bioethics, or rather in "the field" of bioethics, for that word describes—or rather reveals—the linguistic echo of a particular sort of relationship among us, in which the human work had to do with land, borders, property, and the harvest or the failure of the crop. Taking a careful, word-by-word, moral-gesture-by-moral-gesture account of bioethics begins with looking at what kind of question it is to ask: "what is the ethics of the field?" And this is all carried by that word/work of being "in the field," which carries all the irony of plows and swords. Our work is as tangible as digging furrows in the earth. The ethics of bioethics needs to begin with the actual and particular other, and also to go beyond—for, if the way we act in the world shapes what we create in our field, surely the way we act in the field shapes the way we are in the world. What we sow and reap is a production of a set of ideas and cultural practices about human obligation, desire, sociability, and judgment. It is my contention that bioethics can be doubly responsible. We as a field are called to account for two necessary but unaccomplished tasks. The first is the task of the praxis of social justice in the American project of health care, and the second is the task of the theory of ethics to turn our attention from the narrowness of autonomy to the reciprocity and rigor of hospitality: to both the suffering presence of the actual, particular person in the clinical world—the patient—and to the difficult and demanding nature of collegiality. My aim in this brief chapter is to begin with theory and suggest some ramifications that might emerge if in our intensely inner-directed field we held one another accountable to the fervor of our words.

Let us begin with the most basic equation of ethics: the obligation of the self to the other. How then does one treat one's neighbor in the field? And with this question, one may hear an echo of the Western religious tradition: "If your brother grows poor and his hand falters with you, you shall support him" (Leviticus 25:35). The first gesture I must make is to listen. Here we are in this book of bioethics, both this actual book and the book of the larger public narrative of bioethics, thinking of one another, how we speak, what it is that we do, how we have failed and how we succeed. The editors of this book have asked us to reflect on the ethics of our work, its telos and its process. For this, I want to explore the theory that ought to support the moral philosophy that applies itself to the medicine: its research, policy, and delivery.

First, at the core of the problem that is all inquiry into how we know something, and especially how we know how to act morally, is a paradox. For a search for truth is based on the idea of an ultimate witnessing of both the real world and of the one who, self-referentially, maps the world. Here we are, blinking into the light as subjects, surrounded by the non-selfness of the world, the utter "objectivity" of other beings. One can reduce this self/non-self knowing of the world to the simplest of forms: *I see you*. I / see / you. When I claim that the first claim in bioethics is to tell the truth, I mean the ethical truth that Emmanuel Levinas calls "the optics," an ethics based on the gaze of the Other (Levinas 1969, 38).

In bioethics, this equation has an open frame—a thing built into the genetics of the gaze itself. If our theory of bioethics rests on a core idea of liberal thought, the principle that the autonomous self is endowed with freedom and moral agency, then self-hood begins with freedom. It is this sort of gaze itself that begins the "knowing" of the autonomous being, and in turn the conversation of the autonomous being as a free consumer, who then chooses from the world, which of course reduces the infinity of the world and its anarchy to a series of things one can possess. Hence the theory of the free self creates a desiring self: is this *I see you* so far from *I want you?*—meaning both *"I want (to have) you"* and *"I want (to have what) you (have)"*? For a justice theory, concerned with the relationship between possession and power, neither sentence is so far from the command *"I want you to do. . . . "* The problem with a being that is called into being in freedom is that that freedom is shaped by its capacity for power and enactment. For there is the inherent need within the call for autonomy that is a hidden request for the action of the other on one's own behalf. Autonomous desire—in heath care as surely as in statecraft—is a call for power, to be sure, and it is the power of the rule-maker, of the ruler, toward the world. As our world gets more complex, this is more the case. Can any desire be achieved without the use of the other in the service of the self?

Let me begin with a brief review of why this sort of doubled wanting—which, when looked at word by word, seems such an odd violation of the very thing it claims to be—is a credible moral gesture in modernity, perhaps *the* moral gesture of modernity. The idea of autonomy is a good one, and much has been said about it, its noble history, and the critical link to liberal theory, freedom, and consent. The idea of autonomy could, of course, lead us toward the idea of a strong moral agent with some particular set of responsibilities, duties, and tasks. For Kant, upon whose sensibilities the theory of autonomy in bioethics is largely based, the autonomous moral agent is one who is self-governing, as opposed to heteronymously driven. The agent is also one who is responsible for his human flourishing, for his person-in-the world, possessive of the duty never to fail his *own* talents, station, and gifts. This Kantian idea favors heavily the first principle of The Belmont Report, in which the National Commission on the Protection of Human Subjects articulated the first principle of the secular consensus of bioethics, that the human subject at the core of research must be respected.

This principle was then expanded and extrapolated in ways more narrow. What was a largely Kantian argument about the nature of being and moral action was used to solve the problem of who ought to have power in contractual relationships between strangers in medicine. The way that modernity altered medicine affected this turn as well, and in several ways. First, the contract between doctor and patient was indeed increasingly estranged, for all the calls for caring, covenant, and compassion that bioethics advocated and taught. Second, the economic incentives of managed care, which operated in terms of groups of patients and groups of doctors, as well as standard treatment cadences and evidence-based praxis, meant fewer friends, and even fewer neighbors, faced one another in the clinic. Third, evidence-based medicine and the increasing understanding of the power of pharmaceutical intervention needed a set of large-scale clinical trials to prove their efficacy. Fourth, the potential of abuse haunted such research, leading to a certain urgency regarding the protection of the right to refuse treatment—for this was the one, frail capacity that might protect the vulnerable subject from the powerful agency of science (understood, in this model to be increasingly motivated by sources other than the moral gesture of healing) and of the state.

At the core of this use of consent is the idea that each subject was possessed of *dignity*, an idea that exalts the self beyond the self, for it is a self that is at all times "regarded" by an other—the self is the subject of the gaze of the other, and it is the gaze of the other toward the one, who possesses status imbued by that gaze. This sense of being gazed upon, as the core of the meaning and measure of a human being, has increasingly become the main concern of bioethics, and it is because of the turn toward a principle of "dignity" that autonomy has come to occupy such a place in the literature of bioethics. The richer account of the principle of autonomy, which was a Kantian idea based in respect for persons, has been taken to some distant, Aristotelian model of dignity. For some who have taken this turn, dignity is then linked to study of the nature of the gaze of the other, who, because he gazes toward us, regards the subject as the one to whom the gaze should be properly driven (which is then linked to the circular narcissism of so much of our writing). In the writings of many in bioethics, for whom the turn to dignity is key, the dignity of the subject is the core principle of bioethics. In fact, many have written that the core issue of authenticity or integrity is dignity—related to the root for "dignitary"—and that is a tragic error as well, for every nobleman is such only because of the gaze of serfs. For *dignity* is a word with other definitions: pride, self-regard, decorum, formality, nobility, self-esteem—with all that it tells us about the deep fear of humility, about "shamefulness," and the need for the other to look upon the subject from subjugation, in which the self is esteemed above all. This is the final end of autonomy rendered only as dignity, as winning the gaze of the other as a goal, although perhaps it signals the final end of the troubled dream of autonomy itself.

For if all is relative to a social contract made by the "I," then the claim of the other vanishes. Your auto-nomy, your whatever I say *is (is—as existence)*, erases the difference that opposition insists upon. To worry about dignity is to be concerned with form—both ideal form and the corporeal form; it is a principle that is entirely self-directed, for dignity only existed as a signification. It is why, perhaps, the consistency of concern for embryos and patients in persistent vegetative states, who can be entirely theorized, are the Platonized subjects of so much of the literature (as opposed to children in actual poverty, whose disturbing facticity one is tempted to easily walk past, averting the gaze). Autonomy simply as "dignity" is a thin account of moral agency, for it reduces the call for "respect for persons" to autonomy without justice, or the complexity of the judgment of the third, without the need for complex choices of justice, for it is the assertion of the ipseity as the real. It is, ultimately, the defensive or acquisitive principle of the adolescent, not the adult, for whom the preparation, the intention, and the realized act in history and community is always a part of the moral gesture.

Yet the words we create in "the field" make a claim, a serious one, to the terrain (biological science, medicine, its policy, law, and literature). That claim is a moral activity, not merely an academic description, or a critique, or a cool thing to say. We have made a moral claim that *we know better,* in a language of a particular type, with a particular history, and hence some duty to all that is carried by the words we opine, that we profess: that the autonomous eros and the legal right of the one-who-is-all-liberty must be heard. While that has merit indeed, as the expression of all freedom does, there will be a hollowness at the core of the claim unless we understand that an autonomy without a duty is the name of aloneness, of alienation, of estrangement, of facing the stranger as a stranger.

Let me suggest an alternate principle, and it is that of hospitality, and let me briefly suggest a theory of the hospitable (in all its closeness to the hospice and hospitals in which we witness the core moral activity of bioethics, healing, and repair). Hospitality is the principle that can address the silence under the words of bioethics. I first return to the idea of how the self begins in freedom. For Levinas reverses this idea of being: justice is prior to freedom. What is meant by this? In Levinas's terms, it means that the obligation we are born into actually precedes our defining liberty:

> The essential contribution to the new ontology can be seen in its opposition to classic intellectualism. To comprehend our situation in reality is not to define it but to find ourselves in an affective disposition. To comprehend being is to exist. All of this indicates, it would seem, a rupture with the theoretical structure of Western thought. To think is no longer to contemplate, but to commit oneself, to be engulfed by that which one thinks, to be involved, is the dramatic event of being in the world . . . we are thus responsible beyond our intentions. (Levinas 1996, 5)

It is hospitality that actually turns us away from the self and toward the other, toward service, and not fear of the next thing that walks toward our door. (Which, by the way, is why our bioethics literature is so fearful of the next thing that walks in the door, of each new idea or inquiry in the reflexive way that one sees in so much of the contemporary work of bioethics.) If we say we know better, then bioethics has a responsibility for our word/work: we will have to answer for what we have done, how we allocate our time, and for whom we speak and care.

In thinking about the problem of bioethics, one can look for models. For Levinas, the critique of philosophy and of ethics began with the crisis of having nowhere to go in the face of danger. As the doors of Europe closed one by one on Jewish students and faculty, Levinas, the gifted student of Martin Heidegger, was forced to hide his family, just before his own capture. The link between the Heideggerian sense of being—once the very core of his own work (as the translator of Heidegger's work as well as his student)—and the utter failure of the academy (even that, even there!) to provide a safe haven for Jews was direct. For Levinas, the danger of the Heideggerian impulse was a large part of both his obsession with death as our defining telos and his turn from positive law. Heidegger writes, like so many in the current work in bioethics, of how a self ought to be uneasy about technology and modernity and its choices. In fact, many who are most insistent on this auto-nomy—read: dignity—are also the most mistrustful of technology, and this mistrust is spoken about in the terms that Levinas would call "pagan," the sense that the Gaia of the natural world has a lesson for us, or that hidden intuitive forces direct our proper gaze. Yet let us note that the gaze of this sort of pagan bioethics is often a gaze away from the quotidian authority of the actual case, from the actual need that would demand everything.

For Levinas, this great theorist of ethics, whose work was the culmination of German philosophy, the turn away from the face of the other, the actual fact of the other in need, was fatal, and Levinas could not forgive this choice. For the problem, we are reminded, is not how to be righteous, as it clearly is for so many who critique bioethics, or how we must "look righteous" to the ones who gaze upon us; the problem is why is it righteous, why is it defensible *to be*. How can we justify our existence as morally useful? For this, one needs an entirely other-regarding task, else bioethics too (like philosophy, medicine, law) will fail to respond to the ordinariness of hunger, cancer, TB, infant diarrhea. We will be thrilled by the virility of responding to death, but not to suffering. We may, worst of all, not offer a simple, a mere, a just home—hospitality—to the worker who just needs a health care policy, a child in foster care who just needs a checkup, because we are busy with how the wealthy in the year 2060 might make a clone.

How to restore an ethical bioethics? One of justice in intent and in method? In the Levinasian sense this could begin with the simplest act of awakening to the "difficult freedom"—the work that is the seeing of the other, which would lead us to the suffering of the other, and to our duty, our imperative, to address this suffering, to acknowledge that justice is prior to freedom. For Levinas, and I would argue, for us in bioethics as well, the justification for being must lie in duties that emerge from the brokenness of being itself, which pulls us not to concern for our own perfection or toward a vague spiritual journey, but toward the facticity of the needs of the other. We are pulled toward the other in her complete need not because she is a pathetic victim but because her interruption defines and authorizes our being. Our abundant capacity for response is created by the way we must come up with what she needs even in a situation of scarcity. I stand (knowing better) with more than enough, for I have enough to give to you in your hunger. An ethics of hospitality means an interruption of desire; it means first of all seeing the suffering presence, the one who comes to you with all of her need. I am already asked, when I begin to speak, and if I do not hear clearly enough, I will be interrupted by the call in the middle of the night—where are you? When so many need health care, clean water, foster care, vaccination? Are you there? Or are you off having an interesting, first-world time thinking about our gadgets and our cool new stuff: cloning, implants, and the ever-present worry, our "designer babies," or our science fiction novels?

For Levinas, philosophy and science share a common sort of work: the finding of the true world. "Every philosophy seeks truth. Sciences, too, can be defined by this search, for the philosophic *Eros,* alive or dormant in them, they derive their noble passion" (Levinas 1996, 88). Yet the problem in this search is that truth "implies experience"—meaning that a thinker must understand the self living in a reality that is separate from him and "absolutely other," able to be explored and discovered—and yet "truth also means the free adherence to a proposition," meaning that one must be free to maintain one's being despite the "unknown lands" to which the pursuit takes one. Here is the troubling prospect of the reduction, of all to the Same.

It is the irreducibility of the other that then limits freedom. Without the resistance of the other, the Same and the Self are understood as being, and the being then shifts, for example, in Heidegger, to an ontology that "thus continues to exalt the will to power, whose legitimacy the Other can alone unsettle, troubling good conscience. . . . This is an existence that takes itself to be natural, for whom its place in the sun, its ground, its site, orient all signification—a pagan existing. Being directs its building and cultivating, in the midst of a familiar landscape, on maternal earth. Anonymous, neuter, it directs it, ethically indifferent, as a heroic freedom, foreign to all guilt with regard to the Other" (Levinas 1996, 104). For Heidegger, freedom and "the freedom that is identical with reason" precedes justice (Levinas 1996, 105).

But for Levinas, and I would argue for bioethics, it ought to be precisely the reverse: the beginning of justice, which is the core moral gesture of all ethics, is the recognition of the infinity represented by the face of the other. Here, I would add: by the broken body of the other, for that is the justification for the whole show of bioethics, the witness to the broken body of the other, and to the need which is literally infinite and also theoretically without border. It is this which limits my freedom—the brokenness which I am implicated in, if not that I was causal to as a participant in a system of power in which I am largely the beneficiary, as professor and scholar, at least, as the person standing right here and clearly seeing that brokenness. It should be that bioethics is a refusal to turn one's gaze away (and the failure of bioethics could be named as the great turn toward the self, toward the trivial, or at the worst, toward the angst at the condition of most privileged).[1]

Let me suggest that we ought to look for truthful narrative, and for principles of philosophy from some earlier sources, and to suggest that the line from "respect for persons" should run directly from The Belmont Report to a principle and praxis of hospitality. To think of hospitality is to theorize from respect for persons, indeed, but outward toward them, with real goods in hand. This is hospitality, not protectionism, in which the self must be protected from malevolent intrusion. This is hospitality, not pity, and it is not the story of Eden—of perfection ruined by curiosity, or by technology or the marketplace of trade—but a story from the part of the Hebrew Scripture in which moral agency is first given voice. It is here, in the story of the tent of Abraham and Sarah, who live at the messy, complex crossroads, whose tent is lit by fires that are seen for miles, so that any traveler can knock at the door, that human beings demand justice in the world, asking the question (even of Divine Visitors) that should ground bioethics—*why is the world not just?*

It is the task of the host in that narrative to be an adult in a hungry world, to live in the sort of tent that is open on all sides. Why is this? Levinas would remind us that I am most free when I am entirely bound to this principle of hospitality, which interrupts my opining, even my reading, always my sense of my dignity, precisely because it is impossible to understand, really, the borders of the self if one has no sense of hospitality (Gibbs 2000). One might think she is alone, or worse yet, endlessly entitled without restraint. It is the other who constrains me, who restrains me, not with force but with need. For philosophers from the tradition of Judaism, such a claim is resonant with the Hebrew Scripture, and as I mentioned before, resonant with history, with the locked doors of European modernity and the very philosopher of Being, Heidegger himself. For Maimonides, and for Hermann Cohen, the attention to the specifics of the command to bring the entire community into one's pilgrimage feasts was the core of joyfulness itself, a joy commanded to be shared with those in desperation (Cohen 1995, 456). Hence at the core of the ethical life of service/prayer (which are the same word: *avodah*, in Hebrew) was not the radical aloneness of the New Testament but the act of feeding the whole crowd.

How far is justice from this claim of hospitality? Not far. For Levinas, the nature of the relationship presupposes that a third, and then the many, will come into play, and with the entrance of the other, and the other to her, comes the need for justice. Could a primary claim, such a basic principle as justice, derive its power in this way, from the first intrusion? For Levinas, the answer is clear: the problem of the one (the real problem of being) begins with the privilege to have in the first place. In this sense, one's advantage is temporal, but not truly spatial: we begin with equal shares in our essential beings, of course, but we are born into a course of events, born into history. We end up, then, in debt to one another, to that history and to the future, in the sense that the events that allow and shape our knowledge are acquired by way of the other. It is not the self we need to theorize, it is the self turned inside out—giving "the very skin of our bodies" if it is needed to clothe the other. It is not dignity that we need to theorize, but nakedness.

This will be, perhaps, just too hard a task—or rather it may seem deceptively easy. In the first version of this chapter, an anonymous reviewer was dismayed by such calls. After all, the reviewer noted, how could one *prove* this hospitality thing? Where was the gear of bioethics, the "real numbers" that needed to be generated by "hard data" or quantitative research? Perhaps it would be prudent to ask, thought this reviewer: how many in the field feel hospitable, or ask: how much money exactly should be spent per poor stranger? How much would this cost, this "abundance"? The reviewer's position was that "ultimately, this claim requires not poetic philosophy, but some empirical work and some cost-benefit analyses: What are we investing, and what return are we getting?" But this idea that quantities of opinions, like so many commodities, are the real truth of bioethics is so clearly a part of our problem that moral philosophy can seem too passionate to be important, in that we don't get enough "return" on the "investment." Yet moral philosophy—ontology and the question of being—is actually what I am proposing is the core of our work. Justice theory is about sacrifice, or it is actuarial.[2]

How to create such a bioethics? Here are notes, without, alas, numbers, on what would be needed.

A TERRIBLE FEARLESSNESS

What would bioethics look like if it were truly unafraid, in the Socratic, hemlockian sense of the term, by which I mean, if one were to risk one's position, but never the real citizenship of the terrain in which our field exists, in the country which risks all? What does this mean? Elsewhere I have noted the time that I left a position rather than withdraw a report or give the identities and work stations of the nurses who confided in me. I did this because of a conversation I had with

Benjamin Freedman, who reminded us that such acts of heroism would be required of us if we are to work in the clinical setting. I have been told this is not wise, that it is impudent. It is difficult to teach such acts. I have seen colleagues respond to students who come to them with their tales of cruelty witnessed, which we all know to be valid, but we believe the investigation of which would get them demoted in some way or another. Far too often the students are told to just witness, but not to speak, told not to trust what they are seeing, told it must be only partially the case. What if we did not just say "this is how it is in medical school; you cannot challenge it yet, but when you get in power, you could be different"? What if students and colleagues who offered our sharpest clinical critiques were not labeled "difficult" but were carefully heard? This is actually very odd in a field that spends hours thinking about distant corporate financing or marketing issues (and they are outrageous, to be sure) but very little about the actual conflict of interest in the daily deal made, the sale made, by everyone who thinks "if I really spoke honestly here, I could lose my job."

A TRAGIC SENSE

Always, we should aim toward the real, toward the target of the real at the center of the world, and always (for there is a real at the center of things) we will miss; we are always in peril, always failing. This sense of the tragic—and not one of false humility or cheap salvation—comes because we have a sense that our work could have gone better, that our errors are manifest. Of course what is to be feared in bioethics is the not-even-trying praxis of repetition, in which only the ordinary, the expected errors can be made and nothing is attempted, and the path to error is so worn that it is like the trails in the High Sierra, sunken into the meadows—the grass at our shoulders, we walk in trenches. It is in this sense that an error in bioethics is a kind of sin, in the sense of its being a miss or *chet*, the Hebrew word for sin/error. Such *chetim* are largely a plural matter—it takes the collective error to make a real blunder, and so in our field as well, for we are so social that we can create a sense of rumor, or attention to one narrative after another, the sense of the narrative being so powerful that it carries us along, past the clarity of seeing the target of the real, much less the face of the other.

Bioethics is in need of a tragic sense, for we are engaged in a tragic exercise, ultimately. Our work is within the *clinic*, after all, for even if we are not doing clinical ethics, is it not true that our hands are covered with blood? that we are watching the blood of the neighbor being spilled, and we simply cannot stand idly by? Lest we forget why we have the warrant to claim expertise in how a pharmaceutical company can run or what a scientist should rightly be thinking about, let me note it here. It is not because these are interesting things to write about. It is because we are driven to witness and help if we can, in the great answer that medical research and therapy is supposed to be to the complex question of suffering. Let me say this simply: the finality that is morbidity and mortality defines us. Because we are humans, we see this as tragic and as repairable, in part with our cleverness and skill with tools, and in part because of our decency and skill with words. It is a privilege as a moral philosopher to be allowed access to the conversations about needing and healing in medicine, and it is what medical research is aimed at—which is why it is our business to be in the laboratory as well. It is healing that draws us, the primal capacity to heal that allows us permission to speak, for it is our claim that our words matter in that way.

A LOGOS OF ABUNDANCE

If, as Paul Ricoeur says, and as extrapolated by theologian David Ford (2005), one can move from the "logic of scarcity to the logic of abundance," then bioethics can account for, must account for the sense of abundance that our research can give. One of the many reasons that we should not fear a research imperative is this sense of scarcity, which might give us the idea that hoarding our wealth, or our world, or our capacity is a sort of justice, and not, as Ford would say, a sort of self-aggrandizement. It is only in the risk of failure and of experiment that one is truly prudent. What does this mean? For Ford, failure in a moral sense is to make a mistake in the idea of possession. If we think that what we have is never enough, and yet what we have is ours, we have erred, for we live in a world in which each of us (even the poorest American) actually has more than enough to share. This logic could lead us in several fruitful directions. First, in research ethics, we would understand the slowness of the pace of research and allow for failure without our abandonment of the project. In academia, we might allow for a generosity of discourse, understanding that an honor for one's colleague is not a diminishment of oneself. A more humble and generous spirit in bioethics would allow us, perhaps, more simple kindness and joy in one another's work.

ACTS OF HOSPITALITY

Most of all, we need a bioethics that is—larger. For what we have is a xenophobic bioethics in the simplest sense of the term, in that we hire our friends and think within our small epistemic circles. The who-I-knowness of the field is both its sweetness and its trouble, for it can too easily slip into high school clique. But in the largest sense it is to create praxis of hospitable action. What would this look like? This is an odd question to find in a book about theory, but I am suggesting a theory shot through with pragmatics. What if, reader, you were to finish this essay and make a call. It could be to the local shelter, and you could offer to feed someone there. It could be to the foster care agency in your city, and you could tell them you are ready to care for a child, even for a night, even for a day. It will be that these small acts are nearly unimaginably difficult. They are far harder than calling for the restructure of the entire American health care system. But a bioethics based on sacrifice, on our real work, and not only our ideas about the work of others, would be transformative.

Let me give three examples, in that concrete and daily way. (In this, I recall Levinas's essay on time, in which he notes after a long passage about being and time that while it is nicely necessary to think about "the hypostasis and the problem of death and time," it is also necessary for a man to buy a watch.) Here are my challenges, which I want to briefly mention as grounds for more research. I contend that in addition to our lack of a good theory of justice, in which I have suggested we understand hospitality more deeply, we also indulge in three unhappy practices that must be rethought if we are to make a more ethical bioethics. My sense of the lack in bioethics has grown over the year that I have written this chapter—we have become a field both far more gilded and far more self-involved. First, we have allowed colleagues to play out the politics of academia without consequence or comment, and it is a subject so covert that it cannot be spoken of even here, in this very volume. Second, we sit at a far remove from the grief at the bedside and give our opinions and theories without even a factual account of the problems and without a promise to bear the consequences of our theoretical ideas. Third, we have abandoned the needs of the poor—their malaria and their crops, for the concerns of the rich, even worse, for rich bioethicists.

Let me, finally, demonstrate how just one challenge of bioethics can be reconsidered, given my idea of hospitality, so that, reader, you will know that I actually mean it: here are my next concrete directions for our field. The first directive is to ask: could we rethink the way that organ and gamete donation is considered? In the act of donation, one can see how the petty bourgeois, actuarial stance of bioethics has utterly dominated the entire set of ideas that burden and constrain the moral gesture. We are turned away from the most blinding act of hospitality—the offering of one's body, and moreover, in the case of the donation of gametes, the offering not only of the cells of the body but of the infinite generativity of the body, what Levinas knows (speaking in a gendered way) as "pater-

nity"—by a fistful of papers, of informed consent, of the need for liability insurance, by the problem of risk accounting. All of this is beside the point, for of
course what is created with the act of donation is the opportunity, now that we
have become clever and adept enough, to give parts of our bodies—blood, bone
marrow, eggs, sperm, even a kidney or piece of our liver. We are worried about
the marketplace, and yet we allow the act of donation to be seen as a social contract between strangers who need lawyers—that would be bioethicists—to advocate and argue the case. How much can one give the donor? Bus money? Fifty
thousand dollars? But once the thing has become a thing, a piece of gear exchanged, a thing to buy and sell to make us happy, the entire point is lost.

Donations are sacrifice itself, the act of sacralization of the flesh, the making
holy the acts of the flesh. They are really a risk, to be sure; it can make you sick
to give so utterly, and we know this, as good members of bioethics, because we
write the informed consent forms. But here is what the consent forms do not say:
will you give your body to another as an act of love? Do you know that your body
is the body of the other, do you understand his captivity is ended or deepened by
what you will do with your very body? Here is what I want on the donation forms:
"YOU AND THE STRANGER ARE REVERSIBLE." That they are not written this way, not
seen as alluding to a theological choice is only because modernity obscures
sacrifice as surely as it obscures sex and song, and tricks it all out in the prosti-
tute's garb, and sells it back. And we in bioethics help to think it so—we act as if
we fear exploitation, but we are edgy because we might be called on to speak about
God, and the nakedness of the suffering who needs even our bodies, or just our
cells, which, like the fruit trees of Gan Eden, can bear and bear, red flesh and uncountable seeds, each one a mitzvah, and still bear more. Why would it be, we are
led to ask, that human persons are so constituted, with uncountable eggs and
sperm, far more than could ever be used for children? Could it be so that the very
skin of ourselves, the very half beings that are ourselves, can be for the other if
we will it to be so? It is an idea born of a bioethics that begins by asking about our
duty to heal, and asking what could be more important than risking oneself to
heal the other in need? More important than being interrupted by this need?

The second directive is to rethink the foster care system in America. This is a
large task, but since we have had two decades of thought on embryos, IVF,
cloning, and the theoretical designer baby of the distant future, it would be just,
I argue, to devote at least the next decade to the plight of the poor children—over
500,000 who are left waiting as "clients" in the foster care system. Their health
care is sporadic, their numbers growing, and we lack a policy to care for them.
Most of all, they lack homes—and we know this and yet do not take them in to

ours. I believe that there will be a time in bioethics that we will remember this small moment in which we had still so much to do: so many unmet needs, still no universal access, still no plans for crisis, and still so many children orphaned into desperation. I believe we have the capacity to use our theory of hospitable moral acts to solve these difficult issues, and to at least in this interim measure our loss and our grief at the way we have failed as yet to achieve what we could be.

FINAL ACCOUNTS

You could argue that this idea is mere poetics. Are we responsible for this level of insistence? For this level of demand? The rabbis of the Talmud raise this question: how much are we responsible for the failures of our colleagues to be decent, or for the failure of a society to be just? (Talmud, Shabbat 54b–55a).[3]

> Rab and R. Hanina, R. Johanan, and R. Habiba taught: "Whoever can forbid his household to commit a sin but does not, is held accountable for the sins of his household; Whoever can forbid his fellow citizens to commit a sin, but does not, is held accountable for the sins of his fellow citizens; Whoever can forbid the whole world to commit a sin, but does not, is held accountable for the sins of the whole world." R. Papa observed: "And the members of the Resh Galutha's household (who are responsible for all the Jews in exile) are seized for the sins of the whole world." Even as R. Hanina said: "Why is it written, 'The Lord will enter into judgment with the elders of his people, and the princes thereof'—Because if the Princes sinned, how did the elders sin? He will bring punishment upon the elders because they do not forbid the princes."

It is the contention of bioethics that we have the right to comment on and judge the world—look in any newspaper account of a dilemma or advance in medicine or science and you will find our field queried. But this passage reminds us that if we fail to rebuke, we are held to account for the acts themselves; it is as if we did them, for we allow them to continue when we could have done otherwise. In this volume you will find arguments for our intervention into a wide array of subjects and debates, and I, too, hold our field accountable for the sins of injustice. Yet the wisdom of this commentary is in its humility; one first must attend to the errors of one's own house, then one's fellows, then "the world." If bioethicists lay claim to speaking for all reasonable persons, or take positions within the halls of power, or act as critics of the house of power (whatever these powers are named), then we have to bear the weight of failure as well.

Notice here that I have returned you, reader, to the first place of my narrative—

a moral philosophy rooted in the oldest traditions of production, suggesting the use of the metaphor in various ways as we reconsidered research, donation, and the theory that undergirds our opinions about the moral activity of medicine. There will be many other chances for renegotiation about things we have considered, if we trust one another. This would begin with telling one another the plain truth, and if we can see one another as colleagues engaged in an act of generativity we will give birth to a new generation—if we are wise, with enough to share, instead of a group of grasping, desperate strangers. If we see the harvest as possible only if the work is shared and if we see that our field is bounded by the poor, we will know that we are encircled by those who wait at the corners for what is due to them—the attention of our scholarship, the goodness of ethical teachers. But without a robust turn to a hospitable bioethics, one in which we are in the messy thick of things, willing to do difficult and actual work to feed the hungry and willing to understand that such work is endless—unless we act in concert with colleagues for whom we care—we ultimately will not be in the field at all: we will be alone.

NOTES

1. Olympic athletics! Concert violinists! The children of the privileged!

2. The Society of Bioethics Consultation, a precursor for the present American Society for Bioethics and Humanities, once had a serious workshop about the morality of the argument that clinical ethics consultants could "prove their worth" by showing how much money a hospital could save if the ethicist could "facilitate" things so families would turn off life support sooner. My thanks to my colleague Susan Rubin, who noted that we may in fact be called on to do precisely the opposite—support calls for more care.

3. Soncino Talmud, Balvi, Shabbat 54 and 55. Judaica Collection, Davka Press CD. Translation is my own. Thanks to Rabbi Joshua Fiegelson for his insistence on this point.

REFERENCES

Cohen, H. 1995. *Religion of Reason.* Translated by Simon Kaplan. Atlanta: Scholar's Press.

Ford, D. 2005. Paper given at the Society for Scriptural Reading Seminar, Cambridge, England (June).

Gibbs, R. 2000. *Why Ethics?* Princeton: Princeton University Press.

Levinas, E. 1969. *Totality and Infinity.* Pittsburgh: Duquesne University Press.

———. 1996. Is ontology fundamental? *Basic Philosophic Writings.* Bloomington: Indiana University Press.

Soncino Talmud, Balvi, Shabbat 54 and 55. Judaica Collection, Davka Press CD.

CHAPTER EIGHTEEN

Learning to Listen

Second-Order Moral Perception
and the Work of Bioethics

JUDITH ANDRE, PH.D.

Bioethics is a practice, in Alasdair MacIntyre's sense of the word: a complex social activity that changes through time and has its own internal goals and excellences (MacIntyre 1981). I have argued elsewhere that a central, defining goal of our field is encouraging moral development in ourselves and in those we serve (Andre 1992). Moral development comprises the abilities to see what matters, reason about it, and act accordingly. In order to promote this growth we do not simply write papers; we take part in ethics consultations, sit on policy task forces, teach at many levels, conduct in-service education, speak to the public, deal with the press, and do many other things. One goal of these activities is a deepening and sharpening of moral perception: recognition of an adolescent's emerging autonomy, of subtle injustices, of the difference between support and paternalism, and so on. Seeing such things clearly is a precondition for moral reasoning and moral action, which are defining goals in bioethics. I argued for all these points in *Bioethics as Practice* (Andre 2002).

In this essay I step back and ask about preconditions for moral perception itself, or rather, preconditions for engaging our audiences in such a way that their moral perception sharpens. I argue that doing so demands deepening *our* moral perception of *them*, and in a particular way: not just as having moral worth, but as themselves moral perceivers. Seeing someone as having moral worth I will call first-order moral perception; seeing them as perceiving moral worth I will call second-order moral perception.

Critics of bioethics claim that attention in the field is too narrow. Although they're right about this, the solution demands more than exhortations to pay attention to other things, like chronic disease, the situation of nurses, or the perspectives of the poor. Unless we understand *why* such topics receive little attention, exhortations are futile. The usual explanations point to cultural, institutional, or disciplinary blind spots. I believe we need to approach our myopia at a deeper level.

The foundation of my analysis is that undertaking a project is relational: our writing, teaching, speaking, and consulting require an audience, require uptake.[1] I suspect that most of us assume that we have only two options about choice of topic: either wait for an invitation from already interested audiences, or create interest by speaking (teaching, writing) powerfully. This assumption suggests two restraints on what we talk about: lack of interest in the audience, and lack of charisma or rhetorical power in the bioethicist. But there is a third kind of restraint, my subject in this essay: a failure to recognize the particular moral terms in which our audiences understand the world. This failure leads to simplistic efforts and frustration: We say, "Look at this! Notice how much it matters!" And we go unheard. Intertwined with this kind of failure is another: we can fail to understand ourselves, to notice how we distance and block out those who turn a deaf ear to us. A look inward might reveal a seductive picture of ourselves as prophets, as those who call the people to righteousness. That is a picture that most of us need to abandon. Perhaps a few in bioethics can be prophets, but for the rest of us the work is slower and more relational: less patriarchal and more maternal, as Sara Ruddick (1989) uses the term—the offering of support for the growth of others, support which demands sensitive attention and allows room for the other to build his or her own identity, worldview, moral stance.

LEVELS OF MORAL PERCEPTION

Moral perception has been an increasingly important concept in moral philosophy. The term refers to the ability to recognize what has moral significance. For Iris Murdoch (1970) moral perception was loving attention to particular persons; for Michael DePaul (1988) and Lawrence Blum (1994) the concept included the recognition of morally relevant facts (such as suffering) and the understanding of the moral nature of actions (such as the kindness or cruelty of an action). Moral perception is intrinsically tied with taking action, for instance with trying to relieve suffering or restore dignity. This ability I will call first-order moral perception.

My subject here is second-order moral perception, or the perception of perception: of the fact that the people to whom we are paying attention are themselves seeing a moral landscape, a world whose features are marked by moral valence: some things matter more than others, some do not matter at all. Second-order moral perception, like first-order, is intimately tied with action, in this case with protecting and nurturing the ability to see clearly. Both types are intersubjective and particular. Some specific person, right now, is seeing the world in detailed moral terms.

Those audiences whom we cannot reach may seem morally blind. The metaphor invites a certain understanding of our own job: to tear the veils from their eyes. My argument is that, on the contrary, seeing audiences as blind is a sort of blindness on our own part—or better, deafness. It is through language, rather than physical movement, that a person most reveals her moral world. We will do better and understand the world more clearly when we understand *why* the resisters do not see it as we see it. Resistance is rarely "blindness"; having a different gestalt is the better metaphor. And our job is to understand that gestalt, sometimes disrupt it, but more often help it gradually recenter and refocus.

I will explore these claims in terms of three areas often overlooked within bioethics, and argue that second-order moral perception is essential to getting them the attention they deserve. Each involves intense and avoidable suffering. The first is the burden of disease in the developing world, and the second is the lack of universal health care within the United States. That these topics belong to bioethics is uncontroversial. More surprising is the third site: the suffering inflicted on production animals in intensive agriculture. Although it is obvious that their suffering is ethically important, it is not obviously our job to take it up; bioethics paradigmatically centers on the good of human beings. What puts the suffering of production animals within our domain is the fact that veterinarians are health care professionals. Issues in veterinary medicine are a lot like issues in human medicine: confidentiality, informed consent, decision making for patients who cannot speak for themselves. Our particular moral stake in the suffering of production animals is the fact that veterinarians help sustain that form of agriculture.

Since our work is relational, requiring uptake, success requires identifying the relevant audience and recognizing its moral landscape—in other words, engaging in second-order moral perception. Teaching veterinary ethics recently provided me with a vivid illustration of that point.

TEACHING ETHICS IN VETERINARY MEDICINE

For almost twenty years my colleagues and I have been involved in ethics teaching in the College of Veterinary Medicine (CVM) at Michigan State University (MSU). The experience was often, although not always, frustrating. Some of the problems were obvious: We had only a few classroom hours, and key CVM personnel had only a vague understanding of ethics education. Students were required to attend the sessions but not to do any reading or writing. Some CVM faculty members were resistant to us as outsiders who were intent on criticizing work we do not do ourselves. A final factor was the growing public activism against animal research and "factory farming." Public protests naturally cause defensiveness. From the perspective of veterinary faculty, such protests seek to end their livelihood.

For all these reasons, the course was never very successful. One year, however, things changed dramatically. Many of the factors that led to its sudden success were things we knew we needed: new involvement by committed veterinary faculty members, the pairing of veterinary and ethics faculty for every component of the course, the addition of required reading and of written assignments. But the change in the course most relevant to my topic addressed a need we did not know we had; the improvement came from the textbook we used, *An Introduction to Veterinary Medical Ethics* (1999). In it Bernard Rollin, drawing on some thirty years in veterinary schools, constructs a framework that respects the perspective of veterinarians. That respect, and the difference it made, led me to formulate the concept of second-order moral perception.

Rollin begins not with the suffering of animals but with the lives of veterinarians. He is not accusatory, but inspiring; veterinarians are dedicated to the care of animals, and as such, he argues, should take the lead in changing agricultural practice. He sketches the relevant technological history: during the last century it gradually became possible to profit from animals without respecting their nature. (Antibiotics, for instance, allow us to house thousands of animals in a single facility. Before, such crowding would have quickly resulted in death from infectious disease.) This transition from "animal husbandry" to "food production" resulted in suffering for animals, but of a new kind, motivated by efficiency rather than by cruelty. Our moral vocabularies, and our laws, have been inadequate to the new reality.

Rollin classifies himself as an animal rights advocate, but not as an abolitionist: "Animal rights advocate" because his moral position requires respecting the nature of animals, and hence their needs; but not an abolitionist, because he be-lieves respecting animals is compatible with profiting from them, as farmers have done for millennia. His approach allows him to discuss the issues without mak-ing readers defensive. Rollin argues that veterinarians would serve themselves, their clients, and animals best by helping production farmers change to more hu-mane agriculture. Farmers will otherwise be caught in the surge of public out-rage, and possibly subject to misconceived regulations. As for veterinarians, he argues, there would be more jobs (because the animals would get more individ-ual attention) and more rewarding professional lives.

Rollin's respect for his audience flows from second-order moral perception. He not only recognizes their idealism and calls upon it; he also understands their fears and the way it interferes with their own moral perception. Finally he speaks to their self-interest, recognizing both its legitimacy and the way it can block a broader vision. Rollin respects not only veterinarians but also the farmers for whom they work. Other philosophers have attributed factory farming to Carte-sian dualism—to the belief that mind is entirely different from body, and animals are only bodies. But farmers are too close to animals to believe any such thing. Intensive animal agriculture arose not from mistaken metaphysics but from the development of technology in a competitive economy.

From what happened in the CVM we can learn a great deal about fostering moral perception in other areas of bioethics. Translating the lessons into other arenas is not straightforward, however. The first step is being clear about just who our audiences are.

"ECONOMISM" AND TWO OTHER OVERLOOKED TOPICS

About awareness of the global burden of disease there is good news. About universal health care in the United States there is not, or not much. But dealing effectively with either issue demands dealing with what has been called econ-omism (Gasper 2004): the simplistic exaggeration of the role of markets in hu-man well-being. To be more precise, however, we must deal not just with a con-cept but also with an audience (and a set of collaborators) for whom a certain conception of markets is central. And just as in the CVM course we had to learn to see veterinarians not as blind but as perceiving the world differently, so we must do with these other audiences. Only through our own second-order moral perception can we effectively encourage first-order moral perception in them, along with more sophisticated moral reasoning and more effective moral action.

Public awareness of global health issues has never been higher; for a single example, consider the high profile of Jeffrey Sachs and his book *The End of Poverty* (2005). There is also growing attention to the issue in the bioethics literature (London 2005; Turner 2003, 2004; Murphy and White 2005). In encouraging further attention to the issue we have many natural audiences, from biologists and international health workers through our own students.

Our students bring the natural idealism of youth; our challenge is to relate issues in international health to the choices they face in their own lives. A teacher could, for instance, raise the question of whether to volunteer abroad, and if so, under what auspices. That last question is crucial. It connects bioethics with the new and important field called Ethics and Development, focused, to put it crudely, on efforts by rich countries to help poor ones. The central issues in the field have considerable theoretical interest, particularly about what the goals of "development" should be. There are also painful questions of practical ethics, for instance whether humanitarian missions simply prop up corrupt regimes or prolong armed conflict.

All work in Ethics and Development requires second-order moral perception. Most obviously, the work involves listening to "The Voices of the Poor" (Narayan 2000). It also requires listening to practitioners, to those doing development work in the field. For my purposes, however, it is most significant that the work requires listening to public discourse about policy (Bigelow 2005). This involves understanding the moral vision behind neoliberal economics, until recently entrenched in development circles and now under intense scrutiny. As is the case in veterinary ethics, the most effective critiques come from those who know and respect the field. A particularly luminous voice is that of Amartya Sen, Nobel Prize–winning economist and philosopher, who speaks the language of those he criticizes. He also respects them, acknowledging that markets have a central place in any flourishing economy, and that a vigorous economy produces many things of fundamental value to good human lives. Furthermore, markets are valuable not only for the goods they make available but also for the choices they provide. Those of us aware of the great damage done by idealizing and absolutizing markets can forget that allegiance to them has its own moral grounds. Recognizing that fact is a form of second-order moral perception. Until we recognize what others see in markets, we cannot enter into productive discussion: which is to say, without second-order moral perception we cannot promote growth in first-order. A three-dimensional view of the role of markets is crucial for thinking productively about development work, and therefore for anyone concerned with global health, health being so intricately related to living conditions. The "structural readjustment" of the 1990s, imposed by the World Bank and the International

Monetary Fund, required a radical privatization throughout the economy. These changes forced many into destitution (itself a powerful source of illness) and deprived them of health care (which had been privatized). Contemporary debates about patents and pricing of antiretroviral drugs involve the same issues (Stiglitz 2002).

This intense and sophisticated discussion of issues in global public health is not matched by discussions of the need for universal health care in the United States. But if we are to be true to our mission and try to stimulate discussion, it is again economism with which we must deal. Commitment to markets is part of the cultural landscape in the United States, and is a constant silent participant in any discussion of the role of the government in health care. Here, as in the case of animal suffering and global illness, if we are to address the subject we must think carefully about our audiences. I try to make some mention of the topic in every talk I give. But here let me address again the audience, or perhaps collaborators, presented by our graduate students. Questions of health care justice could (and should) be a standard topic in every undergraduate bioethics course, since virtually every health care ethics textbook addresses the topic. Yet not every instructor uses the opportunity. For instance, I recently noticed some graduate students ignoring the topic in the bioethics courses they teach. As their teaching mentor, I first responded by haranguing. Then I sat down to listen: to attend to their own moral perception of their students and of issues in bioethics. I learned that they were not indifferent to the plight of Americans without health care, as perhaps I assumed. Instead their motives were twofold: the graduate students were deeply interested, morally and philosophically, in other issues (and any course has only so much time); furthermore they didn't know how to engage a class of undergraduates in the issue of the uninsured (and a resistant, bored set of students is what most of us fear most). It is easier to capture undergraduates by talking about the headline issues than the relatively simple issue (morally speaking) of health care justice. I shared some teaching techniques with them, a much more helpful strategy than haranguing; and one of them incorporated the issue in his course.

But our most important audiences are health care professionals and the general public. Many bioethicists, in my observation, have backed away from the issue of national health care, partly from moral fatigue, most having lived through the hopes and ultimate defeat of the Clinton health care plan in the 1990s. But another reason for avoiding the topic is the difficulty in engaging audiences at a time when health care reform seems politically dead. My own semi-solution, as I described it in *Bioethics as Practice*, has been to introduce one factual point into just about every public talk I give: that most of us receive our health insurance from our employers, and this benefit is not taxed. If it were classified as taxable income, the resulting federal revenue (more than $150 *billion*) would easily cover health insurance for every American now without it (Reinhart 1997, 1446–47). This point is little known, and shocking enough to register with an audience, to unsettle the gestalt a little. It may also be that the national debate is reigniting; Massachusetts has just legislated early universal health insurance within its boundaries. A rekindled public discussion would make our jobs much easier.

However that may be, we will need to continue to engage in second-order moral perception. Americans who resist government-provided health care (or insurance) do so because they are responding morally to the freedom of choice and the individual responsibility that they believe is fostered by "free markets." Understanding and dealing with economic theory is as crucial here as it is in the case of global public health. In fact this knowledge is required for dealing with many topics in bioethics, from talking intelligently about pharmaceutical policy to the commercialization of scientific research.

Helping ourselves and others grow in moral perception is a defining task for bioethics, and a complicated one. We do it constantly, by attending for instance to what it is like to become a parent of an impaired newborn, or by describing particular instances of compassion. In this paper I have argued for another way of encouraging moral perception, a tool I have called second-order moral perception. It is the perception of moral perception, the recognition of someone's moral view, and it entails respecting that perception and engaging it. Moral reasoning, so often called the heart of practical ethics, presupposes parties who share basic premises sufficiently that they can listen to and respect one another's logic. Moral argumentation assumes that there is a substantial overlap in the moral perception each party has of the world. Second-order moral perception helps us identify and enlarge that overlap.

In Arthur Miller's *Death of a Salesman* Willy Loman's wife cries out, "A man is suffering. Attention must be paid." Sometimes such a cry is enough: this sow is in pain, Africans are dying of AIDS, many people living and working in the United States cannot get health care. But often much more is needed. For those of us in bioethics, whose professional responsibility includes expanding moral perception, the task is twofold. First we must identify our audience, ask whom we can legitimately and with some hope of success ask to pay attention. Then we must listen to them. Only then do we have a chance of being heard.

NOTE

1. I borrow this concept from Marilyn Frye, who uses it for other purposes (Frye 1983).

REFERENCES

Andre, J. 1992. Learning to see: Moral growth during medical school. *Journal of Medical Ethics* 18: 148–52.

———. 2002. *Bioethics as Practice*. Chapel Hill: University of North Carolina Press.

Bigelow, G. 2005. Let there be markets: The evangelical roots of economics. *Harper's Magazine* 310: 33–38.

Blum, L. A. 1994. *Moral Perception and Particularity*. New York: Cambridge University Press.

DePaul, M. R. 1988. Argument and perception: The role of literature in moral inquiry. *Journal of Philosophy* 85: 552–65.

Frye, M. 1983. *The Politics of Reality: Essays in Feminist Theory*. Trumansburg, NY: The Crossing Press.

Gasper, D. 2004. *The Ethics of Development: From Economism to Human Development*. Edinburgh: Edinburgh University Press.

London, A. J. 2005. Justice and the human development approach to international research. *Hastings Center Report* 35(1): 24–37.

MacIntyre, A. 1981. *After Virtue*. Notre Dame, IN: University of Notre Dame Press.

Murdoch, I. 1970. *The Sovereignty of Good*. London: Routledge and Kegan Paul.

Murphy, T. F., and White, G. B. 2005. Dead sperm donors or world hunger: Are bioethicists studying the right stuff? *Hastings Center Report* 35: inside back cover. Or, p. 0–3 (as a search engine gives it).

Narayan, D., ed. 2000. *Can Anyone Hear Us? Voices of the Poor*. Volume 1. New York: Oxford University Press for the World Bank.

Reinhart, U. 1997. Wanted: A clearly articulated social ethic for American health care. *JAMA* 278: 1446–47.

Rollin, B. 1999. *An Introduction to Veterinary Medical Ethics: Theory and Cases*. Ames, IA: Iowa State University Press.

Ruddick, S. 1989. *Maternal Thinking*. Boston: Beacon Press.

Sachs, J. 2005. *The End of Poverty: Economic Possibilities for Our Time*. New York: Penguin Press.

Stiglitz, J. 2002. *Globalization and Its Discontents*. New York: W.W. Norton.

Turner, L. 2003. Has the President's Council on Bioethics missed the boat? *British Medical Journal* 327: 629.

———. 2004. Bioethics needs to rethink its agenda. *British Medical Journal* 328: 175.

CHAPTER NINETEEN

Global Health Inequalities and Bioethics

LEIGH TURNER, PH.D.

What moral issues belong at the heart of bioethics rather than on the periphery of the field? Although priority setting and resource allocation in medicine and health care are important topics for bioethicists, few publications in bioethics explicitly address what priorities ethicists should have when crafting research agendas, teaching, publishing, and engaging in public debate. Amid a sea of possibilities, which topics should bioethicists address and strive to bring to the attention of journalists, policy makers, health care providers, citizens, and politicians? Furthermore, just who is entitled to make such judgments about the relative merits of particular domains of research? Should funding agencies seek to influence research programs in bioethics? Should directors of bioethics centers play leading roles in establishing pathways for more junior scholars to follow? Does the concept of academic freedom mean that bioethicists are entitled to cultivate whichever academic gardens they choose to till? How much scholarship in bioethics is driven by careerism and the reward structures of academe rather than larger moral and social concerns?

Sociologists interested in the emergence of bioethics ask just such questions about the intellectual substance and disciplinary boundaries of bioethics (Bosk 1999; De Vries 2004). However, such matters are not simply for scholars interested in the sociology of bioethics. Bioethicists need to critically assess what they do, why they pursue particular agendas, and whether they might make better use of their capacities as researchers and educators.

LIMITS TO BIOETHICS

I became interested in questions concerning research agendas in bioethics as a result of my gradual realization that, although bioethics addresses important topics, it also neglects the study of many urgent moral issues related to health and illness. For example, bioethics directs considerable attention to risks associated with gene transfer technology but pays little attention to how homelessness and poverty affect mortality, morbidity, and everyday life, even though social welfare programs have normative dimensions. Similarly, while many bioethicists attend to ethical issues raised by the creation of genetically modified organisms, they neglect ethical dimensions of marketing and distributing fast food and cigarettes to low-income populations. Increasing numbers of bioethicists address ethical issues related to biotechnology, nanotechnology, and neuroethics. Though global health ethics is emerging as an area of scholarship within bioethics, even this subject is attracting scholars interested in exploring how nanotechnology, genomics, and the life sciences are going to transform the developing world. Anyone with even a rudimentary understanding of population health in developing societies would be astonished at this choice of focus for global health ethics. The shape of bioethics could be much different from its current form. There is much to be said in favor of encouraging bioethicists to critically assess what they do, what they study, and whether they ought to conform to the field's existing reward structure.

Bioethics needs to become much more engaged in addressing global health inequalities. "Global health" is the term sometimes used to draw attention away from the study of particular individuals or populations and toward a more cosmopolitan, transnational mode of analysis. A full discussion of this topic would require a detailed exploration of globalization processes, the development of an international network of human rights organizations, and the establishment of such transnational institutions as the World Health Organization and the World Medical Association. Here, I do little more than sketch what deserves to be a major area of study in bioethics.

GLOBAL HEALTH INEQUALITIES

Most bioethics scholarship emerges within wealthy, technologically advanced societies. Bioethics research within these countries predominantly addresses ethical issues situated within resource-rich social orders. In describing such countries as Australia, Canada, Great Britain, and the United States as "developed" and "wealthy," I recognize the existence of major health disparities within these nations (Isaacs and Schroeder 2004). Acknowledging the importance of addressing health inequalities within wealthy countries, I want to draw attention to the profound inequalities in the health of populations and access to health care around the world.

The burden of disease is differentially distributed across populations (Michaud, Murray, and Bloom 2001). Some populations have managed to largely escape from long-standing causes of morbidity and mortality. In these countries, chronic diseases rather than infectious diseases and malnutrition are now leading causes of death. In contrast, other regions have never undergone the demographic transition toward increased life expectancy. To the contrary, in some settings, life expectancy has declined as a result of HIV, tuberculosis, malaria, malnutrition, and violence. Bioethicists need to more competently address the complexities of global health; they need to expand their frame of analysis from wealthy societies and engage ethical issues emerging in a globalizing world of extreme inequalities in wealth and health.

Global Burden of Disease and Health Research

In 1990, the Commission on Health Research for Development reported that just 5 percent of the $30 billion in total global funding spent on health research in 1986 was directed toward addressing health problems of developing societies (Neufeld et al. 2001). At the time, research indicated that 93 percent of the global burden of disease was borne by these societies. By 1998, global health research and development rose to $70.5 billion. Despite increases in global funding for health-related research, funding for the health problems of poor societies remains low in comparison to the burden of disease suffered in these settings.

The literature on global health reveals some shocking findings. In 1998, approximately one-third of deaths in low- and middle-income countries—16 million deaths in total—were attributable to communicable diseases, maternal conditions, and various nutritional deficiencies (Jha et al. 2002, 2036). Tremendous disparities exist between expenditures on health-related research and health care in wealthy, developed societies and expenditures within poorer regions of the planet. These discrepancies in the resources poured into health research, health care delivery, health care institutions, and public health programs in different societies occur in a world with enormous variations in burden-of-disease and life expectancy rates. In 1999, estimated average healthy life expectancy for the top five countries in the world was 74.5 in Japan, 73.2 in Australia, 73.1 in France, 73.0

in Sweden, and 72.7 in Italy (Mathers et al. 2001, 1688). At the bottom of the list, estimated average healthy life expectancy rates for Botswana, Zambia, Malawi, Niger, and Sierra Leone were, respectively, 32.3, 30.3, 29.4, 29.1, and 25.9. The gulf between the top and bottom of the list might lead one to assume that bioethicists around the world must be dedicated to addressing global health inequalities. To the contrary, when bioethicists address the topics of inequalities, priority setting, allocation of resources, and social justice they quite commonly focus upon health systems in wealthy societies.

Not surprisingly, child mortality rates differ vastly around the world. Within industrialized societies, in 2000, the child mortality rate was 6 per 1,000 live births. In sub-Saharan Africa, the rate was 175 deaths per 1,000 live births. Amazingly, just six countries account for 50 percent of worldwide deaths of children under five (Black, Morris, and Bryce 2003, 2226). A profound discrepancy exists between how funds are allocated for health-related research and actual sources of suffering around the world.

Questions related to the transnational allocation of biomedical resources receive little scrutiny from bioethicists. However, considering variations in average life expectancy rates around the world, and given differences between wealthy and poor societies in the burden of disease, it seems obvious that scholars concerned with social justice and the amelioration of treatable forms of illness and suffering would want to contribute to debates about how communities with substantial resources should help impoverished societies.

EXPLORING CONTRIBUTIONS

In contributing to scholarship on global health inequalities and practical means of addressing such inequalities, bioethicists could make two extremely valuable contributions. First, they could engage various stakeholders and determine what steps might be taken to address suffering and complex social problems in poor societies. Second, they could explore how health-related research and health care resources should be used to address health inequalities and, perhaps more importantly, argue that reductions in the burden of disease will not simply be a result of increasing funding for health research and health care resources. The standard biomedical focus on diseases risks missing "upstream" influences on health.

Medical Journals

One modest role bioethicists could play in challenging global health inequalities involves questioning publishing agendas of leading medical journals. These journals are not merely repositories for specialized information. Articles published in high-profile medical journals such as the *New England Journal of Medicine*, the *Journal of the American Medical Association*, *The Lancet*, and the *British Medical Journal* are widely covered by popular news media. Publications in top medical journals influence broader patterns of public debate.

Given the long-standing interest among bioethicists in questions of priority setting and resource allocation, the priorities of medical journals are a rich topic for ethical analysis. Several studies suggest global health inequalities and diseases of poverty are neglected by medical journals (Horton 2003; Rochon et al. 2004; Sumathipala, Siribaddana, and Patel 2004). Leading medical journals consistently publish articles on health interventions intended to treat diseases in wealthy, developed societies rather than poor regions with high rates of morbidity and mortality. Bioethicists could play a role in critically examining the overall focus of biomedical research and biomedical publishing. Of course, they might well want to reorient the priorities of bioethics journals before asking why it has taken so long for leading medical journals to begin consistently publishing articles related to global health and international inequalities in health status, access to health care, and life opportunities.

Beyond a Focus on Biotechnology

Too often, bioethicists gravitate toward the study of ethical issues posed by the emergence of novel biomedical technologies. A global focus could prompt bioethicists to challenge dominant research agendas in developed, wealthy societies. Bioethicists could contribute to a more thoughtful ethical analysis of funding priorities, objectives of major health research organizations, international aid programs, development initiatives, and goals of biomedical research.

Scholars working in international health and public health sciences place considerable emphasis upon addressing international health inequalities. Researchers in various fields explore moral issues raised by poverty, malnutrition, perinatal and maternal mortality, and millions of deaths due to preventable infectious disease. Bioethicists have contributed little sustained ethical analysis to intellectual debates and policy analysis concerning global health, international health inequalities, and the need to improve access to essential medicines. Why, it seems fair to ask, have bioethicists historically neglected global health inequalities?

CRITICIZING BIOETHICS

Too often, bioethicists make a fetish of topics related to genetics and biotechnology and neglect issues related to global health and the health of populations. Discussing with colleagues in bioethics my reservations concerning the state of the field, I have encountered various reactions to arguments that bioethicists need to much more fully engage moral issues and policy considerations related to global health inequalities.

Academic Freedom

One response to critiques of bioethics scholarship is based on a sense of indignation. According to this line of reasoning, individual scholars should not be so presumptuous (and moralistic) as to tell other academics what they should study. Intellectuals must have the freedom to address whatever topics they wish to explore. However, to advocate for greater attention toward global health inequalities is not to argue that all bioethicists must always address topics related to global health, poverty, and social justice. Proponents of a more critically, transnationally engaged form of bioethics make the more limited claim that important issues are missing from the agenda of bioethics. As a community of scholars, bioethicists could better engage such topics as international inequities in health, the role of major transnational institutions such as the World Bank and the International Monetary Fund in improving or undermining the health of communities, and the role of intellectual property regimes in promoting or hindering access to essential medicines in resource-poor countries. It should be possible to add the study of global health ethics to the field of bioethics while retaining a sense of appreciation for other areas of inquiry.

One of the great benefits associated with working in academic environments is the freedom scholars have to explore whatever topics they find interesting and worthy of exploration. However, it is inadequate to claim that academics are intellectual "free agents" entitled to follow their whims and study whatever topics they please. Such an account misses important features of academic life. First, universities receive substantial public support because citizens and politicians assume that academics will address matters of broad social significance. While not every act of scholarship needs to be an exercise in public service or a contribution to the public good, academics should have some accountability to the constituencies providing financial and institutional support for their existence.

Second, this claim overlooks how particular topics acquire cachet whereas other topics are broadly perceived as uninteresting, "unphilosophical," "merely empirical," or marginal to a field. Individual decisions about what topics are worth exploring do not occur in a vacuum. Choices about research and teaching are situated within institutional, cultural, and social niches.

Academic Fields as Opportunities and Constraints

As the director of a graduate program in bioethics, I have learned from more than half a decade of reading applications from prospective students that most newcomers to bioethics wish to pursue topics already broadly accepted as legitimate subjects for bioethicists to address. As a reviewer for various journals, I have likewise noticed how often scholars working in bioethics address topics that are already exhaustively explored. When scholars address "canonical" topics in bioethics, they are not obliged to convince skeptics that their work deserves to be published in bioethics journals or discussed at bioethics conferences. Rather, editors, authors, reviewers, and readers already tacitly agree that some topics fall within the scope of bioethics. Here, I wish to identify what might be called an intellectual founder effect.

Pioneers in emerging academic disciplines play an important role in shaping the intellectual boundaries and terms of debate in their field. They play key roles in bringing a field into existence, differentiating it from other areas of scholarship, defending it from critiques, and building institutional niches. They help mold its boundaries and entry pathways, act as gatekeepers in their capacity as mentors, advisers, and employers, and help determine the early topography of a discipline. Past scholarship in bioethics does not dictate the present and future of bioethics. However, previous work plays an important role in providing a stock repertoire of questions, topics, and research programs. The entrepreneurial "Cool Hunters" of bioethics are free to explore "novel" research programs such as biosecurity, nanoethics, and neuroethics. Some of these emerging research programs will become part of mainstream bioethics. Meanwhile, more risk-averse scholars reap the benefits associated with addressing topics already accepted as legitimate objects of study. At present, "global health ethics" is a peripheral subject in bioethics. Skeptics can still argue that this subject is best left to scholars in international health, health economics, public health, and development studies.

Though bioethics has never been exclusively about the clinic, perhaps a bias toward micro issues, the medical domain, and the moral concerns of middle-class citizens make it difficult for bioethicists to "see" moral issues related to health inequalities in such countries as Malawi and Zambia.

Start-up Costs and Branding Exercises

Just as the current structure of a field influences future research programs by providing ready-made topics for deliberation, previous choices by academics can shape their future research trajectories. Within contemporary research universities, scholars are encouraged to specialize. Grants and awards flow to those scholars able to articulate highly focused multiyear research programs. Though generalists survive in some contexts, the contemporary organization of academic research exerts pressure to choose focused research agendas. Successful bioethicists, like scholars in other domains, succeed in "branding" themselves.

Developing expertise in a specific domain takes time; there are start-up costs, opportunity costs, and ongoing "expenditures" of intellectual capital required to become and remain an authority in a particular domain. Decisions about research agendas made at one point in an academic career can have long-term consequences. Early career decisions can have a tethering effect, though some scholars break free of the pressure to specialize and become "public intellectuals" whose views are solicited on a variety of topics. Critical ethical analysis of international health inequalities has historically not been a major area of bioethics scholarship, and thus it has not been a field in which professional reputations could be established. The very complexity of "global" issues is another deterrent to scholarship in this area.

Funding Opportunities and the Shaping of Research Agendas

Funding opportunities also play a role in shaping research programs in bioethics. Within the contemporary university, academics in many fields experience pressure to obtain external funding for research. This pressure seems less palpable in some fields. My colleagues in medieval studies and comparative literature seem less driven than scholars in bioethics to attach their names to as many grant applications as possible. Where researchers are compelled to seek funding, scholars understandably feel drawn toward areas of scholarship promising high levels of financial support. In the recent history of bioethics, two areas of scholarship—end of life care and ethics and genomics—provided significant sources of funding.

I am not suggesting that researchers are crass opportunists who simply follow funding opportunities. Ideas and arguments also drive initiatives. Without claiming that availability of funding determines research programs, I wish to make the more modest claim that funding opportunities can act as an important influence upon the choice of topics. The location of many bioethics positions within medical schools, the pressure within medical schools to obtain funding for research, and the need at many institutions to obtain salary support and not just funding for specific projects likely only places further pressure on bioethicists to pursue "fundable" research agendas.

The existence of funding for particular areas of scholarship raises questions about the extent to which scholarship in bioethics is influenced by sources of financial support. Do bioethicists neglect global health issues because they are drawn to better-funded areas of scholarship? Is the current fascination in bioethics with "genomics and global health" driven in part by the recognition that while there might not be much funding available to study the ethics of global health there are plenty of opportunities to tap funding for the study of ethical, social, and legal issues related to the study of genomics?

Class and Bioethics

A great deal of scholarship in bioethics is set against a backdrop of wealthy, "high-technology" societies. Ethical analyses of withdrawing medical interventions in intensive care units presume that such costly and specialized health care settings are available. Many articles in the bioethics literature assert the right to refuse invasive medical procedures. Far fewer publications provide arguments for improved international access to essential medicines, adequate food supplies, clean water, unpolluted environments, and shelter. The vast majority of publications in bioethics address ethical issues emerging in societies with considerable wealth, infrastructure, and advanced biomedicine.

Bioethics addresses questions that matter to particular stakeholders within specific communities. Moral issues facing middle-class families in Canada or the United States do not resemble the everyday moral challenges facing communities in Sierra Leone or Sudan. Most of the "cutting edge" issues in contemporary bioethics are far removed from the living conditions of humans in poor regions around the world. Why do bioethicists play such marginal roles in discussions of global health? One possibility is that bioethicists typically "see" the moral issues facing middle-class inhabitants of relatively wealthy societies. Embedded in specific social and economic arrangements, they have great difficulty looking beyond the borders of the social worlds they inhabit.

Bioethics or Techno-ethics?

Another possible reason why global health inequalities receive limited scrutiny by bioethicists is that *bioethics* is interpreted in relatively narrow terms. Instead of attending to how housing, food distribution, social welfare, employment, social security, and education shape patterns of health and illness, everyday social life, and the experience of morality, bioethicists construe their field in a circumscribed fashion. They focus on medicine, biotechnology, and health care far more often than they address social determinants of health. Within this framework, notwithstanding the encompassing label, the study of bioethics refers to the study of ethical issues related to the emergence of high-technology biomedicine. However, it lacks tools for critically investigating how less visible social, economic, and political factors shape health and illness. Here, bioethics is an ethics of *techne*, or technology, rather than an ethics of *bios*.

Microanalysis and Macroanalysis

Yet another possibility is that by paying attention to cases and the institutional settings within which particular events such as the withdrawing of feeding tubes or the removal of ventilator support unfold, bioethicists fail to traverse the distance from addressing local, "micro-level" moral dilemmas to "meso-" and "macro-level" analysis of global moral issues (Reich 2002). Perhaps the clinical and case-based orientation of bioethics has hampered efforts to explore more global, transnational concerns related to the health of populations. This focus on micro-contexts might hinder bioethicists by discouraging them from paying closer attention to transnational ethical issues and globalization processes. If this characterization is accurate, then a "corrective" shift in emphasis should not involve replacing one interpretive lens with another frame of analysis. Rather, it requires paying attention to local settings while learning how to place moral issues within larger contexts.

The Complexity of Global Health

Finally, one reason why some scholars might question efforts to develop research programs in global health ethics is the sheer complexity of the topic. Most bioethicists are not trained in macroeconomics. They have no special insight into globalization, social epidemiology, development economics, international aid, debt relief, public health, international health, global finance, human security, and the creation of stable political entities. Their limited toolbox of methods and theories leaves them ill-equipped to grapple with the complexities of global health. However, bioethics is not static. Over time its practitioners have acquired the capacity to knowledgeably address complex issues that require understanding across disciplinary lines. Many bioethicists can speak in an informed manner about the appropriate use of medical technology in the care of dying patients even though few of them are trained in critical care medicine. Many bioethicists have learned to grapple with the ethics of biotechnology even though they are not experts in molecular biology. Similarly, bioethicists have the potential to make valuable contributions to the study of global health ethics. For example, many articles make reference to health inequalities, but they offer little insight into what might constitute "health equality." Publications in journals of medicine and public health sometimes make reference to "health equity." However, they are often quite vague about what "equity" means. Critics of health inequalities seek to address social injustices, but reasonable people can sometimes disagree about what might constitute "just" social arrangements. In short, genuine ethical issues exist in global health, and bioethicists, with new forms of education, might be able to make more effective contributions to the study of complicated ethical issues related to the health of populations around the world.

I have not offered a detailed analysis of "global health" and "global health ethics" or provided a full characterization of what shape a bioethics more attuned to global health and international health issues might take. Rather, I have attempted to identify some shortcomings of contemporary bioethics and suggest why particular research programs are promoted or neglected. In asserting that bioethics addresses specific types of questions—moral concerns that are important in wealthy, resource-rich social settings—I do not mean to suggest that scholarship in bioethics is altogether trivial. However, it seems reasonable to suggest that a more humane, responsive bioethics would address the many ethical issues that unfold beyond the borders of wealthy, "developed" societies. Other intellectual disciplines have adapted in response to globalization processes, the emergence of transnational institutions, and the growing recognition of massive international inequalities in health and wealth. Often content to instruct other disciplines and professions, in this case bioethics has much to learn from scholars working in international health, global health, development studies, international political economy, and public health. Early examples of critically engaged scholarship in global health ethics already exist. The further promotion of scholarship and teaching in this area might help bioethics respond to accusations that it too often attends to the preoccupations of middle-class members of wealthy, technologically advanced, consumer societies.

REFERENCES

Black, R., Morris, S., Bryce, J. 2003. Where and why are ten million children dying every year? *The Lancet* 361: 2226–34.

Bosk, C. 1999. Professional ethicist available: Logical, secular, friendly. *Daedalus* 128(4): 47–68.

De Vries, R. 2004. How can we help? From sociology "in" to sociology "of" bioethics. *Journal of Law, Medicine, and Ethics* 32(2): 279–92.

Horton, R. 2003. Medical journals: Evidence of bias against the diseases of poverty. *The Lancet* 361: 712–13.

Isaacs, S., and Schroeder, S. 2004. Class—the ignored determinant of the nation's health. *New England Journal of Medicine* 351(1)1: 1137–42.

Jha, P., Mills, A., Hanson, K., Kumaranayake, L., Conteh, L., and Kurowski, C., et al. 2002. Improving the health of the global poor. *Science* 295: 2036–39.

Mathers, C., Sadana, R., Salomon, J., Murray, C., and Lopez, A. 2001. Healthy life expectancy in 191 countries, 1999. *The Lancet* 357: 1685–91.

Michaud, C., Murray C., and Bloom, B. 2001. Burden of disease—Implications for future research. *Journal of the American Medical Association* 285(5): 535–39.

Neufeld, V., MacLeod, S., Tugwell, P., Zakus, D., and Zarowsky, C. 2001. The rich-poor gap in global health research: Challenges for Canada. *Canadian Medical Association Journal* 164(8): 1158–59.

Reich, M. 2002. Reshaping the state from above, from within, from below: Implications for public health. *Social Science and Medicine* 54: 1669–75.

Rochon, P., Mashari, A., Cohen, A., Misra, A., Laxer, D., Streiner, D., Dergal, J., Clark, J., Gold, J., and Binns, M. 2004. Relations between randomized controlled trials published in leading general medical journals and the global burden of disease. *Canadian Medical Association Journal* 170: 1673–77.

Sumathipala, A., Sirabaddana, S., and Patel, V. 2004. Under-representation of developing countries in the research literature: Ethical issues arising from a survey of five leading medical journals. *BMC Medical Ethics* 5: 1–6.

CHAPTER TWENTY

White Normativity in U.S. Bioethics

A Call and Method for More Pluralist and Democratic Standards and Policies

CATHERINE MYSER, PH.D.

When reflecting on the cultural practices of academics, we cannot separate questions about knowledge construction from questions about standpoints based on ethnicity, class, gender, sexual orientation, physical abilities or disabilities, religion, nation, and/or academic discipline. In bioethics, however, we have not paid much attention to the origins of dominant theories and methods in the field. I believe such self-reflection and self-remedy is an ethical imperative, especially for those working in ethics. This reflection is important for individual academics, but it is even more important for the majority of "the field" constructing "mainstream" theories and methods. Ironically in this field for which norms are a central focus of study, we have inadequately recognized and questioned the normativity of whiteness in the cultural construction of bioethics. By theorizing from this un-self-questioning white standpoint, we risk reproducing white privilege and white supremacy in the methods and theoretical structures we create to identify and manage ethical issues in biomedicine.

What I am writing about here may seem controversial if misunderstood. I would therefore like to specify what I am not doing and what I am doing in this chapter. Although the 2001–2002 American Society for Bioethics and Humanities member survey found that responding members working in the field of bioethics are overwhelmingly white/Caucasian, and although I regard this as a serious concern for the field, I am not focusing here on skin color, or white people, or "white Anglo-Saxon Protestant" (WASP) people per se. Those would be different endeavors. Rather, by talking about whiteness[1] I am focusing on a marker of location within a social and racial hierarchy—to which privilege and power attach and from which they are wielded—and how this is complicated by forgetting the history of whiteness in the United States and by its current *invisibility*. Furthermore, by focusing on the dominance of whiteness in the cultural construction of bioethics in the United States, I do not wish to imply that whiteness does not operate in bioethics in other countries. The question of whiteness concerns not only those who are shaping bioethics theory and policy but also those who will be affected by this theory and policy—in the United States and elsewhere.

DEFINING WHITENESS

When I lament that the majority of those working in bioethics in the United States are white/Caucasian, I do not lament the color of that bioethics, so much as the *invisibility* of the normativity of whiteness in bioethics. To understand what I am problematizing, it is instructive to recall that moment in United States history when "the first Congress . . . under [its] Constitution voted in 1790 to require that a person be 'white' in order to become a naturalized citizen." In other words, "the very claiming of [Americanness] involved . . . a claiming of whiteness" (Roediger 1994, 181, 189), which referred not to *color* but to a relational and hierarchical position or location conferring social and legal status, rights, privileges, and power. The social standpoint in question was that of the dominant white Anglo-Saxon Protestant (WASP), who was at that moment in United States history declaring the British-American white as white—as the real American self. Against this center of whiteness and Americanness, ethnic "others" from blacks to Irish to Jews were differentiated and denied status and privileges, although the latter two groups eventually won the rights of "new white" ethnics.[2] WASP dominance and normativity was accorded actual legal status, "[converting] whiteness from privileged identity to a vested [property] interest" and relationship. That is, "[the] law's construction of whiteness defined and affirmed critical aspects of identity (who is white); of privilege (what benefits accrue to that status); and of property (what legal entitlements arise from that status)" (Harris 1998, 104).[3]

Accordingly, W. E. B. Du Bois (1920) could assert: "The discovery of personal whiteness among the world's peoples is a very modern thing—a nineteenth and twentieth century matter . . . whiteness is the ownership of the earth forever and ever" (184–85). Much more recently James Baldwin reminded us that "[no] one was white before he/she came to America. It took generations, and a vast amount of coercion. . . . White men—from Norway, for example, where they were Norwegians—became white . . . and we—who were not Black before we got here either, were defined as Black by the slave trade" (Roediger 1994, 177–80). Thus WASP whiteness and Americanness operated interchangeably in the history of this nation as locations of cultural and racial dominance and normativity, and to become American, one had to assimilate WASP whiteness, culture, values, and practices (Brookhiser 1997).

MARKING WHITENESS IN THE CULTURAL
CONSTRUCTION OF BIOETHICS

If white academics in particular forget this ever-unfolding United States history, and operate in a race-and-power-evasive manner while constructing bioethical theories, methods, and policies, we risk reinscribing white privilege and supremacy into our own cultural practice. Thus we need to be more self-reflective regarding our production of knowledge within the largely ethnically homogeneous (i.e., Caucasian) zone of bioethics in the United States.

Lest anyone doubt the ongoing reverberations of this history in U.S. bioethics, I will demonstrate its continuing influence by reconsidering Renée Fox's work highlighting the "American" ethos of bioethics in the United States as an important initial marking of its whiteness and WASP ethos. Although explicit discussion of race and class are—quite surprisingly for a sociologist—almost absent from Fox's analysis of bioethics in the United States, the fact and status of who is in the field shaping its ethos does not go unnoticed: "Its major intellectual shapers and spokespersons have been professionals . . . and academics [and the] literature and commentary . . . generated [by them] tend to be 'locked into . . . upper middle class professional and guild enclaves'" (Fox 1990, 210). Tellingly, Fox notices this because philosophers, theologians, jurists, physicians, and public policy officials form a dominant center in bioethics of which she, as a social scientist and thus "othered" academic, is not a member (despite the fact that she is of similar class, education, occupation, and race).

Fox highlights the American values and cognitive characteristics of those shaping bioethics, linking these to their conceptual frameworks and to what issues they see or do not see as "ethical." For example, she argues that individualism is a "paramount" value in bioethics in the United States, one that circumscribes more socially oriented principles (e.g., beneficence and justice); it structures concepts of "self" as "individual" and "relationships" as "contracts between individuals"; and it "de-lists" social issues from being recognized or treated as "ethical" (206–9). These and other values, concepts, and cognitive characteristics of "American" bioethics resoundingly echo white Anglo-Saxon Protestant values, concepts, and cognitive characteristics. For example, as McGill and Pearce (1982, 458, 466) argue, "hyperindividualism" is the "major cultural distinction" of white Anglo-Saxon Protestants; it delimits interpersonal and social relationships and structures its concepts of "self" as individual and "relationships" as contracts between individuals.

According to Fox's analysis, the basic values of American bioethics include: self-determination and autonomy as the "highest moral good," individual rights, privacy, veracity ("rights to know truth and bad news"), justice, and cost containment—all "structured around an individualistic, rights-oriented conception of the common good." Beneficence and nonmaleficence, also key values, are "structured and limited by supreme individualism." Paternalism is a negative principle that "interferes with and limits individual freedom." Values not emphasized include empathy, caring, service, and altruism (Fox 1990, 206–8). According to McGill and Pearce, the basic values of white Anglo-Saxon Protestants—based on their myth and model of pioneer ancestors—similarly include self-determination, autonomy, self-reliance, self-sufficiency, and self-control. These values are reinforced by the beliefs of white Anglo-Saxon Protestants that "to feel, think and behave correctly is to do so according to principles" and that the "truth is good to hear," no matter how painful (McGill and Pearce 1982, 458, 462, 472).

As described by Fox, the *concept of self* in American bioethics emphasizes rationality and self-interestedness. Social and cultural factors serve as external constraints limiting individuals, as opposed to forces shaping personhood (Fox 1990). Similarly, according to McGill and Pearce, for white Anglo-Saxon Protestants, the meaningful issues and struggles of life all lie within the self. Only individuals have problems and only individuals are responsible for them. Accordingly, white Anglo-American Protestants wish to control all aspects of life, and do not know how to cope with the uncontrollable in themselves, society, or nature. They do not possess the adaptive fatalism to accept and submit to larger forces or the unknown (McGill and Pearce 1982).

Fox outlines the *concept of relationship* in American bioethics as a contract between autonomous individuals, the archetype being informed consent. Benefits to others are circumscribed by deference to individual rights, interests, and autonomy. Socially oriented values and ethical questions, as well as concepts of the collective good, responsibility, obligation, and duty, are secondary to individual rights. The skein of relationships, the socio-moral importance of persons, reciprocity, solidarity, and community are overshadowed by individualism. There is little emphasis on feeling, connectedness, relatedness, or interacting with others in a self-transcending way (Fox 1990). According to McGill and Pearce, for white Anglo-Saxon Protestants, the model of relationship is also a contract. Marriage, for example, is the contractual relationship for negotiating and meeting individual needs. The role of family is to raise self-contained, self-reliant, self-determining, independent, and principled individuals who are empowered to dominate the world. Family is thus valued to sustain individuals, not vice versa. Individuals keep pain, suffering, and problems to themselves, and respect the right of others to do the same: sharing trouble is not part of the interpersonal contract. White Anglo-Saxon Protestants fear aging and incapacity, loss of self-sufficiency and self-esteem, dependence and becoming a burden to family. They are less good at maintaining mutually giving relationships, tolerating dependency, integrating and expressing emotion. Law and litigation are the means of negotiating and regulating relationships. The doctor-patient relationship is contractual, and thus expected to be reasonable, fair, technical, and mercantile (McGill and Pearce 1982).

The *cognitive characteristics* of American bioethics, Fox argues, begin with the capacity to think rationally, logically, and objectively. Rigor, clarity, and consistency are valued, as are principles and the rules of science. Deductive, formalistic, and positivist methods are preferred. Applied pragmatism is favored to manage complexity and uncertainty for decision making and action, with a predisposition toward utilitarian reductionism. Lastly, Fox claims that American bioethics defines ethical "issues" or "problems" as those caused or created by medical science and technological advances. "Problems" are logically reduced or technicalized to make them more amenable to logical analysis and technical solutions.[4] To reduce complexity and ambiguity, and to control strong feelings, analysis is distanced and abstracted from human settings. Since "social" problems are thus "de-listed" from "ethical" problems, there is no focus on, for example, the realities of poor, disadvantaged, nonwhite, single mothers in neonatal intensive care units ethics (Fox 1990, 206–9). McGill and Pearce argue that white Anglo-Saxon Protestants similarly emphasize thinking versus feeling and value reason and control. They are rational and orderly, believing in science and the efficacy of scientific discoveries and methods to solve life's problems. A "problem" is defined as a situation that disrupts autonomous functioning as something "out of control" (McGill and Pearce 1982, 462, 467, 472).

No doubt the sociology of American bioethics has evolved in the fifteen years since Fox's analysis. Similarly, McGill and Pearce's cultural and psychological portrait of "WASPs" in America should not be taken as essentialist or static, inasmuch as ethnic groups are dynamic and ever evolving. Nevertheless, the similarities and overlaps in the cultural ethos of "American" bioethics and a "white Anglo-

Saxon Protestant" ethos are unmistakable. To this extent, I believe Fox's analysis of the "Americanness" of U.S. bioethics is an important initial marking of its whiteness and WASP ethos.

Fox notes that the positioning of "upper middle class" and overwhelmingly white (although she does not mark this fact) academics in the United States confers considerable power to generate ways of thinking about self and other; ways of understanding health and disease; bioethical norms and guidelines controlling access to biomedical technologies—such as the new reproductive technologies and genetics—all of which have far-reaching implications for human nature and society. The importance of class as an epistemological starting point and the ethical issues resulting from that have been inadequately attended to in the field of bioethics, wherein a WASP "white" and "American" ethos tends to overlook or obscure issues of class (McGill and Pearce 1982, 458), given the myth of equality in the United States (Fussell 1983, 10).

Furthermore, and particularly applicable to my argument about whiteness as a category of unmarked dominance and normativity in bioethics, Fox argues: "there is a sense in which bioethics has taken its American societal and cultural attributes for granted, ignoring them in ways that imply that its conception of ethics, its value system, and its modes of reasoning transcend social and cultural particularities. In its inattention to its 'Americanness,' and its assumption that its thought and moral views are transcultural, American bioethics has been more intellectually provincial and chauvinistic than it has recognized" (207–8). The remedy Fox seeks is greater inclusiveness of other academic disciplines, such as the social sciences. This suggested remedy has been echoed by other social scientists and philosophers working in bioethics, including Marshall (1992), Hoffmaster (1992), and Muller (1994). Although I agree that the social sciences have extremely valuable intellectual contributions to offer bioethics, this recommendation for the "evolution . . . of the field" is not an adequate corrective.

SOCIOCULTURAL DIVERSITY: GENUINE CORRECTIVE OR MERE INOCULATION?

Social scientists and other professionals in United States bioethics have gone beyond Fox's remedy of increased disciplinary diversity, recommending sociocultural diversity as a further corrective in the field. The hope is that "ethicists [will be] made to rethink their agendas" (De Vries 1990, 636) and adjust their theorizing and practice by incorporating the "unique" and "varying" sociocultural standpoints, values, beliefs, and practices of, e.g., African American, Asian American, Hispanic American, and Native American "others." However, unless diversity scholars additionally problematize white dominance and normativity, and the white-other dualism, when studying and describing the beliefs and practices of other ethnic groups, their work merely legitimates and maintains "minoritized spaces" in bioethics that remain marginal in relation to the unmarked "majority space" of white theory and practice in U.S. bioethics. This includes the work of African American academics[5] marking their own African Americanness in bioethics as another attempted remedy, because even African American scholars mark whiteness only implicitly, ironically maintaining rather than displacing the whiteness and white-other dualism that continue to marginalize them.[6]

Introducing sociocultural diversity without recognizing and problematizing the dominance and normativity of whiteness in U.S. bioethics merely *inoculates* (Barthes 1972) difference in bioethics. It ignores (a) the question of against whose invisible and seemingly neutral norms such "difference" is defined and (b) the need to subject whiteness to the same kind of surveillance and description. Accordingly, rather than challenging mainstream bioethics theory and practice as intended, diversity research merely stimulates a kind of immune response, leaving the main body of white bioethics intact.[7] This is true because diversity researchers fix our gaze on the other, allowing whiteness to stand as the unmarked or neutral category (unrecognized absence) in relation to which the "difference" of "others" (recognized presence) emerges in high relief. The dominant gaze never reflects on itself, and white theorizing and practice in bioethics—deceptively neutral and invisibly normative—remains wholly unaffected and unchanged. Thus, the dominant white center must be displaced for diversity work to make a difference, reconsidering or revising dominant bioethics values (e.g., hyperindividualism and truth telling) and concepts (e.g., autonomy), and broadening the scope and context of issues recognized as "ethical" (e.g., including broader social issues and injustices).

A related problem with diversity research in bioethics that neglects to problematize white dominance and the white-other duality can be seen in the example of Carrese and Rhodes's work on Native American bioethics. After highlighting differences in the sociocultural values, beliefs, and practices of Navajo Native Americans—specifically "to consider the limitations of dominant Western bioethical perspectives"—Carrese and Rhodes (1995) conclude by quoting medical anthropologist Arthur Kleinman. They argue that health care providers interested in understanding their patients' values and perspectives should "practice an intensive, systematic, imaginative empathy with the experiences and modes of thought of patients who may be foreign to [them], but whose foreignness [they come] to appreciate and humanely engage" (844–45). Carrese and Rhodes's Navajo research subjects are thus maintained in minoritized space, dependent on the "empathy" of "interested" providers from the majority space of U.S. bioethics and health care. Thus, as in the colonial and "orientalist" relations Edward Said has revealed to continue between the non-European Orient and the European West, the very "Western" (and white) bioethics theory Carrese and Rhodes seek to displace remains in a "flexible positional superiority which puts [it] in a whole series of possible relationships with the [theory and practice of minoritized others] without ever losing the relative upper hand" (Said 1978, 7).[8]

Indeed, all too often, "cultural differences" associated with research subjects in minoritized spaces are represented as "obstacles," "difficulties," and/or "challenges" for "us" in the majority space of dominant U.S. bioethics and health care culture, requiring "translation" or "interpretation" by social scientists and others operating in (and ironically maintaining) majority spaces. One example can be found in the work of Marshall (2001): "Results of the [literature] review and . . . case study . . . in Nigeria suggest a number of obstacles to informed consent. . . . [I]nvestigators . . . may encounter difficulties because of cultural traditions. . . . The challenges associated with the application of informed consent are heightened in international settings because of language barriers. . . . Differences in beliefs about who has the authority to give permission to participate in research may also create obstacles to obtaining individual informed consent" (2, 27).

I want to be clear that by making these critiques of existing sociocultural diversity research in U.S. bioethics, I am not arguing that such research is unwelcome. Rather, I am arguing that such diversity research cannot be truly effective until it is accompanied by equal efforts to recognize and decenter unselfreflective white theorizing and practice in the field, against whose norms such sociocultural "difference" is currently defined and constructed. Ironically, it is through this very discursive process—a legacy of colonial discourse—that whiteness actually maintains and reinscribes itself in bioethics.

All who work in the field of bioethics need to recognize whiteness and consider its implications for the theories and practices of the field to enable bioethics better to serve a pluralistic society in the United States and elsewhere. We must also create more democratic methods by which to engage equal collaborators from a full range of voices currently suppressed, silenced, or excluded in U.S. bioethics. "Other" or "different" voices should not be sought out merely in the "hidden niches, separate channels, [and] alternate arenas" of minoritized spaces (Laguerre 1999), to be interpreted or translated in and through the majority space. Rather, such voices should be sought to participate as equal agents in defining, revising, and creating "mainstream" bioethics issues, paradigms, theories, policies, and practices.

CHALLENGES TO SELF-REFLECTION AND SELF-REMEDY

I do not assume that the above endeavors will be easy or that they will lead to quick fixes of bioethics theory and practice. To the contrary, such endeavors pose extremely complex challenges. MacIntyre (1997), for example, describes and warns of "white talk" as a means of "actively subvert(ing) the language white people need to decenter whiteness as a dominant ideology." Tactics include "derailing the conversation, evading questions, dismissing counter-arguments, withdrawing from the discussion, remaining silent, interrupting speakers and topics, colluding in creating a 'culture of niceness' that makes it very difficult to 'read the white world' . . . resisting interrogation . . . switching topics, tacitly accepting racist assumptions, talking over one another, joining in collective laughter . . . to ease the tension, hiding under . . . camaraderie . . . to repel critical conversations." Themes include "construct[ing] difference from 'the Other' . . . reconstruct[ing] myths about whites and people of color . . . privileging [our] own [dominant social practices, belief systems, and cultural norms] over the lived experiences of people of color." White talk can insulate white people from examining their own individual and collective roles in racism and from related self-examination and critique. The "dilemmatic nature of white talk" is such that "white people [need to be engaged] in conversations about whiteness while simultaneously being cognizant of the strategies we use to derail those discussions" (45–48). Keeping in mind that "theory is always written from some 'where'" (Clifford 1989, 1–2), we need to decolonize our minds, imaginations, theories, concepts, and practices.

Commentators responding to earlier versions of my argument about whiteness in U.S. bioethics serve as examples of such challenges to self-reflection and self-remedy. One example is the editors of *The New Atlantis* (2003), and a second example is Robert Baker (2003). The editors of *The New Atlantis* speak from outside the profession of bioethics in a neoconservative journal of technology and society. Their critique, "Navel Gazing: Bioethics and the Unbearable Whiteness of Being" (2003), ambitiously targets not only my arguments about whiteness in bioethics, commentaries by like-minded *American Journal of Bioethics* (AJOB) authors, and the whole bioethics profession, but the entire body of white studies, critical race theory, and other "highfalutin theorizing" (2003, 100) by "postmodern" thinkers—all of which are dismissed in two pages. Although *The New Atlantis* editors are to be credited for engaging in this important debate rather than remaining silent, their critique exemplifies the unquestioned assumptions and biases that can prevent honest and rational consideration of theories and arguments questioning a preexisting (and perhaps unrecognized) worldview.

For example, the editors warn that by "succumb[ing] to . . . whiteness studies" and critical race theory (2003, 99) "bioethics risks becoming a profession worthy of Carlyle's derision—a dismal pseudo-science" (2003, 100). Invoking Carlyle's "dismal science" sneer in the context of this debate is more problematic than the editors may have intended. The sociohistorical context of Carlyle's beef with economics was the emancipation of slaves and ensuing labor market debates on colonial plantations, and Carlyle coined the phrase in his vividly racist tract "Occasional Discourse on the Negro Question" (Carlyle 1849).[9] Antislavery economists had argued that the forces of supply and demand and not physical coercion should regulate the labor market, leading Carlyle to rail against "the social science . . . which finds the secret of this universe in 'supply and demand' . . . led by any sacred cause of black emancipation" (Carlyle 1849). Carlyle rejected such "benevolent twaddle and revolutionary grapeshot," derogating economics as "the Dismal science," and arguing rather that "Black Quashee . . . indolent, two legged cattle . . . will have to be servants to those that are born wiser . . . born lords . . . the whites [the Saxon British . . . manful industrious men] . . . what relations the Eternal Maker has established between [His] two creatures" (Carlyle 1849). It is conceivable that the editors of The New Atlantis are unacquainted with the colonial context and racist bias of Carlyle's argument and language while they invoke it. However, this raises the question that tacit racist assumptions and biases are at work in this critique, leading them to resist interrogation from critical race theory as applied to bioethics, and to dismiss consideration of the "unbearable whiteness" of bioethics as mere "navel gazing" whose theoretical and practical value is unimaginable.

As for the claim that bioethics risks being a "pseudo-science" as well as a "dismal" one, this seems to have more to do with these editors' knee-jerk bias against "trendy academic theory" (2003) than any genuine exploration, sustained engagement, or analysis of white studies or critical race theory, particularly in relation to bioethics. This bias is further evident from the superficial engagement and argumentation comprising the New Atlantis critique. First, the AJOB cover photo is compared to "the artist formerly known . . . as Prince" (Editors 2003), an apparent "white talk" strategy to inspire ridicule and to undermine opportunity for critical engagement (MacIntyre 1997). Core concepts are dismissed as "buzzwords" with no consideration of their meaning or implications, and the contributions of Roland Barthes, bell hooks, Cornell West, and Toni Morrison are dismissed as "lard" (Editors 2003). The historical "arrival" of "whiteness studies" is misplaced "in the mid-1990's" despite my citing multiple sources from the 1830s onwards. Lastly, sole AJOB critic Robert Baker is praised by the editors for his "bracing bit of pruning for this over theorized thicket." However, the only support offered for this judgment aside from "noting" his critiques and suggestions is concluding that "his instincts seem right" (Editors 2003).

Such unquestioned assumptions and biases can disable self-reflection and self-remedy, leading the editors of this journal to repel critical conversation about whiteness in bioethics. In the future I hope that we will see more substantive, respectful engagement, particularly in relation to the intellectual taboo that white studies, critical race theory, and other "postmodern" theory seems to represent for The New Atlantis editors. I agree with them that "a conservative ethics [should] begin . . . to lean less on implicit intuitions and develop for itself a very clear and explicit sense of . . . the dangers it seeks to avert" (Levin 2003), although I would add that it should distinguish between real and imagined dangers. Recognizing the whiteness and WASP ethos of U.S. bioethics is not a "crisis of self-confidence" for a "dismal science." Rather, it is healthy recognition of and honorable disavowal of white privilege—beginning with the privilege of being culturally "invisible" to oneself, and thus believing one's own norms and values to be "neutral," dominant, and universalizable without further exploration or negotiation. These are important first steps that majority bioethics can take with very practical implications for building trust in complex relations between minorities and the majority health care system in a pluralistic democracy.

Another example of whiteness, white privilege, and "white talk" as challenges to the self-reflection and self-remedy I recommend can be seen in Robert Baker's "Balkanizing Bioethics" (2003). Although Baker also can be credited for engaging in rather than withdrawing from this important debate, his commentary is a clear attempt to insulate white academics in bioethics from self-reflection and self-remedy regarding white normativity in U.S. bioethics. Indeed, Baker would derail the conversation all together, asserting: "there is no problem of difference to be addressed, and thus no need to remedy the presumed 'whiteness' of American bioethics" (2003).

Most troubling of all, Baker engages in the "white talk" tactic of reconstructing myths about whites and people of color—in this case that they live in a "pluralist context where cultural authority is divided among groups . . . [and] . . . no one group has the strength to impose its conceptual framework on all of the others" (2003). Thus Baker seeks to erase the U.S. history that I and others have presented to the contrary, including the reality of a historical and ongoing racial hierarchy privileging WASP whiteness. Baker reveals his historical revisionism when he argues: "Only discourses that shed their parochialism sufficiently to become pluralistically acceptable [can] predominate" (2003). A core problem emerges when he argues that it is the "more neutral cosmopolitan discourses . . . borrowed from the language of analytic philosophy" that are "acceptable to a preponderance of groups" (2003). Not only does he offer no argument for this empirical claim, but he also, through his own analysis, illustrates the very argument about whiteness that I have been making. "Analytic philosophy" is by definition Anglo-American, and no more "neutral" or "cosmopolitan" or "acceptable" than Continental European, African, or Asian philosophy. All the same, Baker clearly assumes Anglo-American philosophy and culture appropriately to form the core of "mainstream" U.S. bioethics and "mainstream America," against which all other "theological traditions . . . ethnic, class, and racial discourses" are to be defined as "[regressive] . . . parochial . . . babble" (2003). Against his assumption of an Anglo-American core, Baker's entire earlier argument about the possibility of "other" religious and ethnic groups in U.S. bioethics and society "sharing mainstream" cultural values and traits (2003)[10] is revealed to be a requirement for assimilation into a dominant and falsely "neutral and cosmopolitan" Anglo-American whiteness, lest others "regress" into "balkanization,"[11] merely to "marginalize" themselves and "alienate" the "mainstream" in bioethics and in "America" (Baker 2003). Again, unrecognized or unquestioned assumptions and bias disable Baker's self-reflection and self-remedy.

Baker's language of "neutrality" is telling because it assumes the very invisible dominance of WASP whiteness in U.S. bioethics that I have been trying to highlight. His language of "cosmopolitan" (worldwide) versus "parochial" (local or restricted) applicability is equally telling because it assumes the very universalizability that is also linked to white dominance and normativity. Baker, therefore, illustrates rather than undermines the reality and dangers of whiteness—and the need to problematize white dominance and normativity—in U.S. bioethics and society, because he unjustifiably privileges white social practices, belief systems, and cultural norms over the lived experiences of people of color.

Karen Anijar (2003), a cultural studies scholar, concludes from Baker's commentary that majority (white) bioethics is incapable of self-reflection and self-remedy regarding whiteness and white normativity. Anijar issues a powerful challenge to "traditional" bioethics, and one that I believe majority bioethics (traditional or otherwise) should take seriously. However, while I welcome Anijar's overall analysis and insights, I disagree with her generalization from reading Baker that the field cannot scrutinize and critique whiteness. What I do agree with is Anijar's suggestion that it will be necessary to get outside what she calls "the [filter of the] Eurocenter," and I have previously called the elitist epistemology of "bioethics through a lens whitely." Thus I would agree with Anijar—with the addition of my own qualifiers—that white bioethics *alone* cannot adequately interrogate whiteness, and moreover should not be solely determinative of bioethics theory and policy in a pluralist democracy.

COMMUNITY BASED PARTICIPATORY RESEARCH

Community based participatory research (CBPR) is one epistemological method to venture "outside the Master's house"[12] of majority U.S. bioethics and to achieve greater pluralism and democracy in bioethics theorizing and policy making. Such practical bioethics and social justice work directly evolves from and complements the theoretical work of this chapter, and is being conducted in collaboration with professionals and laypersons from within and outside of bioethics. As such, it can answer the question posed by the editors of *The New Atlantis:* "What does all this [white studies and critical race theory] have to do with bioethics . . . what practical effect . . . does it have for confronting and understanding the central dilemmas of bioethics . . . [e.g.] to eliminate [racial] mistrust some groups have toward medicine . . . [and] . . . useful medical research studies or health screening programs?" (2003, 1–2).

In my former position as research director at the Tuskegee University National Center for Bioethics in Research and Health Care, I spent two years (2001–2002) adapting CBPR for bioethics work in collaboration with CBPR expert Douglas Taylor, of the Southeast Community Research Center in Atlanta, Georgia. Our goal was to develop CBPR to serve as an instrument for public engagement and racial/social justice—to elicit and incorporate the values and priorities of marginalized ethnic and socioeconomic communities—to build greater trust and democracy in and through bioethics research. This project was funded by the U.S. Department of Public Health, Centers for Disease Control, as part of the late 1990s U.S. governmental apology for the Tuskegee syphilis study.

CBPR is a practical mechanism for redistributing power and increasing social and racial justice in bioethics, a method to engage more "different and equal" voices in the cultural construction of bioethics, for greater democracy and more useful service in and through such research. CBPR has been employed successfully in related fields such as public health. The basic idea involves building equal and mutually trusting collaborations between professionals and laypersons (from marginalized communities) to: (1) identify what count as compelling bioethics issues for the community in question; (2) determine what research method(s) can best explore and/or remedy such issues; (3) address relevant inequities affecting the community in question in relation to such issues; and (4) develop and disseminate any research "products" to the mutual benefit of all parties. CBPR embraces the collaborative creation of bioethics knowledge and action for the mutual benefit of all partners, with a special focus on decreasing inequities and increasing benefits to marginalized communities.[13] So key methodological distinctions of CBPR concern how knowledge is produced, by whom, and to what end it is disseminated.

CBPR opens up a space of contact between the "majority space" of U.S. bioethics and "minoritized spaces" currently lacking a decision-making voice. "Researchers" and "participants" are interactively linked, without a hierarchical relation serving as a means of cultural control. Thus social meanings, values, and bioethics issues, standards, and policies must be relationally negotiated, and bioethics "knowledge" is democratically created and constructed.[14] CBPR thus manages "diversity" between equal collaborators who may possess different but equal voices so that various partners are seen not as "othered" challenges, obstacles, or problems for "our" work, but rather as sources of opportunity for knowledge and policy enrichment.

One of the successes of this more dialogic approach to standard setting and policy making is that some of those who have previously been "acted upon" (e.g., African American "research subjects," relatives, and other community members affected by the Tuskegee syphilis study) are, through CBPR, becoming actors and agents contributing to the construction of bioethics knowledge, theory, and practice. There are complex challenges for such pluralistic and democratic collaborations to decenter the whiteness of U.S. bioethics, especially in a politically fraught setting such as Tuskegee. Sandra Garcia (2003) strikes a chord—resonating with issues raised by faculty, staff, administrators, and community members at Tuskegee—in her caveat that "decolonizing the minds of both colonizers and . . . colonized has been, and probably always will be difficult." This strikes at the heart of a whole range of "trust" challenges that must be sensitively addressed and respectfully managed throughout such a CBPR project. In Tuskegee these challenges are particularly painful given the ongoing psychological, political, and ethical reverberations of the Tuskegee syphilis study (from the 1930s to the 1970s).

Our CBPR project has had to address issues of mistrust relating to: (1) race/ ethnicity; (2) regional (North-South) differences; (3) class/educational/occupational differences; and (4) community-institution mistrust. The last issue of mistrust was raised by various community members and acknowledged by former Tuskegee administrators, who attribute such mistrust to Tuskegee University's inability to acknowledge whatever responsibility it may have shared for the syphilis study. All these issues need to be explored at greater length by the partners to our project, but in order to respect the CBPR process and not usurp communal decisions regarding the exploration, analysis, and dissemination of these and other issues emerging out of our work, I respectfully put this discussion aside for future collaborative presentations and publications. Suffice it to say, the "practical effect" of the effort to better understand and overcome minority mistrust toward majority bioethics and medicine, and to understand and confront "the central dilemmas of bioethics" through incorporating the views and experiences of previously excluded and violated minorities, could be considerable.

I am currently involved in another three-year CBPR-inspired project in collaboration with Susan Rubin (co-founder, The Ethics Practice, Berkeley) and the Ethnic Health Institute (Oakland and Berkeley, California)—funded by the Walter and Elise Haas Fund and Aetna. The goal of this project—being done in collaboration with lay "ambassadors" in six African American churches in the East Bay, an African American physicians' organization, a majority physicians' organization, and a local organization of clergy and physicians—is to empower African American individuals, family members, and spiritual leaders in end-of-life decision making and to tailor advance directive practices where appropriate for greater "cultural competency" relative to African Americans. It is anticipated that this project may expand to include members of other ethnic groups through the broad-reaching community networks of the Ethnic Health Institute. Our first-year outcomes reveal fascinating West Coast, urban, and other cultural "disruptions" that occur when we compare local African American collaborators (according to their own systematic comparison of their own views and experiences to key themes highlighted in a comprehensive literature review) with "African American norms" previously reported in the bioethics and medical literature regarding advance directives and end-of-life decision making. One risk we thus seek to avoid is further stereotyping African Americans and other minorities through "ethnic study" and "cultural competency" initiatives. It is important to remain vigilant about attendant risks of essentializing and stereotyping minorities as unintended and ironic consequences of such initiatives. However, because CBPR involves African American laypersons and professionals as equal collaborators, it is hoped that more sophistication revealing an evolving range of "African American norms" will emerge.

A final point worth noting is that the Tuskegee syphilis study remains a powerful memory and source of contemporary mistrust for urban, West Coast African Americans (many of whose families migrated to the Bay Area from the Deep South) regarding their interactions with majority medical professionals and institutions. In this practical CBPR-inspired project there is, then, great potential for better understanding and overcoming minority mistrust toward majority bioethics and medicine, and improving bioethics theories and practices on the basis of the views and life experiences of previously excluded minorities. Through this account of my own collaborative research I hope to encourage all in bioethics to work in partnerships with the public that are more diverse and egalitarian[15] as part of our obligation as citizens and professionals in a pluralistic democracy.

ACKNOWLEDGMENT

This chapter is adapted from several of my articles previously published in the *American Journal of Bioethics* from 2003 to 2004.

NOTES

1. As such, "whiteness" may vary across other relational categories, such as ethnicity, gender, class, sexual orientation, region, occupation, religion, language, abilities or disabilities, and historical circumstance, and thus should not be understood as an essentialist category.

2. See, for example, Ignatiev 1995; Brodkin 1998; and Sacks 1998.

3. Harris expounds: "Property is a legal construct by which selected private interests are protected and upheld . . . [enforcing] or [reordering] existing regimes of power . . . [e.g.,] the settled expectations of whites built on the privileges and benefits produced by white supremacy . . . [reproducing] Black subordination . . . disguised as . . . natural law and biology rather than as naked preferences" (107–8).

4. For examples, the definition of "death" is transformed into medico-legal criteria, and "viability" is defined as a biological concept rather than a philosophical question.

5. See, for example, Murray 1992; Dula and Goering 1994; Sanders 1994.

6. Part of the challenge in the case of African American scholars may be what Eagleton et al. (1990) call the problem of the "double optic, at once fighting on [and seeking . . . to prefigure within] a terrain already mapped out by . . . antagonists." At best, perhaps traditions formed in these minoritized ideological sites of overt resistance and dissident cultural practice can be "strengthened before being carried into the mainstream" to begin the process of revising dominant norms (compare Laguerre 1999). Indeed, hooks (1990) argues that such "counter hegemonic cultural practice . . . offers the possibility of radical perspectives from which to see and create, to imagine alternatives, new worlds . . . a site of creativity and power, that inclusive space where we recover ourselves, where we move in solidarity to erase the category colonizer/colonized."

7. Susan Wolf raised a similar concern during the first panel on race and class in bioethics (at the Fall 1996 American Association of Bioethics meeting in San Francisco) in her talk entitled "Race, Gender, and Class: Reintegrating Empiricism into the Core of Bioethics," when she worried aloud that explorations of "other" bioethics had not informed or changed "the core" of bioethics theory and practice. So one might argue that "difference" is "present" in bioethics, but without "making a difference." Wolf's central concern, how-

ever, was that such "diversity" would lead to a kind of "balkanization" of bioethics. So it would seem that she too recognizes and problematizes neither the dominance and normativity of whiteness (at "the core") nor the white-other dualism in bioethics.

8. As Laguerre explains this phenomenon: "Minoritized space becomes such because of the relations the majority maintains with the minority community. It is the linkage between the majority and minority that creates majoritized and minoritized spaces. . . . The villain is the relations, the mechanism through which people become minoritized. They are related to a hegemonic system that in turn converts them into minorities occupying a minoritized . . . status distant . . . space . . . and site of containment, surveillance, and control. . . . [S]tatus distance maintains a space between the majority and minority that prevents the latter from achieving parity. Status defines the positionality between the two groups, the asymmetry of their relations, and reproduces the [hierarchical] spatial distance between them."

9. This history and debate is fleshed out in much fuller detail by contemporary historians of economics. See, for example, Dixon 1999, Levy 2001, and Groenewegen 1998.

10. Here too Baker begs the very questions and argues the very cases I have been arguing. Historically "new white ethnics" including Catholics and Jews are well documented illustrations of assimilation into WASP whiteness and Americanness, as described in full-length books I cite in my original article such as Ignatiev (1995) and Brodkin (1998) and in articles such as Brookhiser (1997) and Sacks (1998). Thus it is no surprise that contemporary non-WASP white ethnics would "share" assimilated WASP values, norms, etc.

11. We can hope that this analysis will enable other commentators who echo Baker's concerns about "ethnic and racial . . . babble" and "balkanization" to hear such concerns in a new light. For example, Howard Trachtman argues against "[diminishing] the whiteness of bioethics and [broadening] the language and application of the discipline to include the perspectives of other constituent ethnic, racial, and class groups in the United States," suggesting that it will have an "adverse impact on individual liberty in the practice of bioethics" on the basis of concerns "that instead of encouraging people to seek a common bioethical language accessible to all [universal versus heterogeneous representative ethical standards] . . . [it] will lead to a proliferation of bioethical dialects . . . [loosening] the ethical fibers that connect us to one another as citizens of the United States . . . in favor of a gray tone color for bioethics" (Trachtman 2003, W13–W14).

12. This language is taken from Anijar (2003).

13. All descriptions of CBPR in this section are adapted from Israel et al. (1998).

14. One product is to make nonneutral and noninnocent assumptions and meanings of "majority" concepts (sites at which the meaning of social experience is negotiated and contested) explicit. Thus multiple meanings ("polyvalent concepts") with no privileged angle more essential than others can be discovered or created (Laguerre 1999, 21).

15. I regard CBPR's greater ethnic and socioeconomic diversity and egalitarianism as more effective and representative of a pluralistic democracy than, for instance, the "public" discussions of the President's Council on Bioethics—involving only the positioned elites of U.S. society—and IRB's inadequate "community" representation to date (a problem addressed elsewhere in the bioethics literature). In the context of the President's Council's "public" discussions, however, I do laud the call from neoconservative William Kristol (chairman, The Bioethics Project) for more "serious public [political] debate . . . beyond

specialists and beyond experts . . . about [a] whole range of questions in the field of bioethics . . . shaping our nation's future and . . . the future of the human race" (Kristol 2003). However, Kristol is more concerned to advance political rather than public debate (with a particular neoconservative ideological agenda), and this with the goal of slowing scientific research until ethical/political debate can manage science more rationally. My own concern is for more public debate, with the aim of engaging more ethnically, culturally, and socioeconomically diverse voices from among the nation's pluralist democracy. Thus I explicitly seek less elitism and greater pluralist and democratic representation in bioethics debate and policy making.

REFERENCES

Anijar, K. 2003. Into the heart of whiteness. *American Journal of Bioethics* 3(2): 29–31.

Baker, R. 2003. Balkanizing bioethics. *American Journal of Bioethics* 3(2), www.bioethics .net/journal/index.php?jid=10.

Barthes, R. 1972. *Mythologies.* Trans. A. Lavers. New York: Hill and Wang.

Brodkin, K. 1998. *How Jews Became White Folks and What That Says about Race in America.* New Brunswick, NJ: Rutgers University Press.

Brookhiser, R. 1997. Others and the WASP world they aspired to. In R. Delgado and J. Stefanic, eds., *Critical White Studies: Looking behind the Mirror.* Pp. 362–67. Philadelphia: Temple University Press.

Carlyle, T. 1849. Occasional discourse on the negro question. *Fraser's Magazine for Town and Country* 40 (February).

Carrese, J. A., and Rhodes, L. A. 1995. Western bioethics on the Navajo reservation. *JAMA* 274(10): 826–45.

Clifford, J. 1989. Notes on travel and theory. In J. Clifford and Dhareshwar, eds., *Inscriptions 5: Traveling Theories, Traveling Theorists.* Santa Cruz: UCSC Center for Cultural Studies.

De Vries, R. 1991. Book review of *Social Science Perspectives on Medical Ethics,* ed. G. Weisz. *Social Science and Medicine* 33(5): 635–36.

Dixon, R. 1999. The origin of the term "Dismal Science" to describe economics. University of Melbourne, Department of Economics, Working Paper Series.

Du Bois, W. E. B. 1920. The souls of whitefolk. In N. Huggins, ed., *W. E. B. Du Bois: Writings.* New York: Library of America.

Dula, A., and Goering, V., eds. 1994. *It Just Ain't Fair: The Ethics of Health Care for African Americans.* Westport, CT: Praeger.

Eagleton, T., et al. 1990. *Nationalism, Colonialism, and Literature.* Minneapolis: University of Minnesota Press.

Editors. 2003. Navel gazing: Bioethics and the unbearable whiteness of being. *The New Atlantis* 1(Summer), www.thenewatlantis.com/archive/2/soa/navel.htu.

Fox, R. 1990. The evolution of American bioethics. In G. Weisz, ed., *Social Science Perspectives on Medical Ethics.* Boston: Kluwer Academic Publishers.

Fussell, P. 1983. *Class: A Guide through the American Status System*. New York: Touchstone.

Garcia, S. 2003. "Decolonizing" the minds of bioethicists: Reflections on psychosocial challenges. *American Journal of Bioethics* 3(2): 27–29.

Groenewegen, P. 1998. Thomas Carlyle, "The Dismal Science," and the contemporary political economy of slavery. Pp. 74–94. Department of Economics, University of Sydney, Festschrift to honor Ray Petridis.

Harris, C. 1998. Whiteness as property. In D. R. Roediger, ed., *Black on White: Black Writers on What It Means to Be White*. Pp. 103–18. New York: Schocken Books.

Hoffmaster, B. 1992. Can ethnography save the life of bioethics? *Social Science and Medicine* 35(12): 1421–31.

hooks, bell. 1990. *Yearning: Race, Gender, and Cultural Politics*. Boston: South End Press.

Ignatiev, N. 1995. *How the Irish Became White*. New York: Routledge.

Israel, B. A., et al. 1998. Review of community based research: Assessing partnership approaches to improve public health. *Annual Review of Public Health* 19: 173–202.

Kristol, W. 2003. Remarks, Presidential Council for Bioethics public discussion, Session 4: Biotechnology and public policy: Embryo and related research. Thursday, June 12. P. 14.

Laguerre, M. 1999. *Minoritized Space: An Inquiry into the Spatial Order of Things*. Berkeley: University of California, Institute of Governmental Studies Press.

Levin, Y. 2003. The paradox of conservative bioethics. *The New Atlantis* 1(Spring): 53–65.

Levy, D. 2001. *How the Dismal Science Got Its Name: Classical Economics and the Ur-Text of Racial Politics*. Ann Arbor, MI: University of Michigan Press.

MacIntyre, A. 1997. *Making Meaning of Whiteness: Exploring Racial Identity with White Teachers*. Albany: State University of New York Press.

Marshall, P. A. 1992. Anthropology and bioethics. *Medical Anthropology Quarterly* 6(1): 49–73.

———. 2001. The relevance of culture for informed consent in U.S.-funded international health research, commissioned paper. In *Ethical and Policy Issues in International Research: Clinical Trials in Developing Countries*. Volume 2. Bethesda: National Bioethics Advisory Commission.

McGill, D., and Pearce, J. K. 1982. British families. In M. McGoldrick et al., eds., *Ethnicity and Family Therapy*, 2nd ed. New York: T Guilford Press.

Muller, J. H. 1994. Anthropology, bioethics, and medicine: A provocative trilogy. *Medical Anthropology Quarterly* 8(4): 448–67.

Murray, R. F. 1992. Minority perspectives on biomedical ethics. In E. Pellegrino et al., eds., *Transcultural Dimensions in Medical Ethics*. Pp. 35–42. Frederick: University Publishing Group.

Roediger, D. 1994. *Towards the Abolition of Whiteness*. New York: Verso.

Sacks, K. 1998. How Jews became white. In P. S. Rothenberg, ed., *Race, Class, and Gender in the United States: An Integrated Study*. Pp. 1000–1114. New York: St. Martin's.

Said, E. 1978. *Orientalism*. New York: Random House Vintage Books.

Sanders, C. 1994. European-American ethos and principlism: An African-American challenge. In Du Bose et al., eds., *A matter of principles? Ferment in U.S. bioethics*. Pp. 148–63. Valley Forge: Trinity Press International.

Trachtman, H. 2003. The Berlin Wall. *American Journal of Bioethics* 3(2): W13–W14.

CHAPTER TWENTY-ONE

Mentoring in Bioethics

Possibilities and Problems

JAMES F. CHILDRESS, PH.D.

While delaying the preparation of this essay on mentoring in bioethics—and wondering why, in a moment of weakness, I had blithely agreed to write it—I had opportunities to interact with several former graduate students, as well as a few former teachers, and these interactions reminded me just how much I have benefited from both sets of relationships. The debt to former teachers, advisers, and mentors is obvious: The careers we now have as teachers and scholars in ethics would not have been possible without their efforts. Though less obvious, the debt to former graduate students, and to newcomers to the field, is nonetheless quite important. It is gratifying to witness young ethicists' progress in research, teaching, and other activities. Comments by former graduate students—during my visits to their current institutions or in letters or in copies of their recently published books—helped to focus and shape my reflections on mentoring.

Usage of the term *mentor* as "wise counselor," which dates to the mid-eighteenth century, derives ultimately from the character Mentor in the *Odyssey* and penultimately from the prominence Fénelon gave the same character in a French romance at the end of the seventeenth century. When Odysseus decided to undertake the expedition against Troy, Mentor, a long-time friend, agreed to oversee his household and take care of his young son, Telemachus. Mentor's noteworthy characteristics included friendship, integrity, honesty, and a willingness to speak out. When the goddess Athena wanted to assist Odysseus or Telemachus, she sometimes assumed Mentor's bodily form and spoke through his voice—for instance, to provide instructions to the young Telemachus about his journey to find out about his father.

Despite this derivation, there is considerable uncertainty about the nature, possibilities, and limits of mentoring, and hence about the responsibilities and privileges of mentors and mentees. I will draw on a small portion of the vast conceptual, theoretical, and empirical literature. Much of the literature focuses on specific contexts of mentoring, and I recognize that conclusions about mentoring clinical psychologists or high school teachers, for instance, may not fully apply to graduate training and professional development in ethics and bioethics. Nevertheless, several points from this literature are useful and may be illuminating.

NARRATIVE OF A SUCCESSFUL MENTORSHIP

W. Brad Johnson (2002) presents the following narrative as an example of a "successful mentorship." It offers a way into several conceptual, normative, and empirical questions and observations about mentoring. A first-year graduate student (Tim) approached an associate professor (Dr. Guide) in a clinical psychology doctoral program about the possibility of a mentoring relationship, in part because Dr. Guide was known as both "an excellent teacher and a productive scholar." However, because she was concerned about the demands on her limited time and recognized the importance of compatibility between mentor and mentee, she was selective in making a commitment to mentorships. Hence, she informed Tim that she would be unable to accept a new protégé until one of her current protégés graduated and, in addition, she would need to spend a year as his formal adviser in order to determine their "potential match in scholarly interest, career objectives, and personality."

> After a year Dr. Guide determined that Tim was hard working, capable, sincerely interested in her research, and able to contribute constructively to her scholarly projects. She agreed to mentor Tim and scheduled a meeting to discuss mutual expectations for the relationship—included anticipated duration, her policy on confidentiality in mentorships, frequency of contact, and cross-gender concerns. For example, she elicited agreement from Tim that both would work to maintain good professional boundaries. Dr. Guide further solicited from Tim a description of his "ideal" career trajectory, with emphasis on his early career dream (a faculty position in a medical school or clinical graduate program). Dr. Guide began directing Tim toward important professional opportunities, including teaching and research assistantships, coauthorship on articles and conference papers, and top-notch clinical

practicum placements. She introduced him to colleagues at conferences and included him as a cotherapist, coteacher, and coresearcher on different occasions so that she could clearly model her approach to professional activities. Moreover, Dr. Guide was encouraging and supportive of Tim. Although honest in her feedback, she communicated a vision of Tim's competence and potential that markedly bolstered his self-perception and subsequent performance.

Although clearly quite positive over time, the relationship did not escape all tensions and conflicts. As Tim was finishing his graduate studies, he was able on his own to get an article published in a prestigious journal in psychology. After initially "responding coolly" to Tim's good news, Dr. Guide "realized that Tim's increasing independence and pending graduation were difficult for her. She took the initiative in processing this with Tim and warmly congratulated him. She wrote excellent letters of recommendation for him. When Tim departed the program, the two continued to collaborate at times and enjoyed a continuing friendship." I want to use this narrative as a way to explore definitions and types of mentoring, ideal mentorships, and ethical considerations in mentoring.

WHAT IS MENTORING?

The term *mentor* has served as a "buzzword" for the last couple of decades. As a result, sociologist Judith P. Swazey (2001, 481) bemoans "the extensive and dysfunctional overuse and misuse of the term in graduate education." Even though all graduate students have teachers who instruct them in courses and advisers for their programs and their dissertations, as Swazey notes, not all have mentors, at least "in the full, classical sense of the concept." Because the term has so many different meanings for different people, some commentators avoid it altogether and focus instead on the kinds of assistance students receive in their development in two major domains: career and psychosocial domains (Kram 1985). Such assistance includes advice, counsel, and support, typically provided over time by an experienced person (mentor) to a less experienced person (mentee).

Distinctions among types of mentoring relationships tend to emphasize differences in intensity, scope, specificity, and duration as well as in degree of formality. For instance, *primary mentorships,* according to Brad Johnson, "are enduring and bonded relationships between a single mentor and a protégé that often last for several years" (Johnson 2002, 89). This is the paradigmatic conception of mentorship, embodied in the character Mentor and represented in the modern example of Dr. Guide.

Even if primary mentorships are paradigmatic, we should not overlook or neglect *secondary mentorships*, which are "less intense, less comprehensive, and of shorter duration," or *tertiary mentorships*, which, in a more defined period, implement one or more tasks or functions of mentoring (Johnson 2002; see also Russell and Adams 1997, for "primary mentorship"). It appears that Dr. Guide was only willing to embark on primary mentorships, which involve greater commitments and promise larger rewards for both parties. However, secondary and tertiary mentorships are also very important for graduate students and new professionals, particularly because, as I will argue, multiple mentorships are probably both necessary, given limitations on potential mentors' time and commitments, and valuable, given the variety of needs and preferences of mentees.

The value of multiple mentorships is arguably even greater in bioethics, a relatively new and uncharted field that continues to evolve in part because of its close connection to practice in medicine and health care, in research, and in public policy. After all, coming from a variety of disciplines, the first and second generations entered (or better created) "bioethics" without any intention of doing "bioethics" as such, since the field was still emerging and lacked a unifying term until the early 1970s. Many current graduate students still have varied disciplinary backgrounds and varied career goals under the broad rubric of bioethics. In addition, the academic, professional, and practical contexts for doing bioethics are immensely varied. For all these reasons—and perhaps others—multiple mentorships, including secondary and tertiary ones, are quite promising.

The primary mentorship involving Dr. Guide and Tim was mutually arranged; they selected each other rather than being assigned by a third party, such as an academic department. Much of the literature characterizes mutually selected mentorships as "informal," in contrast to "formal mentorships" assigned by third parties. This language is unhelpful and misleading. The mentorship in this case was highly formal—the "mutual expectations" were spelled out in some detail and both Dr. Guide and Tim agreed to them. It would have been even more formal if it had included a contract. Other less formal mentorships may involve only tacit, though nevertheless real and important, expectations. Mutually selected mentorships may result from a process of negotiation. Over time, through the year-long formal adviser-advisee relationship and their conversations and discussions, Dr. Guide and Tim examined their mutual expectations and reached an agreement about how to proceed; they had, in effect, tested each other.

The available evidence suggests that protégés in nonassigned, mutually selected mentorships "receive more career and psychosocial functions from mentors and report greater effect from, and satisfaction with, the mentorship" (Johnson 2002, 89). As a result, many propose that, instead of assigning or matching mentors and mentees, institutions should encourage and facilitate the formation of such mentorships by creating a "climate of mentorship" and by providing appropriate incentives for faculty to accept and cultivate such mentorships.

WHAT COUNTS AS SUCCESSFUL MENTORING?

Recall that Brad Johnson presented his example of Dr. Guide and Tim as a "successful mentorship." However, the criteria for success are not clearly specified. It is unsettled, for instance, whether the relevant criteria should focus on the qualities of the two parties in the mentorship, on features of their relationship, or on outcomes. It might seem appropriate to focus on outcomes, since mentorships are goal oriented: Their aim is to foster development in career and psychosocial domains (Kram 1985).There are other considerations, though, since a graduate student's success in a career generally depends on a variety of personal factors (such as ability and personality) and contextual factors (such as the availability of positions in particular fields at particular times) more than on the qualities of the mentor or of the mentorship. Furthermore, some outcomes, such as career advancement, are more objective, while others, such as the mentee's satisfaction or dissatisfaction, are more subjective.

It is also appropriate to evaluate mentoring in terms of the qualities of the participants, particularly the mentors, and of their relationship. Let's start with mentees' ideal preferences for mentors. It is immediately evident from the literature and from personal experience that there is wide variation among the qualities mentees attribute to ideal mentors and presumably seek in actual mentors. Interestingly, the available evidence does not support a claim that some qualities are universally desired in mentors. One study identified two "core features of the ideal doctoral student mentor": The ideal mentor would have good communication skills and offer honest feedback about the student's work (Rose 2003). Both qualities were evident in Dr. Guide's mentorship with Tim. However, even these qualities did not receive universal endorsement in the study; instead, they received "strong endorsement"—over 75 percent of the respondents gave them a 5 (on a 1–5 scale). No other qualities were strongly endorsed even though other items on the list were also generally positive (Rose 2003).

Instead of seeking an ideal mentor for a primary mentorship—and often being frustrated in the search—graduate students and young professionals might more fruitfully seek multiple mentors, who perhaps can collectively discharge the several functions of mentoring and meet their needs and preferences. According to Rose, "Anecdotal reports support the phenomenon of 'multiple mentors.' The experience of having one person who provides a comprehensive mentoring relationship appears to be relatively less common than the experience of forming re-lationships with several individuals, either sequentially . . . or perhaps simultaneously, who each provide some aspect of mentoring. The holistic combination of these many relationships may be experienced in the protégé as constituting mentoring, but the various aspects of the relationship may not originate from a single person" (Rose 2003, 491). In contrast, then, to the case of Dr. Guide and Tim, who appeared to have a single, primary, exclusive relationship, multiple partial mentors—secondary or tertiary mentors—may be more appropriate in many if not most cases.

For any kind of mentorship, matching is very important, whether the two parties make the match, based on identified interests, or others do so. For instance, the announcement of the "mentoring program" of the American Society for Bioethics and Humanities (ASBH) in 2002 stated that it gives "students and early career scholars opportunities to meet distinguished faculty in bioethics and the medical humanities throughout the conference" and that it includes a separate "mentoring session" of an hour and a quarter. It further noted that "students will be assigned mentors based on the area of interest selected on the registration form: clinical ethics, philosophy, policy, law, history, literature, religion, social science, cross cultural ethics, empirical research, education, or research ethics." Matched students were asked to send their biographical information to the matched mentor prior to the meeting to minimize the amount of time spent on introductions (www.asbh.org).

The mentors were not selected by the mentees but were assigned by the professional organization on the basis of submitted information. Presumably the mentoring session involved groups of matched students, rather than one-on-one interactions, but other interactions were also possible outside the formal mentoring session. As is usual in third-party mentoring assignments, the matching was based on areas of intellectual interest. Other concerns also arise in mutually selected mentorships and should arise in departmentally arranged mentorships. These include gender, race, and ethnicity, as well as personality and style of mentoring, some of which were assumed or explicitly addressed in the process of negotiation between Dr. Guide and Tim. Even within the guidance function, there is a range of styles, for instance, from directive to nondirective. Certainly, Dr. Guide tended to be very directive. Nevertheless, given what I have called a process of negotiation in this case, it is reasonable to assume that Tim was aware of her style and accepted it.

A related matter of style concerns independence/dependence. There are risks when the mentor takes, or wants to take, excessive responsibility for the mentee's progress—as Dr. Guide apparently did. One risk is that the mentor will not encourage the mentee's independent initiatives and will be troubled by the mentee's independent achievements. Dr. Guide at first, before recognizing that her response was inappropriate, appeared to view Tim's independent preparation and submission of an article to a prestigious journal, which accepted it, as a betrayal of their relationship. What should have been a reason for elation instead, at first, produced disappointment.

WHAT IS ETHICAL MENTORING?

Even when established bioethicists mentor developing bioethicists, ethical issues may arise and require attention. Some issues—e.g., honest feedback—have already received passing attention in this essay. Here I will briefly consider confidentiality, conflicts of interest, and conflicts of loyalty, exploitation, and fairness in mentoring.

Confidentiality

Not surprisingly, confidentiality is an important issue in mentoring because of the need for open and frank discussion. If the mentor and mentee do not negotiate the nature and limits of confidentiality, the mentor should declare his or her policy, just as Dr. Guide did, so the graduate student's decision about entering into the mentorship can be adequately informed. After all, the policy on confidentiality may affect the extent to which the mentee discloses relevant information to the mentor and hence may affect the outcome of the mentorship.

Conflicts of Loyalty, Conflicts of Interest, and Avoidance of Exploitation

A conflict of loyalty is a situation in which an agent has loyalties to X and to Y and these loyalties come into conflict, while a conflict of interest is a situation that may create a temptation for an agent to act against another person's interest in order to benefit himself or herself. For example, if a faculty member has obligations to the department that conflict with his or her obligations to the mentee, this is a conflict of loyalties as well as of obligations. Although perhaps rare, a situation could emerge in which a mentee's acknowledgment of personal or academic problems and request for help in addressing those problems could lead to a negative judgment about a student's suitability for fellowship aid and for other opportunities; such a situation could also raise questions about a junior faculty member's fitness for contract renewal or for promotion and tenure. Hence, wherever possible, we should separate the evaluation that is part of mentoring from the evaluation that is used to measure a person's progress in a graduate program or in a faculty position. Even though such separation is not always feasible, it is still worth affirming as an ideal.

Turning to conflicts of interest, I would note that it is not illegitimate for potential mentors, such as Dr. Guide, to be "quite selective" in choosing mentees and, in the selection process, to consider the benefits of the mentorship to themselves, as Dr. Guide did when she determined that Tim would be "able to contribute constructively to her scholarly projects." However, such an arrangement creates a conflict of interest. The mentor may be tempted to provide advice that favors the graduate student's potential contribution to the mentor's projects over advice that would help him or her develop independent projects.

In the absence of clear guidelines, a process of transparency and continuing negotiation may offer the best solution to such a conflict of interest, and thus prevent exploitation of the mentee. Other kinds of exploitation are more easily identified and rejected—most notoriously sexual exploitation. Even though the narrative does not indicate that Dr. Guide and Tim explicitly addressed sexual relations between mentor and mentee, their discussion of "mutual expectations" included "cross-gender concerns" and "good professional boundaries." Excusing sexual contact in mentorships on the basis of the mentee's consent fails to appreciate the significant power differential—a mentor, especially one who promotes a mentee's career as Dr. Guide promoted Tim's, has tremendous power over the mentee, whose freedom of choice might be substantially compromised.

Fairness in Mentoring

Once we move beyond concerns about exploitation, it may be surprising that fairness remains so central in an ethical assessment of mentoring. The principle of fairness can apply to the professional field as a whole or to particular graduate programs or even to particular individual mentors. To be sure, mentoring is an interpersonal activity and practice, and potential mentors generally have discretion about which graduate students and other newcomers to mentor. Potential mentors can be "quite selective," as Dr. Guide was, but questions of fairness will arise if this selection reflects some ethically suspect classification, such as preference based on gender, race, or ethnicity. Nevertheless, as we have seen, mentoring may be more successful when matches are based on mutually appreciated qualities or characteristics. Rather than offering a firm a priori resolution of this tension, we should continue to struggle with it in policies, practices, and particular decisions.

Mentors may face other questions of fairness. A faculty member who is mentoring more than one graduate student may have to determine which mentee among several mentees or among other students in the same program to recommend for a particularly attractive fellowship, internship, or opportunity in research or teaching. Within a particular graduate program, fairness requires that all graduate students have an opportunity to receive mentoring if they want it. Yet many graduate programs fail to ensure the availability of mentors, much less the quality of any mentoring that does occur. For various reasons, institutions should create a "climate of mentoring" and encourage and facilitate mentoring, rather than mandating it for faculty and for graduate students and assigning them to particular mentorships.

Given the uneven mentoring in graduate programs, professional organizations can and should help plug the gaps. One example may be relevant: Many of us who had not directly studied with the late Paul Ramsey nonetheless greatly benefited from his interest in and support for newcomers to the field and his willingness to interact with us—indeed, to mentor us—at professional meetings. While such professional mentoring is voluntary and discretionary from the standpoint of the individual bioethicist, the profession as a whole can and should take steps—as ASBH has done—to increase opportunities for graduate students and young professionals to receive mentoring.

Commentators on Mentor's actions in the *Odyssey* often note the place of divine intervention, for example, when Athena takes over Mentor's bodily form and voice to provide needed guidance. There is no deus ex machina for mentoring in bioethics. In view of what Judith Swazey nicely calls the "deinstitutionalization" of mentoring in graduate programs, a modern substitute for divine intervention might be collective faculty, departmental, and institutional action to ensure the availability and quality of mentoring, both for the benefit of the mentee and for the future of the field. (In focusing on the potential benefits for individual mentees, we should not overlook the potential benefit to the field from the early and easy incorporation of graduate students and young professionals into the profession and its ethos.) In Swazey's view, this deinstitutionalization results in part from the increasing separation of education and research (Swazey 2001).

I do not oppose a separate role or activity of mentoring—indeed, mentoring can often be performed by someone who is not also the graduate student's teacher or adviser. In general, however, I think we ought to see mentoring as an aspect of teaching and advising graduate students. In accepting the role of teaching and advising graduate students, faculty members, in my judgment, also implicitly accept mentoring responsibilities. Still, a single faculty member can teach and even advise many more students than he or she can helpfully mentor—at least in the sense of primary mentorship. While primary mentorship, exemplified in the narrative of Dr. Guide and Tim, remains an important ideal, we should not overlook or neglect the important secondary and tertiary mentorships, which provide specific mentoring functions without the holistic commitment of the primary mentorship. In addition, several features of bioethics that I have noted perhaps make multiple, partial mentorships even more important in this field than in some others.

Except as an implication of the obligations and responsibilities bioethicists assume in accepting roles of teaching and advising, mentoring is not, strictly speaking, obligatory. Nevertheless, based on gratitude, if nothing else, experienced and established bioethicists should feel an obligation to mentor newcomers to the field who may or may not be their own students. Furthermore, a commitment to advance the field of bioethics also implies a commitment to secondary and tertiary mentoring if not to primary mentoring. Potential mentors may even discover that mentoring is not an unwelcome task but a rich opportunity.

REFERENCES

Anderson, E. M., and Shannon, A. L. 1988. Toward a conceptualization of mentoring. *Journal of Teacher Education* 39: 38–42.

Johnson, W. B. 2002. The intentional mentor: Strategies and guidelines for the practice of mentoring. *Professional Psychology: Research and Practice* 33(1): 88–96.

Kram, R. E. 1985. *Mentoring at Work: Developmental Relationships in Organizational Life.* Glenview, IL: Scott Foresman.

Rose, G. L. 2003. Enhancement of mentor selection using the ideal mentor scale. *Research in Higher Education* 44(4): 473–94.

Russell, J. E., and Adams, D. M. 1997. The changing nature of mentoring in organizations: An introduction to the special issue on mentoring in organizations. *Journal of Vocational Behavior* 51(1): 1–14.

Swazey, J. P. 2001. Graduate students and mentors: The need for divine intervention: Commentary on "Mentoring: Some Ethical Considerations" (Weil). *Science and Engineering Ethics* 7(4): 483–85.

Weil, V. 2001. Mentoring: Some ethical considerations. *Science and Engineering Ethics* 7(4): 471–82.

CHAPTER TWENTY-TWO

Obligations to Fellow and Future Bioethicists

Publication

HILDE LINDEMANN, PH.D.

Ludwig Wittgenstein once likened doing philosophy to swimming under water—there is an almost irresistible temptation to come up for air. Many bioethicists, I dare say, feel the same way about writing for publication. We're tempted to surface when we stare for an hour or so at that blank first page, when the dreadful suspicion grows on us that everything we're saying has already been said much better by everybody else, and when we hit the point where, in the vivid image of a friend of mine, we've set our hair on fire and are trying to put it out with a tack hammer. What keeps us going is our desire to participate in the ongoing debates and discussions in the field, intellectual curiosity about some topic that we want to understand better, or a rash promise to an editor or granting agency. The standing expectation at our various institutions that we will be productive scholars doesn't hurt, either.

As a reasonably well-broken-in author, the current editor of *Hypatia*, former editor at the *Hastings Center Report*, editor of a number of collections of essays, general coeditor of two book series, and—worst of all—a moral philosopher by trade, I've developed some tolerably fixed views over the years about the ethics of academic publishing. In what follows, I'll identify what I take to be the more important, commonly shared understandings of the responsibilities attached to the five roles that make the wheels of bioethics publishing go round: the author, the publisher, the editor, the reviewer, and the graduate student mentor. As it's largely through publishing that bioethics defines itself as a field, our professional identities, relationships with our colleagues, and the public's trust in bioethics all hinge on these role-related responsibilities. I begin with the most important role—that of the author, as it's the author's work that lies at the very heart of publishing.

AUTHORS

As Alasdair MacIntyre might have said but didn't, bioethics publishing is a *practice*—a settled, socially recognized, rule-governed activity involving a number of people in the exercise of a set of skills aimed at some specific end. MacIntyre argues that unlike such external goods as money and social prestige, a practice's internal goods can only be attained by exercising the virtues that inhere in the practice (MacIntyre 1984, 187–91). If this is so, authors can't have the satisfaction of getting the argument just right, of understanding something difficult, of contributing to a growing body of knowledge, and the like unless they possess the requisite virtues.

The ancient Greek virtues of courage, practical judgment, and temperance surely attach to publishing: it takes courage to subject one's work to the scrutiny of peers and to keep writing even when reviewers have panned one's most recent book. It takes practical judgment to structure one's arguments properly and to be a good critic of one's own work. And it takes temperance to refrain from becoming self-important and to allow for the reasonableness of other opinions. Add to these the Christian virtues of faith, hope, and love—faith in one's work, for example, hope that the scholarly enterprise increases understanding, and love of the written word—and it becomes clear that she who would reap the benefits internal to publication must be well steeped in the virtues.

Because virtues are qualities of character, however, they can't show us our responsibilities to others except in the most general terms. To understand more specifically what authors owe the other participants in the practice of publishing and to the reading public, we have to identify the socially normative expectations that seem to be operating at the moment and then assess those expectations to see whether they withstand moral scrutiny. JM

First and most importantly, authors are expected to be honest. They violate this expectation when they write things they know to be false, or fudge their data, or misrepresent other bioethicists' positions. Second, authors owe their colleagues consideration as their work undergoes prepublication review. Most journals in which bioethicists publish operate on a shoestring, with no extra money in their budgets for paying their referees, yet the work of refereeing is a critical part of how the field monitors itself. Because it's burdensome and time-consuming to do a decent job of refereeing, it's inconsiderate of authors to submit a paper to several journals simultaneously. To do so is to make promiscuous demands on what is, after all, a limited resource. For the same reason, authors shouldn't rely on the journal's referees to help them revise their work, nor should they submit a new, improved draft after the earlier one has already gone out for review.

Book publishers sometimes have the same expectation as journals: that authors will submit their manuscripts to only one publisher at a time. Here, however, the expectation isn't warranted. Book publishers are business people who expect to make money on the books they acquire and they pay their referees to assess a book's marketability as well as its scholarly soundness, so they operate in a rather different environment from academics who edit journals for love and not money. It's greatly to the book publisher's advantage, of course, to have an exclusive right to accept or refuse a manuscript without having to compete with other publishers for it, but this puts the author at an unfair *dis*advantage. Bioethicists aren't going to make much money from their published books anyway (unless, possibly, from a textbook), which is a reason to favor shared moral understandings that allow authors to strike the most advantageous bargain they can.

Once when I was an editor at the *Hastings Center Report*, a well-known bioethicist who shall remain nameless missed a deadline for a paper he'd been invited to write. When I nudged him, he replied, "Oh, promises to editors are written in water." Editors are used to this attitude, and I think it's healthier than panicking, losing sleep, and pushing oneself to the breaking point to turn something in on time. All the same, authors, like the rest of us, are expected to keep their promises. And it's worth remembering that promises to editors involve follow-through: writing to length as well as to deadline, responding to editorial queries promptly, reading page proofs quickly and carefully, turning in the author's questionnaire (for books) in a timely manner, letting editors know one's whereabouts during the production process, and so on.

Identifying some aspect of health care practice that is a cause for moral concern, developing a piece of bioethics theory, doing empirical research that allows us to understand better how patients or health care providers actually think, feel, and act—this sort of research becomes accessible to fellow and future bioethicists only through the shared cooperative activity of many people. Ultimately, then, it's the obligation of authors to do their share of cooperating.

PUBLISHERS

If the author's activity sits at the center of the practice of publishing, it's the publisher who provides the infrastructure—the compositors, sales or subscription managers, printing firms, warehouses, financial record keepers, and all the rest—that allows us to get our work into print at all. Although from an author's point of view it sometimes looks as if academic book publishers are in the business of thwarting any attempt to publish anything except textbooks that sell a hundred thousand copies in their first year, they actually do a pretty good job, given the current economic climate, of making available books that are of interest mainly to scholars in the relatively small field of bioethics. In addition to putting books in the hands of the reading public, though, publishers have a number of other responsibilities, not all of which are discharged equally well by each.

For starters, book publishers are expected to provide authors with acquisitions and production editors who support their work rather than impeding the process of getting the book written and into print. They are expected to use copyeditors who actually know how to edit copy and book designers who can—well, design. Then they are expected to market books intelligently, targeting the readers who are actually likely to buy them. And finally, they are expected to keep books in print for a reasonable length of time and reprint them if there's a continuing demand for them.

Those responsibilities (except for competent copyediting) apply primarily to publishers of books. Other responsibilities apply to publishers of books and scholarly journals alike. Both sorts of publishers are expected to respond promptly to requests for permission to reprint excerpts from previously published work. And in that connection, neither sort is supposed to demand permission from authors to reprint their own work, though the author is expected to acknowledge the publisher in a note saying that the work is reprinted. Although some book and journal publishers require authors to seek their permission to quote short passages from material to which the publisher holds the copyright, I can't see the justification for this expectation, as it impedes the free circulation of ideas. Because publishers are expected to *promote* the free circulation of ideas, they ought, in addition to setting generous quotation policies, to charge reasonable reprint fees—say, no more than a hundred dollars for a chapter or a journal article—so that the cost of keeping work accessible to other scholars doesn't become prohibitive.

Publishers, then, are expected to make available, to the bioethics community and the larger public, the results of bioethicists' scholarly activity—the activity that in large part defines the field and our place in it.

EDITORS

Editors are the people who sign rejection letters and so are universally hated. Book acquisitions editors are expected to produce a list of books of high scholarly quality, while at the same time limiting their acquisitions to books that will sell reasonably well. Journal editors are expected to take responsibility for the quality of the journal's contents, while at the same time making rationing decisions about how and to whom the limited space of an issue is to be allocated. Mediating between these somewhat contrary expectations requires both kinds of editors to function, under conditions of moderate scarcity, as gatekeepers to a resource whose value they are charged with preserving.

Editors' most important moral responsibility is to maintain the integrity of the editorial review process. Editors must not discount unfavorable reviews simply because the author is well known in the field, or is one of the editor's protégées, or is someone the editor likes. By the same token, however, since reviewers are no more virtuous than the rest of us, the editor must, to the best of her ability, set aside or assign less weight to reviews that are based on a sloppy reading of the submission, or that are malicious and spiteful.

It's a mark of editorial irresponsibility to keep authors waiting for many months, even years, before a decision is made whether to accept their submissions. Because it can take a couple of months to find two or three competent scholars who are willing to read a manuscript, a four-month review period is reasonable for journal submissions. For book submissions, which take longer to assess, six months may be needed. Equally irresponsible is to keep authors waiting several years before their work sees print. This can't always be avoided, especially by prestigious journals with high rates of submission, but it's a state of affairs that editors are expected to address rather than shrugging it off.

The moral expectations surrounding editors' gatekeeping functions are, I think, quite widely shared, even if in practice editors don't always do a very good job of living up to them. There is, however, another moral understanding that I would like to see between editors and authors that is, as far as I can tell at the moment, not widely shared at all. That is the expectation that editors will *help* authors. That when the book is under contract, the editor will read as much of the manuscript as she can and provide encouragement and intelligent feedback. That when the article has been accepted for publication, the editor will work with the author to get it into first-rate final shape. That when authors ask for advice or help, it will be cheerfully—and promptly—forthcoming. I've been blessed with a num-

ber of such editors and am deeply grateful to them all. What they have in common, in my experience, is their ability to forge a bond with their authors of trust,
mutual respect, and even affection.

In the broadest terms, the editor's role is to help authors maintain high standards for work in bioethics, both by how they conduct the peer review process and
by what they accept for publication. Ultimately, then, editors owe it to present and
future bioethicists to be honest brokers.

PEER REVIEWERS

If they play their cards right, peer reviewers are almost as likely as editors to
break an author's heart. Leigh Turner (2003) has written a wonderfully wicked
guide for the sadistic reviewer. To make sure that a submission is rejected, or at
least sent back for numerous rounds of revisions, Turner recommends that the
reviewer make impossible demands. If, for example, a medical journal imposes
a 2,000-word limit and the author does a splendid job of discussing health inequities, globalization, and social justice within that limit, the reviewer can reject
the piece on the grounds that it does not sufficiently address the literature in epidemiology, feminist ethics, public health, cultural studies, and research ethics. A
second strategy is to review manuscripts lying far outside the referee's area of expertise, but to criticize the author for not using the referee's preferred topics and
methods. And, since anonymous review protects referees from accountability,
Turner invites them to be as vicious and venomous in these comments as they
please.

Turner claims that "most journal editors send revised manuscripts to a new
set of reviewers" (208) who need not confine themselves to determining whether
the problems identified originally have been resolved, but this (I hope) is just
Turner's fun. While I know of no journal editor who sends a revised manuscript
to any but the original reviewers, Turner may be keeping lower company than I.

He closes his essay by arguing, seriously this time, for a system whereby reviewers' identities are known to the author. On this point, he and I disagree.
While there is much to be said for the forced accountability that attends this sort
of transparency, I believe it asks too much of authors, who are often and understandably protective of their work and touchy when it is criticized. When a review
is negative, even if authors have the self-discipline to refrain from arguing with
the reviewer (and many don't), they are bound to direct their resentment at the
reviewer and feel uncomfortable on occasions where they and she find themselves on the same panel or working group. I once naively revealed my name to

an author whose manuscript I gave a negative review, and not only did he send me a lengthy e-mail to explain, unconvincingly, why he was right and I was wrong, but I discovered several months later that he was on the search committee for a job for which I'd applied.

Reviewers are the invaluable judges who keep bioethicists from their own worst errors and, with editors, are directly responsible for maintaining the quality of published work in bioethics. Their obligation to present and future bioethicists is to put a "not" in front of everything Turner recommends.

GRADUATE STUDENT MENTORS

I close with a brief reflection on what senior bioethicists can do to initiate their graduate students into the mysteries of academic publishing. When I agree to become a student's director, I extract a promise that he or she will never, ever send a manuscript out for publication without showing it to me first. That saves inflicting raw or half-baked work on a busy editorial staff and its reviewers. Sometimes the students do it anyway, but mostly they see the sense in allowing me to help them make it their best work before submitting it to a journal.

Students might also be encouraged to look at a journal's Web site to see if it accepts unsolicited book reviews, what editorial style the journal uses, how long a paper should be, and how to send a submission. In addition, professors sometimes ask students to write their seminar papers as if they were going to submit them to, say, the *Hastings Center Report* or *Bioethics*. Another strategy is to ask students to write critical reviews of books as a requirement for a bioethics course, and then to show them how the reviews can be improved.

Mentors often involve their graduate students in their own editorial projects, relegating certain chores such as assembling the bibliography, reading proofs, or even preparing the index to their research assistants. Even more valuable is the experience of working with a graduate student on an edited collection, so that the student learns how to send papers out for review, select the ones that will appear in the collection, assist in establishing a coherent order for the papers, write the introduction, and shepherd the collection through the production process. Less ambitiously, Laura Purdy suggests that when a journal asks the mentor to review a submission, the mentor might give a copy of the manuscript to his graduate students and ask them to write up a set of comments. Then, when the mentor has written his own comments, the students can trade papers with him and learn how it's done.

Do bioethicists owe this sort of mentoring to bioethicists-to-be? Arguably they do, not only because they are expected to professionalize their students, but because the future of the field depends on how successfully they fulfill this expectation. Bioethics consists to no small degree in what bioethicists do in the classroom, in the courts, and in the clinic. But what gives it its basic identity as a well-established and growing field is the accumulating literature that marks it as a distinctive, interdisciplinary endeavor. To the extent that this endeavor is worth pursuing, bioethicists owe it to each other and to future bioethicists to contribute as authors, editors, reviewers, and mentors to the settled, socially recognized, rule-governed practice of bioethics publishing.

ACKNOWLEDGMENTS

Many thanks to Lisa Eckenwiler, Felicia Cohn, and Margaret Urban Walker for their useful comments on an earlier draft. Portions of this essay appeared in *Hypatia* 21, no. 1 (Winter 2006).

REFERENCES

MacIntyre, A. 1984. *After Virtue: A Study in Moral Theory*. 2nd ed. Notre Dame: University of Notre Dame Press.
Turner, L. 2003. Cloaked journal referees: Esteemed goalkeepers of the scholarly world. *Soundings* 86(1–2): 203–10.

PART VI

Assessing Bioethics and Bioethicists

CHAPTER TWENTY-THREE

The Virtue of Attacking
the Bioethicist

TOD CHAMBERS, PH.D.

Recently I was working on an essay in which I wanted to examine the criticism raised against bioethics by Renée Fox and Judith Swazey. In an article titled "Medical Morality Is Not Bioethics" (1984), these two sociologists of medicine describe their fieldwork experience in China and compare it to H. Tristram Engelhardt's reflections in the *Hastings Center Report* about a trip to China that he took with a group of bioethics scholars (1980). Fox and Swazey argue that Engelhardt profoundly misunderstood the moral basis of Chinese medicine because of his particular Western philosophical bias. The authors then analyze the way bioethics has developed in the United States, and they conclude that it has not taken into account broader communal values outside of the analytical philosophical framework. When I mentioned to various colleagues what I was working on, several responded that Fox and Swazey's argument is motivated by the resentment that they felt having lost a disciplinary battle with bioethics. One of these humanities scholars argued that this was best illustrated by the way they had lost in the decisions about medical school curricula, where the humanities is now more often taught than the social sciences. I confess that I wondered, assuming that these critiques were correct, how I should respond. Does the motivation for the argument matter at all in our evaluation of an argument? When I spoke of this criticism with a sociologist of medicine he replied by questioning the motivation of my colleagues' criticism.

This method of critique is an example of a class of argument referred to as ad hominem, which literally means "to the man." Ad hominem critiques are those that criticize the speaker of an argument rather than focusing on the validity of an argument itself; generally such critiques are considered a fallacious form of rebuttal. The Western tradition of philosophy strongly denounces such critiques, for it is argued that statements should be judged and scrutinized without regard to the kind of person making the statement. If a person presents an argument for the validity of a new medication, the fact that he or she also happens to be racist should not be considered relevant. Ad hominem arguments are thought to divert our attention away from relevant matters in evaluating claims being made; the academic world cares primarily about the character of ideas, not the character of their promulgator. In fact, in my example of the social science criticism of bioethics, the sociologist was himself employing a form of ad hominem attack on the ad hominem attack, the *tu quoque* form ("you too"). In his book *Ad Hominem Arguments,* Douglas Walton (1998) argues that one needs to distinguish types of ad hominem attacks, and, by doing so, one can discern that certain forms of these attacks are not necessarily fallacious, that we may desire to include some forms of ad hominem arguments in the range of valid forms of criticism. For example, there are areas of knowledge in which most would agree that the identity or character of the person presenting information is a relevant consideration in evaluating the information. We would think it important to be informed that this same person has a monetary stake in the success of the drug being proposed, for we worry that the financial benefits the person may receive from the drug's success may lead to biased results. A second common exception that is made for ad hominem attacks concerns the issue of expertise. In a legal setting, the assessment of a person's credentials is seen as an essential step in accepting the testimony of that person. Finally, ad hominem critiques are often considered relevant when we doubt the personal ability of the person making the claim to the knowledge. Suppose a physician tells us that a patient who speaks only Spanish has given informed consent for a medical procedure. If I tell you that I doubt that the physician's high school Spanish is adequate to have gained this information, then you might agree that we should distrust the validity of the informed consent.

Ad hominem critiques are thus valid in the evaluation of certain types of knowledge claims when the acquisition of the evidence is contingent upon the character or skills of the investigator. So in disciplines like physics, we may believe (assuming that we do not wish to engage in the science studies debate) that ad hominem critiques are generally irrelevant, whereas in cultural anthropology, the knowledge acquired is directly related to the character of the fieldworker and that person's relationship with the people being studied. I do not wish to suggest, however, that we should judge any argument *solely* by ad hominem standards. I think that there are fields in which such critiques would be a distraction in evaluating knowledge claims. Philosophers, however, have engaged in debates such as whether Heidegger's silence on the Nazi genocide should influence our understanding of his philosophy (Lang 1996). In an article on that patron saint of the ad hominem, Nietzsche, Robert Solomon contends, however, that, "ad hominem critiques expand, they do not limit, the field of philosophical argumentation. Instead of restricting the focus to mere thesis, antithesis and argument, the ad hominem approach brings in the motives, the intentions, the circumstances and the context of those who have a stake in the outcome" (1996, 189).

Should ad hominem critiques be a part of how we evaluate bioethics? Is it appropriate to ask questions about the character of the speaker in moral issues? Should we evaluate the ethics of bioethics by looking at the bioethicist? The critique of Fox and Swazey examines the issue of motivation, which I wish to return to later in this essay, but I would like to mention two other forms of ad hominem critiques that we may also wish to consider in relation to bioethics.

In June 1996 the disability activist group Not Dead Yet protested a conference at Michigan State University. Stephen Drake (1996), one of the protesters, states the reason that he went to the conference: "The agendas of the conferences were especially outrageous as these discussions were to take place without any representative from the group of people the discussions would affect." This kind of ad hominem critique relies upon the importance of personal experience in moral evaluation and questions the possibility of moral arguments being made without consideration for how one's experiences (in this case as a nondisabled person) affect the kind of analysis made. This is known as "bias ad hominem," and in the case of the attack against bioethicists by such groups as disability activists it can entail what might be further classified as an oblivious bias ad hominem, for the people being attacked are unaware of the way in which their life experience influences their present position. In a recent essay, Howard Brody (2004), one of the bioethicists inside the Michigan conference, submitted an apology for his position in relation to disability and some bioethics cases. He notes that "the key lesson that disability advocates are trying to teach the rest of us" is that the bias one has toward disability affects how one looks at cases. Brody's article represents an acknowledgment of the truth of the earlier ad hominem attack by the disability community.

Valerie Saiving is essentially stating an oblivious bias ad hominem argument when in her classic theology essay she begins by stating baldly, "I am a student of theology; I am also a woman. Perhaps it strikes you as curious that I put these two assertions beside each other, as if to imply that one's sexual identity has some bearing on his [sic] theological views" (1979, 25). Once such biases are revealed, one has a moral obligation to acknowledge them as a part of one's subsequent arguments about a subject. In "European-American Ethos and Principlism: An African-American Challenge," Cheryl Sanders (1994) faults American bioethics for being biased in promoting the perspective of European Americans. On a more personal level, Paul Lauritzen (1996) has discussed how he became the subject of a bias ad hominem attack in bioethics when he wrote in the *Hastings Center Report* a critical assessment of assisted reproductive technology. In this article he described his personal failure with these technologies when he and his wife tried to have a child. He received a "curious response" when individuals who had read the article (and liked it) found that his wife and he had recently become the biological parents of a son; on hearing of his happy news the listeners reacted in a hostile manner. The reaction seems related to a form of bias ad hominem. Here was the bioethicist who spoke from experience but now it appeared that the bioethicist lacked that experience, had provided false biographical information, and thus his observations about reproductive technology were themselves questionable. These examples suggest that a "personal turn" has taken place in bioethics, a movement in which bioethicists wish to admit to some degree that one needs in some manner to embrace ad hominem arguments and admit bias. Judith Andre's book *Bioethics as Practice* (2002) exemplifies an attempt to reveal not simply what bioethicists believe but how their way of life influences the way they approach problems.

A second kind of ad hominem critique that bioethics may also wish to consider valid is the relationship of the ideas proposed and the life lived, or what might be termed "moral identity ad hominem." In a cover story in the *New Republic*, Peter Berkowitz analyzes the work of Peter Singer. Berkowitz notes that the amount of resources that Singer has put into the care of his mother, who had suffered from Alzheimer's, seems to contradict his published philosophical positions. Berkowitz contends that "it is hard to imagine a more stunning rebuke" to Singer's moral positions on economic justice and personhood than this telling biographical feature in which his actions for his mother "seems [sic] to proclaim that what is right and what is rigorous applies only to other people's mothers" (2000, 37). If we think of philosophy or ethics as merely a series of disembodied statements about the world, such an attack would be of course meaningless. If instead we think that philosophy is something that should be lived, that ethics should be applied and evaluated in relation to one's personal life, then the degree to which one argues for a particular moral response to the world and the degree to which one embodies such statements radically alter how one's bioethics is evaluated. One would be forced to look for the relation between rhetoric and habitus. As this volume itself demonstrates, there has been increased interest in the ethics of the bioethics world, but this form of ad hominem is different from ad hominem attacks raised with bias. It is one thing to ask if one has a financial stake in the research study one is supervising the informed consent for and quite another to ask if one's beliefs in social justice necessitate that one should be living with the poor. To admit this latter form of ad hominem argument into bioethics is to raise larger questions about what it means to be a bioethicist. Recent criticisms about the issue of conflict of interest between bioethicists and the medical industry are a form not merely of bias ad hominem (as they would be for any academic who benefits financially from evaluating research) but should also be viewed as an attack on personal integrity and thus a form of moral identity ad hominem (see Turner 2004; Elliott 2001).

However, to attack a person's motivation for making a particular argument is an even more subtle kind of argument. That my colleagues ascribed "resentment" to the Fox and Swazey article is particularly interesting, for it corresponds to what is perhaps the most renowned ad hominem critiques in philosophy: Nietzsche's attack on Christianity, which is in essence a psychological exegesis of the religion's development. He argues that those Christian values that are deemed in the West to be universal are the direct result of the resentment of slaves toward their masters. But Nietzsche (1986) took this tack with many philosophical arguments, for he came to conclude that all philosophy is "the personal confession of its author and a kind of involuntary and unconscious memoir" (*Human, All Too Human* 1: 6). His interest in "what kind of person would hold this belief" resulted in an approach to philosophy that was blended with psychology. With this perspective, Nietzsche argued that every philosophy reflects a particular stage in one's life: Schopenhauer reflects "ardent and melancholy youth—it is no way of thinking for older people" and Plato "recalls the middle thirties" (*Human, All Too Human* 277). Ironically Nietzsche scholars have at times turned their attention to Nietzsche's own life to determine why he thought the way he did (Köhler 2002). In a similar way, James Miller's (1993) biography of Michel Foucault brought into stark light the relation between his approach to knowledge and his sexuality. Can we—and ultimately should we—apply these ideas to bioethics?

As mentioned above, one can see the beginnings of a personal turn in bioethics, as some scholars step forward to reveal how their life stories have affected their intellectual histories. Arthur Frank (1995), Paul Lauritzen (1990), Sue Rubin (2000), Kathryn Montgomery (2005), and Adrienne Asch (1998) have all contributed significantly to this issue. Yet attention to the ad hominem raises questions not so much about the genesis of one's understanding of issues, the angels of our insight, as it exposes the limits of our understanding, the demons of our prejudices. For unlike the personal turn, the turn toward the ad hominem is not self-revelation but rather the exposé of the influences and biases of someone else's work. To welcome the ad hominem attack into bioethics would interestingly force others to take a more personal turn as a form of preemptive strike.

If the ad hominem attack were admitted into bioethics, perhaps not only accepted but expected, then the construction of bioethics texts would be radically changed. The kind of bioethics texts that have become the norm in the discipline, a cool detached writing style that is expressed by an impersonal narrator, would be thought a suspicious one for a bioethicist. *Principles of Biomedical Ethics* (2001), a classic textbook in the field, is often referred to not by title but by its authors: "Do you have a copy of Beauchamp and Childress?" Yet it seems on the surface not to matter who the authors of this work are, for one could as easily be asking for a copy of Rosencrantz and Guildenstern. Someone armed with the ad hominem critique would counter, however, that it does matter who the authors are even if a text strives to keep the narrators as impersonal as possible. Nietzsche's admonition that all of philosophy is in the end "involuntary and unconscious memoir" should be considered in relation to all bioethics texts. The choice of an impersonal narrator is simply an attempt to put on a mask that conceals how personal the narrator truly is. A reader of "What Price Parenthood? Reflections on the New Reproductive Technologies" by Paul Lauritzen (1990) is continually reminded that this article could be written only by Lauritzen. The narrator in the Lauritzen essay can be said to be, to borrow a term from narratology, a "dramatized narrator," a narrator who is not effaced but a part of and related to the world described. Such a narrator, I believe, provides the possibility of an embodied bioethics and thereby a richer presentation of what makes applied ethics complex and intellectually exciting. The ad hominem attack should be welcomed into bioethics primarily because of the kind of texts that will be written to thwart its efficacy.

REFERENCES

Andre, J. 2002. *Bioethics as Practice.* Chapel Hill, NC: University of North Carolina Press.
Asch, A. 1998. Distracted by disability. *Cambridge Quarterly of Healthcare Ethics* 7: 77–87.

Beauchamp, T. L., and Childress, J. F. 2001. *Principles of Biomedical Ethics.* (Originally published in 1979.) New York: Oxford University Press.

Berkowitz, P. 2000. Other people's mothers: The utilitarian horrors of Peter Singer. *New Republic,* 10 January: 27–37.

Brody, H. 2004. A bioethicist offers an apology. *Lansing City Pulse* 2004 [cited 6 October 2004].

Drake, S. 1996. Demand to be heard. *Medical Humanities Report* 18(1).

Elliott, C. 2001. Throwing a bone to the watchdog. *Hastings Center Report* 31(2): 9–12.

Engelhardt, H. T., Jr. 1980. Bioethics in the People's Republic of China. *Hastings Center Report* 10(2): 7–10.

Fox, R. C., and Swazey, J. P. 1984. Medical morality is not bioethics: Medical ethics in China and the United States. *Perspectives in Biology and Medicine* 27: 336–60.

Frank, A. W. 1995. *The Wounded Storyteller: Body, Illness, and Ethics.* Chicago: University of Chicago Press.

Köhler, J. 2002. *Zarathustra's Secret: The Interior Life of Friedrich Nietzsche.* New Haven: Yale University Press.

Lang, B. 1996. *Heidegger's Silence.* Ithaca, NY: Cornell University Press.

Lauritzen, P. 1990. "What price parenthood? Reflections on the new reproductive technologies." *Hastings Center Report* 20(2): 38–46.

———. 1996. Ethics and experience: The case of the curious response. *Hastings Center Report* 26(1): 6–15.

Miller, J. 1993. *The Passion of Michel Foucault.* New York: Simon and Schuster.

Montgomery, K. 2005. *How Doctors Think: Clinical Judgement and the Practice of Medicine.* New York: Oxford University Press.

Nelson, H. L. 2002. What child is this? *Hastings Center Report* 32(6): 29.

Nietzsche, F. W. 1986. *Human, All Too Human: A Book for Free Spirits.* Cambridge: Cambridge University Press.

Rubin, S. 2000. Pulling back the curtain: Crossing boundaries between the personal and the professional. Third Annual Meeting of the American Society for Bioethics and Humanities. Salt Lake City, Utah.

Saiving, V. 1979. The human situation: A feminine view. In C. P. Christ and J. Plaskow, eds., *Womanspirit Rising: A Feminist Reader in Religion.* San Francisco: Harper and Row.

Sanders, C. 1994. European-American ethos and principlism: An African-American challenge. In R. P. Hamel, E. R. DuBose, and L. J. O'Connell, eds., *A Matter of Principles?: Ferment in U.S. Bioethics.* Valley Forge, PA: Trinity Press.

Solomon, R. C. 1996. Nietzsche *ad hominem*: Perspectivism, personality, and *ressentiment* revisited. In B. Magnus and K. M. Higgins, eds., *The Cambridge Companion to Nietzsche.* Cambridge: Cambridge University Press.

Turner, L. 2004. Beware the celebrity bioethicist. *Chronicle of Higher Education,* B18.

Walton, D. N. 1998. *Ad Hominem Arguments: Studies in Rhetoric and Communication.* Tuscaloosa: University of Alabama Press.

CHAPTER TWENTY-FOUR

Social Moral Epistemology and the Role of Bioethicists

ALLEN BUCHANAN, PH.D.

As a species of practical ethics, bioethics aims not just at achieving a better understanding of ethical problems, but at understanding ethical problems in ways that contribute to morally better actions and policies. Given that the ultimate aim of bioethics is practical, those who claim the title of bioethicist ought to think hard about whether the modes of understanding they characteristically employ are adequate to the practical task. In this chapter I argue that the conventional methodologies bioethicists employ are deficient from the standpoint of the practical aim of bioethics, because they do not incorporate what I have elsewhere labeled social moral epistemology. I also want to argue that social moral epistemology is a valuable tool for self-examination by bioethicists—and that bioethicists have a responsibility to apply social moral epistemological analysis not just to the problems they characteristically grapple with, but also to themselves.

SOCIAL MORAL EPISTEMOLOGY: A BRIEF INTRODUCTION

Social epistemology is the comparative evaluation of the efficiency and effectiveness of institutions and social practices in promoting the formation, preservation, transmission, and effective utilization of true beliefs (Goldman 1999).[1] To take only a few examples, social epistemologists critically evaluate the comparative advantages of adversarial versus inquisitorial criminal proceedings as mechanisms for the discovery of truth, try to determine which practices of a scientific community are most effective for progress in scientific knowledge, and examine the effectiveness of alternative democratic institutions in providing relevant information to policy makers.

Social *moral* epistemology, in its most inclusive form, is the comparative evaluation of the efficiency and efficacy of alternative institutions and social practices in promoting the formation, preservation, and effective utilization of true beliefs so far as true beliefs facilitate right action or reduce the incidence of wrong action (Buchanan 2002). A special department of social moral epistemology is the comparative evaluation of social practices and institutions that promote (or impede) the functioning of the moral virtues, so far as their functioning depends upon an agent having relevant true beliefs. For example, the virtue of sympathy does not function properly when one's ability to recognize the humiliation that one's behavior inflicts on certain people is undercut by the belief that they are not fully human. More generally, webs of false beliefs about supposed natural differences between men and women or blacks and whites can result in excluding some individuals from the scope of certain moral principles or from the moral community altogether. The processes by which individuals come to have and to sustain such beliefs are social: They learn them, and they learn to disregard evidence that conflicts with them, through the operation of various social practices and institutions.

Social moral epistemology is a *normative* enterprise, because it evaluates—not merely describes or explains—the epistemic performance of social practices and institutions. It is a species of *moral* epistemology because its concern is not with true belief generally but with true beliefs so far as they play a role in right action. The nature of social moral epistemology and its potential for strengthening bioethics will be made clearer by considering two examples of the ways in which this methodological approach can be applied within bioethics and then suggesting how it can be employed to cast a critical light on bioethics itself and on the role of bioethicists.

THE RELEVANCE OF SOCIAL MORAL EPISTEMOLOGY
TO BIOETHICS: TWO EXAMPLES
Understanding Medical Paternalism
as an Epistemic-Institutional Phenomenon

Medical paternalism is usually defined as the view that physicians may withhold information (e.g., of a grim diagnosis) or even lie to patients, or otherwise preempt their making a free, informed choice regarding medical care, when this is done for the good of the patient. In the early years of bioethics, philosopher-bioethicists, including this author, advanced powerful objections against medical ethics *as a moral view.* In other words, they proceeded as if the bioethicist's contribution to making medical practice more respectful of patient autonomy was to refute the justifications that were or could be given in support of the statement that physicians may lie to their patients or preempt their choices for the patient's good. This was not an especially difficult task. The justifications for the medical paternalist view were flimsy, resting either on unsubstantiated empirical generalizations about the inability of otherwise competent individuals to cope with bad medical news, on an implausible characterization of the physician-patient relationship as one in which the physician is an agent with unrestricted discretion to act on the patient's behalf, or on a failure to distinguish between the patient's medical good (which is within the physician's domain of expertise) and his good overall (which is not) (Buchanan 1978). Having demolished these patently unsound justifications for the medical paternalist view, bioethicists thought their work was done, except for the educational task of informing physicians as to competent patients' rights, showing them how these rights are grounded in "the principle of autonomy," and an occasional bit of remedial argumentation whenever a physician showed signs of invoking flimsy pro-paternalist arguments.

This response to medical paternalism was inadequate for two reasons. First, the argumentative critique apparently did not have much direct effect on physician behavior. Second, the argumentative critique shed no light on a disturbing puzzle: Why did otherwise highly educated, intelligent individuals, who routinely engage in sophisticated chains of reasoning about complex medical matters, appeal to such patently defective arguments to justify their paternalistic behavior? A plausible hypothesis is that both the tendency to act paternalistically and the tendency to justify paternalistic action by appeal to patently deficient justifications are effects of the institutional processes that form the physician's professional identity.

From the standpoint of social moral epistemology, the epistemic functions of these institutional processes are not likely to be limited to the inculcation of scientific and clinical knowledge. They may also include the transmission of beliefs and forms of reasoning that serve the interests of physicians as socially recognized experts and that can be in conflict with the legitimate interests of those who seek their expertise: in this case, false factual beliefs about the coping abilities of competent patients and indefensible justifications to fend off challenges to the physician's power. Understanding how these processes work may suggest interventions that are much more effective than merely critiquing bad medical paternalist arguments.

Deepening the Ethical Autopsy of Eugenics

Bioethicists have proceeded on the reasonable assumption that understanding what went wrong in the eugenics movements of the late nineteenth to the middle of the twentieth century has a practical point—that it can help us avoid moral errors as we grapple with new genetic technologies that were beyond the wildest fantasies of eugenicists.[2] According to what might be called the conventional "ethical autopsy," the chief error of eugenicists was that they were too willing to infringe individual rights for the sake of the social good, uncritically assuming a consequentialist "public health" normative framework that gave short shrift to justice.[3] In slogan form, the practical message of the conventional view is "More Kant, less Bentham!"

The conventional view is incorrect. It is true that, like many would-be social reformers of that period, some eugenicists were sympathetic to utilitarian reasoning. However, it would be a mistake to think that the chief error of eugenics was the abandonment of "rights-based" moral thinking in favor of consequentialism. Instead, eugenicists managed to justify immoral actions and policies, not by repudiating rights-principles, but by subverting them. They achieved this subversion by disseminating false principles in the name of science, relying upon existing patterns of epistemic deference to putative scientific experts, and in some cases creating institutions, such as the Cold Springs Harbor Laboratory and Eugenics Record office, that helped give credence to these false beliefs.

The two false beliefs most central to eugenic thinking were (1) that the human gene pool is suffering a catastrophic decline and (2) that many if not most of the more serious social problems (from alcoholism to crime to sexual immorality) are caused by behavioral traits that are genetically determined in simple, Mendelian fashion. If one has these two beliefs, one need not be a consequentialist to conclude that there is a dire emergency for humankind and that under such conditions ordinary moral constraints, including some of those imposed by respect for individual rights, do not apply. Even the staunchest "rights-based" theorists, including Robert Nozick (1974), concede that the most basic rights may be infringed to avert a "moral catastrophe."[4] The normative flaw here was not that the eugenicists were consequentialists who ignored rights. Rather, the primary error concerned the ethics of belief. Given the moral gravity of the actions they recommended on the bases of these two beliefs, their standards of evidence were remarkably low. The greater the moral risks of acting on a belief, the higher is the evidentiary burden.

The distinction between rights-based and consequentialist moral theories and principles does little to illuminate such a subversion of conventional morality. We need to understand why so many well-educated laypeople, across the political spectrum, trusted the wrong "experts." In social moral epistemology terms, we must explain the phenomenon of *unwarranted epistemic deference*—showing how it came to be that certain individuals managed to present themselves to the public as scientific experts on human heredity and why the public was ready to accept what they said. Also needed is an explanation of why the supposed experts steadfastly sustained these false beliefs in the face of repeated, clearly articulated scientific refutations of them. We need an account of the *epistemic vices* of the supposed experts. Finally, a comprehensive social moral epistemological analysis would have to explain why the scientific refutations of false eugenic beliefs had so little effect on the public. In other words, we need to understand why the accurate information that was produced was not utilized effectively. Similarly, we might well ask today whether repeating arguments to refute genetic determinist fallacies is adequate, or whether something also must be done to critique and reform the social and institutional processes, including those involving the media, by which the public comes to think in deterministic ways.

CRITICALLY EVALUATING BIOETHICS
AS AN EPISTEMIC INSTITUTION
The Institutional Growth of Bioethics

In the past three decades bioethics has become institutionalized in a number of ways: There are bioethics centers, state and federal bioethics commissions and advisory committees, institutional review boards, and hospital ethics committees. Although bioethicists sometimes humbly aver that there are no moral experts, the institutionalization of bioethics is based on the assumption that bioethicists are experts and that they make a distinctive and valuable contribution to the task of identifying and responding to ethical issues in the life-sciences—a contribution that cannot be made or generally is not made as effectively by clergy, scientists, physicians, politicians, lawyers, or bureaucrats. Even if few assume that bioethicists uniquely grasp moral truths, the rationale for institutionalizing bioethics includes the assumption that bioethicists play an important role in the division of epistemic labor.

Even when bioethicists are not functioning as part of particular institutions, there is a sense in which they play a distinctive social role. Because this social role is recognized not just by bioethicists but by the public generally (thanks in part to the media's reliance on bioethicists as producers of "sound-bites") and by various private and public institutions, it is accurate to say that bioethics is an institution.

Self-Reflective Social Moral Epistemology

If this is the case, then the critical resources of social moral epistemology ought to be brought to bear on the institution of bioethics and thus on the role of bioethicist. What is needed is a systematic inquiry into the reliability of the processes by which individuals become socially identified as bioethicists and are therefore regarded as having the distinctive expertise that bioethicists are thought to have.

The application of social moral epistemology to bioethics itself would also require a critical analysis of the relationship between what bioethicists do and the preservation and enhancement of their status as valued experts. To the extent that being recognized as an expert brings not only employment opportunities but also the power to influence decisions and policies and the status that goes with this, all experts—bioethicists included—have an incentive to "sell" and indeed oversell both the quality and extent of their expertise. As with other forms of expertise, there is not likely to be a perfect congruence between optimal performance as source of reliable beliefs, judgments, and forms of reasoning, on the one hand, and doing what serves one's interest in preserving and enhancing our status as bioethical experts, on the other.

Consider one important aspect of the self-proclaimed and socially recognized expertise of bioethicists: the ability to identify important ethical issues. The reliability of bioethics as an epistemic institution depends in part upon how well bioethicists perform this task. However, the kinds of institutions within which bioethicists work influence not only which problems they prioritize but even which problems they are aware of. For example, when most clinical bioethicists are based in university medical center tertiary care hospitals, the ethical issues that are most salient in those environments tend to receive more attention than population health ethical issues, global health inequities, or ethical issues that arise in home care. The highly contingent way in which bioethics became institutionalized in the United States has resulted in a morally arbitrary narrowing of the range of ethical problems bioethicists have identified and addressed. To that extent, U.S. bioethicists, instead of being reliable identifiers of ethical problems, may in fact have foisted a distorted conception of what the chief ethical issues are on the public, thereby diverting attention from more morally urgent issues. If this is the case, then bioethicists have not lived up to their claims of expertise in identifying and addressing important ethical problems. Furthermore, this failing cannot be understood within the conventional bioethics perspective. From that perspective, bioethicists are seen as influencing institutions, not as being influenced by institutions. How well bioethicists perform their role in the division of epistemic labor will depend upon the epistemic features of the institutions within which they function.

When the critical scrutiny of social moral epistemology is focused on bioethicists as socially recognized suppliers of epistemic goods, it becomes possible to consider whether they also stimulate demand for those goods—and whether this can compromise their performance. To the extent that they have a stake in preserving and enhancing their status as experts, bioethicists, like other experts, have an incentive to stimulate demand for their services. Yet their opportunities for stimulating demand are constrained by their capacities. In particular, as I have already noted, it seems fair to say that bioethicists are, for the most part, better at identifying moral problems than at providing solutions to them. If this is the case, then bioethicists have an incentive to proclaim problems where none exist or at least to exaggerate the seriousness of problems that do exist. Moreover, even though they can rarely offer solutions to the problems they identify, they can often recommend ways of coping with them, for example by developing oversight institutions— which, coincidentally, almost always involve important roles for bioethicists.[5]

It should not be assumed that such tendencies detract from the social benefits that the institution of bioethics confers, all things considered. It might be the case that the tendency of bioethicists to exaggerate ethical problems plays a valuable role in counterbalancing the tendency of scientists, health care workers, and biotechnology entrepreneurs to minimize the moral risks of what they are doing. Similarly, under certain conditions, rivalries among scientists that exhibit "impure" motives may in fact contribute to scientific progress, through complex but ultimately productive adversarial relationships (Kitcher 1990). Whether the existing institution of bioethics is optimal or suboptimal in this regard can be determined only by a social moral epistemological analysis. What is clear, however, is that there is no reason to assume that the existing institution is optimal and therefore no reason to be smugly confident that the way bioethicists currently operate best achieves their avowed practical goal of moral improvement. Only if the work of bioethicists is submitted to social moral epistemological analysis can they be confident that they are in fact succeeding in doing what they profess to do.

To summarize: The existence of the social role of bioethicist is grounded in the assumption that bioethicists supply important epistemic goods. They identify ethical issues, propose procedures and institutions for coping with them, help private individuals and institutional actors think about moral issues in a constructive way, and produce reasoned defenses or critiques of actions and policies. The practical goal of bioethics is to contribute to morally better outcomes by supplying these distinctive epistemic goods. The way in which bioethicists supply these epistemic goods is shaped by the institution of bioethics, which in turn is constituted by the various particular institutional settings within which bioethicists work and the connections among them. Therefore, how well bioethicists fare in achieving the practical goal of bioethics depends upon the epistemic reliability of the institution of bioethics. To assess the epistemic reliability of an institution is to engage in social moral epistemological inquiry. Accordingly, assuming that bioethicists have a responsibility to try to ensure that they are pursuing the practical goal of bioethics effectively, they also have a responsibility not only to incorporate social moral epistemology into their engagement with the problems they characteristically grapple with, but also to focus its critical resources on themselves.

The conventional conception of bioethics ought to be expanded to include social moral epistemology. This methodology has the potential to further the practical goal of bioethics, not only by illuminating the problems bioethicists have characteristically addressed but also by casting a critical light on the institution of bioethics itself and on the role of bioethicist.

NOTES

1. In this section I draw on Buchanan (2002).

2. This discussion of the importance of social moral epistemology in understanding the moral pathology of eugenics is taken from a much more detailed treatment in Allen Buchanan, "Institutions, Beliefs, and Ethics" (unpublished paper).

3. See, for example, Buchanan et al. (2000, 28–29). The author of the present chapter was not the primary author of the chapter of *From Chance to Choice* in which the conventional ethical autopsy of eugenics was advanced.

4. Nozick uses the phrase "moral catastrophe" to denote an evil of such magnitude that its avoidance would justify the infringement of even the most basic individual rights. See Nozick (1974, 30n).

5. I am indebted to Lance K. Stell for focusing my attention on this form of conflict of interest among bioethicists.

REFERENCES

Buchanan, A. 1978. Medical paternalism. *Philosophy and Public Affairs* 7(4): 370–90.
———. 2002. Social moral epistemology. *Social Philosophy and Policy* 19(2): 126–52.
Buchanan, A., et al. 2000. *From Chance to Choice: Genetics and Justice.* Cambridge: Cambridge University Press.
Goldman, A. I. 1999. *Knowledge in a Social World.* Oxford: Oxford University Press.
Kitcher, P. 1990. The division of cognitive labor. *Journal of Philosophy* 87: 5–20.
Nozick, R. A. 1974. *Anarchy, State, and Utopia.* New York: Basic Books.

CHAPTER TWENTY-FIVE

The Glass House

Assessing Bioethics

NANCY M. P. KING, J.D.

People who live in glass houses shouldn't throw stones.

Anonymous proverb

Bioethics is a relatively young field that is principally concerned with moral reflection upon and reform of practices associated with medicine and biomedical science. Despite its youth, it seems to have acquired quite a reputation. Significantly, bioethics is often viewed as more willing to critically examine others than to serve as the object of critical examination by others, whether from within or outside the profession. And in a climate of ever-increasing attention to measurement and evaluation in medicine and elsewhere, bioethics' apparently unexamined status has become a contended issue. In other words, the people who do bioethics live in a glass house, and collectively we have been throwing stones for over thirty years now. What should follow from that? Should we stop letting fly at all or some of our targets? Should we put stone deflectors up around the property line? Or should we take our chances like everybody else, and just start budgeting for necessary repairs?

What does it mean to say that bioethics—the field, its practitioners, its activities, or its products—needs assessment? Who are we, anyway? Is this a field? What kind of tongue-twisting creature is a "bioethicist"? Why are standards wanted—or needed? How can standards be set, and applied, without standardization?

As a member of one of the first academic generations to choose bioethics as a career path (as opposed to drifting or falling into it from someplace else), I have a keen interest in these questions, as well as a healthy skepticism about them. My skepticism is both sincere and self-interested. That is probably a decent pair of adjectives to apply to bioethics as well: People who do bioethics are, generally speaking, deeply and sincerely interested in the questions we address—and accustomed to framing them in ways that fulfill our personal and professional goals, as well as the goals of academia or of our various other employers. The challenge we try to rise to is that of critically examining and, when necessary, shifting that frame. This includes examining ourselves and our own work; hence this volume.

The variety of claims about and challenges to bioethics are themselves challenging to organize, encompassing as they do scholarly critiques of bioethics' positioning and achievements, as well as calls for codes of ethics, standards, accreditation, and conflict of interest and disclosure policies. What is intriguing about this range of concerns is that it signals some lack of agreement about the nature of the problem with bioethics—and about what could solve it.

If bioethics needs to be assessed, we have to consider the subject of the assessment—that is, just who and what should be assessed. In addition, we must consider the objectives of assessment, to determine why it is needed, what its goals are, and how it ought to be done.

THE SUBJECT OF ASSESSMENT
Assessing Whom?

When I was in college, I started reading the *Hastings Center Report* and found the issues and ideas discussed in its pages irresistible. So I looked at the degrees after the names of the people who published in it, and decided that getting a J.D. suited me better than getting an M.D. or a Ph.D. It is no longer quite that simple, since degrees and certificate programs and degree combinations relating to bioethics continue to proliferate. And perhaps it never was really that simple; I know full well that the educational path I chose has important implications for what I do in bioethics, how I think about what I do, and how I do it.

This is as it should be; what would be troubling would be the idea that bioethics is or can be unaffected by the perspectives of those who engage in it. By our perspectives I most emphatically do not mean our politics (Elliott 2004). I mean that lawyers and philosophers have different ways of identifying, articulating, and addressing bioethics issues, whether they are "conservative" or "liberal" thinkers;

and that physicians, nurses, sociologists, anthropologists, persons trained in religious studies, practicing clergy, social workers, and all the rest of those engaged
in bioethics also approach their work differently by reason of their education.

This deep diversity presents particular challenges for any kind of assessment
(see Sharpe, this volume; Andre 2002). Importantly, the challenges are not just
sociological and practical, not just related to keeping track of all the various pathways and educational possibilities and tracing how a given pathway might influence one's views about and disposition toward the work of bioethics. Instead, the
challenges are also epistemological and normative. What is considered most important may well depend on who is asked, but the answer matters a great deal for
assessment.

Nor is it only education that creates this kind of fundamental diversity. The activities in which we engage, the institutions in which and with which we work,
and the experience we gain from these influences also affect our perspectives
about what is important in the field, and why (Buchanan 2002). Clearly, doing
bioethics encompasses many very different kinds of activities, which might perhaps be divided into three categories: academic, applied, and advocacy.

Many of those who do bioethics consider themselves simply to be academics.
They teach in academic settings (whether in undergraduate education, graduate
education, a health professional school, or a non-health-related professional
school like law or business school), and they expect to be assessed professionally
according to the standards of their academic disciplines and departments. But
many of these same people, as well as others without academic appointments (for
example, ethicists based in hospitals or other health care facilities, or those who
work in the pharmaceutical or health care services industries or in government),
view themselves as doing applied ethics—that is, context-sensitive and situation-
specific practical application of discrete general and professional moral norms.
And finally, at least some view themselves as advocates, whose role is the deliberate use of moral argument to advance a particular position. Undoubtedly, there
is substantial overlap among these roles, and most people in bioethics play all
three roles at one time or another, but most probably also identify themselves
principally with one in particular. And each has very different implications for assessment.

Assessing What?

Defining roles in terms of activities raises yet another fundamental question.
What should be assessed: the individual or the work? Who we are, or what we do?

The profession of bioethics, or its activities? The nature of assessment, and the choice of assessment tools, depend importantly on whether we mean to assess individuals or their activities or both. Even if we narrow things down to the assessment of activities, there is considerable complexity to encompass. We immediately face another fundamental question: What is the substance of bioethics? What is of critical importance—the process of bioethics, or its products? The questions asked, or the answers?

Activities in all three of the role categories I've identified—academic, applied, and advocacy—might be further divided into several areas for which there already exist assessment standards and tools (though some are more familiar than others). These are: scholarship, research, and writing; teaching; consultation; and the interpretation, evaluation, and development of policy. The process/product question must still be addressed, however. How processes and outcomes are defined and understood is, again, of both practical and philosophical importance. Academics generally have discipline- or profession-specific review processes, built on assessment of particular activities and products. Standard setting focused on different activities—such as ethics consultation—would presumably look quite different, if only because bioethics scholarship is not all that is needed for a good consultation, however "good" is defined.

There's a problem, though, with this parsing of activities. Consider the criticism that is likely to be leveled against the most perfect and complete advance directive check-box form ever developed: "Fine, but that's all about choosing and refusing particular treatments; it doesn't tell us a thing about the goals of treatment, which is what we really need to know!" It's worth noting that many emergency department physicians really like check boxes, whereas most palliative care specialists, and at least some bioethics types, would probably rather talk about treatment goals. Similarly, assessing particular activities and products in bioethics can be appealingly concrete—and also appallingly shortsighted. Perhaps we should ask that assessing bioethics include considering whether its tools and foci are sufficient for meaningful progress on the complex and vexing issues that it seeks to address. Bioethics has been operating at the micro and macro levels, considering individual rights and governmental responsibilities, since its beginnings, and it is only recently that we have attempted to wade into the messy middle between. It is arguably in that middle arena where real progress can be made. But that progress is likely to be slow, halting, complicated, and compromising, as it requires the appreciation of social context and the creation of reflective communities of discourse and action. This kind of bioethics work bears the same relationship to a nice straightforward paper about informed consent that community based participatory research bears to a small and simple pilot drug trial. And assessing this kind of bioethics work can't be easily accomplished either.

Yet this is the essence of one of the most important internal critiques of bioethics, which asks how well bioethics has done in addressing intractable, persistent, and pervasive issues that are not as exciting or trendy (or analytically straightforward) as, say, face transplantation. These issues—consideration of which is an important theme in this volume (see the essays by Andre, Baylis, Buchanan, and Turner)—include justice (international and domestic) in health care and research; whether health care should be a right, a privilege, an entitlement, or a commodity; whether access to health care is as meaningfully related to health as are basics like education, income, and employment; how health disparities should be understood and addressed; what health care is necessary; what the boundaries of health and medical care are; even how and why health is important.

These kinds of messy, enduring questions seem to need that middle-level approach. But taking that approach not only is more difficult but also may go against self-interest. Providing a narrow answer to a question from inside the health care perspective keeps us in business; looking beyond health care to health—or even further, to the nature and meaning of a fulfilling life and how societies might foster fulfilling lives for their members—might not serve us or our employers or funders as well (and maybe isn't even bioethics).

The problem thus begins to resemble that faced by developed-world clinical investigators who wish to conduct research in the developing world. Lately these investigators have been asked—by bioethics—to engage in political work to help ensure that the host country and its people are not exploited by the research, and that the government of the host country will pass on benefits provided by investigators to the research subjects and/or their communities. Investigators might reasonably object that if they had wanted to do all that, they would have joined Doctors without Borders or the Peace Corps, or become politicians, instead of becoming clinical researchers.

There's something to that objection, of course. Yet a range of imperatives from the larger world stage, including HIV research and the pharmaceutical industry, has resulted in a productive explosion of bioethics thinking that has gone beyond the narrow initial questions without expanding beyond the graspable. Closer to home, it's possible to argue that part of the reason we are still facing, over and over, the same kinds of cases that at first seem simple but are apparently intractable—like the Terri Schiavo case and all its many relatives—is because the problem is *not* just who gets to decide or what the right decision is. These hard

cases are really also about compassion and culture and rhetoric and communication and a whole range of concerns that bioethics narrowly construed doesn't
even begin to touch. If we don't begin to construct a broader view, based on social responsibilities at a level intermediate between individuals and societies,
there's a good chance that bioethics will be stuck in an endless feedback loop. But
to find that new level, bioethics has to become even more multifaceted, nuanced,
interdisciplinary, and reflexive than before.

THE OBJECTIVES OF ASSESSMENT

Thus I've come to the "why" question: What is the aim of assessing bioethics?
Why is assessment needed? What is the problem it is meant to solve—or the good
it seeks to increase? By this time, it should go without saying that the why question has different answers depending on how the "who" and "what" questions are
answered. Even so, there are only two general kinds of possible answers: Assessment ought somehow to prevent harm, or to promote good.

In the spirit of multidisciplinarity I must note that considerable scholarly attention, much of it from sociology, political science, economics, and law, has been
paid to public and private credentialing and other forms of professional regulation. Self-regulation has routinely been proposed by professions that come under
scrutiny, as a means of staving off regulation from external authorities. Professional regulation is also routinely proposed as a means of improving the quality
of services provided by the profession. All the available evidence shows, however,
that regulation does not improve service quality; what it reliably does is limit entry into the profession and increase service costs (Havighurst and King 1983a and
1983b). Discussion of assessing bioethics should acknowledge this sociopolitical
backdrop.

Bioethics and Harm?

It has been argued that credentialing is important to the field so that people
who hire bioethics experts will be able to avoid hiring ill-trained or incompetent
people. I am somewhat skeptical about that argument, believing that if a potential employer prefers to deal with an imprimatur rather than a curriculum vitae
and references, there is already a problem. Those who would hire people to do
bioethics should be generally able to assess candidates' qualifications directly, and
must be willing to do so. Yet perhaps that very willingness necessarily entails a

certain understanding of what it means to do bioethics. I may be expecting too much of potential employers; if they don't know how to evaluate us without the shorthand of a credential, then that could well be our failing, not theirs.

And perhaps there is also a deeper concern behind standard seeking: Is it only that someone hired to engage in bioethics work might be badly trained, or incompetent, or wrong, or venal, or a bad person? Or is it that someone working in this area might, for any of those reasons or more, do harm? (See Nelson, this volume.) If harm can be done by people doing bioethics, it's quite important to think about why that might be so. Consider the difference between the activities of a law professor and someone who is engaged in the practice of law. The professor and the practitioner are assessed, credentialed, and regulated differently, even if their areas of expertise are the same, both because the practitioner's activities are different from the professor's and because the practitioner has different, more extensive authority and therefore greater power to cause harm.

The perception of the potential for harm in bioethics strikes me as important and troubling. The harm with which we should be concerned is not harm to the field generally speaking or to its ideas, since inherent in the very nature of an endeavor like bioethics is the premise that ideas are always available for discussion and challenge. But there does seem to be a perception that people engaged in bioethics have some special sort of moral authority that can be wrongly or dangerously wielded and can harm others. This perception comes not only from Dean Koontz (2002) but also from within bioethics. And it troubles me because it is aggrandizing.

Bioethics should not be punditry or soothsaying. Bioethics "professionals" should not be granted or ceded any special moral authority. All humans are moral agents, whose moral responsibilities are related to their activities. People engaged in bioethics have no authority over others by virtue of bioethics, but only the authority wielded (along with commensurate responsibilities) by virtue of teaching positions, committee memberships, scholarly expertise, and the like. We should be concerned with our own moral responsibility, but should not be elevated to a secular priesthood. If we have to worry that authority is being seized by bioethicists—or ceded to us—because we are somehow viewed as more moral than others and therefore should be listened to and obeyed, then there is something very wrong (see Elliott, this volume; Scofield 2005).

What I take from this is that standard setting isn't necessarily helpful. What seems more vital, to me, is to foster a certain disposition about the work of bioethics, a disposition that comports with scholarship, openness, humility, and critical reflection—characteristics and activities that are antipathetic to the gathering and exercise of the power to harm.

Of course, there is an empirical question here. And the evidence seems to suggest that there is little to worry about. If bioethics is supposed to be about thorough, thoughtful, critical examination of important social/medical/moral questions, then we need not fear that bioethics has too much authority. The rhetorical posturing surrounding the sad case of Theresa Schiavo ought to convince us that bioethics never speaks alone, but must enter the marketplace of ideas alongside politics, passion, and media theater. Which is a source of both comfort and frustration, as it should be. The comfort comes from recognizing that people who do bioethics are not likely to be granted any special credibility, so there may not be much harm we can do, except perhaps by sounding stupid in a sound bite. The frustration comes from recognizing that the kind of voice we seek to add to the chorus is likely to be drowned out by those who don't appreciate (or want others to hear) our subtler melodies.

Bioethics and Good?

It seems unexceptionable that bioethics has the capacity to promote good. A number of the essays in this volume consider how the knowledge, skill, and virtue possessed by bioethics scholars and practitioners can produce good (see essays by Stevens, Orentlicher, Baylis, and Lindemann, for example). But what if setting and enforcing standards for the field, though perhaps not needed to prevent harm, is wanted to promote good? If we can develop a reliable and meaningful assessment process, the voices of those who pass muster will be more clearly heard. This is the essence of the argument in favor of permitting bioethicists to testify as expert witnesses in court proceedings (Spielman and Rich 2005). And it is no less aggrandizing an argument when the object is promotion of better decision making than when the object is preventing harm.

I'd certainly be happy if I were consulted more often. I truly believe that it is unfortunate when bioethics is left out of the conversation, whether that conversation is about patient care or stem cells or controversial research or health and social justice. And it is even more unfortunate when the reason for leaving bioethics out is the conviction that it is obstructionist or ideological—that is, when it is not seen as a perspective of inquiry and teaching. It may be extremely difficult at times to separate teaching from preaching; but we ought to work damn hard to at least be sure that our preaching has a lot of teaching in it—as well as a lot of listening (see Andre, this volume). When that effort goes unseen or is misunderstood, something important is lost (see Stevens, this volume). But it is very hard for me to see how any seal of approval can open ears or minds. Again, it seems more productive to foster that disposition of scholarship, openness, humility, and critical reflection, not only to prevent harm but also to model for others that which promotes good.

The 2005 month of March madness that ended with Terri Schiavo's death engendered a lot of reflection, within and about bioethics. The popular Bioethics Discussion Forum listserv became a focus of furious (in all senses of the term) information exchange and discussion, contributed to by academics and practitioners from every bioethics-related discipline. The foci of e-discourse about the Schiavo case included:

- dissemination of complete and accurate information from the courts, medicine, religious teachings and traditions, and the media;
- discipline-based interpretation and analysis of that information (from medicine, law, philosophy, religion, and the social sciences);
- discussions of the relevance of ideology and funding sources to the evaluation of moral arguments;
- discussions of when bioethics functions best through moral analysis and when it functions best through moral engagement or advocacy;
- philosophical examination of the nature of autonomous advance decision making, and comparison of legal and moral decision-making frameworks;
- consideration of different types of bioethics training, different audiences for bioethics, and how best to reach different audiences;

and, finally,

- offering "rules of engagement" for bioethics, to preserve scholarship, civility, and critical reflection. One rule offered was "Do your homework; get your facts right." My favorite rule was "Always respond to an argument as if the argument were made by someone acting in good faith after serious reflection" (Schwartz 2005).

The net result of this discussion reminded me of the story of the blind sages and the elephant. Bioethics is the elephant this time. It is indeed made up of a lot of very disparate pieces, which reasonably appear quite distinct when examined separately. These parts nonetheless fit together into a whole organism that is unique, somewhat ungainly, and at the same time both impressive and even, in its way, quite beautiful.

What's the Solution?

What kinds of assessments and standards are under discussion for bioethics? Well, here's the problem: there are lots. The basic typology seems to include codes of ethics and other forms of behavioral guidelines; core competencies and other educational standards; conflict of interest disclosure and management; certification and other credentials. Each of these can be dichotomized in two ways. First, into "with or without teeth" (that is, mandatory—and therefore enforceable—or optional—and therefore advisory). Second, into "internal or external" (that is, professional standardization or regulatory oversight). To be meaningful, each must also be the product of a credible process of development, including the development of tools for assessing whether standards are met and guidelines adhered to.

The complexities are considerable. This volume alone has touched on guidelines and competencies for ethics consultation (Baylis; Nelson; Baker); rules for management and disclosure of conflict of interest, both financial and nonfinancial (Sharpe; Morreim; Elliott; Turner; Charo). Other kinds of guidance documents are conceivable too, including consensus documents addressing particular bioethics issues, such as UNESCO's Draft Declaration on Universal Norms on Bioethics (2005). Having already confessed to skepticism about the motivations for and the value of formalized assessment, as opposed to the cultivation of a lively conscience (Churchill 1999; King 1999), I have little more to offer.

STONES INTO BREAD: SOURCES OF SUGGESTION

It seems to me that any assessment, whether new and specific to bioethics or based on existing professional or academic assessments, must have two characteristics. First, it must be amenable to searching out those characteristics and capacities that promote thorough and thoughtful critical reflection on bioethics issues. And second, just as the best test of a patient's capacity for informed decision making is making a decision, the best test of anyone's capacity for doing good work in bioethics is doing some work in bioethics. A careful assessment must then be made—but the necessary skill and expertise should have been modeled for the assessor in the work itself.

The Hyphenated Bioethicist

Those who do bioethics work do it in specific and complex social and institutional contexts. And, as has frequently been noted, bioethics began its life as a quintessential outsider—an interloper in the hospital and the clinic. Now many of us are tenured academics, with some prestige, decent incomes, and good positions. Those of us who have gained some turf seek to protect it. In short, bioethics is now at least in some respects an insider (see DeBruin, this volume). If bioethicists have interests to protect, then perhaps the concern shouldn't be harm, but self-interest as a corrupting influence on the work of bioethics. Many in bioethics complain that we don't have sufficient respect, that we aren't understood when it comes to tenure decisions, that we don't get enough grants, that we can't get published in the right places—the whole standard academic litany, complicated by the housing of much of academic bioethics in medical centers and multidisciplinary departments. If bioethics finds its work driven, at least partially, by where the money is, is that worse than when money drives the direction of clinical research or the specialty choices of newly minted physicians? And what if it isn't money that is the driver; what if it is academic prestige, which is a good deal harder to measure? Or the imperatives of one's institution? Or the need to be liked and respected (by colleagues, bosses, clients, constituencies) in order to stay on the inside, which can lead to capture? All of these are issues of academic integrity that are currently very important and vigorously contested. Are they different—or worse—when they appear in bioethics (Andre 2002)?

There is probably a risk that people in bioethics may be used as cover by an organization or institution (see Sharpe and Elliott, this volume). There is also probably a risk of capture that arises from "applied" bioethics: the effort to provide meaningful advice often requires immersion not only in technical medicine and science but in their cultures. The famed "beeper ethicist" in the hospital setting may risk becoming a wannabe M.D.; the research ethics specialist on the IRB may become not only fluent in scientific and regulatory language but a promoter of the institution's research mission to an extent that could militate against raising important questions about the value or validity of particular protocols.

Being different, as bioethics is different from the provision of health care or the conduct of clinical research, is important. The "translation problems" created by this difference are in some sense fundamental to the work of bioethics. Even as they represent an ongoing frustration requiring constant reexplanation, these translation problems signal that engagement with bioethics issues somehow opens up a moral space for thinking together, because everybody engaged in the inherently cross-disciplinary conversations of bioethics has to think twice about what is being said.

People who do bioethics necessarily have to think about how what is said is heard and used by others. Conversations and scholarship that stay within monolithic professional boundaries can at least pretend to avoid responsibility for the readings and uses of scholarly products by "outsiders." Although bioethics has no special authority, by its very nature it seems clearly to have a special responsibility to consider and address the possibility that things may be misheard or misapplied across disciplines. Whether the audience for bioethics discussion or advice is industry, the media, students, health professionals, or those requesting ethics consultation, we must remain aware that the teaching endeavors of bioethics are continual and various. It may even be worth considering whether some version of reader-response theory might be more critical to assessment of bioethics than any other sort of measurement tool.

The Glass House

There are two kinds of glass houses, and bioethics needs to think about both. The proverbial glass house with which I opened this essay is one; J. D. Salinger's Glass house is the other. In Salinger's classic short novel *Franny and Zooey,* the sister and brother of the title, Franny and Zooey Glass, address the problem of judging the moral behavior of oneself and others. Zooey (the brother) accuses Franny of being selfish, even as she appears to be acting selflessly. It is quite possible that those of us who resist standard setting, for what we think are very good and noble reasons, may really just be trying to get away with something.

Zooey reframes his sister's nervous breakdown/spiritual crisis by placing it in the rich and complicated social context and web of relationships that makes up the Glass house, where they grew up. He calls her to account by asking her (and how he asks is as important as what he asks for) to consider what responsibilities she now has, as a young adult, toward her parents, to whom she has come home. And ultimately, he invokes the Fat Lady. Zooey, Franny, and the other Glass siblings were radio performers as children, on a quiz show that seems to have been a cross between *Jeopardy* and *Kids Say the Darndest Things.* Zooey reminds Franny that the audience they imagined as children, the person they really wanted to reach, was the archetypal Fat Lady—somebody whose language, life, and preoccupations might be wholly different from theirs, but for whom they could somehow make a real difference.

The Fat Lady is a singularly sentimental conceit, no doubt. At the same time, however, she may be a pretty useful character against whom to examine some of what should be important about bioethics: our translation capacity; our readiness to address the complex, messy, and unpopular as well as the exotic and the familiar; our humility; and our willingness to examine not only the rest of the world but also ourselves. Maybe we should even consider developing a Fat Lady Assessment for bioethics. I'd start with a version of one of the rules of engagement: "Always engage with others as if they are acting in good faith after serious reflection." A lot could follow from such a beginning.

REFERENCES

Andre, J. 2002. *Bioethics as Practice.* Chapel Hill: University of North Carolina Press.

Buchanan, A. 2002. Social moral epistemology. *Social Philosophy and Policy* 19(2): 126–52.

Churchill, L. R. 1999. Are we professionals? A critical look at the social role of bioethicists. *Daedalus* 128(4): 253–74.

Elliott, C. 2004. Beyond politics: Why have bioethicists focused on the President's Council's dismissals and ignored its remarkable work? Posted Tuesday, March 9, 2004, at www.slate.com/id/2096815.

Havighurst, C., and King, N. M. P. 1983a. Private credentialing of health care personnel: An antitrust perspective, part I. *American Journal of Law and Medicine* 9: 131–201.

————. 1983b. Private credentialing of health care personnel: An antitrust perspective, part II. *American Journal of Law and Medicine* 9: 263–334.

King, N. M. P. 1999. Who ate the apple? A commentary on *Core Competencies for Health Care Ethics Consultation: The Report of the American Society for Bioethics and Humanities* (ASBH). *HEC Forum* 11: 170–75.

Koontz, D. 2002. *One Door away from Heaven.* New York: Bantam Books.

London, A. J. 2005. Justice and the human development approach to international research. *Hastings Center Report* 35(1): 24–37.

Salinger, J. D. 1961. *Franny and Zooey.* Boston: Little, Brown.

Schwartz, R. 2005. Listserv communication, March 2005.

Scofield, G. 2005. Motion(less) in limine. *Journal of Law, Medicine, and Ethics* 33: 821–33.

Spielman, B., and Rich, B. 2005. Symposium: Bioethics in court. *Journal of Law, Medicine, and Ethics* 33: 194–278.

UNESCO. 2005. Draft Declaration on Universal Norms in Bioethics. Available at www.unesco.org.

Index

ABIOMED, xxvii, 181. *See also* independent patient advocacy council

abortion, xiii, 47, 141

Abu Ghraib, 134–37

abundance, logos of, 215

academia: commercialization of, 170–71; politics of, 216

academic bioethics: description of, 299; left bias in, 108–16

academic freedom, 234–35

academic publishing: authors and, 271–72, 275–76; editors and, 274–75; ethics of, 270–71; graduate student mentors and, 276–77; peer reviewers and, 275–76; publishers and, 272–73

activism: aims and methods of, 145–51; bioethics as form of, 144–45, 153–54; traditional methods of, 151–54

ad hominem critiques, xxix, 281–86

Adorno, Theodor, 153

advance directives, 13–14

advisory group, independence of, 186–87. *See also* independent patient advocacy council

advocacy. *See* activism; independent patient advocacy council

advocacy bioethics, 299

agriculture, intensive, 222–24

Agrippa, 123

AJOB (*American Journal of Bioethics*), 249, 250

Alexander, Shana, "They Decide Who Lives, Who Dies," 10

AMA Ethics Institute, 171

American Association of Bioethics, 26

American Association of University Professors, 24, 28

American Enterprise Institute, 99, 100

American Journal of Bioethics (AJOB), 249, 250

American Society for Bioethics and Humanities (ASBH): Advisory Committee on Ethics Standards, 142; annual meeting in 2004, 116n1; G. W. Bush and, 30; bylaws of, xxv, 28, 138; conspiracy of silence in, 137–39; formation of, 9, 26; human rights and, 136–37, 142–43; M. F. Marshall address to, 28; membership of, 241; mentoring program of, 265, 268; October 2002 meeting of, 38n20; politics of, 108; substantive positions and, 140–42, 144; task force of, 30, 31

American Society for Law, Medicine, and Ethics, 30, 31

Andre, Judith, 284

Anijar, Karen, 252–53

animals, suffering of, in intensive agriculture, 222–24

applied bioethics, 299, 307

argument: ad hominem, 281–83; bias ad hominem, 283–84; moral identity ad hominem, 284–85; motivation for, 281, 285; response to, 305

Armey, Dick, 101

Aroskar, Mila, 47

arrogance: courage mistaken for, 194–95, 196; integrity compared to, 201–2; as interpersonal matter, 197–98

ASBH. *See* American Society for Bioethics and Humanities

Asch, Adrienne, 285–86

assessment: characteristics of, 306; Glass house and, 308–9; of individual vs. of work, 299–302; need for, 297–98; objectives of, 302–6; subject of, 298–302

assisted suicide, legalization of, 87